W9-BMW-463

The T.A.T., C.A.T. and S.A.T.
in clinical use

by the same author

Dementia Praecox: The Past Decade's Work and Present Status: A Review and Evaluation. New York, Grune & Stratton, 1948*

Projective Psychology: Clinical Approaches to the Total Personality (editor and contributor; with Lawrence Abt). New York, Alfred A. Knopf, 1950, paperback, Grove Press, 1959.*‡

Manic-Depressive Psychosis and Allied Disorders. New York, Grune & Stratton, 1952.

The Psychology of Physical Illness: Psychiatry Applied to Medicine, Surgery and the Specialities (editor and contributor). New York, Grune & Stratton, 1952; London, Churchill, 1953.†

Schizophrenia: A Review of the Syndrome (editor and contributor, with P. K. Benedict). New York, Logos Press; now distributed by Grune & Stratton, 1958.*†

Contemporary European Psychiatry (editor). New York, Grove Press, hardcover and paperback, 1961.

A Handbook of Community Psychiatry and Community Mental Health (editor and contributor). New York, Grune & Stratton, 1964.

Emergency Psychotherapy and Brief Psychotherapy (with Leonard Small). New York, Grune & Stratton, 1965.†§

The Broad Scope of Psychoanalysis: Selected Papers of Leopold Bellak, ed. Donald P. Spence. New York, Grune & Stratton, 1967.

The Schizophrenic Syndrome (editor, with Laurence Loeb). New York, Grune & Stratton, 1969.

Progress in Community Mental Health, Vol. I (editor and contributor, with Harvey H. Barten). New York, Grune & Stratton, 1969.

The Porcupine Dilemma. New York, Citadel Press, 1970; Tokyo, Diamond Publishing Company, 1974.§‡

Progress in Community Mental Health, Vol. II (editor and contributor with Harvey H. Barten). New York, Grune & Stratton, 1971. (Vol. III, 1975).

Ego Functions in Schizophrenics, Neurotics, and Normals (with Marvin Hurvich and Helen Gediman). New York, John Wiley & Sons, 1973. □

A Concise Handbook of Community Psychiatry and Community Mental Health (editor and contributor). New York, Grune & Stratton, 1974.

The Best Years of Your Life. A Guide to the Art and Science of Aging. New York, Atheneum, 1975.§·

Overload: The New Human Condition. New York, Behavioral Publications, 1975.

Geriatric Psychiatry: A Handbook for Psychiatrists and Primary Care Physicians (editor and contributor with Toksoz B. Karasu). New York, Grune & Stratton, 1976.

Emergency Psychotherapy and Brief Psychotherapy, with Leonard Small. New York and Larchmont, Grune & Stratton and C.P.S., Inc., 1978.

The Disorders of the Schizophrenic Syndrome, editor and contributor. New York, Basic Books, 1979. □

Psychiatric Aspects of Minimal Brain Dysfunction in Adults (editor and contributor). New York, Grune & Stratton, 1979.

Specialized Techniques in Individual Psychotherapy, editor and contributor with Tokusz B. Karasu. New York, Brunner/Mazel, 1980. □

Crises and Special Problems in Psychoanalysis and Psychotherapy, with Eleanor P. Faithorn. New York, Brunner/Mazel, 1980. □

Reading Faces, with Samm Sinclair Baker. Holt, Rinehart & Winston; paperback, Bantam Press, 1981.

Handbook of Intensive Brief and Emergency Psychotherapy, with Helen Siegel. Larchmont, N.Y., C.P.S., Inc., Box 83, 1984. □

The Broad Scope of Ego Function Assessment, with Lisa A. Goldsmith, New York, John Wiley & Sons, 1984.

---

* Selection of the Basic Book Club, † Also published in Spanish, ‡ Also published in Italian, § Also published in German, □ Selection of the Macmillan Book Club, · Also published in Japanese.

The Thematic Apperception Test
The Children's Apperception Test
and
The Senior Apperception Technique
in clinical use

FOURTH EDITION

LEOPOLD BELLAK, M.D.

Clinical Professor of Psychiatry,
Albert Einstein College of Medicine/Montefiore Medical Center
Clinical Professor of Psychology,
Postdoctoral Program in Psychotherapy,
New York University

Revised with the collaboration of David M. Abrams, Ph.D.

Grune & Stratton, Inc.
Harcourt Brace Jovanovich, Publishers
Orlando   New York   San Diego   Boston   London
San Francisco   Tokyo   Sydney   Toronto

PHOTO CREDIT: Back Cover Photo by Paula Willey.

Library of Congress Cataloging-in-Publication Data

Bellak, Leopold, 1916–
    The thematic apperception tests, the children's apperception test, and the senior apperception technique in clinical use.

    Cover title: The T.A.T., C.A.T. and S.A.T. in clinical use.
    Bibliography: p.
    Includes index.
    1. Thematic apperception test. 2. Children's apperception test. 3. Senior apperception technique. I. Abrams, David, Ph.D. II. Title. III. Title: T.A.T., C.A.T., and S.A.T. in clinical use. IV. Title: TAT, CAT, and SAT in clinical use. [DNLM: 1. Mental Disorders. 2. Projective Technics. 3. Thematic Apperception Test. WM 145 B435t]
BF698.8.T5B42 1986   155.2'844   86-4763
ISBN 0-8089-1815-X

Fourth Edition
© 1986 by C.P.S., Inc.
Larchmont, New York 10538

Third Edition
© 1975 by C.P.S., Inc.
Box 83
Larchmont, New York 10538

Second Edition
© 1971 by C.P.S., Inc.

First Edition
© 1954 by Grune & Stratton, Inc.

Grune & Stratton, Inc.
Orlando, FL 32887

Distributed in the United Kingdom by
Academic Press, Inc. (London) Ltd.
24/28 Oval Road, London NW 1

Library of Congress Catalog Card Number 86-4763
International Standard Book Number 0-8089-1815-X

Printed in the United States of America
86 87 88 89   10 9 8 7 6 5 4 3 2 1

Nihil est in intellectu quid non antea fuerit in sensibus.
Hume

Esse est percipi.
Berkeley

ACKNOWLEDGMENT

David M. Abrams, Ph.D. is a clinical psychologist in private practice in New Rochelle, New York, and senior psychologist at the Center for Preventive Psychiatry in White Plains. In addition, he is on the faculty and a supervisor in the Child and Adolescent Training Program at the Postgraduate Center for Mental Health in New York City.

I came to know and value David Abrams first when I supervised him as a trainee in the Postdoctoral Program in Psychotherapy at New York University. He has a broad scope in the field, from psychoanalysis to neuropsychology, and I appreciate his contribution to this revision.

Susan Berger, MSW, a graduate student in psychology, was also very helpful in organizing the complex changes in this new edition.

Marlene Kolbert, as so often, oversaw all the details and kept the project coordinated.

I am grateful to all three of them.

Leopold Bellak

CONTENTS

PREFACE TO THE
FOURTH EDITION

It is of course personally very gratifying to be able to write a preface to this fourth edition, over 30 years after the book was first published. Not the least of the satisfaction derives from the fact that projective techniques, apperceptive techniques, have survived a period when there was little interest in diagnosis of any kind. Now they more than hold their own in a burgeoning field of computerized rating scales and questionnaires as well as in the face of a new trend to ignore psychodynamics and to consider panics largely the result of prolapsed mitral valves and phobias as solely the manifestations of abnormalities of neurotransmitters. Single-faceted fads have not and will not survive: Organismic, wholistic thinking prevails.

Aside from an exercise in self congratulation, I want this preface, like the others, to provide a brief overview of the developments since the last preface, over a decade ago, and to provide some perspective on the theoretical foundation of apperceptive techniques at present. I want to bring their use up to date with developments such as those in the field of neuropsychology, object relations theory, the preoccupation with the Borderline concept, and other recent innovations. Above all, I want to align the use of apperceptive techniques with my current views of psychodynamics generally, and psychoanalysis specifically.

Psychoanalysis was always, among other things, a *perceptual theory.* Psychoanalysts usually don't know enough about academic psychology to realize this and many psychologists do not know enough about the basis of psychoanalysis to see that fact. Dream imagery, for instance, is by far best understood in terms of a combination of psychoanalytic theory and Gestalt psychological theory. The dream is a Gestalt, more than the sum of past perceptions, influenced by various fields of forces.

Psychoanalysis, when it is not busy being a theory of *motivation,* or a *developmental theory,* or broadly speaking, a *learning theory,* or a dynamic *theory* of interacting forces, or a *systems theory* as in psychosomatic medicine, is concerned with the effect of earlier perceptions upon contemporary perception. What we study in the three apperceptive techniques are individual differences in perceptual distortion of standard stimuli. By looking for intrapersonal common denominators as well as interpersonal differences we hope to glimpse the unique perceptions of an individual, and his ways of coping with what he perceives. It is as simple as all that. Quantitative content analysis is still not used enough to put these inferences on a statistically respectable basis. One would think some bright young computer specialist would program his gadgets to do not only a word count but also an analysis of clusters of what Henry Murray called syndromes of press and need—units of stimulus and drive. These clusters should give a very lively picture of a personality and keep methodologists happy.

Freud's basic contribution to the field of personality theory and perception was to *establish continuity* between childhood and adulthood, between waking thought and dreaming thought, between "normality" and psychopathology. He established *causality* in psychological science. This is his unique contribution, *unprecedented, unparalleled,* and *unsurpassed.* Apperceptive techniques, projective techniques, are predicated upon these basic hypotheses. The specific responses to the stimuli are determined by specific factors. One need not employ the narrowest kind of mechanistic determinism to maintain these propositions. A high degree of probability of relationships is a very adequate basis for our work.

Systems theory teaches us that input may come from various intersecting fields; biological causes (e.g., neurological deficit), ethnic background, contemporary events (such as just having had an enraging experience), or experiential data from childhood. All these factors must be sought for in analysis of apperceptive responses.

Personality theory holds that "personality" is a relatively stable system. We expect Tom Jones to be approximately the same person today, tomorrow, and the next year, as he was yesterday and a month ago. On the other hand, of course, we know that Joe may have been depressed yesterday and be anxious tomorrow and that successively administered tests, like the T.A.T., would reflect these changes, and still reveal the basic structure. Look at the dramatic evidence in the T.A.T.s of the Nazi leaders Streicher and Rosenberg in this monograph. Both faced hanging, but they told quite different stories to the T.A.T. pictures even so.

In interpreting apperceptive responses it is sound to know something about the subject's current life situation. We want to make sure that she does not have a temperature of 103° while taking the test. All other things being equal, we are betting that the main personality organization is being reliably and validly revealed.

We look for continuities between the patient's life history and apperceptive responses. If we find common denominators between several responses we tentatively assume that they are meaningful and try to relate them to various systems such as the ethnic background, psychoanalytic structure, and dynamics. In a broader sense, it is most useful to see the subject's response to stimuli and to the instructions as a *task* with which the subject has to *cope.* Personality, symptomatology, and style are then best studied as *coping mechanisms.* Their adequacy, usefulness, or pathology are the broadest basis for our diagnostic inferences.

Within the last decade, *Object Relations theory* has attracted a good deal of interest. The present volume has a chapter on Object Relations aspects in the apperceptive techniques. In terms of the discussion so far, this simply means that certain perceptual aspects, namely the percepts concerned with self-representation as well as the interaction of internalized object relations have received more attention in the past decade than they have previously. Object Relations theory has simply emphasized, in various forms by different authors, the specific effect of self-perceptions at different times of one's development and of object perceptions at different stages upon contemporary perception. To use Henry Murray's term, self and object representations have a *"regnant"* effect on perception.

That is very useful to keep in mind, useful in studying responses to the T.A.T., C.A.T. and S.A.T., and not in conflict with basic psychoanalytic theory or the way we have always interpreted responses to these stimuli. Those who like Kohut's contributions to *self psychology* may find it useful to look for evidence of self psychology in the thematic responses.

Neuropsychology is another field that has burgeoned in the last 10 years. Like any new development it has something of a star quality or superior status, the way psychoanalysis, pharmacotherapy, and community psychiatry, for instance had. It has this status especially because of the swing in the direction of biology in the whole field of mental health. The swing of that pendulum I believe has already started on a return trip. Undoubtedly, neuropsychology will continue to play a valuable role. It is not, however, a substitute for other methods of assessment; just as the value of apperceptive techniques for neuropsychological assessment is modest.

Curiously enough, neuropsychology is not that new—it just had an extra spurt. When I was a graduate student in psychology, in 1940, working under F. L. Wells' supervision in Stanley Cobb's Department of Psychiatry at the Massachusetts General Hospital, we used tweezers, Seguin Form Boards, and a number of other performance tests. We carefully tested each child for laterality, searched for any tendencies toward letter reversals and under Kurt Goldstein's instruction, learned to use the Kohs blocks for a study of abstract and concrete ways of thinking. These activities did not keep me from using the T.A.T. and the Rorschach at the same time. Both neuropsychological testing and personality assessment by apperceptive techniques have their merits and their limitations, and complement each other.

David M. Abrams, whose collaboration I enlisted for this revision, contributed many useful ideas to the newly discussed topics. Over several years, he and I have often seen the same adolescent and adult patients for diagnostic evaluation, which has provided a wealth of hard, clinical data for our discussions on the use of thematic apperception tests in the assessment of object relations, and borderline and other preoedipal conditions, and in cases of my special interest, ADD in adults.

The *Borderline condition* has attracted a great deal of interest in the last decade, and therefore there is a new chapter concerning it in this volume. Different authors define the condition by different criteria and have different ideas about the stability of the disorder and its merit as a diagnostic label. This volume is not the place for a major discussion except as it related to manifestations—and their diagnosis—in these apperceptive techniques. If there is "splitting," and one wants to consider it as pathognomonic, it can be seen in some stories; so can "projective identification."

The fact is that the stories people tell are *primary documents:* they are the unique products of the storyteller. By what criteria one wants to study the uniqueness of each production is a matter of the investigator's choice. In that sense, the T.A.T., C.A.T. and S.A.T. are monuments to humanism. To paraphrase what Freud said of the dream, they are royal roads to the understanding of the individual, and thus to *all* of the human spectacle.

I have very often been told, by colleagues and by patients, that the T.A.T. pictures are cheerless, outdated looking, artistically undistinguished—and I agree. They have prevailed, despite several attempts to compete with them. I personally find only 10 of them useful as I discuss in the text. These, however, seem to have some unique ability to stimulate rich and useful responses. To put it in the form of an old saw—if I were on an island and could have the choice of one single diagnostic device only, I would want it to be T.A.T. picture #1, the picture of the youthful Jehudi Menuhin behind a violin.

I can only hope that this volume will help you understand and identify salient features of the infinite variety of human nature. Furthermore, I hope you will enjoy the study of these apperceptive techniques as much as I have for so many decades!

Larchmont, NY.   L.B.
February 1986

PREFACE TO THE THIRD EDITION

Fast change is the hallmark of our epoch. The publisher must be complimented on being willing to incur the cost of bringing out a new revision so soon after the last in order to keep this book as useful for today as possible.*

The major change in this revision is the outgrowth of a new and increasing awareness of one facet of our society, namely longevity. At this writing, the number of people over 65 years old in the United States has passed the twenty million mark and increases by more than 4000 every day. This means that more and more people have to learn one more adaptive phase and master one more identity crisis. This has social, economic, political, medical, and above all, individual human implications.

For the clinical psychologist and related professionals, this means an increased concern with the problems of older people and those who care for them. Whether one works in a hospital, in private practice or a community mental health center, the needs of the aged will increasingly make themselves felt.

The Senior Apperception Technique (S.A.T.) was developed to do for the understanding of the aged what the T.A.T. and C.A.T. have done for the younger age groups. In this revised volume, you will find for the first time apperceptive techniques which, by stimulus character, span psychodynamics, if not quite from the cradle, then at least from about three years of age to the grave.

Aside from this addition, the third revision includes the 1973 revision of the regular T.A.T. Blank published by the Psychological Corporation since 1947 and my Short Form for the C.A.T. and T.A.T. (revised 1974). In both instances, the major change is provision of a practical scoring scheme for ego functions as revealed in the test data and during test behavior.

This holds true also for the revised Psychodiagnostic Test Report Blank—as well as a recognition of the increased attention merited by neurological problems. With a widely held belief that as many as 15 per cent of the population may suffer from some form of dyslexia or the minimal brain syndrome, it is important to look for evidence of it, record it, and take it into pedagogic as well as psychodynamic consideration specifically, and therapeutic planning generally.

Finally, a few selected references have been added specifically to buttress some of the above-mentioned factors, and the equivalence of the animal and human versions of the C.A.T.

I am deeply gratified that this book has been widely used since 1954 and hope that the present revision will make it even more helpful.

Larchmont, New York   L.B.
January, 1975

---

* I gratefully acknowledge the editorial assistance of Caroline Birenbaum in preparing the third edition.

PREFACE TO THE
SECOND EDITION

Seventeen years ago, when this volume was first published,* personality assessment, and especially projective testing, was a rapidly expanding field. Each year brought a new crop of tests; few of these survive today in practice. The Rorschach and the T.A.T. are now without doubt the most frequently used projective tests, followed by the Bender Visual Motor Gestalt Test, the Figure Drawing Test, and the C.A.T. for the testing of children. Many other tests are available but are not in general use; most of them are employed by a few psychologists who are fond of them, skilled in their interpretation, and who find them especially productive.

It would only be a slight overstatement to say that clinical psychology was born during World War II; psychiatry and psychoanalysis simultaneously gained greatly in importance. In the late 1940's and the early 1950's we were in something like the heroic phase of these fields: enthusiasms, discoveries, and new techniques of personality assessment abounded. As we know, however, all new experiences are emotionally overinvested, and even in the most ideal love relationship there is an end to the honeymoon spirit. Not only does one became aware of a wrinkle here and some undesirable features there, but one also tends to take many of the good things for granted. The same pattern can be discerned in science. Specifically, much of what was new in the postwar years has become fully integrated into clinical psychology and psychiatry; this is true to such a degree that at present many are unaware of all the aid and comfort which psychodynamic hypotheses have provided us with. There is practically no one who does not at least misapply psychoanalytic concepts, even while being totally critical of them.

One problem of psychodynamics and personality assessment in the postwar years which contributed to the present disenchantment of some people with them was undoubtedly the fact that their usefulness was overestimated. "Signs" in the Rorschach or the T.A.T. are not an infallible way to truth, and psychoanalysis does not cure all problems, especially not social problems. Nor were these tests, methods, and concepts intended for these purposes, or considered as such by those who were fairly well informed. The less well-trained the person, however, the more inflated his expectations and the greater his disenchantment.

In retrospect, some of the problems of the testing field seem almost comical. Demands of reliability and validity for projective techniques were made which ignored the following basic propositions.

First, repeat reliability makes sense only if one has reason to believe that the *condition tested* remains stable; only when this prerequisite is satisfied can the measure be stable. Personality is a system of dynamic forces which results in temporally quasi-stable structures that may move on the diagnostic continuum *within* the normal or neurotic or psychotic range, or from one to another. There-

---

* I gratefully acknowledge the assistance of Dr. Marjorie Bristol in preparing the first edition of this book.

fore, reliability statements can be assessed only if one makes them within a framework that provides for intrapersonally and externally shifting forces.

Second, psychological tests could not unfailingly identify psychopathological conditions which themselves were ill-defined. In the case of schizophrenia, for example, as long as there is no agreement on what the necessary and sufficient conditions for the diagnosis of this condition are, *no* test can identify its existence by any of the validating methods. Actually, schizophrenia does not represent a single disease entity, but rather a syndrome characterized by severe disturbances of ego functions due to any of several possible causes. If one agrees with my definition, it then becomes possible to somewhat arbitrarily decide what degree and kind of pattern of ego function disturbance will be called schizophrenic syndrome, and then the tests can aid in validly identifying it.

Third, relating manifest content and latent content revealed in testing was difficult due to the early lack of knowledge and understanding of ego pathology. Much of the failure in attempts to relate the manifest and latent contents revealed in our tests was due to ignorance of ego functions as intervening variables. In time, the richest yield came from understanding the value of the discrepancy between what goes on relatively latently and what is manifest: discrepancy helps in assessing the forces of control and those of cognition and aids in the prediction of clinical course.

These methodological considerations have largely disappeared now because projective techniques are better understood. The whole concept of projection and unconscious distortion not only disturbed laboratory psychologists, but also had practically a mystique about it.

In 1944, I was still struggling experimentally with this mystique myself. At first, I resolved the problem by speaking of adaptive, expressive, and projective aspects of responses to tests [12]. Next, I brought ego psychology to bear on the responses [23] by studying defenses in the T.A.T., and then changed from speaking of projection to apperceptive distortion [24]. Eventually I found Kris' concept of adaptive regression in the service of the ego perhaps most useful for understanding the creative process involved in responses. Adaptive regression in the service of the ego can be translated as "a brief, oscillating, *relative* reduction of *certain adaptive* functions of the ego in the service of (i.e., for the facilitation of) other, specifically the 'synthetic,' ego functions." Cognitive, selective, adaptive functions are then decreased. This weakens the sharply defined boundaries of figure and ground, of logical, temporal, spatial, and other relations, permits unconscious material to become conscious, and leads to reordering into new configurations with new boundaries, under the scrutiny of the again sharply functioning adaptive forces [30].

On the broader scene, the interaction between laboratory psychology and clinical psychology similarly came to embrace responses to projective tests as individual differences in perception effected by interlocking motivations. What I had tried to describe as expressive aspects has since been highly developed into the field of cognitive style. Interplay among adaptive functions of the ego, the environment, and drive has become a staple of psychological science, from motivational research to clinical psychology to social psychology.

Projective methods as diagnostic devices are, then, much less of a theoretical problem today than they were 20 years ago and, by that token, also much less of a methodological problem. If one wanted to computerize projective test responses, one would only have to work out good definitions of terms for use in content analytic studies (based on the frequency of words and word constellations) to make these techniques acceptable to the hardest of psychological hardware specialists.

The acute problem in all personality assessment today is the current decrease of interest and sophistication in psychodynamics and in psychodynamic diagnosis and treatment. An excellent review of major factors in this area was made by Molish in his presidential address to the Society for Projective Techniques [188].

In part, this change is simply due to the passage of time, the change in values that usually accompanies it, and especially the devaluation of most values of yesterday, which have become identified with the establishment. What was heady stuff in 1950 just does not intoxicate as much in 1970. Aside from this natural course of history, the advent of such diverse factors as existentialism, behavior therapy, the community mental health movement, and psychotropic drugs has led to an inappropriate downgrading of psychodiagnostic assessment.

Behavior therapy, as an adjunct in certain selected instances, may very well be useful. As an attempt to deal with most disturbances by reconditioning, it is about as rational as treating syphilis by putting penicillin ointment on the superficial syphilitic chancre; since *Treponema* are deeply dispersed through all the tissues, superficial treatment at best merely masks the pervasive disorder.

The psychotropic drugs are a very valuable addition to treatment of practically all conditions in the field of mental health. To use them indiscriminately, and as a cure by themselves, rather than as a means of approaching the patient while using other forms of therapy, is often a misuse. Like behavior therapy, a consequence of this misuse is, of course, that such a practitioner has little interest in diagnosis except the most superficially descriptive and therefore also no interest in assessment by psychological techniques.

Existentialism is in many ways diametrically opposed to random drug treatment and behavior therapy. There is a deep interest in what the patient feels. But practically all problems revolve around feeling of identity and its disturbance, with virtually an antirational attitude and an abundance of undefined neologisms. Again, the nature of the approach is nihilistic as far as precise psychodiagnosis is concerned.

Community mental health is a vast step forward. As an aspect of public health, with eventually increasing emphasis on primary prevention, it is the only approach that promises significant changes in a contemporary society in which emotional illness is of virtually epidemic proportions [38]. Nevertheless, many practitioners of community mental health behave as if the need for epidemiology, pollution control, and immunology in public health medicine would make cardiology and surgery (and training in these fields), not to mention physiology and biochemistry, unnecessary. In community mental health, no amount of day care, night care, storefronts, or anything else will make a difference if there is not a science of psychodynamics and rigorous attempts to diagnose what ails the patient.

A diagnostic concept is an heuristic hypothesis. It should involve propositions concerning the etiology, treatment, and prognosis of the disease or syndrome under consideration. The diagnostic hypothesis must be measured by the traditional scientific criteria of validity and reliability. In the broadest sense, the usefulness of a diagnostic hypothesis is indicated by its ability to help one understand, predict, and control; to understand means to see the particular set of conditions involved in the diagnosis in the matrix of a sequence of causal events. It is in this significance that we speak of psychodynamic diagnosis: relating the patient we meet to the biosociopsychological facts of his life and trying to understand the relationship of his drives, his ego and superego controls, his value systems, and adaptive problems to the complaints that bring him to us.

A diagnosis, to have maximal usefulness, must have nomothetic and idiographic aspects. There must be enough of general propositions to see the symptoms of a person as roughly belonging to a class of disorder—neurosis, psychosis, and specifically what kind of neurosis, psychosis, or other class of maladaptive functioning—so that we may make some general inferences with regard to prediction (prognosis) and treatment. However, within the nomothetic group a person belongs to, there is and must be concern with the idiographic features, the identification of those factors which make him uniquely himself, above and beyond his group membership.

The third important aspect of a dynamic diagnosis is the fact that we are dealing with dynamic forces. The nomothetic diagnosis implies that we are dealing with at least a quasi-stable characteristic—a Gestalt of drives, controls, and environmental input that has enough discreteness to assure more intragroup similarity between people in the given nosological group than intergroup similarity, and that this characteristic constellation is of a stable enough temporal quality to be usefully so identified. However, by virtue of thinking in dynamic terms, it must also be obvious, and stated, that a person has more or less of a propensity to move towards other forms of compromise formation between the different forces. A diagnosis, then, must not only establish nosological class properties which are useful for cataloging a person for statistical purposes, and about which some general statements can be made, it must also state the unique properties at the time of diagnosis and the individual likelihood of continuing or moving, for better or for worse, to another form of adaptiveness—healthier or sicker, or just different qualitatively [40].

To do this kind of diagnostic work may not always be possible—for many reasons. To strive for it is essential, and to aim for less, deplorable.

Personality assessment, with the T.A.T. and C.A.T., among other means, as a method of studying individual perceptual differences and of understanding them as the unique product of the interaction of personal history with external and organismic factors in the present, in the past, and at different points in the future is essential work for a good clinician.

I hope this book will help a little in that direction.

Miss Lynn Lustbader was primarily helpful to me with the review and updating of the literature in the text. Mrs. Ann Noll carried the major editorial responsibility for all the many tasks involved in revising this volume. I am extremely grateful to both for bearing up under and ameliorating my own shortcomings.

Larchmont, New York   L.B.
January, 1971

PREFACE TO THE
FIRST EDITION

This book on the T.A.T. is the outgrowth of work with this instrument since 1940. At that time I came to Harvard and soon made the Harvard Psychological Clinic my headquarters. It is only fair that I should make some acknowledgment of the stimulating and enjoyable time I spent there.

I had previously studied medicine at the University of Vienna, where I had also learned some of the fundamentals of psychoanalysis. I had already been exposed to academic American psychology, first at Boston University and then at Harvard. At Emerson Hall (Harvard) I acquired particularly some measure of methodological superego from Professors G. W. Allport, E. G. Boring, and S. S. Stevens.

Harvard Psychological Clinic, under Henry A. Murray, became the happiest integration imaginable of Emerson Hall and Viennese psychoanalysis, both in substance and in spirit. The tiny Gold Coast house then harboring the clinic seemed to have innumerable rooms, and the outstanding characteristic of these rooms was that the doors were always open (or nearly always; occasionally a hermit state became necessary); work was done by collaboration, by exchange of ideas. The clinic was very much alive; someone was likely to be working there at six in the morning as at midnight, if the spirit so moved him—and then possibly he would not appear for several days, when the spirit moved him elsewhere.

Seminars were often conducted as luncheons or afternoon teas, and ideas were as much a part of the menu as food. At times there would be feverish physical activity, with experimental testees following schedules from one room to another as if they were trotting in a maze, calculating machines ticking away upstairs, and hidden cameras and microphones recording responses.

Such was the atmosphere I was privileged to share.

The war and the impatience of maturing men for ever new fields put an end to this happy existence. The T.A.T., too, moved from this sheltered academic life into the rough and tumble world of the Armed Forces and their personnel needs and, as part of the great upsurge in clinical psychology, changed from a method known mostly around Harvard Square, with a bibliography of 11 items in 1941 [282] to its position as one of the two most widely used personality tests, with a bibliography of 780 in 1953 [259].

There have been attempts to make the T.A.T. more economical and easier to work with. Many methods have been designed, and much has been published. I went on to becoming a practicing psychiatrist and psychoanalyst, thus staying close to the clinical use of the T.A.T. I have taught classes and seminars exclusively dedicated to this one technique at New York University, The New School for Social Research, Veterans Administration installations, etc., and to working clinicians, psychologists, and psychiatrists. An estimate of around a thousand students is probably on the conservative side. What I have to say in this book is largely the outgrowth of these attempts at teaching which, in turn, were aided by clinical experience. My suggestions for using the T.A.T. are based on the facts that the method seems teachable and, if used judiciously, clinically economical.

Methodologic bluenoses (who often mistake obsessive doubt for a scientific attitude and their intellectual sterility for caution and eclecticism) are not quite happy about the T.A.T., and to a considerable extent there is justification for their feeling: The T.A.T., in common with all the other projective tests, is still far from being a properly established instrument. Problems of validity, reliability, norms, and standards have by no means been satisfactorily solved as yet. It is not even clear what would constitute a satisfactory state, as I have occasion to discuss in the text. This book is meant primarily to be of practical use to the student and practitioner of clinical psychology and psychiatry. Much as the utmost in experimental and theoretical refinement is desirable, it should be remembered that there must be a steady interchange between empirical clinical science and experimental theoretical science. The sulfa drugs had saved hundreds of thousands of lives before a satisfactory hypothesis had been established concerning the nature of the lifesaving process. It is now many decades since Konrad Roentgen enriched medicine with x-rays; yet I am unaware of a single study of repeat reliability of the readings of x-rays by several judges, or of statistical studies of validity— although I think it would be very helpful if some such studies were done!

Acknowledgments

In compiling this volume, I have had, unavoidably, to draw upon my previous experience with the T.A.T., including previously published material. The chapter on the theoretical foundations of projective testing has appeared in part in the *Journal of Projective Techniques,* while part of Section B of Chapter 1 and part of Chapters III and IV lean heavily upon an earlier paper in a book edited by Abt and Bellak, *Projective Psychology,* published by Knopf in 1950. Some of the things I have to say about interpretation are also closely related to the chapter on the T.A.T. in the above-mentioned book, and to my *Guide to the Interpretation of the TAT and the Analysis Blank,* published by the Psychological Corporation. The discussion of the effect of contemporary events upon the T.A.T. includes a discussion of the T.A.T.'s of the Nazi leaders Streicher and Rosenberg, which has previously appeared in the *Journal of Clinical Psychology.* Some of the remarks on defenses in the T.A.T. are borrowed from an earlier paper on this topic which was read before the New York Academy of Sciences, and portions of Chapter I have appeared in the *Journal of Projective Techniques* as part of a symposium on failures in projective techniques.

I wish to express my gratitude to the editors of the *Journal of Projective Techniques,* to Alfred A. Knopf, Inc., to the Psychological Corporation, to the editor of the *Journal of Clinical Psychology* for permission to use the material previously published, and to Dr. Shneidman et al. and to Grune & Stratton for permission to use the Case of John Doe for discussion, previously published by them in *Thematic Test Analysis.*

I am particularly grateful to my friends and colleagues, Drs. Leonard Small and M. Brewster Smith for having read the manuscript critically and having made many helpful suggestions.

L.B.

New York City
June, 1954

CHAPTER I

THEORETICAL FOUNDATIONS FOR PROJECTIVE TESTING

A. Toward an Ego Psychology of Projective Techniques in General and of the T.A.T. in Particular

DURING WORLD WAR II THE PERSONNEL NEEDS OF THE ARMED Forces constituted a tremendous task and challenge. Young men with little training had to become experts in clinical psychology in weeks, and older ones with experience and training in the laboratory and in academic chairs became clinical specialists. The same pressure of circumstances produced ever new projective techniques and led to their acceptance as gospel when even the "oldest" were almost entirely unvalidated and poorly understood. This state of affairs paralleled the development of intelligence testing during World War I. After such periods of pressure as both wars produced, pioneering should be devoted to careful scrutiny, to investigations of the tools themselves. Indeed, as one surveys the literature, one sees that fewer new tests are appearing, and that an increasing effort is being directed to validation, testing the limits, and discarding favorite notions. The large number of papers concerned with the nature of the color response in the Rorschach [208, 234, 278, 304] are some examples; Lindzey's review of the Thematic Apperception Test (T.A.T.) [218], Meltzoff's study of the sentence completion test [232], and Weisskopf's study on faking [339] are others.

The requirements for validity and usefulness in projective techniques can be seen as twofold: projective methods are expected to perform as tools of both nomothetic and idiographic sciences.* Formulated by Windleband [350], and notably elaborated by Allport [7], nomothetic science is concerned with general lawfulness—e.g., in physics, chemistry, etc. Idiographic science is concerned with understanding one particular event, e.g., of a historical nature (what led to the unique event of the storming of the Bastille?). The main efforts in American psychology are directed toward making projective methods the tools of nomo-

Concerned with individual

---

* It may not really be useful to speak of idiographic and nomothetic "science." Instead, it may be more helpful to speak of a primarily idiographic or primarily nomothetic "viewpoint" concerning a series of events.

thetic science; the Basic Rorschach Score [183], the development of signs [165, 264], and the work with group Rorschachs [151, 243] bear testimony to that trend. The purpose—extremely valuable in part, and in part carried over from brass-instrument laboratory concepts of the "average" person, and from statistical psychometrics—is to arrive at criteria which are applicable to groups of people or to syndromes. When these signs are encountered, they are to help one to assign a given person to a given group: Mr. Jones perceives in such a way that he must be considered a schizophrenic, or a criminal, or an engineer. Idiographically speaking, one would be satisfied to describe Mr. Jones as a unique specimen who perceives configurations in a certain way and tends to control his impulses under given circumstances, generally constituting a uniqueness of functioning which will not be exactly duplicated by any other individual.

Some projective methods undoubtedly lend themselves more readily to the nomothetic approach than others. Perhaps the generalization can be made that the expressive methods and those scoring schemes primarily predicated upon formal characteristics lend themselves better to valid generalizations than those concerned primarily with content. Surely the Rorschach is relatively easier to harness lawfully than the T.A.T. (which is probably the most idiographic of all instruments). From a clinical standpoint, in fact, one might choose testing procedures according to whether one wants nomothetic or idiographic information.* The nomothetic approach, to be sure, is extremely valuable and necessary. The failures and limitations of projective methods as nomothetic instruments are the main impetus for further research and attempts at better conceptualization. The problem is often discussed as the difficulty of making inferences from the latent (test data) to the manifest (behavioral level). Naturally, if the psychiatrist wants to know if a patient is suicidal or of criminal inclination, he would like the psychologist to be able to tell him whether the signs and dynamics of suicide or criminality in the projective data imply whether or not the destructive impulse will be acted on. Similarly, the personnel executive will want to know if an individual will make a good officer in reality, not in fantasy!

It is quite possible, however, for a technique to fail us idiographically. I have had occasion to study records, primarily T.A.T.'s, of patients whom I have come to know in three years of classical psychoanalysis. Study revealed that, while in many ways the tests were extremely valuable and accurate, they failed to illuminate certain areas of personality at all, or else displaced emphasis. Thus, while nomothetic performance can best be checked statistically, idiographic performance can probably best be investigated by a study of records against data from a prolonged psychoanalysis, the most idiographic of all studies.

The failures and limitations of projective techniques have often been related [22, 25, 88, 271] to a lack of consistent conceptualization. When Frank [126] coined the term projective methods it was certainly the most appropriate available at that time, but it is rapidly proving to be a misleading term. Projection, taken from Freud, was generally formulated in American psychology [54] as a defense mechanism in the service of the ego, designed to avoid awareness of

---

* "Diagnosis" meaning either identification of a person with a given nosological group, or a statement concerning the unique constellation of forces in a given individual.

unacceptable wishes, thoughts, and impulses, accomplishing its task by ascribing such undesirable *subjective* phenomena to the *objective* world. This meaning of projection was primarily taken from Freud's discussion of paranoia in the case of Schreber [133]. Only belatedly did some workers in the field [18, 20] become aware that Freud [134] himself saw projection in a much broader sense as a general perceptual process, whereby *all contemporary meaningful perception is predicated upon and organized by the memory traces of all previous perceptions.* This broader concept, formulated by Bellak [53] as *apperceptive distortion,* might possibly serve as a more useful frame of reference for some of the so-called projective methods. However, perusal of any of the anthologies will show that there are techniques included under this term which are hardly applicable: graphology, the Bender-Gestalt Test, the Szondi, the Mira, the Figure Drawing Test, and even the Rorschach in its noncontent aspects, are not primarily predicated upon apperception.

An attempt at a breakdown of the processes involved in all the tests currently considered "projective" led to five categories of study [53]: (1) content, (2) expressive data, (3) Gestalt formation, (4) body image, (5) a study of choices (Szondi).*

1. Methods based upon the study of *content.* Here we are concerned with *what* the patient says. The T.A.T. and the Make A Picture Story (M.A.P.S.) Test are the best examples. To a certain extent, the Rorschach inquiry and finger painting method also belong here.

2. *Study of expressive, structural aspects.* The main inquiry is directed toward *how* the subject says or does something. Here we refer to techniques like the Mira, Mosaic, Rorschach, and graphology, which belong to the subsemantic levels of myoneural functioning insofar as these are valid procedures for the understanding of personality factors and structure.

3. *Gestalt functions.* These are exemplified in the Bender-Gestalt, the Mosaic, and again in the Rorschach (W, d, dd, S, etc.). In the T.A.T. this function enters only rarely to any extent when the subject is unable to apperceive the picture as a whole or when he leaves the stimulus altogether.

4. *Body image* or *self-image.* The Figure Drawing Test is primarily predicated upon this approach. It enters into the Rorschach when, for example, the subject identifies with puppets, and in the T.A.T. when the subject sees the hero as crippled (picture 3BM), or the violin as broken and/or "dead" (picture 1), or identifies with an athlete (picture 17BM).

5. *Methods of preference.* Outstandingly, the Szondi is based upon a system of selective choices as personality indicators. Color choice in finger painting, selection of figures in doll play, as well as in the M.A.P.S., etc., all come under this category.

It is apparent that all five organismic aspects enter into every one of the projective methods, although in varying degrees.

The problem is to find a consistent body of theory under which five such divergent aspects of psychologic functioning can be subsumed. All these variables—fantasy content as in the T.A.T.; perceptual organization as in the Rorschach; ability to see Gestalten as in the Bender; self-perception and motor expression as in the Figure Drawing Test, the Mira test, or graphology; and recognition and the making of choices as in the Szondi—are functions of the ego and resultants of its interaction with drives.

The answer, then—a broad enough roof to cover the house of projective testing—lies in an ego psychological theory. Projective techniques, similar to

---

* See Section C of this chapter for further elaboration.

early psychoanalysis, have primarily been steeped in id psychology, a concern with drives and their expression. Psychoanalysis made its major step forward when it turned from being solely a psychology of the unconscious drives to a study of the interaction of these drives with the ego [127]. It is equally necessary that projective testing take this step to understand fully our data and their limitations.

The Role of the Ego in Imaginative Production

In order to study the participation of the ego in imaginative productions, we need first a brief review of the psychoanalytic concept of the nature and functions of the ego, most succinctly formulated by Hartmann [153], and discussed by Bellak, particularly from the standpoint of ego strength [27].

We term the ego that aspect of personality which:
1. organizes and controls motility and perception;
2. serves as a protective barrier against excessive and internal stimuli (see no. 6);
3. tests reality and engages in trial action (Freud's concept of thinking) and sends out danger signals (anxiety);
4. has organizing and self-regulating functions which include mediating between ego and super-ego and the id on the one side, and reality and all the variables on the other. This includes frustration tolerance, capacity for detour behavior, and all we comprise under defenses;
5. has some "autonomous functions," which include abilities, intelligence, and an unspecified number of inherited characteristics, possibly including ego strength;
6. has the capacity for *self-exclusion;* not only must the well-functioning ego be able to repress (i.e., exclude) disturbing id (and superego) impulses for the sake of good organismic functioning (e.g., as a driver must not be unduly distracted by a pretty girl, or feel unreasonably compelled to avoid a mud hole) it must also be able to exclude some or nearly all of its own functions. Hartmann [154], and later Kris [204], who described the ego's capacity for self-exclusion and regression in the service of the ego (one of the last discovered and most important functions), have pointed out that it is necessary that cognitive ego functions be excluded in order to be able to fall asleep. A person who is driven by undue anxiety of nocuous stimuli (oedipal fears) to maintain his cognitive functions will keep his muscles tense, hear the clock ticking, see the light flashing, feel the blanket pressing. Under certain circumstances, the withdrawal of the cognitive functions can be subjectively experienced (hypnagogue phenomena, especially Silberer's [305] functional phenomenon.)

Our projective tests, their strength and limitations, now need exploration in the light of these ego functions. The amount of ego participation in various productions, and the type of ego function involved, differ from method to method and from case to case.

The ego participates in varying degrees in imaginative productions in a way which suggests a continuum from minimal to maximal participation, in the following sequence: dream, hypnagogue phenomena, preconscious fantasy, daydream, free association, artistic productions, test behavior on projective techniques, problem solving.

The dream. Little has been said in the literature about the role of the ego in the dream. One could consider Freud's description of "dreamwork" (condensation, symbolization, displacement, and secondary elaboration) as defensive efforts of the ego. (The theory of the ego had not yet been developed when *The Interpretation of Dreams* was written.) In my own analytic experience, I have found that there are other aspects of ego participation in dreams. Some patients may recount a number of dreams of one night, or four or five different parts of one dream, manifestly connected or not. Dream analysis demonstrates that all dreams or dream parts have the same content; sometimes the first one may be the most undisguised statement, and the subsequent ones may be more and more covered up. At other times, *sequence analysis* will reveal the opposite—a decrease of defensive distortion of latent content, and in others, again, there may be a fluctuation back and forth. This greatly resembles phenomena observed in T.A.T. productions [30]. By and large, however, the dream is predominantly a primary process and shows less ego participation than any other mental phenomenon, save possibly psychotic productions.

This, incidentally, is related to the problem of the diagnostic value of dreams, in terms of identification of nosological syndromes from dreams. Most psychoanalysts, including myself, hold that one cannot diagnose a psychosis from the manifest dream content, i.e., the dreams of psychotics are not manifestly differentiable from those of nonpsychotics. Some psychiatrists, notably Kant [264], have suggested that there are typical dreams of psychotics. This problem involves the assumption that there may be more or less pure "primary processes" in dreams and thus, by implication, better or less well-functioning defenses in the dream. I would be willing to assume that in advanced or chronic psychotics there may be such a decided lack of any dreamwork as to be manifestly different; psychoanalysts in part agree with this position when they differentiate children's dreams from those of adults as being manifestly more primitive and more directly wish fulfilling. Similarly if, in a clinical situation, a patient should recount an openly incestuous dream before the analytic process had loosened the defenses, a psychoanalyst would at least carefully consider this lack of defensive dreamwork as a possible indication of psychosis.

*Hypnagogue phenomena** are those associated with the process of falling asleep. Described particularly by Silberer [305] as autosymbolic phenornena, and by Isakower [178], these phenomena are predicated upon partially existing cognitive ego functions: a subjective awareness of the process of falling asleep, of the

---

* The distinction between hypnagogue phenomena, preconscious fantasies, and daydreaming is not an entirely clear one, nor is there agreement on the definition. Silberer stated that the autosymbolic phenomenon comes about in a transitional state between waking and sleeping, in the presence of a struggle between the two states (he did not conceptualize in terms of the ego.) He gives the following example:

He was trying to think through some philosophical problem, part of which began to elude him while he was nearly falling asleep. Suddenly, he had some dream-like experience in which he requests some information from a secretary who morosely disregards him.

He had symbolized and concretized his quest for enlightenment as met by his sleepiness. In response to an internal stimulus, a preconscious fantasy developed autonomously which could be made conscious and brought in relation to a conscious process.

On the other hand, much of what Varendonck [329] reported as preconscious fantasy also took place in the process of falling asleep. Rapaport [272] believes that Varendonck spoke of preconscious fantasies when he really meant daydreams. At any rate, I myself wish to differentiate preconscious fantasies by their quality of being *ego alien,* similar to mild obsessive phenomena, as compared with such fantasy as is *ego syntonic,* and for which I prefer the term daydream. It is, however, entirely possible for a person at one time to run the entire continuum from hypnagogue thinking to preconscious thinking, daydreaming, and problem solving, all possibly related to the same problem. Kris [204], in a discussion of preconscious mental processes, has discussed this continuum and its relation to the creative process and its metapsychologic implications.

withdrawal of the cognitive functions, and of external cathexis. The most frequent type of experience is of having a door shut or a window screen closed—
sudden darkness indicating the closing of the eyes or the narrowing of the visual
perception. Actually, such phenomena occur primarily when the process of falling asleep is disturbed, either in a situation where one should stay awake and thus
struggles against falling asleep, or where anxiety disturbs the smooth self-exclusion of the ego. An even more widespread phenomenon of this type which I also
consider to be a hypnagogue phenomenon is that of having fallen asleep and
waking with a start upon the sensation of falling. This phenomenon is due to a
disturbance in the smooth self-exclusion of the ego functions concerned with
muscular control and awareness.

Preconscious fantasy. By definition, preconscious fantasies are processes which
are not conscious at the time but can easily be made conscious on effort. They
were most extensively described by Varendonck [329] and occur particularly
while some monotonous or semiautomatic task is being performed. Frequently,
upon some additional stimulus, one may "snap out of it" and suddenly become
aware of the fantasies which have lived a nearly autonomous life. Such fantasies
may have started as regular daydreams, or may develop in tangential relation to
some internal or environmental stimulus which may be recognized as related by
subjects who have learned to introspect. People in analysis, people who are
deeply preoccupied, and prepsychotics may experience an abundance of such
fantasies which are to a certain extent an ego function (inasmuch as they are in
some relationship to environmental or originally conscious stimuli) and can be
made conscious upon effort.

Daydreaming. Daydreams are to a considerable extent under the control of the
ego. Many people will reach for ready-made daydreams which they think of
routinely in frustrating situations. Others will keep their daydreams within some
limits of reality. Indeed, controlled daydreams may be the forerunners and con-
comitants of problem solving behavior (e.g., the man who daydreams of success
and in this process hits on a workable formula).

Free associating. The patient who is asked to free associate in the clinical situation is asked to perform a complex task: to let his mind run freely—that is, to
decrease the controlling function of his ego, and at the same time, or in brief
succession, to increase the cognitive function of the ego concerned with self-
awareness. It is the nature of this complex task, of an *oscillating* function or ability
of the ego to change from self-exclusion to control, that makes free association
such a difficult task for some patients. Notably, obsessive-compulsives find it
difficult to "let go" and thus report a dearth of ideas. We may say that in these
cases rigidity is in direct contrast to the flexibility of ego functions necessary for
free associating. Frequently, their ability really to free associate coincides with
the time of their cure. Some other patients, possibly hysterics more than others,
may find it difficult to keep enough distance to do a good job with the observing
function (the tasks for the ego become even more complex when a third function
becomes necessary; aside from "letting go" and observing, insight presupposes
the ability to see new configurations) [37].

The process of free association can be explained in a more lucid way by reform-
ulating the concept of self-exclusion of the ego or, better, of adaptive regression

in the service of the ego [37]; as it involves free association, it involves a relative reduction of certain adaptive functions, one of which is a reduction of secondary process qualities of thinking and an emergence of primary process thinking and unconscious content. The first phase of the process is succeeded or overlapped by an increase in adaptive and synthetic ego functioning. In this way insight emerges, partly due to oscillation from regression of specific ego functions to an increase in others.

The regressive phase consists of two aspects; one is the temporal regression of ego functions to levels characteristic of earlier ages, and the other refers to the topological regression from mainly conscious functioning to functioning at the preconscious and unconscious levels. The topological regression of certain ego functions, frequently simultaneously, involves a temporal regression of these ego functions and often a regression in the libidinal zones and modes.

In the process of free association, metapsychological problems other than the topological are involved; these are the structural, dynamic, genetic, and energetic [37].

Artistic creation. This process, similar to free association, also necessitates both the ability of self-exclusion of the ego and the rapid change to cognitive critical awareness. Kris has pointed out that only in the presence of intact ego functions (regression in the service of the ego) can one speak of art (an accentuated form of *communication of experiences* in distinction to the productions of advanced psychotics). In the case of many borderline or ambulatory psychotics who are artists, there is still enough ego function left so that one can consider their productions as truly artistic.

Projective techniques. In a procedure such as the T.A.T., the subject is again asked to perform a complex task. We ask him to let his mind run freely; that is, to induce some self-exclusion of the ego. Then we continue our instructions to the effect that he is to tell a story about the picture, to tell us about what is going on, what led up to the situation, and what the outcome will be. We ask him to adhere to the stimulus and to maintain a set consistent with our formula. As in free association and artistic production, performance on the T.A.T. and other projective techniques presupposes an *oscillating function* of the ego. The overly rigid patient will not be able to decrease the control, will give only descriptive data and "meager" data altogether; the patient with insufficient ego control will "leave the stimulus and leave the task."

The "letting go" gives us the drive content thus far primarily studied in projective methods. By observing the oscillating functions and the defenses against the drive material, we may infer ego strength and may often observe drive content which does not appear prima facie. The following stories may illustrate the point:

9BM: Group of four men who are running away from something—something the fellow on the left is looking for. Probably they've broken out of confinement. The position—the way they're lying doesn't seem to indicate they're under any great stress or tension. They could just as well be four hunters. The fellow on the left could be watching for whatever they're hunting, duck or game of any sort. Little siesta after working on any kind of on-location job.

This response of an adolescent boy really consists of at least three stories: they are running away from something, possibly escaping confinement; then (a much more innocuous story than the first) they are merely hunting; and (even more innocuous) finally the aggressive connotation of hunting is given up and the picture becomes one of utmost peace and passivity—siesta.

Thus we see one way of meeting, with obsessive elaboration, the threat of (one's own) aggression.

It is by such study that fine features of defense and character may be discovered. (See also Chapter IV, pp. 73 and 74.)

From the ellipse or the omission, or from the sequence of defenses, we may learn the content. A study of the equilibrium of drive and control is the most useful method of investigation.

Similarly, in the Rorschach, we study the ego's ability to perceive, to organize, to perform complex tasks (see later discussion of color shock), and to control anxiety, aggression, and sexual impulses.

In the Figure Drawing Test, graphology, and the Mira test we study the motor executive functions of the ego. In the Bender-Gestalt Test, and to a certain extent in the other tests, the ability to perceive figure and ground properly and the capacity to interpret well are studied (see discussion of signs). In the Szondi, a system of selective choices is the basis for personality indicators. The nature of the choices involved is a matter of disagreement, but there can be no doubt that the activity of choosing between alternatives is always, to a certain extent, influenced by the ego; this holds true cognitively and conatively.*

Projective responses as products and indicators of creativity. There are four central factors in making inferences from projective responses as creative products which are different from those operant in other creative acts. First, the unconscious and preconscious conditions needed in artistic and scientific creativity often require a (conscious) mental set to create which may not be available in objective settings. Second, whereas the creative process generally attains the emergent level only in its own course, in projective testing the administrator commands the subject to create. Similarly, in interpreting projective protocols it is assumed that creativity is composed of continually operant variables of personality whenever it is present. This is not valid for all creative people; creativity may be cyclic. (See item 4, under "Possible Means of Increasing Productivity of T.A.T. Material by an Ego Psychological Approach," below). The third difficulty in inferring general creative ability from projective tests is based on the fact that the creative product is the resultant of many factors, including situational factors, the nature of the stimulus, etc. The fourth problem in making inferences about creativity is due to the fact that personality syndromes are not the same at different times, and that the degree of variability over a period of time is a highly significant personality index. Consideration of these four problems leads to the conclusion that it may be impossible to ascertain creative potential with standard tests [35].

---

* *Problem solving* as an imaginative production is the type of activity involving more ego participation than any of the others. There, reality testing and adaptation, with all the resources of the ego, are involved. Nevertheless, even in this situation a certain ability for self-exclusion of the ego may be helpful. Cases in which a solution to a difficult problem comes to one just prior to falling asleep, or even apparently during sleep, are not infrequent. The capacity for insight—to see new wholes— presupposes some flexibility of the perceived boundaries of existing wholes.

The Latent and the Manifest

The ability to relate *to and from the latent to the manifest* (behavioral) level—from the projective test data to actual behavior—has often been considered the crucial problem of projective testing. However, I do not agree that this is so for clinical practice, since in this situation the psychologist should not be called upon to make blind diagnoses. A good analyst would never interpret a dream from the manifest content without knowing the life situation and the day's residuum, etc. Similarly, a psychologist should only interpret the unconscious data in the light of, and in the complementation of, behavioral data. One can learn the most from a combination of both levels: if a man's T.A.T. drips with blood and gore and he turns out to be a Caspar Milquetoast behaviorally, one can make inferences as to the nature of his tensions, etc.

There are, however, certain situations in which we are legitimately called upon to make inferences from the latent to the manifest: for theoretical, experimental purposes, and for such clinical situations as the prediction of criminal behavior and suicide, and such problems as personnel selection.

The ego must be considered the intervening variable between the latent and the manifest level! A study of ego functions in relation to drive may permit one to see that aggressive impulses are or are not permitted to break through. This can be illustrated by the following story of an obsessive patient given in response to picture 17BM:

> The man shown here is a circus performer and has been one for many years. His ambition has always been to be a solo performer instead of part of a trapeze trio. Until now he has not had the opportunity. In tonight's performance he will save a fellow trouper from a serious accident and as a reward for his bravery will be given the chance to do his act alone.

We can formulate the following: this person wants to be in the limelight and do away with the competitors; this thought is not permitted expression. Instead of the aggressive thought, the hero gives help in an accident, that is, the aggression is impersonalized, the helpfulness appears manifestly, and the original goal is given as a reward. In other words, the sequence of the story demonstrates this subject's use of reaction formation in avoiding expression of manifest aggression. Sometimes a picture of the entire defensive nature of the character structure reveals itself clearly in the T.A.T.

As in the psychoanalytic situation, small breakthroughs of original impulses must be looked for to illuminate what it is the patient is resisting. For instance, in the stories of a young murderer, a slip of the tongue in his story to picture 8BM is illustrative:

> These two boys have gone out hunting. *They shot a lot of boys—I mean, animals,* and decided to split up to get more pheasants. They agreed to meet at 8:30 at night to count the game and to go home. This boy was standing in the bushes. Twenty feet from him he heard something move. He goes to look at what he caught and finds his friend and rushes him to the doctor. The doctor says the boy will be all right and in the end the boy gets okay and forgives him for what he did.

The slip betrays the poorly controlled aggressive impulse which becomes absorbed in a perfectly acceptable hunting story, then breaks through again in the boy's injury. An inquiry into the small detail of 8:30 at night revealed that this was the time for lights out at the institution, and strongly suggested that it is at this time that his fantasies are permitted to emerge. Similarly, he started his story to picture 1 in this way:

> This boy does not like to practice his trumpet—I mean he likes to play his violin.

He changes a negative response immediately to a positive one. The story he gives to picture 15 is as follows:

> An undertaker; he is very sad because he is putting to rest all these people. He goes out one night and looks with remorse at all the work he has done. He tries to find out how he can undo his work. He can do nothing about it.

In this story the undertaker behaves as if he had killed all the people he buries, revealing the original aggressive impulse only by what would otherwise be incongruent guilt feelings.

A relationship among drive and superego and ego may permit one to prognosticate suicide; stories in which the punishment far exceeds the crime, and in which the punishment is immediate and severe (or cruel), are consistent in my experience with real suicidal danger.

The adequacy of the hero in dealing with the task which the subject himself has constructed is an excellent criterion of ego strength. The more adequate the hero and the more appropriate, realistic, and happy the outcome, the safer the inference that one is dealing with a person who will bring other tasks to a good completion. I am not now considering specific aspects of ego strength needed for specific jobs; the ego strength required of a research scientist is concerned with ability for detour behavior, etc., as compared with the abilities required of a combat officer, e.g., capacity for anxiety tolerance and the ability to libidinize anxiety.

Further Problems an Ego Psychology of Projective Techniques May Answer

Barren records. I have had occasion to discuss this problem before in connection with one of the ways in which a projective technique may fail. Murray [246] speaks of "chaff" needing to be separated from the "wheat" in T.A.T. stories. With all due respect, I must disagree with this formulation. To speak of chaff is reminiscent of the days when psychoanalysts still saw resistance as a nasty way in which patients behaved and something which they had to overcome. With the analysis of the ego, the analyst has learned a great deal from the analysis of the resistance. He learns, in fact, how the ego and the defenses are structured as he never could without the resistances. Similarly, analysis of the chaff, of what is considered barren, will give much information about the defenses of the ego, as in the earlier examples. From the standpoint of determinism as an essential axiom of psychological science, every psychological performance—and thus every utterance—must be meaningfully related to the total structure of personality. It is true that, practically and clinically speaking, it will usually not be worthwhile or possible to investigate each detail.

In patients whom I have analyzed for as long as three years, and whose T.A.T.'s and other projective data I also have, I have had occasion to compare production on the couch and on the tests. For all practical purposes, the generalization can be made that the defenses used in the clinical situation and on the projective techniques were identical: those who use avoidance, denial, and isolation, and who gave barren records, also tended to spend hours on the couch reporting apparently meaningless data which had to be interpreted and could become meaningful only by inferring what they were *not* talking about.

Recent experimental studies have supported the fact, long known in clinical practice, that avoidance of aggressive responses to aggressive stimuli is indicative of a great deal of aggression [25].

Inconsistent result. In certain cases, failure to obtain test data which one could expect to find may be understandable in terms of ego psychology. For instance, in lobotomized or topectomized patients, various projective techniques and other tests may fail to show any deficit behavior. Lobotomies in particular, and topectomies to some extent, are still blind procedures neurologically and, particularly, psychologically speaking. The results and effects differ widely from case to case, in my experience, sometimes strengthening and sometimes weakening the ego. When the surgical procedure somehow interferes with the "drive push" of the patient, the ego may be secondarily strengthened and none of its integrating functions impaired in such a way that a disturbance in the ego function would manifest itself in psychological test behavior. In other words, the failure of our tests to reveal expected pathology incident to the surgical trauma is due to the fact that none of the ego functions involved in test behavior were involved in the trauma.

Signs. "Organic signs," in my opinion, are symptoms of ego defect in situations in which the organic lesion involves ego functions. The reliability and validity of "organic signs" will be greatly improved if they will be expected only in such lesions as are likely to involve the ego functions tested in a particular procedure.

Other inconsistencies in test results may consist not only of *not* finding what "ought" to be there, but also, not infrequently, of finding data which "ought not" to be there, in the sense of indicating much more pathology than can be accounted for. For example, if more than 50 per cent of the students of a city high school show "schizophrenic" signs on the Rorschach, *there is obviously something wrong with the signs.*

Signs are a result of the pressure for nomothetic data in the search for the "average" man and the hunted deviant. Many of them are arrived at simply by the use of faulty generalizations by the factor-analysis hunters. Schizophrenia being the most fashionable diagnosis, faulty diagnosis of this syndrome probably constitutes the majority of all misdiagnosis. I willingly make the generalization that the less experienced the psychiatrist or psychologist, the more often he will make the diagnosis of schizophrenia, notwithstanding the fact that he will often enough miss it when it does exist. The main problem seems to me to be that "signs" of schizophrenia are almost all signs of disturbances of the ego, such as poor control, poor reality testing, etc. While I have gone on record describing ego weakness as the main factor in schizophrenia and other disorders [27], it must be remembered that it is not the sole criterion (cathexis also playing a role) and that other conditions of ego weakness may obtain the same ego indicators. Adolescents notably have weak egos, and many phenomena in adolescence would have to be interpreted as schizophrenia in other age groups (which makes the diagnosis of the real adolescent schizophrenic the most difficult one I know). By the same token, an artist who has learned to exclude his ego functions in creative situations may "let go" in the testing situation to the point of giving signs of ego weakness which may be inappropriately interpreted as schizophrenic. Eron [109] has shown that what was reported as schizophrenic in T.A.T.'s by Rapaport [271] could frequently be found in nonschizophrenics of all kinds, including people who must be considered normal.

Another group that is frequently inappropriately diagnosed as schizophrenic on the basis of signs is the mentally deficient. These subjects also have a defect of the ego which often manifests itself in poor control, poor perception of reality, even paranoid interpretation of an environment which they have every reason to fear and suspect of "putting something over" on them. It is not useful to mistake their intellectual deficit state for a psychosis.

Color shock. Color shock is one of the most interesting and most embattled "signs" of the Rorschach. Personally, I am most impressed with Siipola's [304] work on this phenomenon; in essence, she contends that when color and form suggest divergent concepts there may be three different ways of dealing with the situation. The normal individual may be able to achieve an integration nevertheless: an object first suggesting a bear by shape but being green in color may be quickly seen as a chameleon. The neurotic may be stymied and "shocked" into silence by the conceptual conflict; the psychotic may have his judgment impaired to the point where he cheerfully gives the response, "green grass bear." It is Siipola's contention that color shock occurs only where form and color clash, and that it constitutes a response to a more difficult task. I would go further and say that this is best stated in terms of ego psychology, namely, that the normal ego is strong enough to achieve a difficult integration, the neurotic's ego is too weak to accomplish this, and the judgment functions of the psychotic ego are so impaired that he easily combines form and color inappropriately. In line with what was said above about caution in the interpretation of signs, it must be pointed out that a nonrepresentational artist, accustomed to decreasing his ego functions without being psychotic, might well not hesitate to say "green grass bear," and that a psychoanalyzed subject may equate the testing situation with the analytic situation and induce a similar ego-excluding "set" which might permit him the same green grass bear response.

Faking. Superseding questionnaires and rating scales, projective psychologists like to think of themselves as real scientists and of their instruments as practically foolproof. All the more disturbing to them, therefore, are reports of successful faking on the Rorschach, the T.A.T., and other tests. Such faking can be understood and restricted to its limitations by understanding the productions from an ego point of view: to the extent to which conscious attitudes and conscious ego control can be introduced, the subject may alter the record to a relatively small degree in one direction or another, concerning such variables as overall "wholesomeness." Particularly with regard to Weisskopf's work with the T.A.T. [339], it must be remembered that she used only a few pictures, and the most difficult task for the subject would be to fake *consistently* over the whole series of pictures. Furthermore, an analysis of the defenses would probably reveal the basic structure of the character however much faking the subject endeavored to engage in. Naturally, such characteristics, which, though under the control of the ego, are not under its conscious control and not on the semantic level, are unlikely to be affected at all.

Possible Means of Increasing Productivity of T.A.T. Material by an Ego Psychological Approach

If we pick relative "barrenness" of records as the chief complaint of psychologists, we may be able to suggest a number of ways to increase productivity.

1. *An analysis of the defenses* as they appear in the T.A.T. record has already been discussed at some length as a means of increasing the yield.

If barrenness is the result of overly increased ego control, a number of measures capable of decreasing ego control must then increase the productivity. This could be accomplished by:

2. *Providing stronger stimuli.* If the stimuli have more affective pull, the ego will find it more difficult to control the affect. In the T.A.T. this coincides with the need for "better" pictures—primarily a wider range of stimuli to facilitate study of apperceptive distortions of situations not currently provided for in the existing set.

3. Any other form of *increase of pressure* might also increase productivity. Stein's use of tachistoscope exposure [312] is one way in which this might be done, the shorter exposure time causing more tensions, and increasing the ambiguity (see below). Both this approach and the one of stronger stimuli might prove a double-edged sword: while this might decrease the ego control in some subjects, others might freeze up even more. I suggest the standard approach first, and only if this has failed and if there are no other contraindications (such as excessive anxiety) will it be economical to increase the pressure.

4. *Increasing ambiguity* has been attempted by Weisskopf [337] and Weisskopf and Lynn [341] with the T.A.T. and the Children's Apperception Test (C.A.T.). Presenting tracings of the usual pictures and interrupting the outlines to make less good Gestalten may—up to a point—increase productivity to some extent. Murray's recent modification [246] in presenting the pictures for only 30 seconds and then removing them also increases ambiguity and prevents excessive descriptive clinging to the stimulus.

More recent studies have indicated that cards which are medium ambiguous are best for projection. Murstein [251] has suggested that pictures most useful for thematic production are those which are clearly structured as to who is in the picture, but are relatively ambiguous as to what is going on. Such cards are medium ambiguous. Many studies have indicated that highly ambiguous cards are least useful for personality assessment. Lazarus [207] has noted that, because of high ambiguity of stimuli in projective tests, the lack of expression of certain needs, i.e., aggression, could either be due to lack of arousal value of the stimulus or to ego defenses against the related impulses.

5. *Physiological means* of weakening the ego, such as barbiturates or alcohol, have worked well at times in my experience.

6. *A stress inquiry* in the form of a request for controlled associations to any of the stories, and particularly to any specific concrete references in them (after all the stories have been told), may be a useful means of increasing the data of otherwise barren records.

7. Finally, if a certain test fails to give the necessary data, *use another test*. I am not very much in favor of the routine use of batteries. It is reminiscent of the shotgun prescriptions of prescientific medicine. The doctor put dozens of ingredients into every prescription in the hope that, if one would not help, another might. I believe that a test should be fitted to the needs. If one needs content of the psychodynamics, one should use the apperceptive tests; if one wants an assay of ego strength and generally quantitative indicators, one should use the formal expressive tests. But if, for example, aggression is not meaningfully expressed in the T.A.T., it may be very useful to study figure drawings. The verbal expression of aggression may be successfully controlled when its muscular expression is clearly seen. Often enough the problem can be stated in a generalization, namely, that when one fails to obtain data on the semantic level, tests probing the subsemantic area may produce information. There is good reason, on the other hand, not to leave out the semantic tests routinely, since they can elicit much more detailed, more subtle information than can safely be inferred from the organizational subsemantic methods of personality appraisal.

B. Apperceptive Distortion: A Theory Concerning Content of Responses, as Seen Particularly in the T.A.T.

In the preceding section I discussed the general framework of ego psychological theory of projective techniques and the various dimensions of tests subsumed under that term. Since I wish to describe the T.A.T. particularly, and the T.A.T. is characterized as primarily a test of content, we should address ourselves now more specifically to psychological theory concerning *what* the patient says.

Certain theories concerning adaptive and expressive formal test behavior are necessary. It will require special parts of a general ego psychological theory of personality (to be postulated and verified) to determine why outgoing movements on Mira's test should be associated with outgoing, aggressive personalities, or why extensor movements in the Rorschach should be associated with healthy, active striving. Why a preference for Dd in the Rorschach should be related to obsessive-compulsive tendencies might well be satisfactorily explained by psychoanalytic hypothesis. Why color should play a special role may need psychological hypotheses additional to those of Siipola [304] and others. However, projection in its original sense, namely, as referring to content of perception, is our special concern.

The term projection was first introduced by Freud [129] as early as 1894 in his paper, "The Anxiety Neurosis," in which he said: "The psyche develops the neurosis of anxiety when it feels itself unequal to the task of mastering [*sexual*] excitation arising endogenously. That is to say, it acts as if it had projected this excitation into the outer world."

In 1896, in a paper, "On the Defense Neuropsychoses" [131], elaborating further on projection, Freud stated more explicitly that projection is a process of ascribing one's own drives, feelings, and sentiments to other people or to the outside world as a defensive process that permits one to be unaware of these "undesirable" phenomena in oneself. Still further elaboration of the concept occurs in his paper on the case of Schreber [133] in connection with paranoia. In brief, the paranoiac has certain homosexual tendencies which he transforms under the pressure of his superego from "I love him" to "I hate him," a reaction formation. This hatred he then projects onto or ascribes to the former love object, who has become the persecutor. The ascription of hatred presumably takes place because emergence into consciousness and realization of the hatred is prohibited by the superego, and because an externalized danger is more readily dealt with than an internal one. The superego inhibits expression of the hatred because it morally disapproves of it.

While projection thus originated in connection with psychoses and neuroses, it was later applied by Freud to other forms of behavior, for example, as the main mechanism in the formation of religious belief as set forth in *The Future of an Illusion* [130] and in *Totem and Taboo* [134]. Even in this cultural context, projection was still seen as a defensive process against anxiety. While Freud originally considered repression the only defense mechanism, at least 10 mechanisms are at present mentioned in the psychoanalytic literature. Although projection is firmly established as one of the most important defensive processes, relatively little work has been done on it. Sears [300] says: "Probably the most inadequately defined term in all psychoanalytic theory is projection." There is a long list of papers on projection, however, particularly clinical psychoanalytic and some academic ones.

The definition of projection as a defense mechanism served our purposes well until a crucial point arose in connection with attempts at the experimental investigation of the phenomena which are reported elsewhere [20, 31]. The *first experiment* consisted of provoking a number of subjects and giving them pictures of the T.A.T. under controlled conditions. In the *second experiment* the subjects were given the posthypnotic order to feel aggression (without being directly aware of it) while telling stories about the pictures. In both instances the subjects behaved according to the hypothesis of projection and produced a significant increase of aggression as compared with their responses of the pictures when they had not been made to feel aggressive first. Similarly, when the subjects were under posthypnotic orders and were told that they were extremely depressed and unhappy, it was found that they projected these sentiments into their stories. Up to this point there was no need to change the concept of projection as the ascription to the outside world of sentiments that are unacceptable to the ego.

When the experiment was varied, however, and the posthypnotic order was given to the subject that he should feel very elated, it was found that elation, too,

was projected into the stories given to the T.A.T. pictures. At this point it occurred to me that this could not possibly be subsumed under the concept of projection as a defense mechanism, since there was obviously no particular need for the ego to guard against the "disruptive" effects of joy. Such a case can be hypothesized, for example, when joy is inappropriate, as in the death of a person toward whom ambivalence is felt. Such was not the case, however, in the experiment. Therefore, it was necessary to examine further the concept of projective phenomena and to suggest a reexamination of underlying processes.

As so often happens, it was found on careful rereading of Freud (following a reference by Dr. Ernst Kris) that Freud had anticipated our present trend of thought. He said in *Totem and Taboo* [134], page 857:

> But projection is not specially created for the purpose of defense, it also comes into being *where there are no conflicts*. The projection of inner perceptions to the outside is a primitive mechanism which, for instance, also influences our sense-perceptions, so that it normally has the greatest share, in shaping our outer world. Under conditions that have not yet been sufficiently determined even inner perceptions of ideational and emotional processes are projected outwardly, like sense perceptions, and are used to shape the outer world, whereas they ought to remain in the inner world.

and (on page 879):

> The thing which *we, just like primitive man, project in outer reality,* can hardly be anything else but the recognition of a state in which a given thing is present to the senses and to consciousness, next to which another state exists in which the thing is *latent,* but can reappear, that is to say, *the coexistence of perception and memory, or, to generalize it, the existence of unconscious psychic processes next to conscious ones.*

I believe that this thought of Freud's, not further elaborated upon nor systematically expressed anywhere and stated without any of the sophistication of modern semantics, contains everything necessary for a consistent theory of projection and general perception.

Freud's main assumption is that *memories of percepts influence perception of contemporary stimuli.** The interpretation of the T.A.T. is, indeed, based on such an assumption. I believe that the subject's past perception of his own father influences his perception of father figures in T.A.T. pictures, and that this constitutes a valid and reliable sample of his usual perception of father figures. Clinical experience, as well as experimental investigation, has borne out this point. My own experiments have shown that the behavior of the experimenter can bring out sentiments that originally were probably related to the father figure. While these sentiments had a demonstrable but temporary overall influence on the perception of stimuli, individual differences were maintained according to the genetically determined structure of the personality.

It seems, then, that percept memories influence the perception of contemporary stimuli and not only for the narrowly defined purpose of defense, as stated in the original definition of projection. We are compelled to assume that *all* present perception is influenced by past perception, and that, indeed, the nature of the

---

* Herbart antedates Freud on this idea (see p. 16 [289]).

perceptions and their interaction with each other constitutes the field of the psychology of personality.*

It is necessary to describe the nature of these perceptual processes and later to attempt to formulate a psychoanalytic psychology of personality based on these conceptions. Projection as a variant of perception has indeed become an integral part of the psychology of personality. (See below.)

Apperception and Apperceptive Distortion

To use the term projection for the general perceptual processes described above does not seem useful in view of the history of the concept and its present clinical applications. On the other hand, "perception" has been so definitely linked with a system of psychology which has not been concerned with the *whole* personality that I hesitate to use it any further in the context of dynamic psychology. While terminology is certainly not a matter of primary importance here, I propose that the term apperception be used henceforth. I speak of apperception as an organism's (dynamically) meaningfully interpretation of a perception, following the definition by C. P. Herbart in his *Psychologie als Wissenschaft* (Part III, Section I, Chapter 5, p. 15) as quoted in Dagobert D. Runes, editor of the *Dictionary of Philosophy:* "Apperception (lat, *ad* plus *percipere* to perceive) in psychology: *The process by which new experience is assimilated to and transformed by the residuum of past experience of any individual to form a new whole. The residuum of past experience is called apperceptive mass."*

This definition and the use of the term apperception permit us to suggest, purely for the purpose of a working hypothesis, that there can be a hypothetical process of noninterpreted perception, and that every subjective interpretation constitutes a dynamically meaningful *apperceptive distortion.*† Conversely, we can also establish, operationally, a condition of nearly pure cognitive "objective" perception in which a majority of subjects agree on the exact definition of a stimulus. For instance, the majority of subjects agree that picture 1 of the T.A.T. shows a boy playing the violin. Thus we can establish this perception as a norm, and say that anyone who, for instance, describes this picture as a boy at a lake (as one schizophrenic patient did) distorts the stimulus situation apperceptively. If we let any of our subjects go on to further description of the stimulus, however, we find that each one of them interprets the stimulus differently, for example, as a happy boy, a sad boy, an ambitious boy, a boy urged on by his parents. There-

---

* This theory, in its broadest implications—namely, that perception is subjective and is the primary datum of all psychology—is, of course, not original with Freud. Hume's *"Nihil est in intellectu quid non antea fuerit in sensibus"* is virtually a perceptual theory of personality though not meant that way. Similarly, philosophical idealism, such as Schopenhauer's *Die Welt als Wille und Vorstellung* and Kant's transcendental state, represent a similar position.

† We might add that, as long as the formation of a new configuration results in a commonly agreed upon "apperception," we may call it just that—e.g., the apperception of a certain wooden structure as a "table." If there is any disagreement on the nature of an apperception, somebody must be engaged in apperceptive distortion.

fore we must state that purely cognitive perception remains a hypothesis, and that every person distorts apperceptively, the distortions differing only in degree.

In the clinical use of the T.A.T. it becomes quite clear that we deal with apperceptive distortions of varying degrees. The subject is frequently unaware of any subjective significance in the story he tells. In clinical practice it has been found that simply asking the subject to read over his typed-out story may often give him sufficient distance from the situation to perceive that the gross aspects of it refer to himself. Only after considerable psychotherapy, however, is he able to see his more latent drives, and he may never be able to "see" the least acceptable of his subjective distortions, on the presence of which any number of independent observers might agree. It may be permissible, then, to introduce a number of terms for apperceptive distortion of varying degree for purposes of identification and communication.*

Forms of Apperceptive Distortion

Inverted projection. It is suggested that the term "projection" be reserved for the greatest degree of apperceptive distortion, such as paranoid delusions. Its opposite pole would be, hypothetically, a completely objective perception. Projection was originally described in clinical psychoanalysis as pertaining to psychoses in particular and to certain neurotic defenses generally, and to some "normal" maturational processes. We may say that in the case of true projection we are dealing not only with an ascription of feelings and sentiments which remain unconscious, in the service of defense, but which are unacceptable to the ego and are therefore ascribed to objects of the outside world. We may also add that they *cannot be made conscious* except by special prolonged therapeutic techniques. This concept covers the phenomenon observed in a paranoid that can be essentially stated as the change from the unconscious "I love him" to the conscious "He hates me." True projection in this case is actually a very complex process, probably involving the following four steps: (1) "I love him" (a homosexual object)—an unacceptable id drive; (2) reaction formation—"I hate him"; (3) the aggression is also unacceptable and is repressed; (4) finally, the percept is changed to "He hates me." Only the last step usually reaches consciousness.

I suggest calling this process *inverted projection,* as contrasted with simple projection, which is discussed below. The first step in the process usually involves the operation of another defense mechanism, reaction formation. It is sufficient to say here that, in the case of the paranoid, "I hate him" is approved, while "I love him" (homosexually) is socially disapproved and was learned early by him in relation to his father as a dangerous impulse. Therefore in this case "I hate him" extinguishes and replaces the loving sentiment. Thus in inverted projection we really deal first with the process of reaction formation and then with an apperceptive distortion that results in the ascription of the subjective sentiment to the outside world as a simple projection.†

---

* It must be understood that these various forms of apperceptive distortion do not necessarily exist in pure form and frequently patently coexist with each other.

† See Murray's concepts, p. 20.

Simple projection. This mechanism is not necessarily of clinical significance, is of frequent everyday occurrence, and has been well described in the following joke:

Joe Smith wants to borrow Jim Jones' lawn mower. As he walks across his own lawn he thinks of how he will ask Jones for the lawn mower. But then he thinks: "Jones will say that the last time I borrowed something from him I gave it back dirty." Then Joe answers him in fantasy by replying that it was in the same condition in which he had received it. Then Jones replies in fantasy by saying that Joe will probably damage Jones' fence as he lifts the mower over. Whereupon Joe replies . . . and so the fantasy argument continues. When Joe finally arrives at Jim's house, Jim stands on the porch and says cheerily, "Hello, Joe, what can I do for you?" and Joe responds angrily, "You can keep your damn lawn mower!"

Broken down, this story means the following: Joe wants something, but recalls a previous rebuff. He has learned (from parents, siblings, etc.) that the request may not be granted. This makes him angry. He then perceives Jim as angry with him, and his response to the imagined aggression is: "I hate Jim because Jim hates me."

In greater detail this process can be seen as follows: Joe wants something from Jim. This brings up the image of asking something from another contemporary, his brother, for example, who is seen as jealous and would angrily refuse in such a situation. Thus the process might simply be: the image of Jim is apperceptively distorted by the percept memory of the brother, a case of inappropriate transfer of learning. I shall have to attempt to explain later why Joe does not relearn if reality proves his original conception wrong. The empirical fact is established that such neurotic behavior does not usually change except under psychotherapy.

Joe differs from the paranoid not only by the lesser rigidity with which he adheres to his projections but also by less frequency and less exclusiveness as well as the smaller degree of lack of awareness, or inability to become aware of how patently subjective and "absurd" the distortion is.

The following process is certainly not infrequent: Someone arrives late for work on Monday morning and believes, incorrectly, that his supervisor looks angrily at him later on. This is spoken of as "a guilty conscience," that is, he behaves as though the supervisor knew that he had come late, when in reality the supervisor may not know it at all. This means that he sees in the supervisor the anger that he has come to expect in such a situation. This behavior can then be understood again as a simple (associative) distortion through transfer of learning, or in more complex situations, the influence of previous images on present ones.

Sensitization. If we modify the above case of a subject's coming late to work so that we have a situation in which the supervisor feels a very slight degree of anger at the latecomer, we may observe a new phenomenon. Some subjects may not observe the anger at all and thus not react to it, while others may observe it and react to it. In the latter case we shall find that these subjects are the ones who tend to perceive anger even at times when it does not objectively exist. This is a well-known clinical fact and has been spoken of as the "sensitivity" of neurotics. Instead of the creation of an objectively nonexistent percept, we now deal with a *more sensitive perception of existing stimuli.** The hypothesis of sensitization merely

---

* A very similar process has been described by Eduardo Weiss as objectivation.

means that an object that fits a preformed pattern is more easily perceived than one that does not fit the preformed pattern. This is a widely accepted fact, for example, in the perceptual problems of reading, wherein previously learned words are much more easily perceived by their pattern than by their spelling.

Sensitization, I believe, is also the process that took place in the experiment by Levine et al. [212]. When these experimenters first starved a number of subjects and then fleetingly showed them pictures in which, among other things, were depicted objects of food, they found two processes: (a) when starved, the subjects saw food in the fleeting pictures even if there was none, and (b) the subjects correctly perceived actual pictures of food more frequently when starved. Apparently in such a state of deprivation there is an increased cognitive efficiency of the ego in recognizing objects that might obviate its deprivation, and also a simple compensatory fantasy of wish fulfillment which the authors call autistic perception. Thus the organism is equipped for both reality adjustment and substitutive gratification where real gratification does not exist. This is really an increase in the efficiency of the ego's function in response to an emergency—a more accurate perception of food in the state of starvation. I believe that this process can also be subsumed under our concept of sensitization, since food images are recalled by the starvation and real food stimuli are more easily perceived.

An experiment by Bruner and Postman [80] may possibly also follow the same principle. The authors had their subjects adjust a variable circular patch of light to match in size a circular disk held in the palm. The perceptual judgments were made under the influence of varying degrees of shock and during a recovery period. Results during shock did not vary markedly. During the postshock period, however, the deviations of perceived size from actual size became very marked. The authors tentatively proposed a theory of selective vigilance. In terms of this theory, the organism makes its most accurate discriminations under conditions of stress. When tensions are released, expansiveness prevails and more errors are likely to occur. We may make the additional hypothesis that the tension results immediately in a greater awareness of the image in memory, and more acute judgments of equality of size between the percept memory of the disk and the light patch are made.

The concept of the *mote-beam mechanism* of Ichheiser [176] may also be subsumed under the concept of sensitization. Ichheiser proposes to speak of the mote-beam mechanism in cases of distortion of social perception when one is exaggeratedly aware of the presence of an undesirable trait in a minority group although one is unaware of the same trait within oneself. In other words, we can say that there is a sensitization of awareness (coexistent with unawareness of the process itself and of the existence of the trait within oneself, as inherent in any defensive mechanism) owing to one's own unconsciously operating selectivity and apperceptive distortion.

Autistic perception. Whether the perception of desired food objects in the state of starvation among stimuli that do not objectively represent food objects constitutes a form of simple projection or is a process that should be described as distinct from it depends on rather fine points. Both Sanford [292] and Levine et al. [212] have demonstrated the process experimentally. We may see that the increased need for food leads to a recall of food objects, and that these percept memories distort apperceptively any contemporary percept. The only argument that I can advance for a difference from simple projection is that we deal here with simple basic drives which lead to simple gratifying distortions rather than to the more complex situations possible in simple projection.

Externalization. Inverted projection, simple projection, and sensitization are processes of which the subject is ordinarily unaware, and decreasingly so in the order mentioned. It is correspondingly difficult to make anyone aware of the processes in himself. On the other hand, every clinician has had the experience of a subject's telling him a story about one of the T.A.T. pictures similar to this: "This is a mother looking into the room to see if Johnny has finished his homework, and she scolds him for being tardy." On looking over the stories in the inquiry, the subject may spontaneously say: "I guess that really was the way it was with my mother and myself, though I did not realize it when I told you the story."

In psychoanalytic language one may say that the process of storytelling was preconscious; it was not conscious while it was going on, but could easily have been made so. This implies that we deal with a slightly repressed pattern of images which had an organizing effect that could be easily recalled. The term externalization is suggested for such a phenomenon purely for the facilitation of the clinical description of a frequently occurring process.

Murray [247] has formulated a number of hypotheses concerning projection which need mention here. In the first place, he chooses to differentiate between cognitive projection (actual misbeliefs of what he calls the Freudian type) and imaginative projection, which he believes is what we deal with in projective techniques. He feels that when we ask the patient to imagine something, the process involved deserves differentiation from the clinical concept of projection. This seems a good idea to keep in mind for distinguishing the severity of disturbance as it appears in the protocol, but probably does not merit a theoretical differentiation. There are many patients who, when shown the T.A.T., believe that they are functioning cognitively and that their response corresponds to the actual content of the pictures. At best one might say that the degree of ego participation or voluntary exclusion of its reality testing functions varies in the case of response to projective techniques. However, Murray very usefully differentiates between supplementary projection and complementary projection. He reserves the first term for projection of self-constituents, that is, for the distortion of external objects by one's own needs, drives, wishes, and fears. He would speak of complementary projection as the projection of what he calls figure-constituents, which he defines as "the tendencies and qualities that characterize the figures (imaged objects) that people the subject's stream of thought and with which he interacts in fantasy. For the most part these are images of significant objects (father, mother, siblings, friends, enemies) with whom the subject has been intimately related. . . . In short, subjects are apt to ascribe self-constituents to one character (say, the hero) of the story, and figure-constituents to other characters." In other words, Murray's concern centers primarily on the definition of subtypes of projection predicated upon the *specific content* of the projection, while our discussion so far has been primarily concerned with the *degree of severity or complexity* or relative unconsciousness of distortion. It may be profitable to combine the two points of view.

The problem of *degree* of distortion was also investigated by Weisskopf. She wondered how well the T.A.T. pictures lend themselves to projection (by eliciting more than purely cognitive perception). She developed a "transcendence index" as a quantitative measure of this factor. Subjects were instructed to describe each of the T.A.T. pictures rather than to tell a story about it. In order to obtain the transcendence index of a picture, the number of comments about the picture which went beyond pure description were counted. The transcendence index of the picture is the mean number of such comments per subject. Pictures with high transcendence indices make impersonal observation difficult and lure the subject away from the prescribed objective path of the instructions, forcing him to project. Weisskopf found that the pictures which had high transcendence indices were those lending themselves to interpretation in terms of parent-child relationships or in terms of heterosexual relationships between contemporaries.

Purely cognitive perception and other aspects of the stimulus response relationship. Pure perception is the hypothetical process against which we measure apperceptive distortion of a subjective type, or it is the subjective, operationally defined agreement on the meaning of a stimulus with which other interpretations are compared. It supplies us with the end point of a continuum upon which all responses vary. Inasmuch as behavior is considered by general consent to be rational and appropriate to a given situation, we may speak of *adaptive behavior* to the "objective" stimulus, as discussed below.

In my own earlier experiments it was found that aggression could be induced in subjects and that this aggression was "projected" into their stories in accordance with the projection hypothesis. It was further found that certain pictures are more often responded to with stories of aggression, even under normal circumstances, if the experimenter does nothing beyond simply requesting a story about the pictures. It was also found that those pictures which by their very nature suggested aggression lent themselves much more readily to projection of aggression than others not suggesting aggression by their content.

It seems that the first fact—that a picture showing a huddled figure and a pistol, for example, leads to more stories of aggression than a picture of a peaceful country scene—is nothing more than what common sense would lead one to expect. In psychological language this simply means that *the response is in part a function of the stimulus.* In terms of apperceptive psychology it means that a majority of subjects agree on some basic apperception of a stimulus and that this agreement represents our operational definition of the "objective" nature of the stimulus. Behavior consistent with these "objective" reality aspects of the stimulus has been called *adaptive behavior* by Gordon W. Allport [8]. In card 1 of the T.A.T., for example, the subjects adapt themselves to the fact that the picture shows a violin.

Several hypotheses may be formulated:

1. The degree of adaptive behavior varies conversely with the degree of exactness of the definition of the stimulus. T.A.T. pictures and the Rorschach test inkblots are purposely relatively unstructured in order to produce as many apperceptively distorted responses as possible. On the other hand, if one of the pictures of the Stanford-Binet Test (the one depicting a fight between a white man

and Indians) is presented, the situation is well enough defined to elicit the same response from the majority of children between the ages of 10 and 12.

2. The exact degree of adaptation is determined also by the *Aufgabe* or set. If the subject is asked to describe the picture there is more adaptive behavior than if he is asked to tell a story about it. In the latter case he tends to disregard many objective aspects of the stimulus. If an air-raid siren is sounded, the subject's behavior is likely to differ greatly if he knows about air raids, expects to hear sirens, and knows what to do in such a situation. He will differ from the subject who does not know the significance of the sound, and who may interpret the noise as anything from the trumpet of the Day of judgment to the announcement of a stoppage of work, and behave accordingly.

3. The nature of the perceiving organism also determines the ratio of adaptive versus projective behavior, as previously discussed. The experiment of Levine et al. demonstrated sensitization, and we have found that people distort apperceptively in varying degrees. Even the same person may react altogether differently to a stimulus when awakened from sleep than when wide awake.

Other aspects of the subject's production—for example, that given in response to T.A.T. pictures—have been more simply discussed in an earlier paper [20]. I referred there to what Allport has termed expressive behavior.

By *expressive aspects* of behavior we mean, for example, that if a variety of artists are exposed to the same conditions, one would not expect the same creative productions. There would be individual differences expressed in the way the artists made their strokes with their brushes or with their chisels; there would be differences in the colors they preferred and differences in arrangement and distribution of space. In other words, certain predominantly myoneural characteristics, as Mira [236] calls them, would determine some features of their product.

Expressive behavior is of a different nature from both adaptation and apperceptive distortion. Given a fixed ratio of adaptation and apperceptive distortion in a subject's response to either Stanford-Binet picture, individuals may still vary in their style and in their organization. One may use long sentences with many adjectives; another may use short sentences with pregnant phrases of strictly logical sequence. If individuals write their responses, they may vary as to upper and lower length in spacing. If they speak, they may differ in speed, pitch, volume. All these are personal characteristics of rather stable nature for every person. Similarly, the artist may chisel in small detail with precision or choose a less exacting form. He may arrange things either symmetrically or off-center. And again, in response to the air-raid signal, á person may run, crouch, jump, walk, talk—and do each of these things in his own typical way.

If, then, adaptation and apperceptive distortion determine *what* one does and expression determines *how* one does it, it is needless to emphasize that one may always ask *how* one does *what* one does. Adaptive, apperceptive, and expressive behavior are always coexistent.

In the case of artistic production, for example, the ratio of adaptive to apperceptive material and to the expressive characteristics may vary, of course, from artist to artist and, to a certain extent, from one product to the other of the same artist. In a similar way, expressive behavior influences the T.A.T. productions, accounting for individual differences in style, sentence structure, verb-noun ratio [17], and other formal characteristics. Expressive features reveal, then, *how* one does something; adaptation and apperceptive distortion concern *what* one does.

A Restatement of the Metapsychology of Projecting (Apperceiving) as a Variant of Perception

The *adaptive* features of the apperceptive process were long underestimated not only by clinicians but also by academic psychologists when they discovered the effect of motivation on perception. Clinicians have been aware of the fact that there always is a kernel of truth even in paranoid delusions but were concerned primarily with the distorted factors.

A variety of propositions have been advanced for the ratio of adaptive and nonadaptive factors in apperception, such as Weisskopf's study of the effect of ambiguity [337], the formulations of Bruner and Goodman [81], my own [20], and others. Obviously, motivation as well as factors of the stimulus value, such as clarity of definition as compared to ambiguity, enter in. Physiological aspects other than drive motivation enter into apperceptive distortion, such as fatigue, panic, and, of course, drug effects. Much attention has recently been paid to the role of relative sensory deprivation or perceptual isolation or scrambling of perceptions in apperceptive phenomena [68]. Perceptual vigilance as part of and as an antipolar phenomenon to defensive apperceptive distortion, namely as a particularly sharp perception of stimuli due to special motivation, is also relevant here.

The matter of expressive features in apperception generally was discussed originally by Allport and Vernon [6] and, as a corollary of apperceptive behavior, by myself At one time I had occasion to attempt to relate ego psychology to the expressive diagnostic technique of Mira [236]. The matter of "style," of *how* one does what one does, seems relevant in psychological testing, artistic creativity, and many other forms of behavior. This aspect of cognition, called cognitive style, was given particular prominence by the work of Holzman and Klein [171] and others, who spoke of "levelers" and "sharpeners"; this relates to the degree with which persons merge new experiences with memories of earlier experiences. These memories may be either conscious or unconscious, and become either increasingly bolder in relief or "level out."

The concept of leveling is particularly important to us for a general discussion of the process of defense mechanisms. Gardner and Lohrenz [136] have hypothesized that there is a relationship between extreme leveling and the predominance of repression in an individual's defensive organization. Obviously, an extreme of leveling not only relates to repression but to apperceptive distortion of any experience by the previously acquired apperceptive mass. It is likely that leveling is primarily related to the normally present and necessary synthesizing function of the ego, which when absent in part accounts for dissociative phenomena, and when excessive for pathological repression. A relationship of leveling and sharpening to the synthesizing function would make more reasonable the assumption of these authors that leveling-sharpening is an enduring aspect of ego organization. (I consider the synthetic functions to be often primarily congenitally determined.) Selective leveling and sharpening of various composites of one stimulus may play a role in reaction formation where the acceptable features are sharpened and the unacceptable ones leveled.

A cognitive view of projection that is relevant to apperceptive distortion has been put forth by Singer [307], who bases his theory on Festinger's theory [118] of cognitive dissonance. Singer postulates that when people are aroused to a particular emotional state, many experience cognitive dissonance. One way of reducing such dissonance would be for the individual to distort his perception of other people. This can be effected in three ways. When the individual is unaware of his own feelings, projection occurs to people who are different, since attributing the feelings to similar people would bring discomfort, due to the unconscious status of the feelings. This is the case of classic analytic projection, and Singer differentiates from this the second case, that of rationalized projection, in which the affect is recognized by the individual and projected onto similar people, since in this way he can believe that people like himself also share this emotion. The third case is that of the projection of positive emotions, which can occur in people who do not normally conceive of themselves as feeling joy, for instance. The implications of Singer's view are directly relevant to projective testing, particularly to tests like the T.A.T.

The *structural* aspects of apperception can probably be put most succinctly by paraphrasing Eissler [106]. He said that *perception becomes structure.* One might add that, in turn, structure influences perception. When Eissler said that continuing perceptual experiences become the structure of the personality, we may emphasize that the past apperceptive mass continually influences contemporary perception. Aside from the other experimental data, structural aspects of the ego apparatus which may have to be labeled as autonomous also affect apperception; intelligence, the synthetic function of the ego, and the various anlagen, presumably constituting a biological, constitutional, and hereditary precursor of the later ego, also shape apperception.

In this context, we could define *projection as an extreme of apperceptive distortion where the previous apperceptive mass, or certain aspects of the previous apperceptive mass, has so much of a controlling effect on contemporary perception that it seriously impairs the adaptive aspects of cognition.* The primary process "contaminates" the secondary process.

The relative predominance of primary and secondary process can be thought of as on a continuum in a variety of psychological processes. As I have pointed out before [32], in a dream there is a predominance of apperceptive mass and a relative minimum of ego functioning; in hypnotic phenomena, the self-observing functions and other cognitive forces of the ego are decreased as in the process of falling asleep, but at the same time they are structured by some motivational force. Similarly, in a preconscious fantasy, the apperceptive mass has a greater influence than the adaptive cognition; however, since this process is preconscious, it is easily reversed so that adaptive, cognitive functions take over. Déjà vu phenomena and depersonalization, the response to projective techniques, and the process of free association need to be placed in this continuum of relative predominance of apperceptive mass over adaptive functioning, and the role of repression in the service of certain adaptive functions of the ego. An interesting step has been taken by Holt [169] toward extending predictions from cognitive style to evidences of "regressive" thinking. Holt says that perhaps the dispositions to primary-process forms of thought and the varieties of such reversions will be dictated by the conditions and possibilities afforded by cognitive style. He has developed a set of indices concerning the amount, type, and manner of control of primary-process thinking in Rorschach responses. Preliminary findings indicate that "subjects with definably contrasting cognitive styles are distinguishable on the indices" [169].

The *genetic* aspect of apperception and its extreme variant, the process of projecting, are intimately related to the nucleus of all psychological theory. The consensus today is probably that we do not start out as a *tabula rasa* but rather with a set of anlagen and precursors of the ego apparatus as well as drive characteristics.

The hypothesis that all apperception is structured by previous apperception once upon a time left the problem of the first apperception. We know now, of course, that, in terms of Gestalt theory, at first there is little differentiation of figure and ground, and that articulation of percepts and various hierarchical relationships between experiences are only slowly established. The concept of the primary process and the slow emergence of the secondary process are the analytic processes relating to this area of psychology. As a matter of fact, Spitz, with his concept of primal cavity [310], and B. Lewin, with the breast as the original "screen" [213], have proposed specific perceptual hypotheses.

Spitz has offered the proposition that the oral cavity is the first site of perception, first of internal stimuli, and then of external stimuli.

> The earliest sensory experiences of events taking place in the primal cavity are dealt with on the level of the primary process, yet they lead to the development of the secondary process. In its non-differentiation this world is the matrix of both introjection and projection, which therefore appear primarily as normal phenomena, though we become really aware of their proliferation in pathological processes [310].

In this same paper, Spitz reviews much of the relevant literature and discusses some of the antecedents of mature perception. He, like Lewin, sees early memory traces as "more like pure emotion," and made up of deeper, tactile, and dimly protopathic qualities. He suggests an integration of Lewin's concepts and Isakower's phenomenon into his own general genetic theory of perceptual development.

In attempts at genetic models of projecting, the idea of "spitting out" of noxious or unpleasant stimuli has been used [147]. By this token, too, projection has been said to have a certain oral basis. A not-too-dissimilar notion plays a role in Melanie Klein's formulations of projections of the "good breast" and the "bad breast." These formulations seem to have some explanatory value in certain childhood ideas of fear of poisoning, probably related to anal concepts too (dirty, sexual material ingested does harm and may be ejected either orally or anally). Perception, however, also needs to be considered in the broadest perspective of individuation of the differential perception of the self and others. It is on this level that projection and depersonalization need be considered as interrelated concepts [39]. The oral, genetic concept needs supplementation by visual, thermal, tactile, proprioceptive, and other perceptual cues related to the development of the self concept and later interactions between self and nonself.

The qualities of the unconscious thought processes can probably be best understood in terms of the genesis of the apperceptive mass [36]. When we speak of transference phenomena, I think of the apperceptive distortion of the contemporary figure of the analyst by self-constituents or figure constituents (to use Murray's terms) of the past: the analyst becomes the object of oral, masochistic, phallic, or other demands and may be experienced as if he were father, mother, etc. In the transference distortions and in attaining insight and working through apperceptive distortions, we try in essence to isolate various genetic components of the contemporary apperception: the clinically present Gestalt or configuration has to be "analyzed" into its component parts.

As all current apperception is viewed through something like a composite of all experiential data, we find that no contemporary apperception has a one-to-one relationship to a specific experience of the past but is constantly impressed by overdetermination of each experience. Dream imagery, of course, gives the most vivid account of the contamination of contemporary experience by many layers of past images. That the process of distortion follows a certain mechanism has been illustrated by the work of Fisher [121].

The *topographical* aspects of apperception have been briefly touched upon before; if the process ranges from adaptive behavior to sensitization, externalization, simple projection, and inverted projection, it obviously ranges from conscious to preconscious to unconscious spheres of activity.

The strictly *economic* aspects of apperception are clearly important if one remembers that object cathexis is largely a matter of cathexis of internalized objects, and that indeed the increase or decrease of stimulus value is largely affected by the apperceptive mass. Holt [169] has dedicated himself to the rather closely affiliated problem of energetic aspects of changes from the primary to the secondary process.

The problems of the *dynamics* of apperception are of immediate interest. They are related to the entire concept of defense mechanisms. (Academic psychologists have in part approached the problem by speaking of "perceptual defense.") This aspect of the apperceptive process is considered in the next section.

An Attempt to Integrate Concepts of Apperceptive
Distortion and Other Basic Concepts of Psychoanalysis

Apperceptive psychology and its clinical instruments are children both of psychoanalysis and of academic clinical psychology (particularly of the dynamic theories of Gestalt psychology concerning learning and perception). Nevertheless there has been a deplorable lack of integration of the two methods of approach and a lack of understanding between the exponents of psychoanalytic and those of nonanalytic psychology. I wish to show here that the basic psychoanalytic concepts can be stated in experimentally verifiable form as problems of learning theory and, particularly, of apperceptive distortion.

I believe that such a restatement is important since the clinical psychologist using projective techniques often finds it necessary to employ a psychoanalytic approach and does so with unnecessary misgivings and insufficient clarity. At the same time, the clinical psychologist is not infrequently called upon to treat the patient he has tested. The relationship between projective testing and planning for psychotherapy is close, and this will be more fully described in Chapter X. With this thought in mind the subsequent discussion is presented: problems of psychotherapy and a number of special dynamic problems seen in terms of apperception.

We believe it can be said that psychoanalysis is in part a theory of learning especially concerned with the life history of the acquisition of percepts with their emotional tone, their lawful interaction with one another, and their influence upon the perception of later stimuli. This formulation is a rudimentary attempt at present and is merely designed to set the general frame of reference for the theory of apperception advanced earlier. Systematic restatement of all psychoanalytic doctrines and experimental verification must remain for the future.*

The learning of percepts is chiefly stated in propositions implicit in the hypothesis concerning the libido theory, primarily a set of genetic propositions dealing with personality. The complex constellation of the oedipal triangle (and its effect on later apperception) constitutes a nuclear concept. The lawful interaction of percepts and the memories thereof is covertly present in what Freud has to say about parapraxes and symptom and character formation. The influence of past percepts upon contemporary apperception is implied in the concept of defense mechanisms and the genetic interpretation of contemporary behavior.

Gestalt psychologists, particularly Koffka, stated from the beginning that the laws of organization of perception are applicable to learning. In line with Gestalt psychology we can say that the subject's apperception of a father figure in the T.A.T. is frequently related to a memory trace of his own father in accordance with the law of similarity. I proposed earlier in this chapter that throughout the development of the individual he perceives, for example, his father figures in many and various ways, a fact which accounts for a whole series of images and image memories. The contemporary image of the father, in accordance with the law of Prägnanz, is a "figure" which is a composite of all previous "figures" and exhibits a "good" organization, yet still accounts for the complexity of all the factors that entered into it.

The contemporary apperception of a father figure is, then, a Gestalt which is formed from the father-image memory and the contemporary image, according to the concept of transposition. Gestalt psychology is thus able to explain the rigidity and yet the complexity of human responses. It allows us to reformulate Freud's principles of defense mechanisms in general by the law of Prägnanz if we simply substitute optimal organization and equilibrium of the organism for the notion of defense. Freud himself regarded the concept of maintenance of equilibrium of forces as one of the most basic of all his considerations. Inasmuch as the percept memories tend to deal with contemporary stimuli in the light of past experience, we may speak of learning on the part of the organism. Learning is consistent with optimal functioning for survival of the organism, and in this sense

---

* This is not meant to be another attempt at neo-Freudianism; rather, it is an attempt to advance Freud's teaching methodologically.

"defense mechanisms" serve the defense of the organism against catastrophic disturbances of its equilibrium. Thus the whole problem of defense mechanisms can possibly be restated by saying that *it is inherent in the organization of the personality to constitute a system of checks and balances that tends to absorb any new stimulus with a minimum of change.* In essence this principle was expressed in the very early writings of Freud in the form of a constancy principle. It has been extensively discussed by Karl Menninger [233]. All perception follows this principle—just as one more photograph in a series of a thousand would only change the composite picture very little. Exceptions to this rule are mentioned in the discussion of the onset of neurosis below. Defense mechanisms proper are only distinguished from other perceptual processes by the fact that they follow a certain pattern as, for instance, later described in reaction formation.

Postman, Bruner, and McGinnies [267] take a similar view of the defensive nature of perceptions without quite as inclusive a formulation as ours. They say:

> Value orientation not only contributes to the selection and accentuation of certain percepts in preference to others, it also erects barriers against percepts and hypotheses incongruent with or threatening to the individual's values.

The process described for the functioning of the personality factors can be easily likened to the buffer system in our blood; the buffer system permits an adjustment of the pH by complex reshifting of ions. The acid of one lemon, normally ingested, would otherwise be fatal to the average human.

The self-regulating configuration of images that constitutes the personality system accounts for the clinical facts of continuity of the personality structure and, under certain circumstances, for rigidity as a protection against pathological upsets. Obsessive-compulsive neuroses with their very repetitiveness are seen as the ultimate in rigid defensiveness against such complete disorganization as is seen in schizophrenia.

The selection of a percept memory or memory trace by a current apperception and the selective influence of the memory trace upon the present apperception and response are consistent with the feedback principle advanced by Wiener [349] in his exposition of cybernetics. Systematic comparisons between his computation machine problems and those of apperceptive distortion may well become a source for future experimental investigations.

In this light the libido theory may be regarded as involving propositions concerned with the history of the perception of oral, anal, and genital stimuli, and with the reaction of the significant adults (parental figures) to them. Since psychoanalysis developed as a clinical empirical science in which the beginnings of methodology are only now becoming manifest, it does not distinguish between underlying learning hypotheses and the actual results. It describes the effect of early oral frustration of an individual without stating that the law of primacy is consistent with the assumptions of the importance of early experiences. It does not systematically explore, in terms of reward and punishment, the effect of the mother's reaction upon the acquisition of cleanliness, but deals nevertheless, in a manner yet to be experimentally stated, with the effect that the image of the mother will have on this individual's later perception of bodily functions. In other words, the percept memory of the mother will have a determining influence on later perceptions. "The child identifies with the mother" can be restated as "The child perceives the mother and retains a memory of that percept." The child learns to associate pleasure or avoidance of anhedonia with the maternal percept. It learns to behave according to the rules of the mother in order to avoid anhedonia, which can derive from inorganic reality (the child might burn itself) or from the mother's disapproval, which could take the form of withdrawal of love or actual physically painful punishment. The percept memory of the mother becomes a guiding image, motivated by the wish to avoid anhedonia, which exerts a selective influence on behavior; it becomes a part of the self-system of the child, or an ego ideal, in Freud's language. Actually, of course, there is not a single percept of the mother, but a whole series of percepts, as Paul Schilder has pointed out [297]. There is mother giving, mother taking, mother cleaning, mother playing, and so on. The percept of the mother differs with the age of the child, and one percept becomes superimposed upon another. Thus the percept of the mother at, say, age 14 of the child, is the final outcome of all the percepts of the mother up to that time. This composite, according to the concepts of Gestalt psychology, will be more than the sum total of the percepts. It will have its own configuration.

Psychoanalysis has been particularly interested in the selective fate and organization of these memory traces. Freud had discovered that earlier learned percepts had become unrecognizable to the individual and to the outsider in the process of integration of percepts. He spoke of their having become *unconscious*. The psychoanalytic technique was designed to recognize the parts that constitute the whole which is immediately observable. Dream images and their analysis by means of free association are probably the best example. The manifest dream constitutes the final Gestalt. "Free associations" reveal the parts that went into the image and permit us to order the dream events into the continuity of the stream of thought processes. Freud's *principle of overdetermination* can then be stated as merely a demonstration of the Gestalt principle that the whole is more than the sum of its parts.

If the self-system (personality) can be seen as a complex system of percepts of diverse nature, influencing behavior selectively, it makes no difference whether the organism at birth is seen as a *tabula rasa,* to be structured entirely by the later learned patterns, or whether it is thought of as born with a number of determining factors of ontogenetic, familial, or a general biological nature. Which biological drive a theory postulates, whether it speaks of sexual drive, aggression, need for security, or avoidance of anhedonia, any one alone or any number combined, is not essential for our theory. Whatever drive presents itself is modified and shaped by the various learned percepts.* Furthermore, each percept is modified and integrated with every other percept.

Psychoanalysis has chosen to speak collectively of those percepts determining the behavior consistent with the avoidance of reality difficulties and the testing of logical propositions as the "ego."* It has chosen further to identify those ego

---

* Factors other than percepts also enter in. e.g., autonomous factors, etc.

percepts which are more specifically associated with goal ideas of long-range nature, or more closely circumscribed and more definitely patterned after a particular person, as the "ego ideal." The percepts governing "moral" behavior are collectively called the "superego." Originally the parental images (or those of other significant adults taking the parental role) constitute the representation of society which, of course, becomes enlarged later.

At first Freud arrived at the awareness of these perceptions by reconstruction from adults—that is, by breaking down the whole of the patient's percept of a maternal figure into its historical component parts. Later on his reconstructions were confirmed by direct observation of children. Psychoanalysis also treats of the laws of changes of percepts by interaction among themselves into different configurations. The best example of this process is the dream work, in which symbolization, condensation, and displacement are the processes leading to the final configuration of the manifest dream.

The *theory of defense mechanisms* is really a theory concerned with the selective influence of memory percepts on the perception of contemporary events. Each defense mechanism is a hypothesis concerning the lawfulness of interaction of images (and their emotional charge) under certain circumstances. If, for instance, a mother has aggressive feelings toward her child along with affectionate feelings, one of the possible results of this conflict of sentiments may be described by psychoanalysis as reaction formation: the mother may be entirely unaware of her aggressive feelings and may manifest excessive affection. We can restate this in conditioned response theory by saying that the following lawfulness is implied: when a stimulus arouses percept memories that elicit both aggressive and nurturant attitudes, and the aggressive one has met with disapproval, then the disapproved attitude is extinguished and the approved one reinforced. This statement makes reaction formation an experimentally verifiable concept, at least in principle. Of course any number of further supplementary hypotheses may have to be developed to fit the complexities of real life situations. Furthermore, Gestalt principles may possibly be better able to fit the model. It may be experimentally demonstrated that when a "good" image and a "bad" image are simultaneously exposed, the result will be a reinforced "good" image modified by some aspects of the "bad" image [120]. Mother love as the result of reaction formation has the restrictive features of overprotectiveness, that is, some of the originally coexisting aggression manifests itself in the new guise. Reaction formation may, in fact, be adequately expressed, as for instance in the principle of conditioned discrimination, which is stated by Hilgard as follows [166]: "If two stimuli are sufficiently distinguishable, the organism can be taught to respond to one of them and to cease responding to the other. This is done by the methods of contrast. That is, one of the stimuli is regularly reinforced, the other regularly non-reinforced. The selective extinction which results is known as conditioned discrimination because the organism has learned to react differentially to the two stimuli. . . ."

As I mentioned earlier, the paranoid originally reacts to the homosexual love object with love and then with hate—as in the typical ambivalence of the boy to his father. He has an image of the loved father (as the big protector) and an image of the aggressive-sadistic father (of primal scene origin). These images may apperceptively destroy any other perception of males. By conditioned discrimination through the social mores and the fear of the father, love response is extinguished and the hate response remains to be projected.

Freud's theory of neurosis has always been stated as one of a compromise formation, that is, it is a statement of the best possible Gestalt in a given system of forces—the id, the ego, the superego, and reality. Freud's theory of the outbreak of an adult neurosis may be stated as follows: "A neurosis becomes manifest when a contemporary constellation of forces coincides with the pattern of a traumatic childhood situation." Under such circumstances the neurosis is a repetition of the earlier established reaction pattern. For example, a patient was married to a much older woman who dominated him in many ways. He had early been a partial orphan brought up by the mother. When his wife deserted him this otherwise well-adjusted man broke into acute anxiety attacks. When by chance he visited the nearby city in which he had been born and which he had visited frequently in the past few years, he wandered aimlessly in a department store, became uncomfortable and increasingly anxious as he approached the exit. At this point he spontaneously recalled that as a small boy he had one day been lost by his mother and had stood crying in the doorway of the same department store. He instantly experienced a decided relief. It appeared on exploration that being left by his wife had created a terror in him similar to the emotion felt when he had been lost by his mother; that is, the present situation fitted a preexisting pattern.

Freud's original contributions, which were concerned with hysterical amnesia or with the traumatic origin of neurosis, with parapraxes, and with dreams, were really hypotheses concerning learning, forgetting, and the methods of recall (hypnosis, persuasion, and free association).

Some Special Dynamic Phenomena Seen as Cases of Apperceptive Distortion

Hypnosis. Hypnosis is one of the processes in which a subject's apperception can be temporarily altered and in which major distortions can be introduced. While we cannot hope to solve the problems of this highly controversial phenomenon, we can attempt to understand it with the help of the concepts so far advanced [33].

The hypnotic process starts with a gradual narrowing of the subject's apperceptive functions and a final limiting of these functions to the apperceptions of the hypnotist's voice. (Apperception it is indeed, since different subjects often give the hypnotic instructions a different meaning.) In fact, Ferenczi's theory of hypnosis suggests that the hypnotist represents the parental image that once upon a time lulled the child or ordered it into sleep. In our terms, the hypnotist is apperceptively distorted by the image memories of the parent. Accordingly, if the hypnosis proceeds well, these parental images, via the hypnotist, have as highly controlling an influence upon the perception of any other stimuli as did the parents in early infancy, during which there was no differentiation between thought and reality.

Obedience to posthypnotic orders demonstrates conclusively that image memories of which the subject is not aware and of which he is unable to become aware may have a controlling influence over action. The subject's apperception of the hypnotist distorts the present stimulus. When, for example, the hypnotist asks the subject how his seat feels, the subject may obediently jump up with a feeling of heat on his seat. In experiments, I have ordered subjects to feel angry or depressed; the subject recalled a past situation of anger or depression, and the memory of this situation distorted the apperception of the T.A.T. cards in such a way as to suggest social situations involving aggression, grief, etc.

The hypnotic state can also be understood as a state of partial self-exclusion of the ego similar to the process of falling asleep but not identical to it. In hypnosis, the self-exclusion of the ego is not as complete as in sleep; cognition of the hypnotist is maintained, and, in fact, some ego functions of reality testing are delegated to the hypnotist.

The degree of self-exclusion of the ego varies with the "stages" of hypnosis. That is, in the process of being hypnotized, a topological regression occurs from conscious perception to preconscious functioning to hypnagogic reverie to that state in which almost all reality testing is relinquished except for sensory contact with the hypnotist.

All the phenomena produced in hypnosis are under control of the ego. The performance of extra- or intra-aggressive acts under the influence of hypnosis, for example, can be explained by the ego theory. In healthy people, enough ego function remains intact to avoid such acts if they are normally ego alien to them; individuals with weak egos can conceivably be led to harmful acts under any ego-weakening force.

Mass psychological phenomena. Mass psychological phenomena can be understood in a way very similar to hypnosis. As Freud pointed out in *Group Psychology and the Analysis of the Ego* [131], each individual introjects the "mass" or group as a transitory factor into the ego and the superego. We can say that while the individual is a member of the group, he "sees the world through the eyes of the mass." The group is seen temporarily as an authoritarian figure and, as in hypnosis, the apperception of the group gains a controlling influence over most other image memories and the drives related to them. Thus lynching, stampeding, and fighting come about by facilitation of primitive impulses.

Transference. While the term "transference" is frequently used quite loosely, I wish to restrict its meaning to pertain to that part of the emotional relationship of the patient to his psychoanalyst which is predicated upon earlier feelings toward other significant figures. An integral part of this relationship is that the analyst is at least theoretically a figure who does not enter actively into emotional relationships and refrains from punishing, praising, or in any way manifestly reacting to the patient's moods.

Transference implies that the patient transfers to the analyst sentiments that he has learned previously. He may thus expect to hear criticism, punishment, or praise from the analyst and may frequently apperceptively distort the analyst's reactions. It is part of the analytic work to show the patient at plausible points the difference between his distortions and the facts.

The analyst's lack of response has a unique effect which differentiates the transference situation from that of any other apperceptive distortion of a similar parental figure. When a patient has found that one particular way of attempting to manipulate the relationship does not succeed, another pattern of behavior emerges. For instance, one patient bluffed a great deal during a part of his analysis, showed off his considerable knowledge, and tried to amuse the analyst.

When this was pointed out to the patient and when it became clear that the analyst failed to respond to the patient's exhibitions, the patient reacted with aggression and later with plain anxiety and dependence. We can say that this patient had originally developed a number of behavior patterns for dealing with his anxiety. When his most recently learned pattern failed, he regressed to an earlier one, just as Mowrer [242] has demonstrated in another context, and then again to an even earlier one. Eventually his relation to the analyst became similar to the one he had with his parents when he was quite small. His apperception of the analyst was distorted by the various images of the parents at various ages. When, for instance, his oedipal fear of the father was reenacted, he was made aware of his fearful expectations. He learned that these fears are unfounded; that is, he relearned the earlier troublesome patterns by insight and conditioning in the transference situation and by "working through" in his external world.

The transference situation can then be described as one in which the patient distorts his apperception of the analyst with increasingly earlier images of the parents and other significant figures of his early life.

Psychoses. In psychotic delusions and hallucinations we may say that the early images have emerged so strongly as to have a greater distorting influence upon the apperception of the contemporary world than in any other condition.

If we say that our current apperception is a Gestalt, a composite picture of all the previously learned apperceptions, then we can say, schematically speaking, that certain early images of a fearful nature have been so strong in a given patient as to powerfully distort all later ones that might otherwise have been of a more harmless nature.

Usually the apperceptive distortion at first affects only a small group of stimuli. In the early paranoid it still involves only one individual or a very few. Sometimes the original distortion is not necessarily absurd and can keep juries busy checking for long periods. With the progress of the disease the patient's distortions usually become more marked and more nearly all-inclusive. The system formation of the paranoid becomes more and more ramified until it involves the whole world—his whole apperceptive field.

Therapy

The psychoanalytic theory of therapy can also be restated in terms of apperceptive distortion and in relation to the T.A.T. (see Chapter VII).

C. The Basic Assumptions for Diagnostic Inferences from the T.A.T. and Similar Methods*

Basic Principles

A diagnosis is an heuristic hypothesis concerning (a) a variety of causal relationships (e.g., between the present and the past, between several discrete phenom-

---

* See also discussion of the concept of diagnosis in the Preface to the Second Edition and in this chapter under this heading, specifically with regard to the nomothetic and idiographic aspects.

ena and a common base); (b) psychodynamics; and (c) structure (e.g., in the form of ego functions and general adaptiveness). In its broadest sense, analytically speaking, the concept of diagnosis involves a metapsychological formulation of the adaptive, genetic, dynamic, structural, economic, and topographical factors. A diagnostic hypothesis thus involves propositions concerning the etiology, treatment, and prognosis of the disease under consideration. A temporal statement should, therefore, depart from all diagnostic propositions to the extent that, when we are dealing with dynamic constellations, we are dealing only with quasi-stable configurations.

If one accepts an *organismic* view—that any part is a function of the whole—any aspect of human behavior can be used for "testing"; a "test" can be considered a sample situation which permits inferences concerning the total personality.

In principle, asking a subject to stand on his head could be used as a testing situation and inferences drawn concerning his personality. Similarly, in organic medicine, since the fingernails are undoubtedly a part of the bodily organism, a diagnosis could be made by inspection of the fingernail, as someone is said to have done. Presumably with enough experience and detailed analysis, many conditions could be recognized by their reflection in the metabolic changes in fingernails.

Nevertheless, diagnosis in organic medicine is not made by inspection of the fingernails but by physical examination of the whole body and by such tests as tend to be most valid and economical as indicated for specific problems. A final diagnosis cannot be obtained without carefully integrating the various x-ray and laboratory findings with the clinical picture; diagnoses on laboratory evidence alone are often misleading. Similarly, in psychological diagnosis, test findings can never stand alone; they must be integrated with the total picture, whether the clinician is a psychiatrist, a psychologist, or a social worker. *There is no slot machine diagnosis possible*—one cannot put in a coin and get out a diagnosis—either in medicine, in psychiatry, or in psychology. *Integration* of test results with other facets of the personality is an essential principle. Thus, I always recommend that test results be reported as follows: "The results *are consistent with* a diagnosis of . . ."

Psychological determinism is another basic assumption that is absolutely essential to the interpretation of T.A.T. productions. The hypothesis of psychological determinism is regarded as a special case of the law of causality,* namely, that everything said or written as a response to some stimulus situation, like all other psychological productions, has a dynamic cause and meaning. The *principle of overdetermination* must be taken into account in this context since it insists that each part of the projected material may have more than one meaning, corresponding to different levels of personality organization. It is useful to recall, by way of example, that a story may be consciously taken from a movie recently seen and yet may be reported only because it reflects an important conflict of the subject on a preconscious level and also because it may, at the same time, have significant symbolic meaning on an unconscious level. Similarly, a given act may

---

* In the sense of a high probability. Causality remains a useful concept desite the apparent exceptions in quantum mechanics.

have several different unconscious meanings, each of them valid in relation to the whole personality.

Startling as this principle may appear at first to behaviorists, it must be pointed out that it holds in the physical sciences also. In physics, for instance, the flight of an object through the atmosphere is the resultant of a number of factors such as its size, weight, and shape and the wind velocity. In our present language, its final path is overdetermined. In a quite similar manner a psychological act is the resultant of a number of different psychological processes. Saying that a psychological event may have several meanings simply indicates that it may be viewed as causally related to a number of different factors.

Another basic assumption is that of the *continuity* of at least the basic personality of one person. To use an analogy: If a river is sampled at various relatively close intervals, the chemical analysis of the content will be highly similar. Any pailful will be representative of the total content. Now, if a new tributary joins the river (as compared to a new situational or developmental factor in psychological sampling), it may of course add factors about which the assayer has to know in order to account for changes in content. A primarily genetic theory of personality, like psychoanalysis, maintains that the main contents of the stream will remain the primary matrix which, beyond a certain point, tributaries can only modify to a greater or lesser degree.

Some common assumptions. There are certain assumptions basic to the interpretation of the T.A.T. which are commonly held by most practitioners of this method. According to Lindzey [218] these assumptions are the following:

First, the *primary assumption,* that in completing or structuring an incomplete or unstructured situation, the individual may reveal his own strivings, dispositions, and conflicts.

He then lists five assumptions involved in determining revealing portions of stories:

1. In creating a story the storyteller ordinarily identifies with one person in the drama, and the wishes, strivings, and conflicts of this imaginary person may reflect those of the storyteller.

2. The storyteller's dispositions, strivings, and conflicts are sometimes represented indirectly or symbolically.

3. All the stories are not of equal importance as diagnostic of his impulses and conflicts. Certain crucial stories may provide a very large amount of valid diagnostic material, while others may supply little or none.

4. Themes that appear to have arisen directly out of the stimulus material are less apt to be significant than those that do not appear to have been directly determined by the stimulus material.

5. Recurrent themes are particularly apt to mirror the impulses and conflicts of the storyteller.

Lindzey then lists four assumptions involved in deriving inferences about other aspects of behavior from these revealing portions of fantasy material:

1. The stories may reflect not only the enduring dispositions and conflicts of the subject, but also the conflicts and impulses that are momentarily aroused by some force in the immediate present (e.g., the test administration). (See Chapter V, under the heading "The Influence of Contemporary Events on T.A.T. Stories.")

2. The stories may reflect events from the past that the subject has not himself actively experienced, but has witnessed or observed, e.g., street scene, motion picture, story. It is assumed further that, although the subject has not himself experienced these events and is telling them as he observed them, the fact that he selects these events rather than others is in itself indicative of his own impulses and conflicts.

3. The stories may reflect group membership or sociocultural determinants in addition to individual or personal determinants.

4. The dispositions and conflicts that may be inferred from the storyteller's creations are not always reflected directly in overt behavior or consciousness.

All of these points are discussed in various chapters of this book.

One major qualification to assumptions such as the preceding which needs to be recognized is that the cognitive style of the subject often determines whether and how his needs and conflicts will be expressed in thematic content. Klein [199] has noted that cognitive controls function as delay mechanisms and need to be considered in the evaluation of behavior (e.g., projective test responses). This cognitive control approach is consonant with the current psychoanalytic trend of regarding ego processes as determinants of perception, rather than simple need states.

In line with this thesis are Holzman's comments [172] concerning the importance of cognitive controls in perception, specifically in relation to the perceptual dysfunction in schizophrenia. Literature is accumulating on both cognitive styles and proprioceptive feedback disorders in the schizophrenic syndrome. Holzman has stated that the act of perception, defined as the transferring of physical stimulation into psychological information, can be broken down into its component phases of reception, registration, processing, and feedback. The perceiver, due to his particular personality organization, has a unique influence on the organizing and reorganizing of the percept at each of these successive stages as well as in the feedback function. Each individual's personality organization is based on his unique set of cognitive controls that are manifested in any disease process (i.e., through the level of perceptual functioning), including states of disorganization. These controls determine the nature of the individual's psychopathological organization.

The Processes Involved in Diagnosis by Various Projective Techniques

The processes in diagnosis vary greatly and have already been outlined in an earlier section of this chapter (Section A). A mixture of processes is usually used in any given projective technique, although one particular process may be most important.

We have already discussed *apperceptive distortion* as opposed to *adaptation* to the nature of the stimulus. The following is a study of the *content* of the responses and is particularly applicable to the T.A.T. We have also mentioned that one can study not only *what* the patient says but *how* he says it, the latter being the *formal, structural* aspect.

What is seen is of primary importance in the T.A.T. and all related tests, such as the M.A.P.S. Four-Picture-Test (F.P.T.), etc. This is equally true of the Sentence Completion Test. In the Rorschach, although other determinants are often of even greater importance, the content can be very illuminating. If a man sees witches attacking a victim, the inference that he sees women as aggressive witches is certainly of great importance. In a technique as unstructured as finger painting, what is being painted is always an important clue to the total personality. Thus, the *apperceptive content,* what is seen, while primary to the T.A.T., is significantly involved in other projective techniques as well.

Expressive aspects are the primary factors involved in diagnosis in Mira's technique and in graphology. These aspects are also primary in the Rorschach, where one's first concern is not so much *what* does the subject see in the inkblot, but *how* does he see it? Does he envision the blot as a whole or in parts? Is he influenced by color or shading? Does he see a person, an animal, or an object in motion? To a certain extent these aspects are also involved in diagnosis with the T.A.T. Organization of thought processes, sentence structure, bizarre verbalizations, etc., are all useful clues.

However, the expressive aspects are all-important in such techniques as the Mosaic Test, where one is dealing with subsemantic material of nonverbal substrata which are affected by gross lesions.

Expressive movements make up the formal aspects of various projective tests, and these aspects lend themselves to forming typical patterns which can, to a certain extent, be identified with certain nosological entities. However, this can only be done within limits, for instance, in the Multiple Choice Rorschach, where a subject is presented with five possible responses to each plate and asked to pick the one he considers most suitable. This type of short-form testing lends itself to statistical patterning, but only in the sense of uncovering trends. Like statistics of longevity, it may not be at all meaningful for any one individual.

Closely related to the expressive, or structural aspects, is the ability to perceive *Gestalt formations.* This is a more specific function which, if disturbed, may be indicative of gross pathology. In the Rorschach, the function of perceiving the proper figure-ground relationship may be disturbed, possibly apperceptively distorted in addition. A small detail may be seen and transformed into a confabulated whole, disregarding the actual configurations of the rest of the blot. Of even clearer importance is the Gestalt problem in the Bender-Gestalt Test, where the subject is required to copy geometric figures. Inability to carry out this task signifies impairment of the ability to form a Gestalt, and may indicate organic brain damage. This same ability to form Gestalten is necessary in the Mosaic Test. In the T.A.T. this function only rarely enters into the situation, in such unusual cases as when the subject is unable to see the picture as a whole, or when he leaves the stimulus altogether.

Projection of *body image* or *self-image* is another process involved in many projective techniques. In its purest form it can be seen in figure drawing. The subject may see himself as weak and feminine and draw a figure which shows this very clearly. He may separate the head from the body by drawing an unusually long neck, indicating his fear of his instinctual impulses. He may draw a very small or a very large figure; the body line may be thin, weak, and wavering, or sharp, strong, and assertive. Content is of significance here as well, as in whether the figure is clothed or unclothed, indication of sexual organs, etc.

Projection of the body image can also be seen quite clearly in the Rorschach. A woman who sees a dressmaker's dummy in plate 1, where most people see a woman's body, thinks of herself as a dressed-up doll, and not as a real woman at all. Much can often be learned about body image from story 1 of the T.A.T. in comments about the violin and the bow, often in a negative reference (remarks about the violin or bow being broken, etc.) The figure in 3BM may be seen as crippled. The man on the rope in 17BM may be seen as muscular, etc.

Preferences are the basis of the Szondi test, where the subject is shown eight photographs at a time and asked to pick out the two he likes the best and the two he likes the least. The choices are made on some basis of identification or libidinal investment. In other words, the pictures the subject chooses as his "likes" are those faces which seem to him to show qualities that are ego syntonic, and selects the "dislikes" on the basis of qualities that are ego alien.

Preferences of color in finger painting are also revealing, as are the figures in doll play. In the M.A.P.S. Test the element of choice also enters, since the subject chooses the figures for his story.

Bases for Diagnostic Validity of the T.A.T. and Related Tests

Normative, Statistical Factors (Interindividual Factors)

Projective techniques have been a matter of much concern to academic psychologists because they cannot easily be made to conform to the usual methods of establishing reliability and validity.

The collection of norms for intelligence or achievement tests can follow a clear-cut pattern: a representative sample population is tested and the norms established on a distribution curve. Any individual subsequently tested can then be compared to the sample population, and a specific point on the distribution curve assigned to him.

This type of procedure is difficult to follow with projective techniques. For one thing, it is almost impossible to find a sample representative of a large enough segment of the population. While this may not be quite so difficult for the Rorschach, it is extremely difficult for a test like the T.A.T.; the content of psychodynamics is infinitely more affected by the many cultural substructures in the United States than, for example, an intelligence test. New Yorkers of second generation Irish, Italian, or Jewish background will differ markedly from each other, not to mention Midwesterners or Southerners, even if they are all matched for age, sex, intelligence, and economic level.

Further, even if such a normative approach were possible—or to the extent that it is possible—it is hardly very useful. As Rosenzweig and Fleming have pointed out [283], in projective techniques we are not only interested in the definitive value of the subject's standing with regard to group modes of behavior (what they call interindividual comparisons), but also, and primarily, in those aspects of the responses characteristic of this one individual. A statistical approach to projective techniques is of necessity an atomistic approach, whereas the value of projective techniques lies in their molar approach to personality. Thus a breakdown of the responses robs the test results of much of their meaning-fulness.

Sharkey and Ritzler [301] review the general status of studies of the diagnostic validity of the T.A.T. They cite Renaud as having found few differences and Davison as being unable to find consistent differences between neurotics and schizophrenics. On the other hand, they cite Dana [98–100] who found consistent differences between normals, neurotics and psychotics on measures of story organization; popular responses. They are critical of the studies of Eron and associates [110, 137, 277] for using measures of emotional tone, story outcome, and activity level to differentiate normals, neurotics and psychotics. They feel that the story content in response to T.A.T. stimuli is excessively determined by the stimulus characteristics. This is a critique difficult to understand since the rest of us have for decades found great individual differences in response to these stimuli [221].

Lundy's comment regarding studies of reliability of the T.A.T. is that the standard psychometric test, coefficient alpha, is not an appropriate means of determining the reliability of the T.A.T., despite its wide usage. T.A.T. pictures are selected from a domain which is highly heterogeneous and coefficient alpha is most reliable when determining the reliability of a test whose concern is homogeneous. In addition, the T.A.T. test-retest conclusions may be adversely affected by the standard instructions to write a "creative" story.

To a certain extent, any accumulation of statistical data concerning the T.A.T. may be helpful as a frame of reference, particularly in respect to formal characteristics. For example, it may be useful to accumulate thousands of samples to ascertain what percentage of males sees the figure in 3BM as male or what percentage sees the woman on the right in picture 2 as pregnant. If we were to discover, for instance, that only 10 per cent of a large population tested sees the woman as pregnant, we would then hesitate to infer that not seeing her as pregnant signifies a meaningful scotoma; if 50 per cent or more men see the figure in 3BM as a female, we would hesitate to consider such a response as even the merest suggestion of a feminine identification. Nevertheless, even knowing this, we might have to decide that it may mean feminine identification in some and not in others, depending on how much empathy with specifically feminine traits is revealed in making a woman the hero of the story. Even if 90 per cent of all males do not mention the woman in picture 2 as pregnant, if someone describes her as slim and well-proportioned we would still have to interpret this as a denial of pregnancy. In other words, although we recommend accumulation of such data, the final interpretation must be from an idiographic approach. Each response must be evaluated in relation to all the other responses in the test, as pointed out below.

Content Analysis

Content analysis is a method of counting the occurrence of certain words within a given context. One could, for instance, count all the words pertaining to aggression and love on a page of Dickens and a page of Hemingway. One might find that words connoting aggression occur much more often on the Hemingway page. One can apply the same technique counting the frequency of various words in transcripts of psychotherapeutic sessions utilizing apperceptive methods. Within certain limits of usefulness and relative frequency of certain words will tell one something about the narrator if compared to frequency of the same words in other peoples' responses to the same stimuli. The technique therefore lends itself to a quantitative analysis of responses to apperceptive techniques.

Intratest Patterns

The T.A.T. deals, in essence, with a series of social situations to which we ask the subject to respond. In interpreting the results, what we are primarily interested in are any repetitive patterns of behavior in dealing with these various situations. A response gains its meaningfulness in part from its relationship to the rest of the responses and in part from its relationship to similar responses to other situations. For instance, if all stories end on a hopeless note, or if all females are seen as benign and nurturant, or all males as protective, we feel entitled to make the inference that the repetitiveness of the apperceptions are related to a definite variable in the subject's personality. Thus the repetitiveness itself, and any patterning within the test responses, becomes a criterion of reliability (and by implication, of validity) of the responses for the given individual, irrespective of any relationship to population scores. By this token and the facts mentioned below, the responses of one individual to a stimulus may be considered interpretable as psychologically significant. We suggest calling this basis of validity the *intratest validity*. (Rosenzweig speaks of this as the intraindividual comparison, but we prefer to reserve this term for the following variable.)

Intraindividual Comparisons: Behavior Variables and "Fantasy" Test Variables

In addition to the two comparisons mentioned by Rosenzweig and Fleming, I should like to point out that a comparison between manifest behavior and fantasy behavior in the test responses is a valuable basis for inferences. For instance, if we learn that, behaviorally, someone is a Caspar Milquetoast and all his stories are filled with blood and thunder, we may feel entitled to infer that there is a good deal of repressed aggression in the subject. Or if we deal with a manifestly boisterous and aggressive male and find a predominance of themes of passivity, we may make the inference that manifest behavior is in a defensive relationship to the latent variables. This factor again emphasizes the importance of a global approach to personality; in clinical practice there is no place for experimentation. The psychologist should be informed of behavioral data, or final evaluation of test data should only be made by a clinician who has access to both the behavioral and test data.

CHAPTER II

THE CLINICAL USE OF
THE T.A.T.

A. The T.A.T. and Related Methods

THE THEMATIC APPERCEPTION TEST IS A TECHNIQUE FOR THE investigation of the dynamics of personality as it manifests itself in interpersonal relations and in the apperception or meaningful interpretation of the environment. It consists, in its present form, of a series of 31 pictures. Testees are asked to tell stories about some of the pictures, thereby presumably revealing their personal, individual apperception of purposely ambiguous stimuli.

The T.A.T. was originally described by Morgan and Murray [239] in 1935. Tomkins [325] shows that there were earlier attempts by psychologists and psychiatrists to elicit meaningful responses of subjects to pictures. These include workers like Brittain [79], who published such an attempt in 1907, Libby [216], who used such a procedure (like Brittain) with children in 1908, and finally Schwartz [299], who developed his Social Situation Test in 1932. None of these forerunners, however, has attained the popularity of the T.A.T., which at present ranks second only to the Rorschach Test.*

The present T.A.T. pictures are the third set to be used since 1935. Aside from additions and omissions made since the first series was issued, the cards in the second and third series are distinguished by being twice the original size, a fact that probably facilitates the testee's rapport with the pictures.

Aside from the present wide use of the T.A.T., similar verbal and picture tests have been devised to meet the special problems presented by different cultures

---

* The *Newsletter* of the Division of Clinical and Abnormal Psychology, August, 1953, stated that the Rorschach and the T.A.T. were the two most widely used tests. An A.P.A. report on the use of tests *(Report on Survey of Current Psychological Testing Practice,* Supplement to *Newsletter,* Division of Clinical and Abnormal Psychology, A.P.A., Vol. 4, No. 5) indicated that the Rorschach and the T.A.T. were used to about the same extent, with the Rorschach being used somewhat more. That report stated: ". . . in general the TAT runs the Rorschach test a close second . . . but is not as frequently considered 'very important' (62% for TAT versus 85% for Rorschach)." It is likely that the preference has remained in the same order in the succeeding three decades.

{ MAPS

and particular age groups. These include the M.A.P.S. (Make A Picture Story Test) developed by Edwin S. Shneidman in 1947. It varies the T.A.T. material principally by separating the figures and the background, allowing the subject to select and place his figures on depopulated backgrounds before he tells his story. Thus the subject responds to a stimulus situation which he has partly created himself and he has the opportunity for using motor expressive acts in accomplishing the test task. The materials for the M.A.P.S. Test consist of 22 background pictures which comprise both structured and unstructured (ambiguous) situations and 67 figures—adults, children, minority group figures, and silhouettes and figures with blank faces.

The Thompson Modification of the T.A.T. for Negro Subjects is based on the assumption that it is easier for blacks to identify with figures of blacks than figures of white subjects. Accordingly, 23 of the original pictures have been adapted by substituting black figures for the original white ones. Six of the original pictures have been used unchanged, and one has been omitted. The new drawings were made by V. A. Winslow, Director of the Art Department of Dillard University, New Orleans, Louisiana.

In 1942 the U. S. Office of Indian Affairs and the Committee on Human Development of the University of Chicago inaugurated the Research on Indian Education. About 1000 children from 6 to 18 years in 11 Papago, Zuñi, Hopi, Navaho, and Sioux communities were studied. The T.A.T. used was a series of 12 pictures drawn by an Indian artist and representing people and social situations presumed to be within the everyday experience of all Indian children: a picture of two boys facing a man; two adults, one leading a horse; an adult woman with a baby in arms and with two other children seated before her; a group of children and adults around a grinding stone; several young men in dance regalia; a landscape scene, of fields, fences, dried animal bones, and the like. The people in the picture were all American Indians.

A modification of the T.A.T. was also designed by Uma Choudhury of the Department of Anthropology, Indian Museum of Calcutta. The pictures were made from live models and imaginary pictures to suit Indian cultural patterns.

Another cultural modification of the T.A.T. was developed by Boris Iflund of the University of California for use on the University Expedition to South Africa. The same principle was employed, translating the dramatis personnae and the setting to South Africa. Another set of pictures was devised for the South Pacific Micronesian culture.

The basic conception of a projective method for diagnosing group properties was developed at the Research Center for Group Dynamics by Horwitz and Cartwright [173]. The technique, involving a projective picture test with slightly modified T.A.T. instructions, was first employed at the National Training Laboratory for Group Development, at Bethel, Maine, in 1947. The way the interacting group phrases a relatively unstructured stimulus configuration, the kind of relationships it sees, and the feelings it deems relevant may provide important insights into the group's structure and internal processes. A set of five pictures was developed by Henry and Guetzkow [163] to show up different aspects of group processes. They consist of: (1) a conference group—seven men assembled around a conference table; (2) a man standing in the doorway of a house; (3) two men facing each other; (4) an older woman and a younger man; (5) an informal scene of four men in what looks somewhat like a clubroom.

It had long been felt that the T.A.T. was not particularly suitable for young children, and in 1949 Leopold Bellak and Sonya Sorel Bellak developed the Children's Apperception Test (C.A.T.) for use with children between the ages of 3 and 10.*

Symonds' Picture Story Test was designed for the study of adolescent boys and girls. It consists of 20 pictures divided into set A and set B, both of which may be used on successive days, or set B may be used alone. These pictures are designed to facilitate the projection of problems typical of the adolescent: leaving home, coming home late at night, social-sexual rivalry about dating, concern about the future (in a picture showing a young boy and girl consulting a fortune-teller), a girl looking at her new self in the mirror, a boy apparently suffering from *Weltschmerz,* pictures concerned with delinquency and jail, and other situations.

A further variation on the T.A.T. theme (though developed earlier and independently) is the Four-Picture-Test designed by D. J. van Lennep. The task here is not to tell four separate stories, but to tell a single story in which all four pictures appear. The first picture shows two people together, the second one person alone, the third represents being socially alone (a figure leaning against a lamppost in a dark street), and the fourth being together with others in a group (the scene is of two tennis players with others watching).

B. Indications for the Use of the T.A.T.†

The T.A.T. is a complex test which, even in the hands of the most experienced practitioner and when used in an abbreviated form, takes not inconsiderable time and effort in administration and interpretation. Even though the test can be group or self-administered, any systematic interpretation will still take at least half an hour per record, and often longer.

Aside from the economic aspects, it is in the nature of the T.A.T. to deal with the subtle, dynamic factors of the personality which will be the subject of investigation only under specific circumstances. Perhaps we can gain from a comparison of the psychological examination and the physical examination. There are routine physical examinations by inspection, auscultation, and percussion, possibly by taking the blood pressure. A more complex examination may include urine examination, fluoroscopy, a blood count. X-rays of the chest have become routine, but x-rays of other parts of the body, tests of body chemistry, basal metabolism, etc., are requested only when there are stringent differential diagnostic reasons, or a particularly careful evaluation is necessary for especially stressful tasks or prior to undergoing major surgery.

Similarly, for ordinary purposes, paper and pencil tests of ability, intelligence, and achievement may suffice for routine examinations of students, employees, etc. However, if we are called upon to do a special selection for highly demanding

---

* See Chapter X on the C.A.T.
† See also Chapter VII.

tasks, such as those of air pilots, special government personnel, or chief executives, if differential diagnosis is indicated, or if the patient is about to undergo a major form of psychotherapy, then more complex procedures such as a T.A.T. are indicated, and deserve the time and effort invested.

The question of course remains as to which of the major tests should be used when a complex psychodiagnostic task is to be performed. One popular answer to that problem is to use batteries of projective tests. This approach undeniably has some merit. For reasons which we only partly understand, one test may show problems which the other tests do not, even though in principle it should illustrate the same problem. However, the principle of "the more, the better," should not apply. The unnecessary use of whole batteries has bogged down personality testing more than necessary. One principle in assorting batteries should certainly be that the tests included tap the personality structure and dynamics by different means, e.g., a verbal test such as the T.A.T. should be combined with an expressive (myoneural) test like the Figure Drawing Test, for example.

We can, however, state the indications for using the T.A.T. even more specifically: the T.A.T. is a content test. More than any other test in use at present, it shows the actual dynamics of interpersonal relationships. By the very nature of the pictures it gives basic data on the testee's relationship to male or female authority figures, to contemporaries of both sexes, and frequently it shows the genesis in terms of family relationships. It may not so clearly indicate the intensity of fears as does the Rorschach, but it tells one the nature of them—fear of lack of support or fear of attack by males in specific situations—and it shows the hierarchy of needs and the structure of the compromises among id, ego, and superego. The T.A.T. is only incidentally, and not particularly successfully, a diagnostic tool, if diagnosis means the identification of a given patient's disorder within a definite nosological group. This is better done by the clinical interview, the Rorschach, and other techniques.

The T.A.T. and the Rorschach can hardly be considered competitive or mutually exclusive techniques. The Rorschach test is invaluable as a formal, percept-analytic technique; it reveals better than any other test available the formal, expressive nature of thought processes and those of emotional organization. By this token, it reveals patterns that are more or less typical for certain psychiatric syndromes or disease processes. The content analysis of the Rorschach test, although it has its natural limitations, has not been utilized to the extent it deserves in the majority of present methods of interpretation.

C. Varieties of Administration Procedures of the T.A.T.

Individual Administration

As in every testing situation, the subject should be put at ease and a proper noncommittal rapport established. The subject is seated in a chair. Usually it is desirable to have the test administrator seated *behind and to the side* of the subject so that he cannot see the examiner but so that the examiner may have full view of the patient's facial expressions. This position may have to be modified with suspicious and otherwise disturbed patients, and with children.

The instructions for administration of the T.A.T., as suggested by Murray, are as follows: Form A (suitable for adolescents and adults of average intelligence and sophistication): "This is a test of imagination, one form of intelligence. I am going to show you some pictures, one at a time; and your task will be to make up as dramatic a story as you can for each. Tell what has led up to the event shown in the picture, describe what is happening at the moment, what the characters are feeling and thinking; and then give the outcome. Speak your thoughts as they come to your mind. Do you understand? Since you have 50 minutes for 10 pictures, you can devote about five minutes to each story. Here is the first picture."

Form B (suitable for children, for adults of little education, and for psychotics): "This is a storytelling test. I have some pictures here that I am going to show you, and for each picture I want you to make up a story. Tell what has happened before and what is happening now. Say what the people are feeling and thinking and how it will come out. You can make up any kind of story you please. Do you understand? Well, then, here's the first picture. You have five minutes to make up a story. See how well you can do."

The exact wording of these instructions may be altered to suit the age, intelligence, personality, and circumstances of the subject. It may be better not to say at the start, "This is an opportunity for free imagination," as an instruction of this sort sometimes evokes the suspicion in the subject that the examiner intends to interpret the content of his free associations (as in psychoanalysis). Such a suspicion may severely check the spontaneity of his thought.

The instructions I use are in essence identical, except that I always omit "This is a test of imagination, one form of intelligence," since it seems inappropriate in the clinical setting; also, I often add: "Let yourself go freely." Then one may have to answer, in a nondirective way, any questions the subject may ask. It is permissible and even helpful to make some encouraging remark at the end of the first story. Otherwise, it is better for the examiner to say nothing for the rest of the time, unless the subject has become too involved in a long, rambling story. At such times one may remind the subject that what is wanted is a story about what goes on, what leads up to it, and what the outcome will be. If the subject remains entirely on the descriptive level, or tells only very brief stories, it is useful to remind him that we want the story of what is going on, what people are feeling and thinking, what happened before, and what the outcome may be.

Self-Administration

The standard procedure has been for the subject to tell his story orally and for the administrator to record the responses by hand or by means of a recording device. It is economical in many cases to give the selected cards to the subject with written or oral instructions, emphasizing that he should look at only one picture at a time, and then to let him write the stories on plain paper in the office or at home. It is helpful to let the subject know that he is expected to write about 300 words per story as spontaneously as possible. The following instructions may be typed on the front inside cover of the set that is given to the subject for self-administration:

Instructions for Self-Administration

1. Please write a story about each picture in this folder.
2. Do not look at the pictures before you are ready to write.
3. Look at one picture at a time only, in the order given, and write as dramatic a story as you can about each. Tell what has led up to the event shown in the picture, describe what is happening at the moment, what the characters are thinking and feeling; and then give the outcome. Write your thoughts as they come to your mind.
4. It should not be necessary to spend more than about seven minutes per story, although you may spend more time if you wish.
5. Write about 300 words per story, or about one typing-paper page if you write in longhand. If at all possible, please type the longhand story later, without changes, in duplicate, double-spaced, one story per page.
6. Please number the stories as you go along, and then put your name on the front sheet.

The obvious advantage of this time-saving procedure is somewhat offset by such disadvantages as a possible loss of spontaneity by the subject, the inability to control the length of the stories, and the lack of opportunity to intervene if the subject begins to show lack of cooperation in responding. Nevertheless, in psychiatric and psychological office practice the self-administration method has proven quite satisfactory.

Again for practical reasons, it has become more and more the custom to use only 10 or 12 pictures (see Chapter III). These should preferably be such a selection as may seem most indicated, most likely to illuminate the details of presumably existent problems of the patient. (A discussion of the special usefulness of each picture and the special features of personality it is likely to elicit is offered below.) This is particularly true when the T.A.T. is used as part of a clinical practice, where one is likely to know a few things about the subject prior to testing and the practitioner can permit himself as much flexibility as he wishes in obtaining material for his own use.

Group Administration

It is also feasible to use the T.A.T. as a technique for group administration. For this purpose the pictures are projected onto a screen and the subjects are given the same instructions as for individual administration, but are asked to write their stories down. Clark [91] collected 852 stories from a wide group of subjects ranging in age from 16 to 64, and basic themes for each picture were selected. Fifty college students were then shown T.A.T. pictures projected on a screen, given a list of the basic themes for each card, and asked to check the story which most nearly represented their idea of the picture portrayed. The same students were also given a modified form of the usual T.A.T. in which they were asked to write original stories. Clark found a substantial relationship between results obtained by both methods, but the relationships were higher when the clinical form was administered first. She concluded that the group projection test merits further study as a possible screening device when the usual administration is not feasible.

An investigation was made by Eron and Ritter [111] as to the possible differences between T.A.T.'s administered orally-individually and those obtained in a group where everybody wrote his own stories. Using two groups of 30 students each, they found that oral stories were longer, but that the quality and amount of thematic content was identical. The written stories had a somewhat happier tone and seemed to evoke more flippancy. However, the authors felt that because of the similarity of thematic content, the written stories elicited much the same material.

Inquiry

An inquiry into the stories *after* they are completed is most helpful. It is particularly useful after one has had some experience in interpretation and knows what to ask for. As a routine, one would inquire for free associations or thoughts concerning all places, dates, proper names of persons, and any other specific or unusual information given by the subject.

Contrary to statements by other authors, notably Rapaport [271], I believe it most important that the inquiry be conducted only *after all the stories have been told,* and not following each story, otherwise preconscious material might become conscious and interfere with the rest of the test responses. The inquiry may actually become a free association process and part of a psychotherapeutic situation (see Chapter VII).

Psychological Problems of Test Administration

The administration of the T.A.T. is simple in manifest procedure, but it is intrinsically fairly complex. Undoubtedly the relation between the tester and the testee is very important for the richness of the responses. Beginning students almost invariably complain that the stories they get are too short. Aside from the fact that brevity need not be a serious drawback (Murray states in his manual that he considers 300 words as average per story), as the course continues the protocols the students obtain become miraculously longer.

The tester-testee relationship has a certain resemblance in its problems to those of the transference situation. The subject comes for help; he is frightened and does not know what to expect. Rapport is a magic word; in this instance it means that the tester must appear interested, but not overeager or the subject may feel that he is merely there for the interest of the psychologist. The clinician should be friendly but not overfriendly, which may elicit heterosexual or homosexual panic in the patient. The best atmosphere is one in which the patient feels that he and the clinician are working together seriously on something very important which will help him, and not something that will be threatening.

Having had the opportunity to get to know patients well over a long stretch of time in psychoanalysis, I have come to learn a good deal about what test administration means to people who had been tested either by me or by others. One patient with a classical hysteria disappointed me greatly with unexpectedly poor stories. About two weeks later she had a dream in which I was sitting at a front desk of an advertising agency, as a clerk, and she was sitting as she had sat during the test administration. I saw this patient in a hospital outpatient clinic, and her associations revealed that she felt that since I worked in a clinic I could not be any good (just a clerk) and that she was there primarily as a guinea pig, and that I would tell (advertise) all about her to medical students. Naturally such a mental set, whether conscious or unconscious, does not permit good responses.

Another patient had an even more markedly negative dream concerning the test administration: she dreamed that I was peeping into her bathroom while she was defecating. Her T.A.T. stories were very constricted. Judging by what I have learned analytically, a majority of patients do not respond with the first thought or story or impulse to any technique. When they do not tell the first thing that comes to mind and the response is given aloud, the defense operations become clearly apparent. However, it is very encouraging that the preferred substitute is nearly as informative as the suppressed response, and it gives us defenses in addition.*

These processes hold true for all the projective techniques, not just the T.A.T. For instance, Dr. Molly Harrower† asked one patient to draw whatever was most unpleasant to him (as part of her Most Unpleasant Concept Test) and he drew a crab. While free associating in the treatment situation with me the patient stated that actually his first idea had been "vagina." He associated by seeing the crab as a dangerous, cutting, castrating animal. In other words, instead of the object of the drive aim, the patient responded with a concept expressing his idea of punishment for the wish. Thus the response must be seen as the result of the original impulse plus—or rather, substituted by—the superego representation. However, when the patient associated during the testing situation, the fuzziness of the crab's tentacles reminded him of pubic hair, thus constituting more of a breakthrough of the original idea.

If a patient tells a very short, meager story, it may help to indicate to him that he could tell a longer story, or to suggest that he let himself go more, adding some reassuring words to this statement.

Some patients will tell poor stories regardless of how the test administration is carried out, and this is as diagnostic as any other form of behavior. It has, incidentally, been my experience that by and large hysterics take more to the T.A.T. and obsessives to the Rorschach. It also seems to me that this holds true not only for patients but for the choice of method by psychologists, i.e., the more obsessive psychologists prefer to work with the Rorschach.

There are a number of artificial steps that can be taken in an attempt to enrich the responses. Murray** has suggested letting the patient see the card for only 10 seconds, after which he tells the story, thus obviating description. Time pressure has been suggested for the Rorschach and could certainly also be used with the T.A.T. The only artefact with which I have any experience is the use of sedation in the form of oral Nembutal one-half hour before the sitting. For depressed subjects I have sometimes mixed this with a stimulant like Dexedrine, and in rare

---

* In the treatment situation, the patient will often tell me what his real first response was, which he had not given to the tester.

† Personal communication to the author.

** As reported in the T.A.T. Newsletter, *Journal of Projective Techniques.*

cases I have administered Amytal Sodium and caffein intravenously. All these expedients help sometimes and not at other times. A similar effect on the guarding functions of the ego can probably be obtained by asking the patient to have a couple of drinks before he appears, but this suggestion should only be made if one attempt has failed, else the patient's anxious expectations will far outweigh any relaxing effect of the spirits. In all of these instances, the patient should be accompanied by a responsible person.

CHAPTER III

THE T.A.T. PICTURES
AS STIMULI

A. Selection of Pictures for Individual T.A.T.'s

SINCE I PREFER TO DEVOTE ONLY A SINGLE SESSION TO THE AD-
ministration of the T.A.T., both for time-saving in administration
and interpretation, and because I believe that usually an optimum of material is
obtained from about 10 or 12 pictures, some word must be said about the criteria
of selecting pictures for a given case.

I believe there are certain pictures which should be used in every case because
they illuminate so well those basic dynamic problems which one meets in every
case. Naturally, all these statements reflect my own experience. Though this has
been considerable, even more enriched by several thousand records brought by
students of my T.A.T. courses as part of the course requirements, my own
experiences will of necessity differ here and there from those of other investigators. My statements, therefore, should be taken as empirical ones and not as
gospel truth.

The pictures which I consider essential for testing *any* males are: 1, 2, 3BM, 4,
6BM, 7BM, 11, 12M, and 13MF. They should be shown in this order. For
females, I consider essential: 1, 2, 3BM, 4, 6GF, 7GF, 9GF, 11, 13MF.*

The responses I expect from each picture will be discussed in detail below.
Suffice it to say here that the above nine pictures seem to me to illuminate all the

---

* In 1969, A. H. Hartman conducted a survey, as part of which he asked 90 psychologists to rank
order their choices for a standard set of T.A.T. cards. There was a very high consistency in the judges'
top 10 choices, ranked in the following order: 13MF, 1, 6BM, 4, 7BM, 2, 3BM, 10, 12M, 8BM. His
series differs in not having 11, but having instead 10 and 8BM. I have little quarrel with these
differences and would agree now that 11 does not prove useful often enough and, in turn, fairly
frequently use 10 and 8BM in addition to my original choices. Hartman recommends a basic T.A.T.
set of eight cards, namely, 1, 2, 3BM, 4, 6BM, 7BM, 13MF, and 8BM. 12M was ranked in ninth place
by 47.8 per cent of the judges. I still feel strongly in favor of including it if testing is done with an eye
on psychotherapy, as this picture so frequently reveals attitudes towards therapy and therapist. Dr.
Hartman has been kind enough to permit me to quote from his table, which appears in "A Basic
T.A.T. Set" by A. H. Hartman, *Journal of Projective Techniques and Personality Assessment,* Vol. 34, No.
5, 1970.

basic human relationships. Picture 3BM is included for females because I have found it to work as well for females as for males, and it produces infinitely richer stories than its counterpart, 3GF.

To these basic nine pictures should be added those specific one, two, or three others which are necessary to the understanding of the particular person, as far as can be judged from the case history (which should, ideally, be available or very briefly taken). If the patient comes with a marital problem, we will want to include all the pictures likely to elicit problems of male-female relationships. If the patient comes with a depression, all the pictures related to aggression and suicidal themes should be included. If it appears to be a reactive depression to the death of a closely related person, 15 is indispensable; 12M may also possibly elucidate that theme. If a male patient seems to have primarily homosexual fears, 9BM, 10, 17BM, and 18BM may be included. Other problems can be handled in a similar manner with flexibility and some economy.

No doubt there are many areas of life not as fully suggested by the T.A.T. pictures as one might wish. For this reason modifications for other age groups, such as Symonds' M.A.P.S. and the C.A.T. have been designed. Such tests as the Horn-Tomkins test fulfill other (industrial) needs. Murstein [251] discusses the general area of thematic modifications.

No experimentally derived performance standards for "normals" or even for various diagnostic groups have as yet been fully established, although much work is currently being carried on to provide evidence of modal performance for members of various groups. The remarks made below, although not grounded in experimental evidence, do possess a strong background of empirical sanction. The few normative data so far available are based on such small samples as to be misleading. Thus, Rosenzweig and Fleming's [283] study is excellent for its exposition of the method used, but cites norms which are largely so divergent from my own experience as to be surely sampling artefacts.

B. Typical Themes Elicited

Picture 1

A young boy is contemplating a violin which rests on a table in front of him.

This is the single most valuable picture in the T.A.T., insofar as such a statement can be made. If I were to be permitted only one picture, this would be my choice for an attempt to make statements about the total personality.

One great value of this picture lies in the fact that it is a good start to the testing situation. It is nonthreatening and induces a feeling of reverie in adults and adolescents.

As to themes, this picture usually leads to an easy identification of the subject with the boy and brings out the *relationship toward the parental figures.* That is, it usually becomes quite apparent whether the parents were perceived as aggressive, domineering, helpful, understanding, or protective. Aside from learning about the subject's relationship to his parents, we also find out to which parent a certain kind of relationship existed. Frequently, we get themes on the conflict between autonomy and compliance with authority in all its wide variations and different patterns. For example, one subject may try to escape the parental commands to practice the violin by playing in the street, but then he finally feels that he ought to go in and play the violin; or he may run away from home; or the hero might be described as not obeying his parents and doing what he wants. Later on he experiences failure because he did not obey them. Thus one subject may display guilt feelings about his autonomy, while in other cases all may go well after he has broken away. Therefore this card is especially successfully employed with adolescents.

Another need this card frequently brings out is that of *achievement*. It is particularly important to see how the success is achieved, whether just on a fantasy level or on a reality level.

Finally, we find that subjects give *symbolic sexual responses* to this card. The play on the strings of the violin, the play with the fiddle, frequently becomes a symbolic story of masturbation, and castration fears are often brought in when the subject insists that the strings have been broken. The relationship between bow and violin is often seen as that of a male and a female. Mastery of the violin frequently constitutes a fusion of sexual and achievement drives; to be able to fiddle like father did.

Aggression may be expressed, with and without sexual connotations, in breaking violin or bow. Superego *anxiety* may express itself in stories in which the boy is said to be blind; this is probably an expression of castration fears, related to voyeuristic wishes.

The *body image* or, in a wider sense, the *self-image* is frequently significantly illuminated in this picture. Most often the violin, and sometimes the bow, serves in this capacity, although the image of the boy may do so too. There may be references to the violin's having a crack, or being dead inside and mute, revealing a sense of not functioning well, of being muted. Reference to "deadness" usually indicates feelings of very severe emotional impoverishment to an extent which compels one to consider schizophrenia in the differential diagnosis. The figure of the boy is sometimes seen as crippled, also suggesting a literally warped body image.

Obsessive preoccupations may become apparent when the subject is much concerned with the notepaper, or the mussiness of the hair, or a black speck present in most of the reproductions of pictures I have seen. In these instances it is referred to as dirt. Frequently the violin, as lying beneath, is identified as a female and the bow as a male, and the whole story about playing the violin may then be seen as *sexual activity. Neuropsychologically,* picture number one is particularly useful. For years it has been an amazing experience to find that there are a good number of subjects with adequate eyesight, of average intelligence, and nonpsychotic, who *do not recognize the violin,* to judge by their spontaneous stories. Inquiry will often lead them to recognize it correctly. I have never understood how and why this occurs. In none of the cases I had seen has there been valid reason to suspect that cultural factors might have been involved. As a result of my generally increasing interest in minimal brain dysfunction (now also referred to as attention deficit disorder, A.D.D.) [43] I became aware of the fact that such nonrecognition of the violin is apparently pathognomonic for attention deficit disorder (see also neuropsychological aspects, page 126).

Picture 2

Country scene: In the foreground is a young woman with books in her hand; in the background a man is working in the fields and an older woman is looking on.

This picture usually offers excellent indications of the subject's *family relations*. Even males usually identify with the central figure of the young girl because it is so definitely the figure in the foreground. Again, varying themes of *autonomy* from the family versus *compliance* with the conservative, backward existence are extremely frequent. These themes show the type of divergence between the subject and the family. Oedipal themes and sibling rivalry also appear in full bloom.

Most useful for our purposes is the subject's handling of the woman leaning against the tree, who is often seen as pregnant. A great deal of information can be obtained from the manner in which the subject handles apperception of *pregnancy*. It may be completely ignored or it may lead to highly informative notions about it in all ages.

The figure of the man may illuminate heterosexual and homosexual attitudes: men may overly admire his musculature, etc.

In this picture, which contains a relatively large number of objects, obsessive-compulsive subjects will comment on small details such as the lake in the background and the tiny figure in the background among others, in a way that virtually permits the diagnosis of *compulsive tendencies*. Sometimes most of the remarks concern the horse, possibly a regressive and avoidance phenomenon. Similarly defensive may be obsessive preoccupation with the small details, or complaints that the furrows are not straight. Again, stories to this picture are frequently removed in time and place, as a form of removal from one's own conflicts.

The way in which the relationship of the two women to the man is discussed—whether as a farmhand run by the woman, or as a father, husband, or brother—adds a good deal of information about the *role of the sexes*.

Picture 3BM

On the floor against a couch is the huddled form of a boy with his head bowed on his right arm. Beside him on the floor is a revolver.

This also belongs to the group of most useful pictures. As already mentioned, this card may be used for females too—they identify with the figure readily enough, manifestly seeing a woman, or identifying latently. Normative data on the percentage of men seeing it as a man may be most useful for future research. Empirically speaking, most men see the huddled figure as a man; if it is seen by men as a female figure, this may be considered a point to keep in mind—not to make the diagnosis, but to keep in mind factors of possible *latent homosexuality*, which may be confirmed if more suggestive evidence appears in other pictures. How the object on the left is perceived often gives a great deal of information about the problems concerning *aggression*. Officially this object is described as a gun. Some subjects may recognize it as a gun; it is interesting to observe the manner of handling the aggression—whether it is used as extra-aggression (e.g., somebody else is being shot by the hero), or whether it is used as intra-aggression (the hero is being shot or he commits suicide). If it leads to extra-aggression, it will be interesting to see what happens to the hero. Whether he is punished severely or whether he escapes is a kind of protocol that gives us a notion of the strength of the superego of the subject. On the other hand, we want to get some clue as to what leads to the depressive pattern that finally results in suicide. It is obvious that this picture is a must with *depressed patients*. The pistol may be turned into a toy pistol and thus rendered harmless. This might indicate denial, but it is important to find out by checking the consistency with other stories whether it is a superficial escape from really entering into the story or whether this corresponds to the fact that one is simply dealing with a healthy subject who has neither excessive intra- nor extra-aggression. Again, a subject who has to repress his latent aggressiveness may completely deny the presence of the gun by omitting reference to it, seeing it as a hole in the floor, as a cigarette case, or not at all. Sometimes a great conflict around aggression, particularly when it has led to a compulsive pattern, will manifest itself by the subject's hemming and hawing for a considerable time over what the object might be.

Here, again, the body image may become illuminated: the figure may be seen as crippled, extremely ill, etc.

The more fact that a story concerns suicide has, in itself, no prognostic significance. Only if such a story coincides with a great deal of latent intra-aggression, a severe superego, and a great deal of aggression should suicide be considered as a serious possibility.

Picture 3GF

A young woman is standing with downcast head, her face covered with her right hand. Her left arm is stretched forward against a wooden door.

This is a picture which may also bring out *depressive feelings.* Frequently, however, it has been found more useful with females to use 3BM, with which they can easily identify, as stated above.

Picture 4

A woman is clutching the shoulders of a man whose face and body are averted as if he were trying to pull away from her.

This picture elicits a great variety of needs and sentiments in regard to *male-female relationships.* Themes of infidelity are often found, and the male attitude toward the role of women may appear. She may be a protector who tries to keep him from rushing into something poorly thought out or one who tries to hold onto him for evil purposes. Similarly, a woman's attitude toward men as persons who may have been aggressive toward her becomes apparent.

Since the woman looks somewhat unusual, she is often made the member of a *minority group,* and sentiments concerning these are displayed.

Another object of interest is the picture of the seminude in the background, which is perceived by more than two-thirds of the subjects. If it is not perceived or discussed at all, it may be a clue to the fact that there is a *sexual problem.* On the other hand, it may be seen as a poster or as an actual figure in the background, prompting themes of *triangular jealousy.* Whether the difference in depth perception involved in seeing it as a poster or as a living person can be considered a differential criterion of value is not clear thus far. There is a possibility that there is a defensive element in seeing it as a poster.

Picture 5

A middle-aged woman is standing on the threshold of a half-opened door looking into a room.

This is often interpreted as the *mother who may be watching* different activities. At times this becomes a symbolic story of fear of observed *masturbation,* or the mother appears as benevolently interested in how the child is, or she may be seen as reprimanding the subject for being up late. *Voyeuristic material* is quite frequent and may actually lead to disguised stories of the *primal scene.* Again, *fear of attach,* particularly in female subjects, is often reflected in a story of burglary, while in males it may lead to *"rescue fantasies,"* in the psychoanalytic sense.

Picture 6BM

A short elderly woman stands with her back turned to a tall young man. The latter is looking downward with a perplexed expression.

This is an indispensable picture for males, reflecting all the problems of *mother-son relationships* and all their derivatives in relation to wives and other women. Oedipal themes are frequent. The stories given to this picture run such a complete range of this fundamental problem that only a monograph could do it justice.

Picture 6GF

A young woman sitting on the edge of a sofa looks back over her shoulder at an older man with a pipe in his mouth who seems to be addressing her.

This is really meant to be a counterpart of 6BM to reflect the *relationship of females to the father.* Probably because of the apparently relatively slight age difference, however, the man is usually, at least manifestly, not seen as the father image but rather as a contemporary, who may thereupon be invested with any number of qualities, from those of an aggressor, a seducer, to someone who proposes marriage. Frequently this man is made into an uncle, who probably represents the picture of an idealized father, as is so often done in folklore, for instance, Uncle Sam and Uncle Czar. All in all, the picture is not a very useful one, but the best we have on this subject at present.

Picture 7BM

A gray-haired man is looking at a younger man who is sullenly staring into space.

This picture of an old man and a young man is indispensable in bringing out the *father-son relationship* and all its derivatives (in males) in the form of attitudes to male authority.

Picture 7GF

An older woman is sitting on a sofa close beside a girl, speaking or reading to her. The girl, who holds a doll on her lap, is looking away.

This picture will bring out the relationship between *mother and child in females*. It seems to encourage negative attitudes toward the mother because of the fact that the girl is looking off into the distance rather than at the mother. The doll, in turn, may reflect the subject's attitude toward *expectancy of children*. Frequently the theme concerns the mother telling a fairy tale, and the most instructive data may be in this theme within a theme.

Picture 8BM

An adolescent boy looks straight out of the picture. The barrel of a rifle is visible at one side, and in the background is the dim scene of a surgical operation, like a reverie image.

This is a very useful picture. Male subjects usually identify with the boy in the foreground. The essential themes that may be developed center on either *aggression*—somebody was shot and is now being operated upon in the background—or upon stories of *ambition*—the dream of a boy of becoming a doctor, for example. The operation scene may elicit a fear of being mutilated while passive. Whether the rifle at the left is recognized or not, and what is made of it, are problems similar to those of the pistol in 3BM. The way in which the figures are described—for example, the attitude toward the doctor as an older person or toward the person being operated upon—if seen as a paternal figure—frequently gives clues as to the oedipal relationship.

The clinical inference that avoidance of mentioning the weapon in this or other T.A.T. pictures may mean particularly severe latent hostility has frequently been attacked as "Damned if you do and damned if you don't," by academic psychologists. However, this fact has been verified experimentally by Eriksen [108].

Picture 8GF

A young woman sits with her chin in her hand looking off into space.

Almost any theme may be produced to this picture, usually of a shallow, contemplative nature. I rarely find it useful.

Picture 9BM

Four men in overalls are lying on the grass taking it easy.

This is another important picture for disclosing *contemporary, man-to-man relationships*. It may, for one thing, offer a general indication of social relationships—namely, which of the figures the subject identifies with. In extremes the subject may identify with someone outside the group who looks askance at the group, or he may be part of it or even the center. Again, *homosexual drives and fears* may become quite apparent in stories to this picture. *Social prejudices* may be brought to light here, for example, stories of hoboes.

Picture 9GF

A young woman with a magazine and a purse in her hand looks from behind a tree at another young woman in a party dress running along a beach.

This is an invaluable picture in getting a notion of the woman-to-woman feeling, particularly for bringing out sister rivalry or daughter-mother hostility. It is very important in cases in which one suspects *depression* and *suicidal tendencies,* since not infrequently in such circumstances the girl below is made into someone who, in a panic, runs into the sea. Again, suspiciousness, at the least, may be brought out by the fact that stories sometimes raise discussions of how this one person is watching the other maliciously. This factor may at times be strong enough to warrant the *consideration of paranoia.* Men are frequently introduced in stories of this picture, in romantic or aggressive connotations. A male is frequently introduced into the story as a "sexual" attacker from whom one woman flees while the other comes to her rescue. Sometimes, on the other hand, one gets stories of one woman or the other or both running to greet a long-lost lover arriving by ship.

Picture 10

A young woman's head against a man's shoulder.

This will bring out much about the *relation of men to women*. If this is interpreted as an embrace between males by a male subject, it is a strong clue to *latent homosexuality* or even manifest problems of this nature. If it is described as a man and a woman by either males or females, it will be interesting to observe whether it is made a story of arrival or departure, reflecting in the departure theme latent hostile needs.

Picture 11

A road skirting a deep chasm between high cliffs. On the road in the distance are obscure figures. Protruding from the rocky wall on one side are the long head and neck of a dragon.

Picture 11 is particularly useful because it operates on a more disguised plane and puts many people more off guard, although it frightens others. Here are brought out *many infantile or primitive fears,* since the animals permit projection of such emotions. If a patient has *fears of attack,* this is a most useful picture since it will expose the fine features of the fears of being attacked—for example, by the phallic symbol of the dragon. Stories of *oral aggression* are frequent. This picture offers good clues to the mood of the patient, whether or not he escapes and, if so, how.

Anxiety, in common with other psychopathologic symptoms, is often expressed in content changing with cultural factors. For example, in the Middle Ages, hallucinations were primarily thought of as the undue influence of the devil and other supernatural forces. In the early twentieth century, electricity and, later, radio waves entered into hallucinatory and delusional content, and I can vividly recall the first paranoid I encountered who felt that radar was being used on him. Similarly, fear of destruction is frequently elicited by this picture in stories about an atomic holocaust leaving everything desolate in its wake. When such stories refer to everything being dead, it may indicate an intrapsychic state consistent with very severe emotional impoverishment.

Picture 12M

A young man is lying on a couch with his eyes closed. Leaning over him is the gaunt form of an elderly man, his hand stretched out above the face of the reclining figure.

This is a most important picture for indicating the qualities of the *relationship of a younger man to an older man,* particularly regarding *passive homosexual fears* and fears of being under the domination of superior figures.

Stories to this picture may reveal whether passivity is ego syntonic or greatly feared; sometimes the man in the upright position is seen as helpful, administering aid, giving comfort, etc., and no anxiety is expressed. At other times he is seen as exerting an evil influence, e.g., by hypnosis, or as attacking or having attacked a helpless victim.

Rapaport [271] has stated that this picture may prognosticate therapeutic success. Insofar as complete, unthreatening passivity may make therapy much more difficult, this may be correct. As to the stories revealing positive or negative feelings toward the therapist, it must be remembered that the mere fact of an initial positive or negative transference is of no therapeutic significance.

Stories to this picture may indeed nicely reflect the relationship to the therapist, inasmuch as the couch and supine position may be unconsciously related to the psychoanalytic situation or the generally dependent attitude of the patient. Such stories lend themselves particularly well to direct use in therapy, as vehicles for insight and interpretation. The following example will illustrate this point:

This can't have too many stories. He's either dead or being hypnotized. If dead, the person with his hand raised over him is doing a rather uncommon thing. Trying to practice some kind of witchcraft. The other man has his knee raised, so he doesn't look too dead. Reclining on a small bed of some sort. Not too dead. Probably just waiting for some kind of black magic from the other fellow. If he's sick, they're trying to remove whatever his sickness is. If he's dead, this fellow is trying to perform whatever they do to dead men so that he will be acceptable to wherever he's going, if he's going anywhere. This picture seems more abnormal than any of the others. It's so terribly abnormal that I don't see how anybody could tell anything but a terribly abnormal story—not even a story but to keep on going and not necessarily ever to have to finish. I'm struck by this and shocked. The hypnotizing, or black magic.

Picture 12F

The portrait of a young woman. A weird old woman with a shawl over her head is grimacing in the background.

This may bring out *conceptions of mother figures,* but, in all, it is not a picture that I have found to be notably useful. Frequently the evil mother figure is made the hero of a story in the guise of a mother-in-law. To appreciate this tendency it must be understood that mothers-in-law are often the recipients of the negative emotions felt toward one's own mother. The subject may be aware only of positive feelings toward his mother and readily projects all the negative ones onto the less holy figure of the mother-in-law. This, I believe, is responsible for the position of the mother-in-law in so many cartoons and jokes.

Picture 12BG

A rowboat is drawn up on the bank of a woodland stream. There are no human figures in the picture.

This picture is meant, as the initials indicate, for boys and girls, and has not proven very useful in my experience. The fact that none of the T.A.T. pictures were really useful often enough with children below the age of 10 prompted my development of the Children's Apperception Test.

This picture has not been found too helpful in any specific case except in *suicidal* or very *depressed subjects.* It will, then, often elicit stories of someone's having jumped or fallen out of the boat.

Picture 13MF

A young man is standing with downcast head buried in his arm. Behind him is the figure of a woman lying in bed.

This is an excellent picture for disclosing *sexual conflicts in both men and women.* In very inhibited subjects this may virtually lead to "sex shock," which will find expression in the stories. In females it may elicit fears of being raped, attacked, or otherwise abused by men. In males it will often bring out guilt feelings about sexual activity and will easily show the disgust of homosexuals. Feeling between husband and wife may be projected. Not unusual are stories of *economic deprivation* in response to this picture, and *oral tendencies* will frequently appear in discussion of the breasts. Again, since this is one of the pictures containing a relatively great amount of detail, *obsessive-compulsives* will easily be recognized by their concern with details.

Picture 13B

A little boy is sitting on the doorstep of a log cabin.

To a lesser degree, this is not unlike the violin picture in prompting *stories of childhood* and is of some use with young boys, although not markedly. It may induce reverie in adults in much the same way as the violin picture.

Picture 13G

A little girl is climbing a winding flight of stairs.

This picture has not been found to be especially useful thus far in my experience.

Picture 14

The silhouette of a man (or woman) against a bright window. The rest of the picture is totally black.

This silhouette can be a most useful figure. For one thing, it will be interesting to note the *sexual identification* of the figure. It will often bring out childhood *fears in relation to darkness.* Again, it is an absolute must when one suspects *suicidal tendencies,* which may be expressed in a story of jumping out of the window. Frequently it will induce themes of simple contemplation and reveal much of the philosophical rationalization of the subject. Sometimes it may reveal *esthetic interests,* and wish-fulfillment stories may be offered. It may result in burglary stories if someone is seen as coming into the window.

Picture 15

A gaunt man with clenched hands is standing among gravestones.

This picture of a figure in a graveyard is especially important if the subject has had a *death in the immediate family* and the clinician wants to discover his sentiments regarding that death. It is also very useful in that it may disclose notions and *fears of death* in any subject. *Depressive tendencies* manifest themselves clearly. What is clinically particularly interesting and important, and may appear in response to this picture, is the fact that there are many conceptions of death. Psychopathology may differ according to whether the idea of death is one of being violently hurt (castrated or anally hurt) or devoured; or whether the idea is concerned with being dead, as an acceptable or unacceptable fantasy of passivity of an oral nature, as Lewin [214] in particular has pointed out. The most specific and unusual fear of death I have encountered existed in an agoraphobic patient where the exhibitionistic fantasy of lying stark naked on the undertaker's slab was particularly fear arousing. The aggressive and passive fantasies of death are probably represented in the religious dichotomy of heaven and hell. All these considerations are particularly important in those plates concerned with suicidal possibilities.

Picture 16

This *blank card* is of extreme value with verbally gifted subjects, who may really let loose and project freely. If the subject has given previous indications that he has difficulty in expressing fantasy material, however, the blank card is often of no value.

The instructions here are first to imagine a picture and then tell a story about it, producing something like superprojection. One of my initial T.A.T. experiences was with engineering students and students majoring in English. The experience has stayed with me vividly, to the extent that I almost categorically speak of subjects giving meager stories as engineers and of those with lively imaginations as English majors. My experience with the blank card is that it does not help the engineers and is unnecessary for the English majors.

Picture 17BM

A naked man is clinging to a rope. He is in the act of climbing up or down.

There are many useful aspects to this picture. There may be revelations of fears in stories of escape from physical trauma, such as fire, or fleeing from man. The latter often leads to disclosures concerning *oedipal fears,* particularly in children, where this picture may actually be seen as someone fleeing from the "king" or the "prince." Again, *homosexual feelings* are easily brought out even by descriptive details. Not unusual are stories of a competitive nature, making this an athletic meet or the like. In males there will often be an indication of their *body image*—whether or not they feel themselves to be muscular, etc.

It has been suggested that outgoing, active people tell stories of people climbing up, in distinction to others. This makes sense in terms of Mira's [236] observations and those of other expressive studies, but my sample did not permit me a definite impression.

Picture 17GF

A bridge over water. A female figure leans over the railing. In the background are tall buildings and small figures of men.

Here is another useful card when one suspects *suicidal tendencies in women* since it opens the way for stories about jumping from a bridge. Otherwise a great variety of stories may be told to 17GF, which I do not consider one of the more useful cards except for the one purpose just stated.

Picture 18BM

A man is clutched from behind by three hands. The figures of his antagonists are invisible.

This is another of the more important pictures for learning about, or verifying, any *anxiety in males*. Fears of attack, particularly of a homosexual nature, become most apparent. If a subject has any anxiety at all, it is bound to come out in response to this picture. On the other hand, it can be made into something innocuous, such as a story of support, for example, of a man in an intoxicated condition being brought home by his friends. How the problem of supernumerary hands is handled is frequently of great interest insofar as the thought processes of the subject are concerned. Sometimes the story is made innocuous in somewhat the following way: A man was out at a stag dinner and now, inebriated, is being helped home by his companions who have ducked behind him to push him up the stairs. *Viribus unitis!*

Hard luck stories are often related, and of course we want to know what a particular person thinks of or fears as hard luck.

Picture 18GF

A woman has her hands squeezed around the throat of another woman whom she appears to be pushing backwards across the banister of a stairway.

This picture gives an excellent indication of how *aggression is handled by women.* It may be completely evaded by the denial that any aggressive act is taking place. Sometimes stories of how one woman is helping another up the stairs or up from the floor are told in attempts to evade aggressive implications. *Mother-daughter conflicts* may be highlighted.

Picture 19

A weird picture of cloud formations overhanging a snow-covered cabin in the country.

A picture sometimes useful with children, but otherwise not notable.

Picture 20

The dimly illuminated figure of a man (or woman) in the dead of night leaning against a lamppost.

The figure may be seen either as a man or as a woman. We do not have any definite indication of the differential implications of such sexual identification. Females may present stories of fear of men or of the dark. Otherwise fears may be brought out by either sex by making it a gangster story. Again, it may be made an entirely innocuous theme by a story of an evening's date.

CHAPTER IV

INTERPRETATION OF THE T.A.T.

I F WE ACCEPT THE HYPOTHESIS OF DETERMINISM OF PSYCHOLOGI-
cal behavior, it follows that deductions concerning the personality of
an individual can be based on any kind of performance. Similarly, nearly any test
can be analyzed for a great many different aspects and, since each dimension is by
necessity a function of the testee's personality, one is bound to have results. The
crux of the matter, of course, is for tests to combine maximal applicability with
maximum validity, reliability, and economy. By the same token, we need those
analytical variables or scoring categories which will offer the most information
with the least effort.

I like to think of scoring categories as fishnets. If a net has a large, coarse mesh
one may only catch a few very large fish, losing many medium-sized ones. On the
other hand, if a net is exceedingly fine meshed, one may catch so many tiny
organisms as to make it almost impossible to pull in the net and haul in a useful
catch. Therefore one must select the sort of net best adapted to the task at hand
and the desired goal. For research purposes, a very finely meshed set of categories may be desirable. Having very few variables, or none at all, may leave one
almost empty-handed. The ideal set of variables will be one that obtains enough
information for clinical purposes without making the task overwhelming.

Before discussing different methods which have been applied to interpretation
of the T.A.T. it seems appropriate to briefly enumerate some of the working
assumptions held by psychologists concerning the nature of psychological tests.
Interpretations of T.A.T. responses, and the diagnostic inferences based upon
them, are most useful when the interpreter views such responses in the light of
the broader framework provided by the following assumptions, which have been
noted previously by Feifel [116]. First, psychological tests represent a way of
securing behavior samples of the individual. Second, the individual's test responses are the end results of thought processes stimulated by test items. These
end products are causally linked to the person's typical ego-organizing principles,
that is, to the means used in selecting and organizing internal and external stimuli.
Test responses should be differentiated from scores. Scores are "designed to
facilitate intra- and interindividual comparisons and, as such, are extremely useful

in clinical testing," but "to reason only in terms of the score, or even score patterns, is to do violence to the nature of the raw material" (Schafer [296]). Third, interpretation needs to take account of the context in which the test responses are made. For example, the meanings of similar formal test patterns may differ in dissimilar contexts. Fourth, a battery of tests is needed in order to obtain a good picture of the many dimensions of ego functioning; no one test is able to reach all the different levels of psychic functioning.

A. Brief Review of Literature on Interpretive Methods

The original technique used by Murray and his co-workers depended on an analysis of the stories by the need-press method. While it is best to consult Murray's book [244] on the details of the need-press concept, it may suffice here to say that every sentence was analyzed as to the needs of the hero and the environmental forces (press) to which he is exposed. To choose a very simple example, he (the hero) loves her, but she hates him: need (for) love met by (press) hate.

Every story was analyzed thus according to all needs and presses, and each need and press received a weighted score. A rank-order system of the needs and presses could then be tabulated. At the same time the hierarchical relationship of the needs to each other was investigated, with such concepts of Murray's as need-conflict, need-subsidiation, and need-fusion. Nearly a dozen possible schemes of categories were developed by Murray and Bellak in 1941 at the Harvard Psychological Clinic. A test manual [62] and a guide to the interpretation were designed based on an earlier one by White and Sanford [348]. Aside from a page for the recording of the quantitative need-press data, there was also a page for the recording of more molar qualitative data, not unlike some of the categories described in the recommendations for interpretation that are indicated below.

The need-press scheme of interpretation still has many advantages for use in experiments in which detail is most important and time is no object. The method has not become at all popular clinically, however, since it is not easy to master the need concept, and it takes four to five hours on the average to interpret 20 stories with this system. Therefore a great number of attempts to interpret the T.A.T. have been developed. Wyatt [355], in an excellent review of the scoring and analysis of the T.A.T. speaks specifically of Rapaport's, Henry's, Rotter's, Tomkins', and his own method, aside from the need-press analysis.

Rotter's [286] suggestions for the interpretation of the T.A.T. are presented in three steps, of which the first refers to 11 aspects of responses to be utilized for interpretation. These are as follows:

1. Autobiographical quality, coherence, predominant mood, handling of sex; endings and their relationship to the story, repetition of themes, unusual wording, attitude toward the world, characteristics of central figure, typical methods of solving problems, characters that can be identified with mother, father, son, etc.

2. In the second step, five principles of interpretation are proposed: frequency of occurrence of an idea, unusualness (regarding plot, language, misrecognition), determination of identification, determination of clichés, selecting alternate interpretations (decision between two possible interpretations).

3. The third step contains qualitative suggestions for the analysis of personality trends as the final step of interpretation.

In a later paper, *Rotter and Shirley Jessor* [287] proceed in five steps:

1. The entire protocol is read for suggestive leads (mood, unusual plots, unique verbalizations, methods of solving problems, and frequency of specific themes) and for the formulation of tentative interpretations and questions to be investigated further.

2. Each story is analyzed for basic ideas and structural characteristics and is compared with plot norms.

3. Each story is considered as a unit in order to identify the characters, the conflicts, and the relationship, to decide whether the material is wishful, autobiographical, or superficial, and to select hypotheses on the basis of consistency.

4. All the stories are considered as one organized combined unit.

5. The interpretive hypotheses are integrated into a final summary evaluation, under five categories: familial attitudes, social and sexual attitudes, general (educational, vocational, etc.) attitudes, personality characteristics, and etiological implications.

Rapaport's [274] interpretation, according to Wyatt, is predicated upon an examination of the cliché quality of the responses, and the subject's deviation from clichés serves as a base line for orientation. In his "points of view" for scoring, Rapaport suggests two major classes:

A. Formal characteristics of story structure, of which there are three aspects:
   1. *Compliance with instructions* (omissions and distortions; misplacing of emphasis; dwelling on picture rather than on situation; introduction of figures and objects not pictured)
   2. *Consistency within the testee's production* (interindividual consistency, as shown by deviation in expressive and aggressive qualities: deviation from the usual significance of a particular picture, and deviation concerning language and narrative form; intraindividual consistency)
   3. *Characteristics of verbalization*
B. Formal characteristics of story content:
   1. *Tone of narrative*
   2. *Figures of story identifications and memory representations*
   3. *Strivings and attitudes*
   4. *Obstacles*

Henry [164], in the most extensive and detailed scheme for analysis next to Murray's, distinguishes (A) form characteristics from (B) content characteristics.

A. Form characteristics are divided into six major categories, each of which has several subclasses:
   1. *Amount and kind of imaginal production* (length of story, amount and kind of introduced content; vividness, originality; rhythm and smoothness; variation in the consistency of all these factors)
   2. *Organizational qualities* (presence or absence of antecedents of story and of outcome; level of organization; coherence and logic; manner of approach to central concept; contribution of elaborations and of details; variation in the consistency of all these)
   3. *Acuity of concepts, observations, and their integration*
   4. *Language structure* (movement, action, qualifying, descriptive words, etc.)
   5. *Intraception-extraception*
   6. *Relation of story told to total thought content* (condensed, suppressed)
B. Content characteristics:
   1. *General tone* (positive and negative tone of language; passivity or aggressiveness of language; expressed or implied conflict; expressed or implied interpersonal harmonies or affiliative action and thought)

2. *Positive content* (characters described in the story; interpersonal relations; action core of story)
3. *Negative content* (what subject failed to say; what he might have been expected to say)
4. *Dynamic structure of content* (symbols, associations)

In the relation of the form and content characteristics, eight areas are considered: mental approach; creativity and imagination; behavioral approach; family dynamics; inner adjustment; emotional reactivity; sexual adjustment; descriptive and interpretive summary.

Tomkins [325], in a systematic attempt at a logically consistent analysis of fantasy, distinguishes four major categories:

1. Vectors, comprising needs, or the quality of strivings "for," "against," "under," "by," "away," "from," "of."
2. Levels, such as those of wish, daydreams.
3. Conditions that may be either external forces (Murray's press) or inner states, such as anxiety or depression. Conditions do not refer to the goals of strivings but to given states the individual finds outside or inside himself.
4. Qualities, such as intensity, contingency (certainty), temporal considerations.

The principle underlying this system of analysis is that each class can be related to any other class. One vector can be the object of any other vector (for example, the wish to act).

Tomkins' method, which is primarily for training and research, comprises both scoring and interpretation. Each story is scored according to the above-mentioned four main categories: 10 vectors, 17 levels, 12 conditions, and six qualifiers. The interpretation utilizes three main approaches: canons of inference, such as Mill's methods (of agreement, difference, of concomitant variation, etc.) and additional methods (for the study of cause and effect involving two or more factors); level analysis (degree of variance, relative frequency, cause-effect relationships, and sequence analysis of levels) to study the relationship between overt and covert needs, the degree to which the subject is aware of his own wishes and behavior, and the nature of the conflict between repressed wish and repressing force; and diagnosis of personality, which includes relative importance of the family, love and sex, social relationships, and work.

Korchin's [202] use of Tomkins' method is a variant of the above approach. It is less formalized and therefore better adapted to clinical use. It examines the characteristics of the heroes, the more generalized meanings of the main themes, the outcomes, and the levels. It also analyzes the areas of family, social relationships, work, etc.

Wyatt [355] uses 15 variables for the analysis of the T.A.T.: (1) story description, (2) stimulus perception, (3) deviations from typical responses, (4) deviation from self, (5) time trend, (6) level of interpretation, (7) tone of story, (8) quality of telling, (9) focal figure, (10) other figures, (11) personal relationships, (12) striving, avoidances, (13) press, (14) outcome, (15) thema.

Magda Arnold's [13] method of interpreting the T.A.T. emphasizes the content of the stories. Situations involving interpersonal relations, such as parent-child, heterosexual, etc., are examined for the feelings and actions described. Thus information is obtained about the subject's attitudes, conflicts, and dominant problems. The stories are also subjected to a brief "sequential" analysis in order to see whether there is a consistent development of the central theme. The five steps in this procedure are: synopsis, situational analysis, analysis of attitudes (from the situational analysis), sequential analysis, and final integration.

Betty Aron [14] works on the level of manifest story content, deliberately leaving aside, for the most part, formal aspects of the performance. She uses the Murray-Sanford scheme of variables—need and press—with numerous changes intended to bring the scheme into closer harmony with clinical approaches and psychoanalytic theory. Each need or press is recorded together with the characters who are the subject and object of the behavior, so that a given variable can be examined in relation to the context in which it is expressed. Also recorded are surface defenses, such as conflict, denial, rejection of behavior, fantasy, uncertainty, etc.; intensity of variables, which is expressed numerically; and outcomes. The results are analyzed in terms of main features in variable scoring and in variable sequences.

Leonard Eron [112] uses a normative, statistical approach. Norms are based on all 20 T.A.T. cards for adult males administered in prescribed order. Stories are rated for emotional tone (from very sad to very happy) and for outcome (from complete failure to great success). Themes are noted according to a check list of more than one hundred themes classified as interpersonal, intrapersonal, and impersonal; disequilibrium (tension) and equilibrium. Any deviations from the task of making up a narrative and any distortions of the physical properties of the pictures, as well as certain other formal characteristics, are noted. The ratings are then compared with the norms. The basic data for this system are the frequency and unusualness of specific fantasy content. Interpretation of personality structure and content depends on the theoretic orientation of the interpreter and on the behavioral data from other sources.

Reuben Fine's [119] method stresses primarily feelings and interpersonal relationships. It makes use of a checklist for scoring the presence or absence in each story of feelings (affection, anxiety, pain, etc.); interpersonal relations (moving toward, moving against, etc.) between specific types of persons (mother to child, man to woman, etc.); and the outcomes (favorable, unfavorable, or indeterminate). The interpretation is a sort of qualitative summing-up of the results.

A. Arthur Hartman [152] uses a psychometric approach which was originally designed for research and aims at establishing quantitative norms as a basis for interpretation. It consists of the following steps:

1. Each story is rated on a five-point scale for 65 response categories covering thematic elements, feeling qualities, topics of reference, and formal response characteristics.
2. Numerical ratings on each category are totaled for all stories, and consistency and trend of ratings are noted.
3. From a list of over 40 personality variables, which previous research proved significantly correlated with certain response items, those personality variables are selected which are associated with each response category found important in the protocol.
4. Data thus obtained are integrated with other findings, to obtain a clinically meaningful personality picture.

The method used by *Robert Holt* [168] is a clinical approach in which the interpreter reads over the stories, jots down tentative hypotheses as he goes along, and integrates these notes into a final personality summary. There is no formal scoring system, and the method may be described as intuitive. The theoretical bases are those of psychoanalytic theory and Murray's need-press formulations.

The system devised by *Walther Joel and David Shapiro* [181] deals primarily with the functioning of the ego. First, interpersonal warmth and hostility and flight from such interpersonal feelings are translated into scoring symbols. Then the sequence of these interactions is analyzed, and finally the interpretation provides a picture of the process of coping with the social environment.

In *Seymour Klebanoff's* [197] method, intended primarily for research, the content of the stories is tallied on a checklist according to overtly stated themes grouped under such categories as loss of life, aggression, internal stress, and positive themes. Profiles of absolute and percentage frequencies for each thema and each category are then analyzed. Interpretation is based upon that analysis.

Jose Lasaga [205] uses a clinical method intended to discover the psychodynamic causes of neurotic and psychotic disturbances and to be an aid in psychotherapy. It focuses attention on the patient's main conflicts and emphasizes the fact that conflicts may be disguised by a process of symbolic substitution. The actual procedure consists of the following: reading the record for general impressions; underlining phrases which express the main idea or important aspects of the main idea; summarizing each story in terms of the main idea; finding clues for discovering the key conflicts; studying anomalies among the ideas or among reaction times; taking into consideration "basic data" about the patient; and knitting all these impressions together into a summary evaluation.

Helen Sargent [294] has devised two methods. The Sargent Insight Test Scoring Method was originally developed for scoring written responses to the author's Insight Test but is applicable to the T.A.T. Affects (A) are scored under 12 categories (pleasure, aggression, etc.) and three expressive modes (action, manifest, and latent feeling expression); defense activities (D) are scored under three categories (evaluations, elaborations, and qualifications). Maladjustment (M) scores, based on the use of first person pronouns, irrelevant feeling expressions, and "subjectivism," are also obtained. The A/D ratio and the A-D-A/D pattern are evaluated and interpreted in terms of established norms, together with qualitative interpretation of the content.

The *Cox-Sargent* T.A.T. Normative Scoring Method is designed as a research tool for analyzing the normative aspects of responses to individual T.A.T. pictures. It uses the following main categories: feelings (frustration, anxiety, etc.); heroes (man, girl, etc.); needs (security, conformity, etc.); threats (guilt, death, etc.); actions to meet need or evade threat (negative, evasive, etc.); and outcomes (success, failure, etc.).

Percival Symonds' [321] method utilizes the impressions received from careful readings of the protocol as a whole, rather than from the separate stories. The data extracted from the stories are classified largely in terms of themes (aggression, love, punishment, anxiety, defenses, moral standards, conflicts, guilt, depression, forms of sublimation, etc.) and relationships (to parents, siblings, teachers, etc.). The final write-up attempts to synthesize the themes of primary importance and to indicate the dynamic relationships among them.

Ralph K. White [347] has devised a "value analysis" method, wherein the manifest content is rewritten in terms of 50 value words which represent motivating forces. In addition, the notations indicate whose point of view is considered, so as to shed light on the storyteller's identification, and also indicate the terms in which the characters are described, in order to get at the storyteller's "social perception." The data are treated quantitatively by tallying. A frustration-satisfaction ratio is obtained from the frequencies of the positive and negative values. The overall interpretation "depends on the clinical insight and disciplined imagination of the analyst."

Piotrowski [263] does not offer any systematized, formal method of approach to the T.A.T., but he lists nine rules of interpretation, as follows:

1. Proceed on the assumption that T.A.T. stories reflect with much greater freedom and with much less distortion the testee's activities and attitudes than they reflect the actual individuals toward whom his activities are directed and toward whom he assumes the attitudes manifested in the T.A.T.

2. When interpreting T.A.T. stories, proceed on the assumption that every figure in the T.A.T. stories expresses some aspect of the testee's personality.

3. The more acceptable an intended action (drive) is to the consciousness of the testee, the greater the similarity between the testee and the T.A.T. figure to whom the drive is attributed.

4. Bear in mind that the degree of generalization of your conclusions affects their validity. The more specific the conclusions, the more difficult it is to confirm and the more easy it is to invalidate them by facts. The more general and more restrained the conclusions, the more likely they are to be valid.

5. Take into consideration the possibility that the stories may not reflect genuine drives but superficial and stereotyped attitudes developed by the testee in order to hide his specific personality traits.

6. Proceed on the assumption that the stories frequently reflect what the subject thinks and feels about persons represented by the T.A.T. figures, i.e., about the old and the young, the male and the female persons. Of course, the T.A.T. would disclose the testee's ideas about those old, young, male, and female persons who play important roles in his life rather than his ideas about old, young, male, or female persons, as such.

7. The more varied and the more incompatible the drives in a subjects stories, the greater the possibility of poor personality integration, of great inner tension, of fear that the unacceptable drives will undermine self-control and will prompt the subject to act contrary to his self-interest. The greater the diversity of the T.A.T. drives, the greater the testee's indecisiveness and anxiety.

8. The chances of a T.A.T. thema being manifested in the subject's overt behavior are positively correlated with the frequency of the thema's appearance in the T.A.T., with the consistency of the total T.A.T. record (absence of incompatible themas), and with the emotional intensity accompanying the expression of the thema.

9. Employ all formal rules which have been proven valuable in the study of creative associative power. These rules are not specific to the T.A.T. and refer to a variety of formal aspects of the T.A.T. performance: uneven pace in the production of the stories, long and variable pauses, marked differences in the number and elaboration of ideas elicited by some pictures as compared with those prompted by other pictures, disregarding of picture details which usually produce comments, far-fetched and bizarre notions, sudden or gradual increase or decrease of ideas, etc.

David McClelland [229], addressing himself to achievement motivation exclusively, has devised a measure of this motive as it is expressed in imaginative stories, particularly the T.A.T. First, the scorer must determine whether or not the story contains any reference to an achievement goal which would justify scoring the subcategories as achievement related. Stories are scored for such Achievement Imagery (A.I.) only when at least one of three criteria, all of which deal with manifestation by a story character of "Competition with a standard of excellence," is met.

The scoring subcategories are:

1. *Stated need for achievement* (N). Someone in the story states the desire to reach an achievement goal.

2. *Instrumental activity.* By one or more characters; is scored I+, I?, I− to indicate whether the outcome of the instrumental activity is successful, doubtful, or unsuccessful.

3. *Anticipatory goal states* (Ga+, Ga−). Someone in the story anticipates goal attainment or frustration and failure.

4. *Obstacles or blocks.* Stories are scored for obstacles when the progress of goal-directed activity is blocked or hindered by a personal obstacle (Bp) or environmental obstacle (Bw).

5. *Nurturant press* (Nup). Forces in the story, personal in source, which aid the character who is involved in ongoing achievement-related activity are scored nurturant press.

6. *Affective states* (G+, G−). Affective states associated with goal attainment, active mastery, or frustration of the achievement-directed activity are scored G.

7. *Achievement thema* (Ach Th). Achievement thema is scored when the achievement imagery is elaborated so that it becomes the central plot of the story.

The *n* achievement score for any individual is computed by combining indexes as follows. Unrelated imagery is scored −1, doubtful achievement imagery is scored 0, and A.I. is scored +1. If a story is scored for A.I., the subcategories are scored. Each subcategory is scored only once per story and given a weight of +1. An achievement score for each story is obtained by summing algebraically the category scores for that story. The *n* achievement score for the subject is the total of scores obtained on all the stories.

Fred Pine [261] has devised a manual for rating drive content in T.A.T. stories. Dual significance is posited in the use of drive content in these themes; absence of such content implies a pervasive, rigid, and fragile system of ego defenses, whereas at the other extreme there are two possibilities: (1) a weakening of ego control over impulses, such that results are maladaptive, or (2) drive energies have been neutralized so that they can be used in productive mental activity. The present manual provides a method for rating libidinal and aggressive drive material in the manifest content of stories, and also describes a procedure for rating the degree to which drive content is integrated into the theme (effectiveness of such integration is considered an index of ego control). Three ratings are obtained for integration of drive content, based upon three types of drive content that are distinguished: thematic, incidental, and nonappropriate. Three ratings are also arrived at for three levels of directness of expression of drive content; these levels are, direct-unsocialized, direct-socialized, and indirect-disguised or weak. An especially useful method for a modified, quantitative content analysis of T.A.T. stories of the entire families of schizophrenics, delinquents, and normals has been described by Stabenau et al. [311], and a scoring manual was developed by Werner et al. [346].

T.A.T. responses have obviously been studied in many ways, more or less complex. The simplest procedure is the *inspection technique.* It is frequently helpful merely to read through the stories, treating them as meaningful psychological communications; one simply underlines anything that seems significant, specific, or unique. When an experienced examiner rereads the stories a second time, he can, almost without effort, find a repetitive pattern running through them, or he can find facets of different stories falling together into a meaningful whole. This method becomes easier the more experience one has with the T.A.T. or the more clinical, particularly psychoanalytical, experience one has.

Name_____Story No._____(TAT Picture No._____)

1. **Main theme:**

2. **Main hero:** age_____sex_____vocation_____
   interests_____traits_____abilities_____
   adequacy (√,√√,√√√)_____body image and/or self image_____

3. **Main needs and drives of hero:**
   a) behavioral needs of hero (as in story):_____

   dynamic inference:_____
   b) figures, objects, or circumstances *introduced:*_____

   implying need for or to:_____

   c) figures, objects, or circumstances *omitted:*_____

   implying need for or to:_____

4. **Conception of environment (world) as :**_____

5. **Parental figures**   (m_____, f_____) are seen as_____and subject's reaction is_____
   Contemp. figures (m_____, f_____) are seen as_____and subject's reaction is_____
   Junior figures   (m_____, f_____) are seen as_____and subject's reaction is_____

6. **Significant conflicts :**_____

7. **Nature of anxieties: (√)**
   of physical harm and/or punishment_____of illness or injury_____
   of disapproval_____of deprivation_____
   of lack or loss of love_____of being devoured_____
   of being deserted_____of being overpowered and helpless_____
   other_____

8. **Main defenses against conflicts and fears : (√)**
   repression_____reaction-formation_____rationalization_____isolation_____
   regression_____introjection_____denial_____undoing_____other_____

9. **Adequacy of superego as manifested by "punishment" for "crime" being : (√, √√, √√√)**
   appropriate_____inappropriate_____
   too severe (also indicated by immediacy of punishment)_____
   inconsistent_____too lenient_____
   also:_____.
   delayed initial response or pauses_____
   stammer_____other manifestations of superego interference_____

10. **Integration of the ego, manifesting itself in : (√, √√, √√√)** (see also ego function rating scale on page 6 of Blank)
    adequacy of hero_____outcome: happy_____unhappy_____
                                                   realistic_____unrealistic_____
                       solution: adequate_____inadequate_____
    thought processes as revealed by plot being: (√, √√, √√√)
    structured_____unstructured_____stereotyped_____original_____appropriate_____
    rational_____bizarre_____complete_____incomplete_____inappropriate_____

Intelligence : (√) superior_____above average_____average_____below average_____defective_____

Analysis Sheet for use with the Bellak TAT Blank (Revised)

FIG. 1. Analysis sheet for use with the Bellak T.A.T. Blank.

In psychotherapy (see Chapter VII) it may be particularly helpful to have the patient hold one carbon copy of the T.A.T. stories while the psychotherapist has another, and then have the patient free associate generally to the stories and make his own attempts at interpretation.

Since I believe that the strength of the T.A.T. lies in its ability to elicit the content and dynamics of interpersonal relationships and the psychodynamic patterns, my method of interpretation and my scoring categories are primarily concerned with these dimensions and only to a small extent with the formal characteristics.

The main thing to remember in the interpretation of the T.A.T. is the following: the T.A.T. pictures are best seen psychologically as a series of social situations and interpersonal relations. Instead of responding to real people in real situations, the subject is responding to people in the pictures, which he imagines as certain social situations. Since he is under less constraint of conventionality of reality, his responses are more likely to depict his inner feelings. By this means we get at the contemporary patterns of his social behavior and may be able to infer the genesis of these patterns. Interpretation is the process of finding a common denominator in the contemporary and genetic behavior patterns of a person [22].

Among other things, this definition of interpretation implies what cannot be too strongly emphasized, particularly for the beginner: a diagnostic statement should hardly ever be made that is based on a datum revealed in only one story. Impressions gleaned in one instance can be considered a very tentative inference only, for which one must try to find corroboration in other stories or through some source of information external to the T.A.T. *A repetitive pattern is the best assurance that one does not deal with an artefact.*

To give a more definite frame of reference for scoring and a more objectively comparable scheme of interpretation, I have designed the system that the Psychological Corporation has published as the Bellak T.A.T. Blank and Analysis Sheet* (Fig. 1). I believe that it is a system simple enough to be most easily mastered, to serve as a guide and frame of reference, and to make it possible to glean the most important data of a complete 10 story T.A.T. in about half an hour.

B. How to Use the Long Form of the T.A.T. Blank†**

The Bellak T.A.T. Blank consists of a six-page folder plus separate recording and analysis sheets, of which one page from the folder is duplicated. On the cover of the folder one records the personal data of the client and, when the analysis is complete, one writes a Final Report.

Let us assume that the examiner wishes to secure 10 stories from a client and that he is going to take down these stories himself as the client tells them. The first story will be written on page 2 of the T.A.T. Blank; the second story will be written on the back of an analysis sheet. Story 3 is recorded on the back of another analysis sheet, etc., until the 10 stories have been recorded. The examiner now has the 10 stories recorded, one on the inside cover of the blank and nine on the back of separate analysis sheets. If these are placed in order, printed side up, and laid on top of page 3 in the T.A.T. Blank, the examiner will note that when each sheet is turned over he has an Analysis Sheet opposite the correspond-

---

* I am indebted to the Psychological Corporation of New York City for permitting me to reproduce here material that they originally published as the Bellak TAT Blank, Analysis Sheets, and Guide to the interpretation of the TAT.

  † Published by The Psychological Corporation, 304 East 45th Street, New York, New York 10017.

  ** Revised, 1973.

ing story. The Analysis Sheet for story 1 is on the front side of the paper on which story 2 is written; the Analysis Sheet for story 2 is on the front side of the sheet on which story 3 is written, etc. The analysis of story 10 (or the last story, if more or fewer stories are used) will be made on the Analysis Sheet that is printed as page 3 of the six-page Blank.

After the stories have been analyzed in this fashion, the examiner can write a summary of each of the stories in the space provided on page 4. (If more than 10 stories are used, more summaries can be written on the back of page 4.) It is best to write these summaries after all the stories have been analyzed, because the summary is one of the stages of formally integrating the content of the analysis of each separate story. When the summary sheet has been completed on page 4, one is prepared to write the Final Report. It will be noted that by folding the Blank, the space for the final report and the summary page may be exposed side by side.

When the task is done, the loose sheets may be stapled in the folder for safekeeping, and the final report appears on the cover for convenient reference.

As noted above, some examiners prefer to have their patients write the stories themselves. Since the patients should not have access to the outline on the analysis sheet, they should write their stories on plain 8½ by 11 paper. If the stories are so short that there are several on a sheet, they can be cut up and either pasted or clipped to the back of the separate analysis sheets so that the final arrangement will be the same as if the examiner himself had written on the back of the analysis sheets. If a separate sheet is used for each story, the folder will naturally be a little bulkier unless a typist is available to copy the stories onto the backs of the analysis sheets.

For some items on the analysis sheet, appropriate information from the story must be written in, using whatever short phrase or key word will most facilitate the analytic process. For others, indicated on the Blank by (√), a system of checks is suggested. A single check (√) may be used to indicate the mere presence of a given attitude, conflict, or the like. A double check (√√) or triple check (√√√) may be used to indicate increasing levels of importance to be assigned to the given item in summarizing the story. It is hoped that this approach to quantification will further research studies of interexaminer reliability of interpretation in addition to increasing the flexibility of the analysis form. Blank spaces are provided for adding categories or ideas not given in the outline. Despite the increasing use of the more recent Short Form of the Blank, the Long Form is still highly useful, especially for training and research.

C. Scoring Categories (Ten Variables)

The following suggestions for the use and interpretation of the individual scoring categories of the T.A.T. Blank may be helpful.

1. The Main Theme

The main theme is best understood as an attempt to restate the gist of the story. (It must be remembered that one T.A.T. story may actually have more than one basic theme.) Since beginners in the use of the test go off on a tangent most often in an interpretation of the main theme, a breakdown of the main theme into five levels is recommended.*

a. The *descriptive* level: on this level the theme should be a plain restatement of the summarized meaning of the story, a finding of the common trend restated in an abbreviated form and simple words.
b. The *interpretive* level.
c. The *diagnostic* level.
d. The *symbolic* level.
e. The *elaborative* level.

The example of the following story may help (6BM):

This is a young successful engineer. He is the only son in his family; his father is dead, and his mother is very close to him. He is in the oil business and he has been offered a contract to go overseas to the East Indies. He has signed the contract and is about to leave. He obtains her farewell and they part heartbroken. After a while she feels very lonesome and decides to follow her son to the East Indies. It is wartime and somehow she obtains passage on a ship to the island on which her son is. An enemy submarine sinks her ship and she perishes. Her son had not heard about her intentions but had independently planned to visit her as a surprise. He decides to return home for a surprise. The ship on which he had obtained passage is taking the same route his mother had taken. At the exact spot where his mother perishes, another enemy submarine attacks and he perishes also.

The theme on a *descriptive* level could be briefly restated as: a son lives alone with his beloved mother and leaves her—when they both try to rejoin each other they die on the same spot. On an *interpretive* level one may go a step further and put the meaning in a generalized form, assuming a meaning beyond the story: the patient believes that if one† permits oneself (incestual) fantasies, such as living with the mother, then both parties die. On a *diagnostic* level one transforms these impressions into a definitive statement: this man has incestuous problems and oedipal conflicts that cause him severe guilt feelings. On a *symbolic* level one may choose to interpret symbols according to psychoanalytic hypotheses; extreme parsimony and caution must be strongly recommended since this level takes one relatively farthest away from hard facts. In our example one might, for instance, possibly want to interpret the torpedoes as paternal phallic symbols which endanger and destroy both mother and son for their illicit attempted get-together. On an *elaborative* level one must get the subject's elaborations and free associations to such specific data as: "East Indies," "engineer," to any proper names or dates, and any other associations he can give.

---

* For the beginner it is most helpful to force himself to go through all five levels. However, it may not be necessary to put them all down in writing. The descriptive level, in particular, is a crutch; it may suffice just to state the theme at this level in one's mind. The interpretive level might be recorded on each analysis sheet, and the diagnostic, or higher, level may be the basis for the summary statement. These levels are primarily a learning device. Once one is experienced, the interpretive and diagnostic levels should be enough, just using the blanks for summaries.

† The interpretive level can nearly always be stated as a generalized conditional clause introduced by "If one. . . ."

2. The Main Hero*

The main hero of the story is the one who is most spoken of, whose feelings and subjective notions are most discussed, and, in general, the figure with whom the narrator seems to identify himself. In case of doubt, the figure resembling the patient most closely in age, sex, and other characteristics should be considered the main hero. At times a man may identify himself with a female "main hero"; if this occurs repeatedly, it *might* be considered a sign of latent homosexuality (depending on the total picture). While practically all young men identify in picture 2 with the young girl in the foreground, only some (there is disagreement regarding the percentage) consider the figure in picture 3BM a female. Vocation, interest, traits, abilities, and adequacy as well as body image of the main hero frequently depict qualities or desired qualities of the patient.

By *adequacy* of the hero we mean his ability to carry through tasks under external and internal difficulties in a socially, morally, intellectually, and emotionally acceptable manner. The adequacy of the hero frequently conforms to a pattern throughout the stories and is often in a direct relationship to the ego strength of the patient.

It should also be mentioned here that at times there may be more than one hero in a story. The patient may use a second figure with whom to identify himself, aside from the clearly recognizable hero. This happens rather rarely; usually it involves a figure introduced but not present in the picture itself, and concerns drives and sentiments which are even more objectionable to the patient than the ones pertaining to the main hero. (Other devices for emphatically trying to dissociate oneself from a story are to place it far away geographically and/or temporally, e.g., placing a story in Russia in the Middle Ages.)

The *body image* concept was originally created by Schilder [298], who stated: "The image of the human body means the picture of our own body which we form in our mind . . . the way in which the body appears to ourselves." This concept has struck us as more and more important—for instance, in the work with cardiac, tuberculous, and other subjects' stories to the T.A.T. It reveals itself particularly clearly in the violin picture (picture 1), but also in 3BM and in the rope picture (17BM), as well as in some others. In picture 1 one may learn about the subject's conception of his own body either in the discussion of the boy or often in the treatment of the violin. This instrument seems to become identified with the hero, and may be described as broken or empty, and dead and falling apart. Particularly in this latter case the reference transcends the body image and really becomes a matter of self-image—including the emotional tone and the subject's conception of his role in the world. (Sometimes the violin is identified

---

* Some of the following variables were used by me in an earlier mimeographed scoring blank I designed while at the Harvard Psychological Clinic in 1940–42. Thus a great and not easily specified extent of information and stimulation concerning these variables was received from Dr. H. A. Murray, Dr. R. W. White, and indirectly from Dr. R. N. Sanford who, with Dr. White, had written a mimeographed guide to the T.A.T. which served as the major stimulus for systematic attempts of interpretation. I wish to express my gratitude to these and other members of the staff of the Harvard Psychological Clinic.

with the female body, the bow constituting the male.) Similarly, 3BM and 17BM lend themselves particularly to both the characterization of the conception of body and self and the social role. Since these are images of primary importance for the determination of behavior, it is very useful to discern them in the T.A.T.

3. Main Needs and Drives of the Hero

Experience in teaching the T.A.T. has shown that the inquiry concerning the hero's needs produces three types of data which are frequently confused to the detriment of the accuracy of the observations.

Behavioral needs. The behavioral needs of the hero constitute the rock bottom data: if the hero is extremely aggressive in the story, attacking and hurting a number of people as the theme unfolds, it is worth recording. It is of course useful to remember that the behavioral needs of the hero *may* be the behavioral needs of the subject, but prima facie they are only the fantasy needs of the subject.

The problem of the relationship of *latent needs* in the T.A.T. to overt behavior is an important one. The interpreter of T.A.T. stories is frequently presented with the necessity of deciding whether or not a need expressed pertains strictly to the fantasy level or might be expressed in reality; for example, the need for aggression or for achievement. The psychologist should have available a maximum of clinical and biographical data about the patient. It must be remembered that the clinical situation is not one concerned with testing the validity of the instrument. Problems of the validity of the T.A.T. are dealt with in experiments and must be decided there. If one has sufficient information about the patient, then the T.A.T. stories must be seen as complementary to the behavioral data obtained. For instance, if the subject is unduly shy and retiring and the stories are full of aggression and guilt feelings about the figures, the dynamic implications are obvious.

On the other hand, there are certain indications from intratest situations which permit us to make assumptions about the manifest or latent needs expressed in the T.A.T. For example, in stories of achievement it is extremely important to notice whether they follow the *deus ex machina* mechanism (simple wish fulfillment) or are actually accomplished piece by piece and suggest much more that they correspond to a behavioral need for achievement.

It was R. N. Sanford [293] who pointed out some important rules concerning the relationship between fantasy needs and behavioral needs. He suggested that there are certain needs that are usually high in fantasy and low in behavior: namely, those needs which are usually prohibited and inhibited by cultural pressure from overt manifestation. These are mainly the needs for acquisition, aggression, autonomy, and sexual activity, the wish to be taken care of, and the need for harm avoidance (the last two suffering more cultural repression in men). On the other hand, some needs may find little manifest expression in fantasy but may find much expression in manifest behavior because of reality demands—for example the needs for order, for avoiding social blame, for learning. Again there is a class of needs which may be high both in fantasy and in behavior, indicating that, while these needs are permitted and encouraged socially, they may yet be sufficiently frustrated to require particular gratification on the fantasy level. To these belong especially the needs for achievement, for friendship, and for dominance.

Dynamic inference. If a subject (hero) is frequently very nurturant and supportive to a number of other figures, one may have reason to suspect that these figures are secondary or tertiary identification figures for the subject, and that the nurturance shown is indicative of a profoundly succorant, demanding attitude on the part of the hero, an attitude which he wards off in this way. On the other hand, one may have indications which lead one to believe that the subject who avoids all reference to aggression does so because of a great deal of aggression which he has to keep under control by denying all of it (an inference permitted only if there is supportive evidence).

Figures, objects, or circumstances introduced. A subject who introduces weapons of one sort or another in a number of stories (even without using them in the context) or who has food as an integral part (even without eating it) may be tentatively judged on such evidence as having a need for aggression or oral gratification respectively. Similarly, the introduction of such figures as punisher, pursuer, benefactor, etc., or such circumstances as injustice, deprivation, etc., may be interpreted with due regard to the rest of the record.

Figures, objects, or circumstances omitted. Similarly, if a subject omits reference to the gun in 3BM and to the rifle in 8BM, or does not see the one woman in 18GF choking the other, one may wish to infer a need to repress aggression—or a need to repress sexual stimuli if the seminude in the background of picture 4 is ignored, or if 13MF is seen as entirely devoid of sexual references. Of course, this level of inference can only be tentative until we have a large enough sample to achieve a statistical basis for what the expectations are when a certain object is introduced or omitted, so as to be reasonably accurate in judging when a subject deviates from the norm.

4. The Conception of the Environment (World)

This concept is, of course, a complex mixture of unconscious self-perception and apperceptive distortion of stimuli by memory images of the past. The more consistent a picture of the environment appears in the T.A.T. stories, the more reason we have to consider it an important constituent of our subject's personality and a useful clue to his reactions in everyday life. Usually, two or three descriptive terms will suffice, such as succorant, hostile, exploiting or exploitable, friendly, dangerous, etc.

5. Figures Seen as . . .

The T.A.T. is primarily an instrument which permits a study of the apperceptive distortions of the social relationships and the dynamic factors basic to them. Therefore, an exhaustive study of the hero's attitudes to parental, contemporary, and younger or inferior persons is an integral part of our scheme. This method permits recording these apperceptions and the subject's reactions to his perception, that is, each picture allows the subject to create a situation that can best be understood as a problem ("Tell me what is going on") which he then has to proceed to solve ("And tell me what the outcome will be"), thus baring his ability to come to compromise formations with his own needs, in other words, to show us his defenses. For instance, if a subject chooses to perceive female figures in the T.A.T. as aggressive, then it is worthwhile for us to determine how he proceeds to react to these creatures of his fancy, whether with withdrawal, counteraggression, intellectualization, or other forms of behavior.*

6. Significant Conflicts

When we study the significant conflicts of an individual, we not only want to know the nature of the conflict but also the defenses which the subject uses against it. It is important, in designating which drive or force is in conflict with the superego, also to specify in a word or two the resultant behavior: e.g., if the conflict is between superego and aggression, it may be that the subject reacts with *shyness*. Here, as in the study of the anxieties and in the general structure of the stories' progress, we have an excellent opportunity for a study of the character structure and the prognosis of the patient. Sometimes the conflict may not be between the superego and such drives as aggression, acquisition, sexual desires, or the like, but between two drives such as achievement and pleasure or autonomy and compliance.

7. Nature of Anxieties

The importance of determining the main anxieties hardly needs emphasizing. Again, it will be valuable to note the defenses in this context, whether they take the form of passivity, flight, aggression, orality, or those classically circumscribed ones mentioned below.

8. Main Defenses against Conflicts and Fears

As we had occasion to point out elsewhere [25], the T.A.T. should not be studied exclusively for drive content, but should, in addition, be examined for the defenses against these drives. Not infrequently such a study of defenses will actually offer more information in that the drives themselves may appear less clearly than the defenses against them; on the other hand, the defensive structure may be more closely related to manifest behavior. By means of studying drives and defenses the T.A.T. often permits a very clear-cut appraisal of the character structure of the subject.

Aside from a search for the main defense mechanisms described by Anna Freud [127] it is also valuable to study the molar aspects of the stories. For instance, some subjects choose obsessive defenses against a disturbing picture

---

* After sex has been checked, the other two blanks may be completed with appropriate adjectives. While the list is by no means exhaustive, the following adjectives may be used: abusive, achieving, acquisitive, aggressive, autonomous, compliant, domineering, dependent, friendly, hostile, nurturant, punishing, resistant, succorant, fearful, devoted, supportive.

content; they may produce four or five themes, each very short and descriptive, manifestly different but dynamically identical. Sometimes a succession of themes to one and the same picture shows the subject's attempts to deal with a disturbing conflict; successive stories may become more and more innocuous, showing an increase in the defenses. On the other hand, each successive theme may permit more expression of the forbidden drive as already discussed in part in Chapter I and also discussed in other chapters.

As another illustration, there is the following fascinating response given by a middle-aged scientist as his story to 13MF (the numbers were inserted by me, not by the subject):

(1) A man and woman who may be in a bedroom or living room with a cot. She may have been ill and had been put to bed. The man may have seen to her wants or he may be a doctor who had been with her for a long time, especially through the night, and is now very tired. The woman may be sleeping or resting or may have died, and the man, her husband or the doctor, has just gone through a long siege or, if the woman is his wife who died, he shows sorrow or if she is just sick he shows fear and is tired. (2) It may be that homicide has been committed and the man shows remorse and realization of the gravity of his act. (3) Or there may have been cohabitation, the woman undraped in bed, the man having dressed. (4) Also, a husband getting up early in the morning to go to work, not quite awake, while his wife is still asleep.

In this case we have at least four stories showing a progression from a relatively innocuous apperception to breakthrough of plainly homicidal thoughts. Whether cohabitation is a further progression to an even worse crime in the mind of the subject, or whether it constitutes a renewed vigor of defenses which culminates in the utterly innocuous domestic scene, could not be ascertained.

It is by such study that fine features of defense and character may be discovered.

9. Adequacy of Superego as Manifested by "Punishment" for "Crime"

The relationship of the nature of the punishment to the severity of the offense gives us an excellent insight into the severity of the superego; a psychopath's hero may consistently receive no punishment in stories of murder, with no more than a slight suggestion that he may have learned a lesson for later life, while a neurotic may have stories in which the hero is accidentally or intentionally killed or mangled or dies of illness following the slightest infraction or expression of aggression. On the other hand, a nonintegrated superego, sometimes too severe and sometimes too lenient, is also frequently met in neurotics.

10. Integration of the Ego

This is, of course, an important variable to learn about; it tells us how well able a subject is to function. It tells us to what extent he is able to compromise between his drives and the demands of reality on the one hand, and the commands of his superego on the other. The adequacy of the hero in dealing with the problems he is confronted with in the pictures, and his own apperception of it, tells us what we want to know in this respect.

Here we are interested in some formal characteristics: is the subject able to tell appropriate stories which constitute a certain amount of cognizance of the adaptive aspects of the stimulus; or does he leave the stimulus completely and tell a story with no manifest relation to the picture because he is not well enough to perceive reality or too preoccupied with his own problems to keep them out, whether pertinent or not? Does he find rescue and salvation from the anxiety pertaining to the test by giving very stereotyped responses, or is he well enough and intelligent enough to be creative and give more or less' original stories? Having produced a plot, can he attain a solution of the conflicts in the story and within himself which is adequate, complete, and realistic, or do his thought processes become unstructured or even bizarre under the impact of the problem?

These observations permit an appraisal of what really constitutes ego strength, often contributing a great deal to facilitating possible classification of the patient in one of the nosological categories, in addition to the dynamic diagnosis which the content variables supply as the main contribution of the T.A.T.

Here too belong such considerations as *the distance of the subject from his story;* for instance, if the setting of the story is far away or long ago, or if the hero is merely an onlooker, or if it is reported as a scene from a movie, or if emotional situations are told in a sarcastic tone and embellished with *sotto voce* remarks, all these factors usually imply an attempt to isolate oneself from the emotional content of the story as a defense mechanism. On the other hand, if a subject immediately involves himself personally in the story and says, "That is just what happened to me . . . ," it may mean a loss of distance and implies a very narcissistic preoccupation with the self.

From a formal standpoint, it is useful to consider that telling stories about the pictures is a task which the subject must perform. We may judge his adequacy, ego strength, and other variables from the standpoint of his ability and way of meeting the task.

Clinical interest in *ego functions* has steadily increased. Therefore, a specific ego function assessment scale is provided on page 6 of the T.A.T. Blank. This scale is predicated upon detailed definitions and extensive research reported elsewhere [13]. When ego functions were studied by interview, psychological tests, and laboratory methods, it turned out somewhat surprisingly that ratings derived from the T.A.T. by several raters correlated more highly than those for the Rorschach, WAIS, Figure Drawings, and the Bender Gestalt Test (13, p. 331). Ego functions may be assessed from the T.A.T. stories themselves and entered on the rating scale. If desired, highest may be drawn to connect the ratings (see Figure). One may also wish to assess ego functions from the test behavior. It is suggested that this be recorded and reported separately in the space beneath the scale on page 6.

The twelve ego functions may be briefly defined as follows:

1. Reality Testing

The ability to differentiate between inner and outer stimuli involves continuous selective scanning and matching contemporary percepts against past percepts and ideas. Social contexts and norms will always be relevant in assessing reality testing.

Inner-reality testing is included in this scale. It is reflected here in the degree to which the person is in touch with his inner self. Stated another way, this implies "psychological-mindedness" or "reflective awareness," e.g., of the implications of the T.A.T. stories.

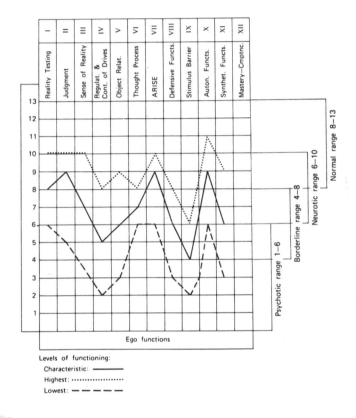

Levels of functioning:
Characteristic: ————
Highest: ·······················
Lowest: — — — — —

II. Judgment

Ratings for judgment are based on data indicating comprehension and appraisals of hypothetical and real situations, and the subject's evaluations of the consequences of action or other behavior related to these situations, as the subject creates them here.

III. Sense of Reality of the World and of the Self

This scale assesses disturbances in the sense of ones' self, as it relates to the outside world. It also assays the sense of reality or unreality of the world. For instance, some T.A.T. stories include talk about ghostly creatures and unreal half-worlds!

IV. Regulation and Control of Drives, Affects, and Impulses

This function refers to the extent to which delaying and controlling mechanisms allow drive derivatives to be expressed in a modulated and adaptive way, characterized, optimally, by neither under nor overcontrol.

V. Object Relations

Optimal relationships are relatively free of maladaptive elements suggesting patterns of interaction that were more appropriate to childhood situations than to the present ones. The most pathological extreme would be essentially an absence of relationships with any people; next would be present relations based on early fixations, unresolved conflicts, and very hostile sadomasochistic relationships. Optimal relations would be the most mature, relatively free of distortions, and gratifying to adult libidinal, aggressive, and ego needs. For Picture #1 of the T.A.T., a story in which a violinst plays with pleasure before an empty Carnegie Hall suggests a great deal of narcissism.

VI. Thought Processes

Disturbances in formal characteristics of logical thinking, as well as the interference of primary process material need to be rated.

VII. ARISE

Adaptive regression in the service of the ego (ARISE) refers to the ability of the ego to initiate a partial, temporary, and controlled lowering of its own functions (keep in mind here the component factors of the eleven ego functions) in the furtherance of its interests (i.e., promoting adaptation). Such regressions result in a relatively free, but controlled, play of the primary process. This ego function can be particularly well observed from the way in which the subject is able to deal with the T.A.T. as a creative task.

VIII. Defensive Functioning

Defenses protect preconscious and conscious organizations from the intrusions of id derivatives, unconscious ego, and superego tendencies. They aid adaptation by controlling the emergence of anxiety-arousing, or other dysphoric psychic content, such as ego-alien instinctual wishes and affects (including depression), which conflict with reality demands. Excessive defensiveness is of course also maladaptive. A notation—whether excessive or defective—is useful.

IX. Stimulus Barrier

Both thresholds and responses to stimuli contribute to adaptation by the organism's potential for responding to high, average, or low sensory input, so that optimal homeostasis (as well as adaptation) is maintained. Stimulus barrier determines, in part, how resilient a person is or how he readapts after the stress and impingements are no longer present. A story of a mother who can't stand the yelling of her child and how it affects her would be very informative here.

X. Autonomous Functioning

Intrusion of conflict, ideation, affect, and/or impulse upon functioning is a major criterion for determining impairment of either the primary or the secondary autonomy.

The basic apparatuses and functions of primary autonomy are:

perception	memory	language
intentionality	hearing	productivity
concentration	vision	motor development
attention	speech	and expression

XI. Synthetic-Integrative Functioning

This ego function fulfills one of the major tasks of the ego as defined by Freud, in terms of reconciling the often conflicting demands of the id, superego, and outside world, as well as the incongruities within the ego. We focus on the reconciling of areas that are in conflict and also on the extent of relating together areas that are not in conflict.

XII. Mastery-Competence

Raters must score competence and sense of competence separately, since a number of different relationships between the two are possible: (1) they may be congruent; (2) actual performance may exceed the sense of competence; (3) sense of competence may exceed mastery-competence.

D. The Summary and Final Report

After all the stories have been analyzed, the main data obtained from each should be noted down in the appropriate space on page 4. When the summary page is studied after the analysis of all the stories has been completed, a repetitive pattern in the subject's responses ordinarily becomes quite clear.*

The final report can be written in full view of the summary page. It is suggested that the form of the final report follow the sequence of the 10 categories on the analysis sheet. The main themes, the second and third variables, permit a description of the *unconscious structure and needs* of the subject, while the fourth and fifth variables show us his *conception of the world and of significant figures* around him. Categories six, seven, eight, nine, and 10 may actually be used as headings for statements concerning the respective dimensions of personality.

The form of the final report will depend, of course, to a great extent on the person for whom it is intended. It is, however, strongly advised that empty phrases and erroneous inferences be avoided by the following procedure: the first half of the report may consist of general abstract statements concerning the subject, following the outline above; a second part of the report should then consist of specific, concrete documentation by excerpts from stories or by specific references to stories from which the main abstract statements have been derived.

This arrangement is particularly useful in instances in which the psychologist reports as part of a team to psychiatrists and to social workers who may not have

---

* Experienced T.A.T. workers, having become familiar with our method, may wish to use only the T.A.T. Blank, using the middle page for a guide to record relevant data on the summary sheet rather than actually filling in the details on 10 analysis sheets.

the time or the experience to read the stories themselves, and for whom a purely abstract statement will not be sufficiently meaningful.*

If a diagnosis must be offered, or if one wishes to state one, I suggest that the following formula be used: "The data represented in the T.A.T. are consistent with the diagnosis of . . ." This expresses my belief that the T.A.T. is not primarily a diagnostic test (diagnostic in the sense of labeling nosologically—of course it is diagnostic of dynamic and structural variables) and also that, preferably, no diagnosis should ever be made on the basis of a single test, or better, never on test evidence alone without additional information provided by a clinical interview.

E. The Short Form of the Bellak T.A.T. and C.A.T. Blank†

The short form of the original Blank has been published mainly for clinical convenience. While it uses practically the same variables as the earlier Blank, it consists only of a three-page form which folds into a single 8½ by 11 sheet, with the summarized facts on the front. When the Blank is unfolded, each of the variables can be recorded in the appropriate boxes for all 10 stories and summarized consecutively under the same headings at the extreme right. The writing of the final report can be simplified by having the summary sheet opened out in full view. It should be noted that the 10 major variables or categories are used primarily as a frame of reference; not all aspects will be relevant to every story and, occasionally, details not included in the Blank will occur and have to be recorded.

The principal function of the Blank is to further facilitate the transition from concrete primary data to the inferential summary and final diagnosis by having all three pages unfolded in front of one. Also the Short Form is easier to handle. In its new revised version, it shows a shift to more interest in ego psychology in that the revised form lists 12 ego functions. These are to be gauged—as many of them, and as well as possible—as a further indication of adaptive capacity. A detailed account of these ego functions can be found in Bellak and Loeb's *The Schizophrenic Syndrome* [61], in *Ego Functions in Schizophrenics, Neurotics, and Normals,* and in a paper called "A Systemic Study of Ego Functions" [58].

Briefly, they can be described as follows**:

Reality testing. The major factors are (a) the distinction between inner and outer stimuli; (b) accuracy of perception (includes orientation to time and place and interpretation of external events); (c) accuracy of inner reality testing (psychological mindedness and awareness of inner states).

Judgment. (a) Awareness of likely consequences of intended behavior (anticipating probable dangers, legal culpabilities, social censure, disapproval, or inap-

---

* I am indebted to S. Sorel Bellak for suggestions and constructive criticism of the revision of this T.A.T. Blank and Manual.

† Published by C. P. S. Inc., P. O. Box 83, Larchmont, New York. For an example of the use of the Short Form, see Case 3, the analysis of Somerset Maugham's short stories (Chapter IX), and Chapter XII.

** The material from here to Section F is reprinted from [58] by permission.

propriateness); (b) extent to which manifest behavior reflects the awareness of these likely consequences.

Sense of reality of the world and of the self. The component factors are (a) the extent to which external events are experienced as real and as being embedded in a familiar context (degree of derealization, déjà vu, trance-like states); (b) the extent to which the body (or parts of it) and its functioning and one's behavior are experienced as familiar, unobtrusive, and as belonging to (or emanating from) the individual; (c) the degree to which the person has developed individuality, uniqueness, and a sense of self and self-esteem; (d) the degree to which the person's self-representations are separated from his object representations.

Regulation and control of drives, affects, and impulses. (a) The directness of impulse expression (ranging from primitive acting out through neurotic acting out to relatively indirect forms of behavioral expression); (b) the effectiveness of delay and control, the degree of frustration tolerance, and the extent to which drive derivatives are channeled through ideation, affective expression, and manifest behavior.

Object (or interpersonal) relations. The components are (a) the degree and kind of relatedness to others and investment in them (taking account of withdrawal trends, narcissistic self-concern, narcissistic object choice or mutuality); (b) the extent to which present relationships are adaptively or maladaptively influenced by or patterned upon older ones and serve present, mature aims rather than past, immature aims; (c) the degree to which the person perceives others as separate entities rather than as extensions of himself; (d) the extent to which he can maintain object constancy (i.e., sustain relationships over long periods of time and tolerate both the physical absence of the object and frustration, anxiety, and hostility related to the object).

Thought processes. The components are (a) the adequacy of processes which adaptively guide and sustain thought (attention, concentration, anticipation, concept formation, memory, language); (b) the relative primary-secondary process influences on thought (extent to which thinking is unrealistic, illogical, and/or loose).

Adaptive regression in the service of the ego. (a) First phase of an oscillating process: relaxation of perceptual and conceptual acuity (and other ego controls) with a concomitant increase in awareness of previously preconscious and unconscious contents; (b) second phase of the oscillating process: the induction of new configurations which increase adaptive potentials as a result of creative integrations.

Defensive functioning. (a) Degree to which defensive components adaptively or maladaptively affect ideation and behavior; (b) extent to which these defenses have succeeded or failed (degree of emergence of anxiety, depression, and/or other dysphoric affects, indicating weakness of defensive operations).

Stimulus barrier. The component factors are (a) threshold for, sensitivity to, or awareness of stimuli impinging upon various sensory modalities (primarily external, but including pain); (b) nature of response to various levels of sensory stimulation in terms of the extent of disorganization, avoidance, withdrawal, or active coping mechanisms employed to deal with them.

Autonomous functioning. The components are (a) degree of freedom from impairment of apparatuses of primary autonomy (functional disturbances of sight, hearing, intention, language, memory, learning, or motor function); (b) degree of or freedom from impairment of secondary autonomy (disturbances in habit patterns, learned complex skills, work routines, hobbies, and interests).

Synthetic-integrative functioning. (a) Degree of reconciliation or integration of discrepant or potentially contradictory attitudes, values, affects, behavior, and self representations; (b) degree of *active* relating together and integrating of psychic and behavioral events, whether contradictory or not.

Mastery-competence. (a) Competence, the person's performance in relation to his existing capacity to interact with and master his environment; (b) sense of competence, the person's expectation of success, or the subjective side of actual performance (how well he believes he can do).

F. Case Illustrations*

Following are some examples of analyzed T.A.T. records.† An attempt has been made to present them as closely as possible to the actual use of the T.A.T. Blank and Analysis Sheets. Since the format of this book is smaller than the actual size of the blank, these pages must of necessity be rather crowded. Another limitation is that the running commentary of a classroom is not easily approximated. The clinical notes are meant to take the place of classroom remarks—enlarging on one aspect or another which might easily appear arbitrary. For instance, in story 1 of John Doe, blindness is scored both as a defense (namely, a form of denial of the voyeurism which is also expressed in the story itself by the subject's failure to recognize the violin) and again as a form of punishment. Psychological acts are over-determined. Fear of blindness, especially in children, must be regarded clinically both as a wish not to have to see (for instance, primal scene events), and also as a fear of being punished for wanting to look. Seeing is sometimes experienced as something active, i.e., the glaring stare of the hypnotist, or as something passive, by the person into whose eyes someone is staring forcefully. The eye may thus serve either as a male or a female sexual symbol. Frequently during psychoanalytic sessions related to the topic of masturbation, patients will rub their eyes and transitory symptoms of compulsive eye rubbing are not uncommon. This usually constitutes a masturbatory equivalent.

The clinical notes accompanying each story are kept to a minimum and where possible printed on the same page as the story itself, as an editorial convenience. *They are not an essential part of the clinical record, but are appended here for didactic purposes.* Similarly, under clinical conditions, the descriptive theme need not be written out at all; the instructions are to write the *interpretive* theme under "Main Theme" on the Analysis Sheet, and to write the diagnostic level of the theme on

---

* In the first two cases, the Long Form is used; in the third case, the Short Form is used.

† These records are by no means exhaustively analyzed, as anyone will recognize. To do so would not be practical here. Indeed, a whole monograph could be written about each T.A.T. record! Different styles of writing the final report are used to illustrate various possibilities.

the Summary Page. *However, for didactic reasons, we are reproducing here the descriptive, interpretive, and diagnostic theme* below each story to show how the final diagnostic level is arrived at by easy stages from the actual story as given by the subject. Then, just to keep the record straight, we also reproduce the interpretive theme on the Analysis Blank and the diagnostic theme level on the Summary Page, where they belong in the actual clinical record.

Thus, the scheme as used here will often be repetitive in the interests of greater clarity.

Case 1

The first case I present is one of "blind" diagnosis, that is, the T.A.T. was administered by someone else in a neuropsychiatric hospital, and sent to me as the protocol of "John Doe," male, age 25, single.* These stories are on the whole quite poor, thematically speaking, and as unsuitable for my type of analysis as could easily be found; I include them to show how much one can derive from the scheme even under poor story conditions.

Although at the time of analyzing the material I knew nothing about this man except his age and sex, I am now including a condensed version of the summary evaluation of John Doe made by the mental hygiene psychotherapist:

The patient is a tall, slender young man of 25 who gives the impression of boyishness. He seems suspicious, indecisive, and unable to relax. There seem to be considerable effeminate mannerisms in his behavior. He had never been able to make secure object relationships. He was very fearful and withdrawn from early childhood. Some of his guilt is in relation to his sexual drives, masturbation, and probably also in relation to incestuous feelings toward a seductive mother. There seems to be considerable guilt in relation to his own hostility. He has established some defenses against this through obsessions, but his defenses are cracking. The patient seemed obsessed with thoughts about death, homicide, and suicide. There were depersonalization, many ideas of reference, and a considerable amount of hostile fantasy. It is felt that this patient is a paranoid schizophrenic who is still able to maintain control over his hostile and destructive impulses, although his control is very tenuous. As long as he can live a withdrawn and sheltered life perhaps he can continue to function outside a hospital; however, in the face of frustration he may become actively psychotic with homicidal and suicidal impulses.

Following is a case reproduced as in the actual T.A.T. Blank, which means that the final report appears on what would be the first page of the blank, so that whoever the report is intended for can read the essentials at one glance. The reader is advised first to go through the stories and then to turn back to the final report. Further on in this book, this case is analyzed in terms of object relations.

---

* Courtesy of Edwin S. Shneidman et al., *Thematic Test Analysis*, New York, Grune & Stratton, 1951 [303]. Since this T.A.T. interpretation was part of a research project, there was no objection to a blind diagnosis.

BELLAK T A T BLANK

For Recording and Analyzing Thematic Apperception Test Stories

Name___John Doe_____ Sex__M____ Age_25_ Date_____

Education_____Occupation_____

Referred by_____Analysis by_____

FINAL REPORT

General:

    This is an extremely disturbed man: he conceives of himself as ill, incapacitated, mutilated, feels depressed, fearful, and dead inside.

    He is exceedingly ambivalent toward both father and mother figures; his oedipal problems are entirely unresolved: he has a tremendous attachment to the mother, whom he sees as dangerous at the same time. He sees the father as cold, hostile, and inadequate.

    The patient has tremendous guilt feelings concerning both sexual and aggressive impulses (which appear fused). He frequently identifies with a female figure. He also has conflicts concerning exhibitionistic and voyeuristic tendencies, possibly related to urethral difficulties.

    His thought processes appear disturbed, tending toward the bizarre. There are data consistent with cosmic delusions and hallucinations.

    The total picture is consistent with a schizophrenic disorder, with potential paranoid and hebephrenic coloring. Suicidal risk is considerable. Homicidal risk should be considered. Sexual criminality, including overt homosexuality, is a possibility.

Specific:

    Illness and mutilation appear in stories 1, 7BM; also in 12M, 14, and 16 (not reproduced here). Depression, fear, and guilt are apparent in every story, usually related to sex, such as prostitution in 7BM, adultery in 4, sex and murder in 6BM; sex and disgust also appear in 13MF, murder and stealing in 14 (the last two stories not reproduced here). Homosexuality is suggested by female identification.

    Blindness occurs in story 1, great notoriety in 3BM, stage acting in 6BM; not looking in 13MF and photography in 14 (the latter two are not reproduced here). These themes are consistent with voyeurism and exhibitionism.

    Water occurs in story 1, fire in 4, slightly suggestive of urethral problems.

    Conflict with parental figures appears in story 1, the female figure is seen as dangerous and seductive in 4, mother seen as dangerous in 6BM, father as cold in 7BM, as inadequate in 7BM (was also sick) and in 13B (not reproduced), and is fought symbolically in 14 (also not reproduced here).

    Thought processes appear most clearly to be disturbed and bizarre in stories 1, 6BM, and 16 (not reproduced here).

Note. The above represents one form of writing the final report, the general statements being separated from the specific concrete references they are based on. The reports for Case 2 and Case 3 show other possibilities.

1: This child is sick in bed. He has been given sheet music to study, but instead of the music he has come across a novel that interests him more than the music. It is probably an adventure story. He evidently does not fear the chance that his parents will find him thus occupied as he seems quite at ease. He seems to be quite a studious type and perhaps regrets missing school, but he seems quite occupied with the adventure in the story. Adventure has something to do with ocean or water. He is not too happy, though not too sad. His eyes are somewhat blank—coincidence of reading a book without any eyes or knowing what is in the book without reading it. He disregards the music and falls asleep reading the book.

Descriptive theme	Interpretive theme	Diagnostic level
A sick child is	(If one) is a sick child	Feels a child, sick, poor body image.
told to study music (ignores fiddle) and	told to work (ignores fiddle),	Feels coerced. Mechanism of denial—re masturbation?
prefers adventure story to studying,	prefers pleasure reading (concerning water) to studying,	Resists authority by withdrawal into fantasy; urethral interests, exhibitionism?
feels not happy, not sad,	without affect,	Anhedonia? Depersonalization?
unafraid of punishment,	unafraid of punishment,	(Fear of punishment), severe superego; denial.
reads without eyes or knows what is in book without reading,	can see without eyes and is omniscient,	Bizarre ideas of magic; severe superego, castration, omnipotence.
falls asleep.	falls asleep.	Withdrawal, passivity.

Clinical notes

The concept of the body image as sick, and merely a child, emerges here, supplemented by the idea of being blind later in the story, probably indicating poor concept patient has of himself, and at the same time probably indicating some intrapsychic awareness of (mental) illness which one finds in patients who seem consciously unaware of being psychotic.

Ignores fiddle altogether: This is rare in adults, usually signifying disturbance re violin playing as sexual symbol, particularly masturbatory.

Instead of studying, prefers fantasy: resistant to parents; unable to study, or unwilling.

Fantasy concerns water, ocean: since this is an entirely personal introduction by the subject, wonder if related to enuresis, urethral complex, and premature ejaculation as sexual disturbance, aside from actual urinary disturbances.

Unafraid of punishment: negation probably means "I wish I were not afraid" (actually quite afraid), as pointed out by Freud (denial).

Not happy, not sad: anhedonia, underlying depression—mechanism of denial.

Name_____Story No. _1__ (TAT Picture No. _1___)

1. **Main theme:** (_Interpetive_) (If one is) a sick child, told to study music (ignores fiddle), prefers an adventure story concerning water, feels not happy, not sad, unafraid of punishment, possibly reading without eyes or knowing what is in book without reading it, falls asleep.

2. **Main hero:** age _child_ sex _male_ vocation _student_ _not happy, not sad._
   interests _reading_ traits _studious, unafraid,_ abilities _reading book without eyes_
   adequacy (√, √√, √√√) _0 ?_ body image and/or self image _ill in bed; blank eyes—no eyes_

3. **Main needs of hero:**
   a) behavioral needs of hero (as in story): _Reads adventure story instead of studying music; falls asleep._
   dynamic inference: _resistant to parents; passivity; withdrawal; prefers fantasy concerning_
   b) figures, objects, or circumstances introduced: _parents, book, water, school_ _urethral_
   problems
   implying need for or to: _illness; to defy parents and withdraw into_ _to study._
   fantasy. Preoccupation with and awareness of illness.
   c) figures, objects, or circumstances omitted: _violin, bow_
   implying need for or to: _Guilt re masturbation_

4. **Conception of environment (world) as:** _coercive, rejecting_

5. Parental figures (m _√_, f _√_) are seen as _coercive - re-_ and subject's reaction is _escape into fantasy_
   Contemp. figures (m___, f___) are seen as _jecting_ and subject's reaction is___
   Junior figures (m___, f___) are seen as___ and subject's reaction is___

6. **Significant conflicts:** _Compliance-autonomy; achievement-pleasure; activity-passivity._

7. **Nature of anxieties:** (√)
   of physical harm and/or punishment___   of illness or injury _√_
   of disapproval___   of deprivation _√_
   of lack or loss of love___   of being devoured___
   of being deserted___   of being overpowered and helpless___
   other___

8. **Main defenses against conflicts and fears:** (√)
   repression___ reaction-formation___ rationalization___ isolation___ _withdrawal,_
   regression___ introjection___ denial _√_ undoing___ other___
   delusional omnipotence) _—of voyeurism) sometimes also a form of castration._

9. **Severity of superego as manifested by:** (√)
   punishment for "crime" _Blind (as punishment)_ immediate___ just___ too severe___
   delayed___ unjust___ too lenient___
   inhibitions___ stammer___ delayed initial response or pauses___

10. **Integration of the ego, manifesting itself in:** (√, √√, √√√)
    adequacy of hero _0 ?_   outcome: happy___   unhappy___
    realistic___   unrealistic _√_
    solution: adequate___   inadequate___
    thought processes as revealed by plot being: (√, √√, √√√)
    structured___ unstructured _√_ stereotyped _√_ original___ appropriate___
    rational___ bizarre _√_ complete _√_ incomplete___ inappropriate___

Intelligence: (√) superior___ above average___ average _√_ below average___ defective___

Analysis Sheet for use with the Bellak TAT Blank

Reading without eyes: bizarre statement; being blind is often punishment for voyeurism (related to exhibitionism) and often consistent with very great masturbatory guilt.

Knows what is in book without reading it: bizarre statement; implies telepathic notions, superhuman power, possibly related to cosmic delusions.

Note. A slightly revised version of variables 9 and 10 of the above blank, to be published as before by The Psychological Corporation, is in process. The changes are identical with those appearing in the revised Short Form.

Falling asleep: resolves conflict situation (disobeying parents) by withdrawal.

Story is far removed from stimulus, poorly structured, bizarre, consistent with severe thought disturbance; flat mood consistent with schizophrenia.

3BM: This is a girl in a cell and she has been jailed because she was found guilty of prostitution. She is in this position in the picture because she is very ashamed, not because of being arrested, because she is quite familiar with the police, but because of the fact that her picture and a newspaper write-up was being sensationally spread across the country. She knew that her sister, who was a nun, would suffer from it, and it made her feel very badly because she, at one time, had a chance and an opportunity to follow her elder sister's example but it was too late now. She grabs a concealed knife from under her blouse and stabs herself.

Descriptive theme	Interpretive theme	Diagnostic level
A girl is jailed for prostitution;	(If a) girl is guilty of prostitution she is jailed;	Great guilt over sex; feminine identification.
is ashamed not for arrest (because she is quite familiar with police) but because of newspaper publicity which would hurt her sister, a nun. Once she could have followed her sister's example but it is too late now.	is ashamed of the publicity and the hurting of sister whom she should emulate in being a nun,	Severe superego concerning also exhibitionism and ambivalence to sibling seen as pure.
Kills herself with knife.	and kills herself.	Intra-aggression.

Clinical notes

Subject apparently considers sex as dirty, in speaking of prostitution here. Apparently feels like an habitual criminal, since he says he is quite accustomed to jail. His fear of the introduced theme of publicity is quite consistent as the exhibitionistic counterpart of the voyeurism in story 1.

Hero identifies with female in this story. This by itself is so frequent in this picture that it can only be considered a most tentative datum. However, this is such a vivid identification and sounds so convincing that it appears to portray something significant.

Name_____ Story No. _2_____ (TAT Picture No. _3BM_)

1. Main theme: (_Interpretive_) (If a) girl is guilty of prostitution she is jailed; is ashamed of the publicity and the hurting of sister whom she should emulate in being a nun, and kills herself.

2. Main hero: age _young_ sex _female_ vocation _prostitute_
interests _none noted._ traits _guilty re sex_ abilities _none noted_
adequacy (√, √√, √√√) _0 ?_ body image and/or self image _feminine identification?_
outcast – criminal – sexually immoral.

3. Main needs of hero:
a) behavioral needs of hero (as in story): _Kills self because sister would suffer from her actions._
dynamic inference: _depression – guilt over sex – suicidal tendencies? aggression against⟶_
b) figures, objects, or circumstances introduced: _sister – publicity – suicide_   ⟵_mother_
implying need for or to: _exhibitionism and ambivalence to sibling (or mother) seen as pure_
c) figures, objects, or circumstances omitted: _object usually seen as pistol is made into a knife (significance not clear – weakening aggression?)_
implying need for or to:_____

4. Conception of environment (world) as: _punishing – shaming – reproving_

5. Parental figures (m____, f__) are seen as _____ and subject's reaction is_____
Contemp. figures (m____, f _√_) are seen as _pure_ and subject's reaction is _ambivalence_
Junior figures (m____, f____) are seen as _____ and subject's reaction is_____

6. Significant conflicts: _guilt concerning sex_

7. Nature of anxieties: (√)
of physical harm and/or punishment_____   of illness or injury_____
of disapproval _√_   of deprivation_____
of lack or loss of love _√_   of being devoured_____
of being deserted_____   of being overpowered and helpless_____
other_____

8. Main defenses against conflicts and fears: (√)
repression_____ reaction-formation_____ rationalization_____ isolation_____
regression_____ introjection_____ denial_____ undoing_____ other_____
projection; identification with aggressor.

9. Severity of superego as manifested by: (√)
punishment for "crime"_____ immediate _√_ just_____ too severe _√_
delayed_____ unjust_____ too lenient_____
inhibitions_____ stammer_____ delayed initial response or pauses_____

10. Integration of the ego, manifesting itself in: (√, √√, √√√)
adequacy of hero _0 ?_ outcome: happy_____ unhappy _√√√_
realistic_____ unrealistic_____
solution: adequate_____ inadequate _√√√_
thought processes as revealed by plot being: (√, √√, √√√)
structured_____ unstructured_____ stereotyped_____ original_____ appropriate_____
rational_____ bizarre_____ complete _√_ incomplete_____ inappropriate _√_

Intelligence: (√) superior_____ above average_____ average_____ below average_____ defective_____

Analysis Sheet for use with the Bellak TAT Blank

4: The girl in the picture is half-caste. She is in love with the man who is going to leave her and return to his wife. They have spent quite some time together in intimacy. She is pleading with him to stay with her or help figure some way to plan for the coming of the child she is going to bear. She is in poor circumstances financially, and he tells her she should make arrangements to conclude the birth and thus everything would iron out because he is definitely determined to leave as the affair in his mind is at an end. She is very broken up by it. She pleads for him to spend one more night, which he agrees to, and in the middle of the night she sets fire to the house, thus solving the problems of all concerned.

Descriptive theme	Interpretive theme	Diagnostic level
A half-caste girl has had a love affair with a man who has impregnated her and now plans to leave her to return to his wife.	(If one) commits adultery, one is "half-caste" (inferior); will be rejected, poorly off,	Sexual guilt; social prejudice; punishment is rejection, poverty.
In their last night together she sets a fire and kills them both.	will kill oneself and lover by fire.	Has intra- and extra-aggressivity; urethral complex (identifies with girl again); but may also say: women are bad, do this sort of thing; endanger one (in secondary identification).

Clinical notes

The reference to the half-caste is intentionally reworded, "If one commits adultery, one is a half-caste," making a causal connection where there had been mere juxtaposition. This is consistent with psychoanalytic practice, e.g., in dream interpretation concerning unconscious modes of thought. The theme is a typical triangular oedipal one; the subject here again identifies with a female in an even more significant way, since here he could easily identify with a male figure.

The introduction of fire again ties in with the urethral aspects of the use of water in the first story, aside from the fact that it connotes uncontrolled emotion. The occurrence of bizarre and unrealistic outcomes, in the presence of structured plots and thought processes, is probably a diagnostic sign of a latent psychotic who can still address himself to a task in an ordinary way even though the pathology underneath is extreme.

Name_____ Story No. _3_ (TAT Picture No. _4_)

1. Main theme: _(Interpretive)_ (If one) commits adultery, one is "half-caste" (inferior); will be rejected, poorly off, will kill oneself and lover. by fire.

2. Main hero: age _young adult_ sex _F_ vocation _none noted_
interests _none noted_ traits _half-caste, poor_ abilities _guilty re sex — pregnant_
adequacy (√, √√, √√√) _O?_ body image and/or self image _strong feminine identifica-_
tion; feels rejected — pregnant.

3. Main needs of hero:
  a) behavioral needs of hero (as in story): _love and support_

  dynamic inference: _fear of abandonment and rejection_
  b) figures, objects, or circumstances introduced: _pregnancy — setting fire to house_

  implying need for or to: _intra- and extra-aggression very strong — possibility of_
suicidal and homicidal impulses; unconscious fear of impregnation.
  c) figures, objects, or circumstances omitted: _half-nude female figure_

  implying need for or to: _sexual guilt — scotoma. repression._

4. Conception of environment (world) as: _hostile and rejecting_

5. Parental figures (m _√_, f ___) are seen as ___ and subject's reaction is ___
Contemp. figures (m _√_, f ___) are seen as _rejecting_ and subject's reaction is _guilt; depression; ag-_
Junior figures (m ___, f ___) are seen as ___ and subject's reaction is _gression._

6. Significant conflicts: _sexual guilt; intra- and extra-aggressivity; urethral complex_

7. Nature of anxieties: (√)
  of physical harm and/or punishment _√_   of illness or injury_____
  of disapproval _√_   of deprivation _√_
  of lack or loss of love _√_   of being devoured_____
  of being deserted _√_   of being overpowered and helpless_____
  other_____

8. Main defenses against conflicts and fears: (√)
  repression _√_   reaction-formation____   rationalization____   isolation____
  regression____   introjection____   denial____   undoing____   other _projection_

9. Severity of superego as manifested by: (√)
  punishment for "crime"____   immediate____ just____   too severe _√_
       delayed____ unjust____   too lenient____
  inhibitions____   stammer____   delayed initial response or pauses____

10. Integration of the ego, manifesting itself in: (√, √√, √√√)
  adequacy of hero _O?_   outcome: happy____   unhappy _√√√_
       realistic____   unrealistic _√√√_
  solution: adequate____   inadequate _√√_
  thought processes as revealed by plot being: (√, √√, √√√)
  structured _√_   unstructured____   stereotyped____   original____   appropriate____
  rational____   bizarre____   complete _√_   incomplete____   inappropriate____

Intelligence: (√) superior____ above average____ average____ below average____ defective____

Analysis Sheet for use with the Bellak TAT Blank

6BM: This is a scene in a play. The two characters are on the stage; one is a famous elderly actress, who has a son about the age of the young man appearing opposite her. The dialogue in the play has suddenly taken on a new meaning for her. She sees now that the play, which was written by her son, has an entirely different meaning in this scene in the picture. The boy is telling the mother that he has just committed a murder. She understands now that this was her son's way of conveying to her the terrifying fact that that is actually what had happened. In the play, as her son had written it, the climax comes when the mother calls the police. But the famous actress decides to put her own climax into action after the play is over. She calls her son and says, "The climax of your play will have to be changed." She says, "I think the audience will prefer this one," so here she draws a revolver and shoots him. (*What kind of murder was it?*) Oh, a girl. Motive primarily to do with sexual. She had been unfaithful.

Descriptive theme	Interpretive theme	Diagnostic level
In a play written by her son an elderly actress suddenly understands that he has killed a girl	If a man kills a girl because she has been unfaithful to him	Aggression fused with sex. Exhibitionism and symbolism.
for being unfaithful to him.	and mother finds out in a play,	Triangular oedipal situation—feels rejected by girl.
Thereupon she kills him.	symbolically the mother will kill him.	Mother seen as phallic, aggressive, dangerous.

Clinical notes

The value of the theme construction is particularly obvious in this story, though cluttered with confusing descriptive detail. The aggressive sexual wishes of the subject toward the maternal figure and the fear of counteraggression by the mother figure become crystal clear. The "sudden understanding" is a typical experience in schizophrenics with paranoid tendencies, as so well described by Sullivan [319]. The patient is in a panic because of many different impulses and apperceptive distortions, finds a new configuration which gives him a measure of stability and a channeling of his fears and aggression—the paranoid constellation. The fact, too, that the information is conveyed symbolically is highly suggestive of a schizophrenic process.

The actor is probably another identification figure for the subject, who attempts at first to keep some distance between himself and the mother in having someone else play opposite her.

Name_____ Story No. _4_ (TAT Picture No. _6BM_)

1. **Main theme:** (_Interpretative_) (If a) man kills a girl because she was unfaithful to him, the mother will kill him.

2. **Main hero:** age _adult_ sex _M_ vocation _playwright_
   interests _writing_ traits _none noted_ abilities _none noted_
   adequacy (√, √√, √√√) _0 ?_ body image and/or self image _not noted_

3. **Main needs of hero:**
   a) behavioral needs of hero (as in story): _to punish (kill) girl who was unfaithful to him._
   dynamic inference: _oedipal theme; feeling of being rejected; aggressive conception of sex._
   b) figures, objects, or circumstances introduced: _actor; audience; police; gun; girl he killed._
   implying need for or to: _punishment for oedipal guilt feelings; aggression; need for exhibitionism._
   c) figures, objects, or circumstances omitted: _none_
   implying need for or to:_____

4. **Conception of environment (world) as:** _hostile; punishing_

5. Parental figures (m_____, f _√_) are seen as _punishing and rejecting_ and subject's reaction is _aggression._
   Contemp. figures (m_____, f _√_) are seen as _rejecting_ and subject's reaction is _aggression_
   Junior figures (m_____, f_____) are seen as_____ and subject's reaction is_____

6. **Significant conflicts:**_____

7. **Nature of anxieties:** (√)
   of physical harm and/or punishment _√_   of illness or injury _√_
   of disapproval _√_   of deprivation_____
   of lack or loss of love _√_   of being devoured_____
   of being deserted_____   of being overpowered and helpless_____
   other_____

8. **Main defenses against conflicts and fears:** (√)
   repression_____ reaction-formation_____ rationalization_____ isolation_____
   regression_____ introjection_____ denial_____ undoing_____ other _projection_

9. **Severity of superego as manifested by:** (√)
   punishment for "crime"_____ immediate _√_ just_____ too severe_____
   delayed_____ unjust_____ too lenient_____
   inhibitions_____ stammer_____ delayed initial response or pauses_____

10. **Integration of the ego, manifesting itself in:** (√, √√, √√√)
    adequacy of hero _0 ?_ outcome: happy_____ unhappy _√√√_
    realistic_____ unrealistic _√√√_
    solution: adequate_____ inadequate_____
    thought processes as revealed by plot being: (√, √√, √√√)
    structured _√√_ unstructured_____ stereotyped_____ original_____ appropriate_____
    rational_____ bizarre _√√_ complete_____ incomplete_____ inappropriate_____

Intelligence: (√) superior_____ above average_____ average_____ below average_____ defective_____

Analysis Sheet for use with the Bellak TAT Blank

Copyright 1951, Leopold Bellak   51-41948 The Psychological Corporation

7BM: This would be a man and his son. The son is very depressed over his health. The father is telling him that as a young man he too had the same illness, and that it can be cured if the son has the will to cure it. The father tells the young man that he himself alone can cure it. The son believes that there is no hope, but replies that he will go away for a little while and think it over. The father replies, "You are not doing a favor to me by saying that. I am thinking about your getting well for the simple reason that you have a wife and children to support, and in the event of your being bedridden, the responsibility for your family will be put entirely upon your mother and me." The young man finally concludes that he will take his wife and family with him and try to make things go better in a healthier climate. *(What kind of illness did he have?)* T.B. *(Did he get better?)* No, I don't think he does. After a few years he dies and the children are old enough to support mother or perhaps he left insurance. Never contacted father again. No correspondence. After not having heard from each other for a long time, the old man dies and leaves the children a large estate. This is his way of having repented.

Descriptive theme	*Interpretive theme*	*Diagnostic level*
A young man suffers from T.B.,	If one is sick with T.B.	Feels sick. T.B. is castration.
and father tells him he used to have it too.	and father had the same illness,	Father also seen as previously sick, castrated.
and that the son will have to cure himself so that his wife and children will not burden father.	father selfishly rejects one.	Feels rejected by father. Father seen as cold, narcissistic.
Son removes himself, angry at father. Both die, father leaving money to children.	One is angry at father. One dies, and father dies too, repenting too late. Wants father to feels sorry about not having been nicer to him.	Aggression toward father. Oral wishes toward father.

Clinical notes

In several years of clinical work with tuberculars, I found that the fantasies of having T.B. are most frequently either those of being invaded (phallically) by the T.B. germs, particularly in an impregnation fantasy, and having holes made in one—i.e., being castrated, particularly in connection with hemorrhages [28]. The fact that the father has also had the illness suggests that patient tended to think of the father also as castrated and weak. Since the father was an identification figure, this may have influenced the subject's emotional growth. T.B. may also mean venereal disease here.

Name_____ Story No. _5_ (TAT Picture No. _78M_)

1. **Main theme:** _(Interpretive)_ _(If one)_ is sick with T.B. and father had the same illness, father selfishly rejects one. One is angry at father. One dies and father dies too, repenting too late. Wants father to feel sorry about not having been nicer to one.

2. **Main hero:** age _adult_ sex _M_ vocation _none noted_
   interests _none noted_ traits _depressed; ill_ abilities _none noted_
   adequacy (√, √√, √√√) _0 ?_ body image and/or self image _ill with T.B.; helpless_

3. **Main needs of hero:**
   a) behavioral needs of hero (as in story): _Help and support because of being ill_
      dynamic inference: _Feels weak, helpless, debilitated, oral needs_
   b) figures, objects, or circumstances introduced: _wife, mother, children, illness, death, money_
      implying need for or to: _heterosexual needs — wanting care from parents — fear of illness and death._
   c) figures, objects, or circumstances omitted:_____
      implying need for or to:_____

4. **Conception of environment (world) as:** _cold, hostile, uncaring_

5. **Parental figures** (m___, f _√_) are seen as _cold, speculating_ and subject's reaction is _withdrawal, anger_
   Contemp. figures (m___, f___) are seen as_____ and subject's reaction is_____
   Junior figures (m___, f___) are seen as_____ and subject's reaction is_____

6. **Significant conflicts:** _Bodily concern (T.B. – full of holes? or is it syphilis?) Strong dependency needs. Aggression toward father._

7. **Nature of anxieties:** (√)
   of physical harm and/or punishment_____ of illness or injury _√_
   of disapproval_____ of deprivation _√_
   of lack or loss of love _√_ of being devoured_____
   of being deserted _√_ of being overpowered and helpless_____
   other _of death_

8. **Main defenses against conflicts and fears:** (√)
   repression_____ reaction-formation_____ rationalization_____ isolation_____
   regression_____ introjection_____ denial_____ undoing_____ other _projection, withdrawal_

9. **Severity of superego as manifested by:** (√)
   punishment for "crime"_____ immediate_____ just_____ too severe _√_
   _____ delayed_____ unjust_____ too lenient_____
   inhibitions_____ stammer_____ delayed initial response or pauses_____
   Sees himself as fatally ill, possibly dies because of anger at father.

10. **Integration of the ego, manifesting itself in:** (√, √√, √√√)
    adequacy of hero _0 ?_ outcome: happy_____ unhappy _√√√_
    realistic_____ unrealistic_____
    solution: adequate_____ inadequate _√_
    thought processes as revealed by plot being: (√, √√, √√√)
    structured _√_ unstructured_____ stereotyped_____ original _√_ appropriate_____
    rational_____ bizarre_____ complete_____ incomplete_____ inappropriate _√_

Intelligence: (√) superior_____ above average_____ average_____ below average_____ defective_____

Analysis Sheet for use with the Bellak TAT Blank

SUMMARY

Record themes and summarize other significant data for each story.

1. Feels a child, sick, poor body image. Feels coerced by parents. Mechanism of denial—re masturbation? Resists authority by withdrawal into fantasy; urethral interests, exhibitionism (?), anhedonia (?). Delusional omnipotence (knowing what is in book without reading it)—severe thought disturbance and flat mood consistent with schizophrenia.

2. Great guilt over sex; feminine identification. Severe superego concerning also exhibitionism and ambivalence to sibling (or mother) seen as pure. Intra-aggession. Self-image: outcast, criminal.

3. Sexual guilt; social prejudice; punishment is rejection, poverty. Intra- and extra-aggressivity. Urethral complex. Identifies with girl again, but may also say: women are bad, do this sort of thing, endanger one (in secondary identification). Possibility of suicidal and homicidal impulses. Unconscious fear of impregnation.

4. Aggression fused with sex. Triangular oedipal situation—feels rejected by girl. Mother seen as phallic, aggressive, dangerous. "Sudden understanding" consistent with paranoid schizophrenic process.

5. Feels ill and helpless with T.B.—full of holes? or syphilis? Father also seen as previously sick (castrated). Feels rejected by father. Father seen as cold, narcissistic. Aggression toward father. Oral wishes toward father. Sees self as fatally ill, disturbed body image.

6.

7.

8.

9.

10.

Ego function assessment from TAT data:

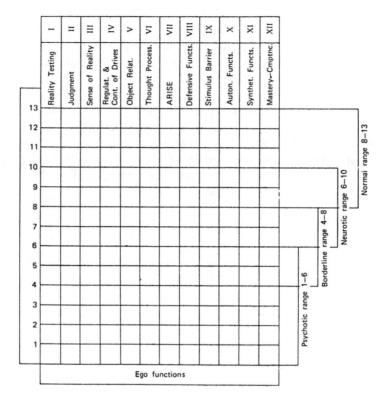

(From Bellak, Hurvich, & Gediman, *Ego functions in schizophrenics, neurotics, and normals.* Copyright © 1973, by C. P. S., Inc. Reprinted by permission of John Wiley & Sons, Inc.)

Ego functions observed during test administration:

Case 2

Following are stories given by a young man in his middle twenties.* We have chosen a few for illustration. At the time of the administration of the T.A.T. he was in a prison hospital. He had gone AWOL from the armed forces because he found it impossible to urinate in the presence of others, and others were always present in the latrines. When he was picked up by M.P.'s he made an inadequate gesture at aggression and was thereupon shot in the abdomen. These few data may suffice to highlight the dynamic material revealed with regard to homosexual problems, problems of voyeurism and exhibitionism, and the handling of the problem of aggression; the subject was just aggressive enough to invite almost suicidal counteraggression on the part of the armed military police. He was intelligent and industrious and came from immigrant stock.

The T.A.T. was not administered by the writer, and unfortunately story 1, the boy with the violin, was not included.

---

* I am indebted to the late Dr. Blaise Pasquarelli for this material.

BELLAK T A T BLANK
For Recording and Analyzing Thematic Apperception Test Stories

Name_____ Sex _Male_ Age_ 26 _Date_____

Education___ high school _____ Occupation___ Army private _____

Referred by_____ Analysis by_____

FINAL REPORT

Choosing just a few of the stories of the subject, one sees his pervasive feeling of inadequacy of his fear of being overpowered running through nearly all the themes. He sees himself either as a woman (#2, 3BM) or as too small (14). When he has aggressive or sexual desires he thinks of himself as bad, inadequate (#13 MF and 18BM).

His needs appear as a need for autonomy (2, 7BM, 14), achievement, and an oedipal type of competitiveness allied to the partial sexual components of voyeurism and exhibitionism.

His conception of the world is one of deprivation (2, 3BM, 14, 18BM), of being overpowered and harmed (2, 7BM), actually representing an image of his parents whom he tries in vain to stand up to.

His main conflicts center around autonomy versus compliance, activity-passivity, and achievement-inadequacy, and he shows a great deal of anxiety of being overpowered and injured. His main defenses are emotional isolation, projection, and attempts at sublimation by intellectualization.

His superego is extremely severe, leading to intra-aggression particularly concerning incestuous sexual wishes.

The integration of the ego is inadequate in that the hero hardly ever succeeds, is usually unhappy, and frequently suicidal. The subject appears to be of above average intelligence.

Impulse control of aggressive and intra-aggressive drives seems so poor that one must consider him potentially suicidal and homicidal, particularly in homosexual panic. The record is consistent with that of a borderline schizophrenic with paranoid features.

Copyright 1947, © 1973. Leopold Bellak, M.A., M.D.
All rights reserved as stated in the test manual and Catalog.

Printed in U.S.A.   Published by THE PSYCHOLOGICAL CORPORATION, New York, New York 10017   73-262AS

Note: In this final report, abstract statements are interspersed with brief references to relevant stories. This procedure may be profitably enlarged, giving the condensed theme or part of the story as an illustration for the abstract statement.

2: What the hell could have happened before in this picture? I don't know . . . (resistance). . . . I would say that this here girl has just come from school and that she has something on her mind which she wants to ask her parents. . . . That's her father and mother in the background—her father on the plow, and her mother leaning up against the tree. She has been brought up very strictly, and her parents probably are of European stock but . . . they are immigrants. She is being held down and doesn't live the normal life that a normal girl should. She is very intelligent and a good student. She probably has just graduated and wants to ask her parents . . . or rather wants to talk . . . she wants to go to college and she doesn't feel that her parents will approve it. . . . Whether or not, she probably has assumed that when she has finished high school that that is as far as a girl should have to go, and what she is thinking now is that she should get married and settle down on the farm the way they did. . . . Her father is a successful farmer who can afford to send her to college . . . but will refuse to do so. This girl is very passionate . . . emotional . . . and unless she is allowed to go to college she will probably develop some psychical ailment (snicker). . . . But that her father refuses in the end to send her to college whereas . . . strike out whereas. . . . They find her a . . . suitor who they think will be suitable for her, and plan to have her married. . . . Is this too long? . . . The father is willing to bestow a portion of his land and the money and materials for a home which they can build on the land. . . . (Long pause.) She is very unhappy, or rather let's say that they become married and she is very unhappy. She refuses to have any children . . . because she doesn't want to bring them up in this backward atmosphere, knowing that her parents will try to bring up her children as they brought her up. Her husband is similar to her father in his attitude towards education and how to bring up a child. . . . He insists that she bear him a child and in time attempts to use physical force to throw a fear into her so that she will do what he will ask of her. She becomes hysterical and ends it all by committing suicide. . . . That's all!

Descriptive theme	*Interpretive theme*	*Diagnostic level*
A very strictly brought-up girl wants to go to college,	(If one) is a young, strictly brought-up girl and wants to be autonomous,	Feels strictly brought up; need for autonomy, achievement.
but is afraid that her parents will be against it	the parents are against it	Parents seen as restricting, coercive.
and will marry her against her will, which makes her sick and unhappy.	and force one into a submissive situation to which one responds by unhappiness, (mental) illness.	Feels unhappy, mentally ill, fearful of sexual aggression.
When her husband, who resembles her father, uses physical force to impregnate her,	When threatened with male sexual aggression (by paternal figure),	Fear of pregnancy, of male sexual aggression. Identifies men too much with father.
she becomes hysterical and commits suicide.	one commits suicide.	Suicidal tendencies.

Clinical notes

Father and contemporary males (husband) are completely equated in this story, in which the subject identifies so vividly with the female figure. There is some awareness of mental disturbance.

Name_____ Story No._____ (TAT Picture No. _2___)

1. **Main theme:** *(Interpretive)* If one is a young, strictly brought up girl and wants to be autonomous, the parents are against it and force one into a submissive situation to which one responds by unhappiness and (mental) illness. When threatened with male aggression one commits suicide.

2. **Main hero:** age *young adult* sex *F* vocation *student*
   interests *education* traits *autonomy* abilities *intelligent*
   adequacy (√, √√, √√√) ___√___ body image and/or self image *feminine; helpless*

3. **Main needs of hero:**
   a) behavioral needs of hero (as in story): *Education; autonomy; to do better than parents.*
      dynamic inference: *curiosity; feeling of helplessness toward parents; competition with parents.*
   b) figures, objects, or circumstances introduced: *college; money; pregnancy; suicide.*
      implying need for or to: *intellectual achievement; suicidal tendencies; fear of impregnation.*
   c) figures, objects, or circumstances omitted: *pregnancy of the older woman leaning against the tree is not mentioned in the story.*
      implying need for or to: *fear of pregnancy.*

4. **Conception of environment (world) as:** *coercive; depriving; aggressive.*

5. **Parental figures** (m √, f √) are seen as *above* and subject's reaction is *attempt at autonomy;*
   Contemp. figures (m___, f___) are seen as ___ and subject's reaction is *intra-*
   Junior figures (m___, f___) are seen as ___ and subject's reaction is *aggression*

6. **Significant conflicts:** *Between autonomy and compliance; extra-aggression and intra-aggression.*

7. **Nature of anxieties:** (√)
   of physical harm and/or punishment __√__   of illness or injury_____
   of disapproval_____   of deprivation_____
   of lack or loss of love_____   of being devoured_____
   of being deserted_____   of being overpowered and helpless __√__
   other *strong homosexual fears*

8. **Main defenses against conflicts and fears:** (√)
   repression __√__ reaction-formation_____ rationalization_____ isolation __√__
   regression_____ introjection_____ denial_____ undoing_____ other_____
   projection   intellectualization

9. **Severity of superego as manifested by:** (√)
   punishment for "crime"_____   immediate __√__ just_____   too severe __√__
                                        delayed_____ unjust_____   too lenient_____
   inhibitions_____ stammer_____ delayed initial response or pauses_____

10. **Integration of the ego, manifesting itself in:** (√, √√, √√√)
    adequacy of hero __√__   outcome: happy_____ unhappy __√__
                               realistic __√__ unrealistic_____
                    solution: adequate_____ inadequate __√__
    thought processes as revealed by plot being: (√, √√, √√√)
    structured __√__ unstructured_____ stereotyped_____ original_____ appropriate_____
    rational_____ bizarre_____ complete __√__ incomplete_____ inappropriate_____

Intelligence: (√) superior_____ above average __√__ average_____ below average_____ defective_____

Analysis Sheet for use with the Bellak TAT Blank

Copyright 1951, Leopold Bellak   51-119AS The Psychological Corporation

3BM: Well, I would say that this was a young girl who . . . is in love with a young man. . . . And they had some disagreement, and in this picture she has committed suicide . . . so she is dead (snicker). I would say that the man distrusted her, or believed that she was unfaithful to him. . . . Oh yeah . . . you might add in there what happened to her fiancé. That after she committed suicide that he was so stricken with grief that he, in turn, committed suicide. . . . That is a pistol by her on the floor. . . . I would say that she shot herself through the head. . . . That's all. . . . The awkward position she is in would indicate that . . . she would not just be sitting there, or laying there like that. . . . I would say her fiancé committed suicide the same way. I can't think of anything else to say. . . . I would say it is a woman because it looks feminine . . . a little wide through the hips . . . the long hair . . . the large bust . . . large legs. . . . That's all.

Descriptive theme	*Interpretive theme*	*Diagnostic level*
Two people are in love with each other, have a disagreement because the man distrusts her faithfulness.	(If one) has a love affair, one cannot trust the faithfulness of the loved one.	Sexual needs; distinct triangular oedipal theme; jealousy.
She commits suicide, and then he commits suicide too.	This leads to disagreement and intra- and extra-aggression.	Intra- and extra-aggression.

Clinical notes

Probably both are identification figures for the hero, since in the last few lines subject feels the need to give reasons for the feminine identification of the depicted figure.

Name_____Story No. *2*_____(TAT Picture No. *3 BM*___)

1. **Main theme:** *(Interpretive)* *(If one) has a love affair one cannot trust the faithfulness of the loved one. This leads to disagreement and intra- and extra-aggression.*

2. **Main hero:** age *young adult* sex *F*_____vocation *none noted*_____
   interests *none noted*_____ traits *none noted*_____ abilities *none noted*___
   adequacy (√, √√, √√√) _*0*_____body image and/or self image *feminine*_____

3. **Main needs of hero:**
   a) behavioral needs of hero (as in story) : *to be loved; aggression.*_____

   dynamic inference: *need to be loved; fear of aggression; oedipal involvement*____
   b) figures, objects, or circumstances introduced: *competitive males*_____

   implying need for or to: *homosexual interests*_____

   c) figures, objects, or circumstances omitted:_____

   implying need for or to:_____

4. **Conception of environment (world) as:** *untrustworthy*_____

5. **Parental figures** (m____, f____) are seen as_____*untrustworthy*____and subject's reaction is_____
   Contemp. figures (m _*✓*_, f _*✓*_) are seen as *Competitive,* ___and subject's reaction is *aggression and intra-*
   Junior figures (m____, f____) are seen as_____and subject's reaction is____*aggression*

6. **Significant conflicts:** *Between need for love and fear of aggression; feeling of inadequacy*_____

7. **Nature of anxieties:** (√)
   of physical harm and/or punishment_____of illness or injury_____
   of disapproval_____of deprivation___*✓*___
   of lack or loss of love___*✓*_____of being devoured_____
   of being deserted_____of being overpowered and helpless_____
   other_____

8. **Main defenses against conflicts and fears:** (√)
   repression_____reaction-formation_____rationalization_____isolation_*✓*__
   regression_____introjection_____denial_____undoing_____other_____

9. **Severity of superego as manifested by:** (√)
   punishment for "crime"_____immediate_*✓*__just_____too severe__*✓*__
   _____delayed_____unjust_____too lenient_____
   inhibitions_____stammer_____delayed initial response or pauses_____

10. **Integration of the ego, manifesting itself in:** (√, √√, √√√)
    adequacy of hero_____ outcome: happy_____unhappy___*√√*__
    _____realistic_____unrealistic_____
    solution: adequate_____inadequate_*√√√*__
    thought processes as revealed by plot being: (√, √√, √√√)
    structured_*√√*__unstructured_____stereotyped_____original_____appropriate_____
    rational_____bizarre_____complete_*√√*__incomplete_____inappropriate_____

Intelligence: (√) superior_____above average_____average_*✓*__below average_____defective_____

Analysis Sheet for use with the Bellak TAT Blank

7BM: In this picture I would say that the younger person is a student who is . . . who is holding some political theories and he is fanatical about them . . . That the older person is probably, I would say, his father, or professor, or teacher, or whatever you want to call him. . . . I would say that it is his father. . . . His father is telling him to give up his wild ideas about the government, but he refuses to give in. . . . The student is in favor of radical changes in society due to some ideals he is holding. . . . The son will probably . . . well here . . . because of his political views will wind up in prison, or become killed . . . in some public forum somewheres where he is trying to arouse the masses more or less. . . . (Long pause.) But anyways, in the end he will learn that he should have listened to his father. . . . That's all . . . I would say that he is just a reformer, that's all. . . . I would say he is against capital. . . . I don't know, I think this is silly myself . . . (snicker).

Descriptive theme	Interpretive theme	Diagnostic level
A young student has radical ideas	If one has aggressive ideas against authority,	Aggression against authority, particularly male figures.
and will wind up in prison or be killed for them, repenting that he did not follow his father's advice to give up such ideas. It's all silly.	one is severely punished and repentant. Should comply with father figure. Tries to laugh it off.	Severe superego. Need for compliance with males. Rationalization, isolation.

Clinical notes

This story illustrates nicely that it is not merely psychoanalytic imagination which considers the government as a parental figure or, in this case, a paternal one, since the subject equates them easily, suggesting that the source of his political ideas also has a parental origin. Again, the snickering is probably used for defensive purposes to dispel the tension.

Name_____ Story No. _3_____ (TAT Picture No. _7BM_)

1. **Main theme:** *(Interpretive)* If one has aggressive ideas against authority one is severely punished and repentant.

2. **Main hero:** age *young adult* sex *M* vocation *student – agitator*
   interests *rebellion* traits *wild* abilities *none noted*
   adequacy (√, √√, √√√) *√√* body image and/or self image *unsuccessful radical*

3. **Main needs of hero:**
   a) behavioral needs of hero (as in story): *aggression; revolt against father*
   dynamic inference: *fear of paternal figures*
   b) figures, objects, or circumstances introduced: *government; jail*
   implying need for or to: *concern with authority; severe superego*
   c) figures, objects, or circumstances omitted:_____
   implying need for or to:_____

4. **Conception of environment (world) as:** *overpowering; punishing; harmful*

5. **Parental figures** (m_____, f _√_) are seen as *powerful;* *advising; punishing* and subject's reaction is *rebellion; repen-*
   Contemp. figures (m_____, f_____) are seen as_____ and subject's reaction is _____ *tance.*
   Junior figures (m_____, f_____) are seen as_____ and subject's reaction is_____

6. **Significant conflicts:** *between autonomy fused with aggression and compliance.*

7. **Nature of anxieties:** (√)
   of physical harm and/or punishment _√_____ of illness or injury_____
   of disapproval_____ of deprivation_____ .
   of lack or loss of love_____ of being devoured_____
   of being deserted_____ of being overpowered and helpless _√_____
   other_____

8. **Main defenses against conflicts and fears:** (√)
   repression_____ reaction-formation_____ rationalization_____ isolation _√_
   regression_____ introjection_____ denial_____ undoing_____ other_____
   identification with enemy

9. **Severity of superego as manifested by:** (√)
   punishment for "crime"_____ immediate _√_ just_____ too severe _√_
   delayed_____ unjust_____ too lenient_____
   inhibitions_____ stammer_____ delayed initial response or pauses_____

10. **Integration of the ego, manifesting itself in:** (√, √√, √√√)
    adequacy of hero _√√_____ outcome: happy_____ unhappy _√√√_
    realistic _√_ unrealistic_____ ,
    solution: adequate_____ inadequate _√√_
    thought processes as revealed by plot being: (√, √√, √√√)
    structured _√_ unstructured_____ stereotyped_____ original_____ appropriate_____
    rational_____ bizarre_____ complete _√_ incomplete_____ inappropriate_____

Intelligence: (√) superior_____ above average _√_ average_____ below average_____ defective_____

Analysis Sheet for use with the Bellak TAT Blank

51-119A3 The Psychological Corporation

13MF: This is a young man who is going to the local university . . . a student. . . . He is very moralistic . . . that is, very virtuous . . . having a highly developed sense of what is right and what is wrong. He is also very religious. . . . He has been brought up very strictly and believes that one of the greatest sins that man can commit is to have sexual intercourse with a woman out of wedlock. . . . One evening, at a party, for some unknown reason, having taken too many drinks and feeling slightly lightheaded, he became very intimate with one of the girls present. He . . . his animal instincts came to the fore and he abandoned all his ideas of virtue, etc. He took this woman up to his room and went to bed with her. The next morning, after becoming sober and having regained his virtuous sense . . . or whatever you want to call it . . . he looked over and saw this woman beside him in utter nakedness. He was filled with anger, and wild . . . let's see (murmurs to himself) . . . and bitter passion at what he had done. A profound hatred swelled up in his chest for this woman that lay next to him. He ordered . . . she by this time had become awake . . . and he ordered her to leave his room. . . . She, not understanding what had brought this attitude of his about, believed that he was joking, and refused to leave in a jocular manner. . . . This man could think of nothing but to clear himself of this sin he had committed . . . cleanse himself of this sin. . . . And as this woman lay there laughing, and being overcome with his guilt, he seized her by the throat and strangled her. . . . Rising from the bed, and putting on his clothes, he became . . . he realized his predicament. He not only had committed a sin . . . a moral sin . . . but he had committed a greater sin by taking her life. . . . He gazed down as she lay there at her statuesque stillness and was filled with remorse. Remembering a few days earlier . . . that a few days earlier he had bought a bottle of iodine, and which was now in the cabinet of the washroom, he went there and gulped down its contents (laughs) and consequently died. That was the end of that. . . . I just said that he strangled her because she was laying in bed next to him, and that was the easiest thing he could have done, by reaching over and grasping her neck.

Descriptive theme	*Interpretive theme*	*Diagnostic level*
A virtuous, moralistic, religious, strictly brought up student, who considers sexual intercourse a great sin, takes too many drinks and is intimate with a girl.	If one is extremely moralistic, one considers sex a great sin which can only be committed under the influence of liquor.	Feels extremely moralistic. Severe superego. Strong guilt feelings about sex. Need for liquor. Strong oral needs. Rationalizes.
Later he is very angry at her, tells her to leave, and when she refuses, strangles her.	Thereafter one is angry at the woman, kills her	Projects (anger) on the woman. Impulse-ridden (it was the easiest thing he could have done).
Filled with remorse, he kills himself by swallowing poison.	and oneself, remorsefully in turn, by swallowing poison.	Strong intra-aggression. Oral needs.

Clinical notes

This story repeats both the orality and the fear of degeneration, as well as the strict superego. When tendencies recur several times in a story, such as oral needs in relation to drinking liquor, and again in the method of suicide, it can usually be considered an indication of the intensity of the problem.

The most ominous feature of this story is the afterthought that he strangled her because "this was the easiest thing he could have done." Together with the realistic detail and the obsessiveness, it suggests that homicidal impulses are not far from the surface in this man.

Name_____Story No. _4____(TAT Picture No. _13 MF_)

1. **Main theme:** *(Interpretive)* If one is extremely moralistic, one considers sex a great sin which can only be committed under the influence of liquor. Thereafter one is angry at the woman, kills her and oneself, remorsefully in turn, by swallowing poison.

2. **Main hero:** age *young adult* sex *M*_____vocation *student*
   interests *religion*_____ traits *virtuous*_____ abilities *none noted*
   adequacy (√. √√. √√√) _0_____body image and/or self image *moralistic; degenerate.*

3. **Main needs of hero:**
   a) behavioral needs of hero (as in story): *drinking; women; aggression; intra-aggression.*
   dynamic inference: *oral needs; severe superego; strong aggression*
   b) figures, objects, or circumstances introduced: *liquor; iodine*
   implying need for or to: *oral needs*
   c) figures, objects, or circumstances omitted:_____
   implying need for or to:_____

4. **Conception of environment (world) as:** *tempting*

5. **Parental figures** (m____, f____) are seen as_____and subject's reaction is_____
   Contemp. figures (m____, f_√_) are seen as *licentious*_____and subject's reaction is *anger*
   Junior figures (m____, f____) are seen as_____and subject's reaction is_____

6. **Significant conflicts:** *between need for sex and superego; extra- and intra-aggression*

7. **Nature of anxieties:** (√)
   of physical harm and/or punishment_____of illness or injury_____
   of disapproval_____of deprivation_____
   of lack or loss of love_____of being devoured_____
   of being deserted_____of being overpowered and helpless_____
   other *of sexual and oral temptation*

8. **Main defenses against conflicts and fears:** (√)
   repression_____reaction-formation_____rationalization_√_____isolation_√_
   regression_____introjection_____denial_____undoing_____other *projection*

9. **Severity of superego as manifested by:** (√)
   punishment for "crime"_____immediate_√_____just_____too severe_√_
   _____delayed_____unjust_____too lenient_____
   inhibitions_____stammer_____delayed initial response or pauses_____

10. **Integration of the ego, manifesting itself in:** (√. √√. √√√)
   adequacy of hero_____ outcome: happy_____unhappy_√√√_
   _____realistic_____unrealistic_____
   _____solution: adequate_____inadequate_√√_
   thought processes as revealed by plot being: (√. √√. √√√)
   structured_√_____unstructured_____stereotyped_____original_____appropriate_____
   rational_____bizarre_____complete_√_____incomplete_____inappropriate_____

Intelligence: (√) superior_____above average_____average_____below average_____defective_____

Analysis Sheet for use with the Bellak TAT Blank

51-119AS The Psychological Corporation

14: Well, I'd say that this takes place in Paris, just for the heck of it. . . . That the papers have announced that there will be a . . . I would say that there will be . . . there will be meteors shooting across the sky on this date. This here person is a man . . . is watching . . . shall we say astral displays. . . . The room he is in is his bedroom and he has put the light out to make it easier for him to see what is going on. . . . He watches for about 15 minutes, closes the window, puts the light on, and gets undressed and goes to bed. . . . And that's the end of that! . . . (resistance). . . . The way the window opened up, I always imagined that windows like that were to be seen in Paris. . . . I would say that before he went to the windows he was laying on the bed, reading a book, until the time came around at which time the newspapers said that meteors would be seen shooting across the sky. . . . I would say that he is more or less of an amateur astronomer and that he has a great interest in the universe and . . . let's say . . . maybe we can make something out of this after all . . . that he is working on some small job which has no future . . . that he has always been interested in astronomy, but due to the fact that his parents did not have the resources with which to send him to school that he could not further his education in that field . . . (resistance). . . . He has some knowledge of the stars, and this display fascinates him and only makes him yearn for that education he might have had . . . that's all!

Descriptive theme	*Interpretive theme*	*Diagnostic level*
A young man in a bedroom in Paris at night is watching meteors appearing according to schedule and feels small in comparison.	If one watches big things at night appearing according to schedule, one feels small in comparison	Patient has witnessed primal scene frequently and has felt insignificant in relation to his father,
This makes him yearn for education which the parents were too poor to give him.	and feels that parents should have given one more (education.)	and blames his parents for not having equipped him better genitally. Information and education are given phallic significance as a powerful tool.

Clinical notes

Paris probably means sex, as in the minds of so many. The meteors probably represent a big phallus. The reference to putting the light out to make it easier to see may well relate to the fact that patient would watch what was going on between parents when it got dark. The window is probably a reference to the female sexual organ and expresses the patient's notion that such (sexual) things would only go on in other dirty places, not in the parental home. He already knows what is going to happen from past experience (the newspaper) and feels himself but an amateur working in a small job (penis) and that it is his parents' fault that they did not equip him better.

Name_____ Story No. _5___ (TAT Picture No. _14___)

1. **Main theme:** _(Interpretive)_ If one watches big things at night appearing according to schedule, one feels small in comparison, and feels that parents should give one more (education).

2. **Main hero:** age _young adult_ sex _M_____ vocation _amateur astronomer_____
   interests _astronomy; education_ traits _curiosity_____ abilities _none noted_____
   adequacy (√, √√, √√√) _√_____ body image and/or self image _small; not having enough_

3. **Main needs of hero:**
   a) behavioral needs of hero (as in story): _to watch; to acquire an education_____

   dynamic inference: _voyeurism; exhibitionism; sexual problems; urethral problems; to be_
   b) figures, objects, or circumstances introduced: _Paris; meteors; parents; newspaper_   _powerful_

   implying need for or to: _sex; problem in relation to parents; voyeurism (newspaper);_
   _interested in phallus (meteors)._____
   c) figures, objects, or circumstances omitted:_____

   implying need for or to:_____

4. **Conception of environment (world)** as: _big; fascinating; depriving_____

5. **Parental figures** (m _√_, f _√_) are seen as _depriving_____ and subject's reaction is _yearning_____
   Contemp. figures (m____, f____) are seen as_____ and subject's reaction is_____
   Junior figures (m____, f____) are seen as_____ and subject's reaction is_____

6. **Significant conflicts:** _Between need for achievement and feeling of inadequacy._____

7. **Nature of anxieties:** (√)
   of physical harm and/or punishment_____ of illness or injury_____
   of disapproval_____ of deprivation_____
   of lack or loss of love_____ of being devoured_____
   of being deserted_____ of being overpowered and helpless_____
   other _of being too small_____

8. **Main defenses against conflicts and fears:** (√)
   repression_____ reaction-formation _√_____ rationalization _√_____ isolation_____
   regression_____ introjection_____ denial_____ undoing_____ other_____

9. **Severity of superego as manifested by:** (√) _not noted_
   punishment for "crime"_____ immediate_____ just_____ too severe_____
                                        delayed_____ unjust_____ too lenient_____
   inhibitions_____ stammer_____ delayed initial response or pauses_____

10. **Integration of the ego, manifesting itself in:** (√, √√, √√√)
    adequacy of hero____ _√_____ outcome: happy _√_____ unhappy_____
                                    realistic _√_____ unrealistic_____
                         solution: adequate _√_____ inadequate_____
    thought processes as revealed by plot being: (√, √√, √√√)
    structured _√_____ unstructured_____ stereotyped_____ original_____ appropriate_____
    rational _√_____ bizarre_____ complete _√_____ incomplete_____ inappropriate_____

Intelligence: (√) superior_____ above average _√___ average_____ below average_____ defective_____

Analysis Sheet for use with the Bellak TAT Blank

Copyright 1951, Leopold Bellak   51-119AS The Psychological Corporation

18BM: This is a young man and he was formerly a successful lawyer. Then due to his bad habits . . . such as women and liquor . . . he began to . . . let's see . . . his talents began to . . . degenerate. Uh . . . He is married and his wife is beginning to turn against him. On this particular night he has . . . he is in a barroom and has become quite intoxicated. It is time for the . . . business to close and the bartender is helping him on with his coat. The man is stupefied and doesn't know what is happening. The bartender, not caring what happens to him, escorts him to the door and leads him out to the street . . . where he drunkenly walks, not knowing where is going, and finally winds up sprawled out on the sidewalk where he is picked up by the police and spends the night in the city jail . . . (snickers). His wife, knowing that he is in jail . . . that is, having been informed that he is in the city jail, but refuses to pay his fine, or to aid him in any way whatever . . . (laughs). He becomes melancholy, and when he is finally let out of the jail . . . knowing that he is . . . where are we? . . . let out of the jail? . . . knowing that he has been overcome by his niggardly condition, he decides to depart . . . to desert his wife and the city that he is in, and decides to go to another city to begin life anew. . . . That's the end of that!

Descriptive theme	Interpretive theme	Diagnostic level
A formerly successful young lawyer degenerates because of bad habits (women and liquor),	If one indulges in bad habits such as liquor and women, one degenerates,	Feels himself a degenerate because of interest in liquor and women.
and his wife turns against him. He is intoxicated in a bar, and an uncaring bartender sends him out	is rejected by one's wife and others,	Feels rejected by male and female figures.
and he is put in jail.	punished,	Severe superego.
His wife refuses to aid him, and he leaves the city to start life anew.	becomes depressed, withdraws, but starts anew.	Depression, withdrawal, counteraction. Oral needs.

Clinical notes

"Bad habits" refer most frequently to masturbation and resultant guilt. This story shows at least a spark of health, in that the hero tries to begin life anew, although it is not told in any convincing detail.

Name_____ Story No. _6_ (TAT Picture No. _18 BM_)

1. **Main theme:** *(Interpretive)* If one indulges in bad habits such as liquor and women, one degenerates, is rejected by one's wife and others, is punished, becomes depressed, withdraws, but starts life anew.

2. **Main hero:** age *young adult* sex *M* _____ vocation *lawyer* _____
   interests *law; women; liquor* traits *drinking; goes with* / *women* abilities _____
   adequacy (√, √√, √√√) _√_ _____ body image and/or self image *degenerate*

3. **Main needs of hero:**
   a) behavioral needs of hero (as in story): *drinking; relations with women; counter-action.*

   dynamic inference: *oral needs and some defensive counter-action to passivity.*
   b) figures, objects, or circumstances introduced: *wife; other women; liquor; jail.*

   implying need for or to: *oral needs and severe superego.*

   c) figures, objects, or circumstances omitted: _____

   implying need for or to: _____

4. **Conception of environment (world) as:** *rejecting; uncaring; hostile*

5. **Parental figures** (m____, f____) are seen as _____ and subject's reaction is _____
   Contemp. figures (m √, f √) are seen as *rejecting* and subject's reaction is *depression; with-*
   Junior figures (m____, f____) are seen as _____ and subject's reaction is *drawal; counter acting*

6. **Significant conflicts:** *Between passivity and counter-action.*
   Sex and Superego

7. **Nature of anxieties:** (√)
   of physical harm and/or punishment _____ of illness or injury _____
   of disapproval _√_ of deprivation _____
   of lack or loss of love _√_ of being devoured _____
   of being deserted _√_ of being overpowered and helpless _____
   other *of loss of control*

8. **Main defenses against conflicts and fears:** (√)
   repression _____ reaction-formation _√_ rationalization _____ isolation _____
   regression _____ introjection _____ denial _____ undoing _____ other *projection*

9. **Severity of superego as manifested by:** (√)
   punishment for "crime" _____ immediate _____ just _√_ too severe _√_
   delayed _____ unjust _____ too lenient _____
   inhibitions _____ stammer _____ delayed initial response or pauses _____

10. **Integration of the ego, manifesting itself in:** (√, √√, √√√)
    adequacy of hero _√_ outcome: happy _____ unhappy _____
    realistic _√_ unrealistic _____
    solution: adequate _√_ inadequate _____
    thought processes as revealed by plot being: (√, √√, √√√)
    structured _√√_ unstructured _____ stereotyped _____ original _____ appropriate _√_
    rational _√_ bizarre _____ complete _____ incomplete _____ inappropriate _____

Intelligence: (√) superior _____ above average _√_ average _____ below average _____ defective _____

Analysis Sheet for use with the Bellak TAT Blank

Copyright 1951, Leopold Bellak   51-119A3 The Psychological Corporation

SUMMARY

Record themes and summarize other significant data for each story.

1. Feels strictly brought up; need for autonomy, achievement. Feminine identi-fication—feels helpless. Fear of pregnancy. Suicidal tendencies. Strong homosexual fears. Extra- and intra-aggression. Parents seen as restrictive, coercive. Feels unhappy, physically ill.

2. Sexual needs; distinct triangular oedipal theme; jealousy. Intra- and extra-aggression. Homosexual interests. Severe superego.

3. Aggression against authority, particularly male figures. Severe superego.

4. Feels extremely moralistic. Severe superego. Strong guilt feelings about sex. Need for liquor. Strong oral needs. Rationalizes. Projects (anger) on the woman. Impulse-ridden (it was the easiest thing he could have done). Strong intra-aggression. Oral needs.

5. Patient has frequently witnessed primal scene and has felt insignificant in relation to his father, and blames his parents for not having equipped him better genitally. Information and education are given phallic significance as a powerful tool. Voyeurism. Conflict between need for achievement and feeling of inadequacy.

6. Feels himself a degenerate because of interest in liquor and women. Feels rejected by male and female figures. Severe superego. Depression, with-drawal, counteraction. Oral needs.

7.

8.

9.

10.

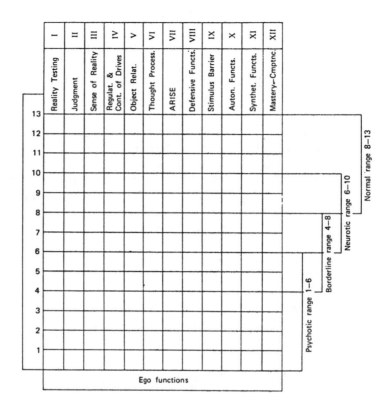

(From Bellak, Hurvich, & Gediman, *Ego functions in schizophrenics, neurotics, and normals.* Copyright © 1973, by C. P. S., Inc. Reprinted by permission of John Wiley & Sons, Inc.)

Ego functions observed during test administration:

Case 3

E.O. is a married man of 25 who came with marital difficulties as his chief complaint. He and his wife were of different religions, although this did not enter into the problems except for some difficulties with the in-laws on both sides. Both families, however, were several thousand miles away. The subject had suffered from depressive episodes of borderline nature and also from premature ejaculation. He had no specific complaints against his wife except that she was not a very good sexual partner, but he did have serious questions concerning his preference for another girl. It became clear dynamically that the other girl was probably a representation of a sister two years older than he and, in the long run, an image of his mother. Together with his ambivalence toward his wife went considerable jealousy (apparently unfounded) concerning her feelings toward other, usually older, men. At times the relationship to the wife was a clearly competitive one, with him equipping her in his fantasy with masculine features. They were both in the entertainment field.

The patient responded favorably to a 6-months' course of psychotherapy. Final diagnosis: cyclothymic personality with some tendency towards a borderline manic-depressive syndrome.

For Case 3 we are using the Short Form (see also Chapters IX and XII). The Short Form, as mentioned, is especially useful for the working clinicians. They are likely to make themselves brief notes in their personal shorthand, for which the space provided will usually suffice. In print, for public consumption, it is impossible to put all the necessary observations into the boxes. Therefore, the diagnostic theme also appears below each story, and only token references to it show in the boxes of the Blank.

The same limitations of printing versus personal notes limit the utilization of the other spaces in the Blank.

For the didactic purposes of this book, we are also reproducing the individual pages of the Long Form to allow the space necessary for printing some of the comments which might otherwise be personal abbreviations. Furthermore, also for didactic reasons, we chose some stories which by their richness allow more than an average of observations.

For those whose personal style runs counter to the small space provided in the Short Form, the Long Form remains the ideal record.

Note. All three final reports have been kept fairly brief in the interest of conciseness and because experience has shown that much longer reports are found objectionable by psychiatrists, etc. Some T.A.T. workers may prefer a more rigid organization of the final report, under the specific headings referred to under "summary," namely, unconscious structure and needs of subject, conception of world and of significant figures, significant conflicts, nature of anxieties, main defenses against conflicts and fears, severity (and integration) of superego, integration of ego, diagnostic impression (this record is consistent with . . .).

SHORT FORM

BELLAK T.A.T and C.A.T BLANK

For Recording and Analyzing Thematic Apperception Test and Children's Apperception Test

Name_____ E. O._____ Sex__M__ Age _25_ Date_____

Education_____High School_____Occupation__Professional Athlete__ (circle one) m. s. w. d.

Referred by_____Analysis by_____

After having obtained the stories analyze each story by using the variables on the left of Page 2. Not every story will furnish information regarding each variable: the variables are presented as a frame of reference to help avoid overlooking some dimension.

When all ten stories have been analyzed it is easy to check each variable from left to right for all ten stories and record an integrated summary on Page 4 under the appropriate headings. That way a final picture is obtained almost immediately.

Then, keeping Page 4 folded out, the Final Report: Diagnostic Impressions and Recommendations can be written on Page 1 by reference to Page 4. Page 5 gives available space for any other notations. The stories then can be stapled inside the blank against Page 5. For further instructions see *Manual for T.A.T. Interpretation*, Psychological Corporation, by Leopold Bellak or *Manual for the C.A.T.*, C.P.S. Inc., or *The T.A.T. and C.A.T. in Clinical Use*, 2nd edition, Grune & Stratton, 1971, N. Y. C. by Leopold Bellak;

FINAL REPORT: Diagnostic Impressions and Recommendations

The main problems of the patient are a low self-esteem and in seeing himself as an object of deprivation and aggression, as seen in stories 2, 13MF, and 18BM. He has a need to express his aggression, but there is a strong conflict in this regard and he frequently turns the aggression against himself (as in 18BM).

His oral needs are very pronounced, manifesting themselves in a need for acquisition of money and fame (1, 2, 13MF). He sees the paternal figure as aggressive and depriving. Contemporary male figures are seen as competitive, and there is a strong homosexual interest in them. Maternal figures are seen with considerable ambivalence and guilt over his aggressive feelings toward them, and also with strong oral demands toward them.

His main conflicts center around activity-passivity, the expression of aggression, and the expression of his oral demands. He shows distinct fears of physical harm and of loss of love.

His main defenses are reaction formation (stories 2, 6BM, 13MF, 17BM, and 18BM) and denial (1, 6BM, and 18BM). He has an extremely severe superego.

This man's extreme narcissism is highlighted in stories 1 and 17BM. His only real need for people seems to be in their capacity as an audience. His exhibitionistic needs thus seem considerably stronger than his heterosexual needs (this is particularly clear in story 17BM, where he states that his interest is not in the girls per se but merely in their admiration of his prowess). Certainly his strong oedipal attachment impairs his heterosexual adjustment quite severely.

Ego strength is of such a nature as to enable him to tell structured, rational stories with, on the whole, perfectly adequate solutions. He deals well enough with reality problems but employs many pathogenic defense mechanisms in order to achieve some equilibrium, especially denial. He appears to be of above average intelligence with a great deal of verbal facility (approaching the verbose), inspiration, and considerable superficial affect.

The dynamic and ego psychological picture is consistent with an affective disorder without manifest psychosis.

•The combination of orality, low self-esteem, and aggression against himself suggests some feelings of depersonalization, but they do not appear marked enough to constitute serious suicidal problems.

Dynamic psychotherapy centering on the problems highlighted above should offer very good chances for considerable improvement and some structural changes.

	Story No. 1	Story No. 2
1. Main Theme: (diagnostic level: if descriptive and interpretative levels are desired, use a scratch sheet or page 5)	Picture 1 Dissatisfied with life. Fantasizes.	Picture 2 Wants to do better than family.
2. Main hero: age <u>10-11</u> sex <u>m</u> vocation <u>musical genius</u> abilities <u>____</u> interests <u>____</u> traits <u>____</u> body image <u>boy feeling empty</u> adequacy (√, √√, √√√) and/or self-image <u>(violin as his image)</u>	Adequate on manifest level.	Female 19. Student
3. Main needs and drives of hero: a) behavioral needs of hero (as in story): <u>to be a genius</u> implying: <u>a great musician to be famous</u> b) figures, objects, or circumstances *introduced*: <u>unseen instruments, money fame</u> implying need for or to: <u>fantasy gratification, artistic striving need for financial and other success</u> c) figures, objects, or circumstances *omitted*: <u>people playing the instruments, or even an "audience"</u> implying need for or to: <u>narcissistic gratification</u>	Feeling of failure of emptiness.	Need for autonomy. Oral needs. Money. Success. Succorance. Reassurance. Pregnancy of older woman. Repression of sexual themes
4. Conception of environment (world) as: <u>mere backdrop for his needs</u>		Poor, but giving opportunity.
5. a) Parental figures (m____, f____) are seen as ____ and subject's reaction to a is ____ b) Contemp. figures (m____, f____) are seen as ____ and subject's reaction to b is ____ c) Junior figures (m____, f____) are seen as ____ and subject's reaction to c is ____		Restrictive Between nurturance and succorance
6. Significant conflicts: <u>between reality and fantasy between strong affect, need for achievement and affection and their denial</u>		Contradiction of "eking out" and plentiful food
7. Nature of anxieties: (√) of physical harm and/or punishment ____ of disapproval ____ of lack or loss of love ____ of illness or injury ____ of being deserted ____ of deprivation ____ of being overpowered and helpless ____ of being devoured ____ other <u>of emptiness</u>		
8. Main defenses against conflicts and fears: (√) <u>some secondary withdrawal from people</u> repression ____ reaction-formation √ regression √ denial √ introjection ____ isolation ____ undoing ____ rationalization ____ other <u>excessive fantasy</u>	Mentions "no people." Doesn't realize he is wealthy and famous.	Reaction-formation. Denial
9. Adequacy of superego as manifested by "punishment" for "crime" being: ( ) appropriate ____ inappropriate ____ too severe (also indicated by immediacy of punishment) ____ inconsistent ____ too lenient ____ also: ____ delayed initial response or pauses ____ stammer ____ other manifestations of superego interference ____		
10. Integration of the ego, manifesting itself in: (√, √√, √√√) Hero: adequate √√ inadequate ____ outcome: happy √√ unhappy ____ realistic ____ unrealistic √√ drive control ____ thought processes as revealed by plot being: (√, √√, √√√) Stereotyped ____ original <u>/imaginative</u> appropriate √ complete √ incomplete ____ inappropriate ____ syncretic ____ concrete ____ contaminated ____ Intelligence <u>superior</u> Maturational level <u>immature</u>	Thought processes intact. Good intelligence.	Adequacy √√√ happy √√√ Realistic √√√ Thought processes appropriate and structured. Superior intelligence.

2

Ego function assessment from TAT data:

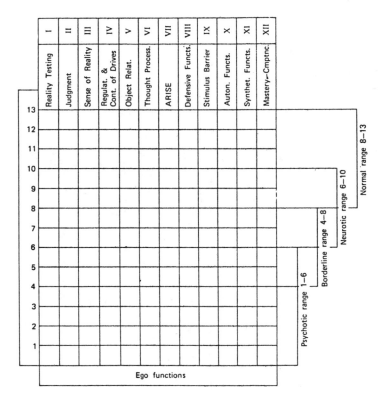

(From Bellak, Hurvich, & Gediman, *Ego functions in schizophrenics, neurotics, and normals*. Copyright © 1973, by C. P. S., Inc. Reprinted by permission of John Wiley & Sons, Inc.)

Ego functions observed during test administration:

Story No. 9	Story No. 10	SUMMARY
		1-3. Unconscious structure and drives of subject (based on variable 1-3)
		A markedly oral, passive person of low self esteem and high aspirations who reacts with a mixture of exhibitionism and mostly (secondary) narcissistic withdrawal, with similarly alternating depressive and elated moods.
		4. Conception of world: A's depriving, restrictive, aggressive. Wishes it to be his audience.
		5. Relationship to others: Need for anaclitic, oral relationships. Wants to be admired and may experience some alienation. Often quite narcissistic.
		6. Significant conflicts: Between passivity and activity. Desire to be taken care of and its denial. Between aggression and superego.
		7. Nature of anxieties: Of emptiness, of inadequacy, of failure, of deprivation, and of his own (oral) passivity and homosexual concerns.
		8. Main defenses used: Reaction-formation. Denial. Rationalization. Mood swings are result of relative weakness of defenses.
		9. Superego structure: Consistently severe.
		10. Integration and strength of ego: Thought processes intact. Defenses rather weak but not enough so as to impair reality testing or judgment. Autonomous functions good. Impulse control good enough to avoid acting out. Some creative ability. Little sense of competence, or self esteem.

Story No. 3	Story No. 4	Story No. 5	Story No. 6	Story No. 7	Story No. 8
6 BM Attachment to mother conflicting with marital adjustment	13 mF Feels deprived orally.	17 BM Body narcissism. Exhibitionism.	18 BM Need for verbal aggression.		
Young, indecisive male	Male student	Male athlete. Seen as skinny and funny.	Young male labor leader		
To please mother and wife. Dependence on female. Problems with wife. Fear of phallus.	For education to help wife make money. Implying: curiosity, nurturance, acquisition. Poverty. Illness.	Exhibitionism. Competitiveness. Second man. Girl.	To speak truth. Sway people. Further justice. Implying strict conscience. Wife workers beating. Masochism. Aggression to mother. Problem with male authority.		
Pressuring. Demanding. Mother nagging, poor, omnipotent, aggressive. Anger. Remorse. Passivity.	Depriving. Non-supporting. Dead. Remorse shown.	Audience Contemporary figures seen as competitive	Punishing. Exploiting. Aggressive. Parents seen as aggressive. Revolt. Contemporary figures seen as passive-aggressive. Reaction: aggressive - passive		
Between mother and wife. Aggression toward female figures.	Between aggression and guilt toward female figure.	Being strong and capable or small and funny as means of gaining approbation.	Between passivity and aggression.		
Aggression. Fantasies. Grief over anger towards mother. Fear of disapproval. Loss of love.	Physical harm. Punishment. Deprivation. Being helpless and overpowered.	Fear of lack or loss of love.	Fear of physical harm and punishment and fear of being helpless and overpowered.		
Reaction - formation. Denial. Projection.	Reaction - formation. Rationalization. Projection.	Reaction - formation	Reaction - formation. Denial.		
Immediate. Too severe.			Immediate. Too severe.		
Happy ✓ Realistic ✓	Unhappy ✓ Inadequate ✓	Realistic ✓ Unhappy Inadequate ✓	Happy ✓ Realistic ✓ Adequate ✓		
Thought processes complete.	Thought processes structured and complete.	Thought processes structured and complete	Thought processes structured and complete		

3

121

SUMMARY

Record themes and summarize other significant data for each story.

1. Feels like a 10 year old boy. Dissatisfied with his life. Feels own shallow affect (poor sexual performance? mild depersonalization?). Denies being temperamental. Switches from activity to grandiose fantasies of fame in a narcissistic way. Denies interest in money. Defenses: regression, denial.

2. Need for autonomy, self-improvement. Wants to do better than family. Family seen as restrictive, later proud of one's success. Need for success, including money. Wish-fulfillment fantasies, rescue fantasies re mother. Need for nurturance, oral needs. Defense: reaction-formation.

3. Has attachment to mother, conflicting with marital adjustment. Projects own aggression toward mother on wife, rationalizing. Mother seen as nagging, poor. Identifies himself with child. Guilt over anger toward mother. Fearful fantasies of aggression (fellatio). Mother seen as omnipotent. Can feel peaceful only if conflict between attachment to mother and wife (and ambivalence toward both) is resolved. Defenses: reaction-formation, denial.

4. Feels deprived orally. Aggression against wife. Projection. Unconscious guilt feelings. Need for acquisition (money), for security. Guilt. Defenses: reaction formation, rationalization, projection.

5. Great body narcissism; exhibitionism. Little heterosexual interest. Homosexual competitiveness. Great stress on being thought entertaining. Feeling of inadequacy. Defense: reaction-formation.

6. Need for aggression denied. Sees female figure (mother?) as being against aggression against authority. Authority is seen as depriving (inviting aggression—masochism). Severe guilt feelings. Socially acceptable aggression permissible (after self-punishment). Defense: reaction-formation.

7.

8.

9.

10.

STORY 1

1: This young lad of 10 or 11 years does not know that he is a genius of the music world to come—via his violin. He has been practicing a piece of music. This particular piece does not please him. He isn't temperamental—but he puts down his violin and stares at the music—it's emptiness—just a cute little melody—no feeling—no warmth—no excitement—just an empty melody. As he sits there—he starts—in his mind—to fix it up the way he feels it should have been written—and the melody is going through his head. The way he sees it, it's very sad, but beautifully so. . . . And as he goes further on . . . different instruments join in—and very soon he has a whole orchestra in the background, with the violin crying out its sad and beautiful melody—he isn't even conscious of the fact that there aren't any *people* playing—just the music and the instruments! As he grows older—he makes a name for himself in the music field—and later on, he tires of playing—and starts composing the music that is constantly in his head—he becomes famous but this doesn't move him particularly—he doesn't even realize that he is wealthy—music is his life, and he is happy, because he is doing what he wants.

Descriptive theme	*Interpretive theme*	*Diagnostic level*
A 10 year old boy is dissatisfied with his music piece, which feels empty, not warm. Stops it (though not temperamental).	If a boy is dissatisfied with his status because life is empty, cold, unexciting,	Feels like a 10 year old boy. Dissatisfied with his life. Feels own shallow affect (poor sexual performance?) Denies being temperamental.
Fantasies writing a better one (sad and beautiful); instruments (not people) join in.	fantasies of resounding effect (without social participation).	Switches from activity to grandioise fantasies of fame in a narcissistic way.
Becomes very famous, happy with music, uninterested in money.	He achieves fame and money, without caring for the latter.	Denies interest in money and recognition.

Clinical notes

It is questionable whether one is justified in identifying the self-image with that of a boy in view of the fact that the picture actually shows a boy. However, subjects frequently tell stories of an adult thinking back to boyhood, thus clearly thinking of themselves as adults, and making the consideration of boyish self-image tentatively possible.

The repeated reference to emptiness suggests subject's feeling of emptiness, probably involving some depersonalization. The different "instruments" might well refer to the proximity of people he needs to dispel this feeling, but at the same time the shallow, narcissistic relationship to them (they exist only as need-fulfilling objects) is suggested by the fact that it turns out that only the instruments themselves, without people, are playing.

STORY 2

2: This girl, about 19 years old, would probably be named Olga, of Ukranian parentage and stock. For generations her family has farmed this piece of land . . . just barely eking out an existence on this tired overused land. But food was plentiful, pure, and wholesome, and they were satisfied, all, until Olga grew up. She was the first in the family to get full schooling. At first the family thought it was useless to keep sending Olga to school, year after year—there was so much work to be done, and at 13 she was almost full grown—but Olga wanted to study and learn more. Finally they conceded, and four years later it was with pride that they watched their Olga graduate from the town school! It was indeed difficult to allow her to go to school all these years. Of course she helped after school hours, but that wasn't enough. And now, now, Olga wanted to go to Normal School to become a teacher! This was ridiculous—but—finally, after Olga showed them how, in another two years, she would graduate and get a job earning a hundred dollars a month as a teacher, they gave in again. We see Olga coming from town—Normal School! It is almost sunset—and as she comes across the field, she sees her brother, stripped to the waist, tilling the land, and her mother, tired and with an aching back from seeding—resting for a moment—Olga sees this and turns away for a moment . . . she hates to see them slave, just to eat and sleep. . . . Soon, she thinks to herself, I'll be earning money and we can buy a tractor—with automatic seeder . . . and there are many kinds of farm equipment that could make work easy, and do it quickly; maybe we'll buy the adjoining piece of land and start making a living instead of an existence. She walks over to her mother, takes the seeds from her, and starts seeding. . . . Her mother, now holding Olga's books, looks at her young educated daughter, who is bent over covering the seeds with the earth, and a light shines in her eyes, as she thinks, "Good, she is not spoiled, my daughter with her books—soon she'll finish and all will be well"—and turns to go down to the house to prepare the evening meal!

Descriptive theme	Interpretive theme	Diagnostic level
A girl of simple European stock wants to study and improve herself. Food important.	If a girl wants to do better than her family by studying (though having enough food?),	Need for autonomy, self-improvement. Wants to do better than family. Oral needs.
A first the family objects but then concedes and watches her succeed with pride.	the family first objects, then concedes, and is proud of her success.	Family seen as restrictive, later proud of one's success.
The girl sees the family toil, dreams of helping them, and actually relieves mother of work.	One feels sorry for the family, fantasies of helping them, and actually helps mother.	Need for success, including money. Wish-fulfillment fantasies, rescue fantasies re mother. Need for nurturance.
Mother is happy about her and prepares a meal.		Oral needs.

Clinical notes

It is frequent for males to identify with the female figure in this picture, so that this by itself does not permit any particular inference. The need for success and money is repeated here, this time without denial of the latter. But denial appears in the contradiction of "eking out" and plentiful food. The need for nurturance [24] may simply stand for need for succorance.

This is a rather verbose, lively story of cheerful mood, probably typical of the somewhat hypomanic mood the patient was in (as compared with the meager, constricted, brief, often merely descriptive stories of obsessive-compulsives, for instance). This story is also to a certain extent autobiographical in that the patient did come from immigrant stock and helped support his family.

STORY 6BM

6BM: This is an old folks' home, and the young man is visiting his old mother. She was only to have stayed for a short while. Till he had moved his family to the new house. . . . Then, when he thought of bringing his mother to the new home . . . his wife had started talking . . . "Grandma was spoiling the kids . . . She kept everyone awake with her nerve-wracking cough, and she was very untidy, and made so much extra cleaning work around the house." . . . At first, the young man was shocked to hear his wife speak that way of his mother . . . he wouldn't think of letting her live in the old folks' home . . . while he had a new house with plenty of rooms in it . . . but . . . after a few weeks . . . he got used to hearing his wife speaking in this manner . . . and he wasn't shocked to hear the words, but he was still upset about his mother living in the old folks' home. . . . His wife was stubborn and insistent . . . there wasn't anything he could say or do that would change her mind, well . . . there wasn't much he could say now . . . he was tired . . . she kept yelling and making scenes. . . . So finally one day he went to see his mother . . . to tell her . . . the easiest way he could, that it was inconvenient for them . . . for her to live with them. . . . After much hemming and hawing . . . he finally blurted out his case. . . . The mother is very hurt, but she sees how difficult it is for her son, and for his sake tries to make it all sound very trivial . . . and actually she likes it at the home! . . . But the man can see through her kind but obvious front. And finally the mother starts talking . . . about how you bring children into the world . . . and no matter how much they love you . . . and no matter what they try to do for you, you always feel that you are unwanted . . . and yet . . . what can an old woman with no income do? The man is feeling very bad . . . his little old mother going through all this pain because his wife didn't want to clean an extra room! He is disgusted with himself for not being man enough to make his wife take his mother in . . . and at the same time he is angry with his mother for making it so difficult for him.

Well, time wore on. The grandma would come to the house Sundays . . . play with the kids . . . enjoy their laughter and their tears. Stay for Sunday dinner, and around about eight . . . the son would drive her to the home.

About six months after the above incident . . . on a Sunday . . . they were having fish for dinner . . . when suddenly . . . one of the children started coughing and spluttering . . . everyone started pounding him on the back . . . the young mother started getting hysterical . . . and the father kept yelling . . . "He's got a bone stuck in his throat." . . . The child started getting blue in the face. . . . The grandma ran into the kitchen . . . went to the bread box . . . took a piece of stale bread back to the choking child, put a good-sized piece of stale bread in his mouth . . . told him to chew it a couple of times, and then swallow . . . no matter how difficult. . . . The child by this time was almost unconscious but, hearing its grandmother's calm voice it did as it was bid . . . and the bread forced the bone down . . . and the child was all right, 'cept for fright. . . . The young mother looked at the man . . . who was her husband . . . and said . . . "If it weren't for your mother's old-fashioned remedies . . . we might have lost our son. I could feel what it was like. I know how she must feel . . . living away from you . . . us . . . now! I think I can manage to clean one more room . . . !" So, the grandma moved back. . . .

Descriptive theme	*Interpretive theme*	*Diagnostic level*
There is a conflict between hero's mother and wife. Hero gives in to wife and mother has to move to old folks' home.	If there is a conflict in one's loyalties to mother and wife, one relucantly gives in to wife.	Has attachment to mother conflicting with marital adjustment. Projects aggression toward mother on wife, rationalizing.
Mother feels son is ungrateful. He doesn't dare stand up to wife and is angry at mother.	and rejects mother, who complains about it.	Mother seen as nagging, poor. Identifies himself with child. Guilt over anger toward mother.
When mother saves life of grandchild when it has a bone stuck in its throat, wife and mother make peace.	If there is trouble with the child (who has object stuck in throat), mother helps. If mother and wife can be reconciled, all is well.	Fearful fantasies of aggression (fellatio). Mother seen as omnipotent. Can feel peaceful only if conflict between attachment to mother and wife (and ambivalence toward both) is resolved.

Clinical notes

This story is most illuminating with regard to the subject's chief complaint of marital problems. Obviously, he is as ambivalent toward his wife as toward his mother and denies both. His relationship to the latter interferes with his relationship to the former. In his oedipal wishfulness, the father is out of the picture. Probably as a punishment both for his oedipal wishes and also because he conceives of the mother as a somewhat phallic woman, the phallus gets stuck in his throat. Making this happen to his own child removes the full impact from himself.

The story of the bone is not unlike the apocryphal story of the origin of the Adam's apple—the forbidden (sexual) fruit getting stuck [19]. It implies a breast-phallus equation. The Kleinian school would speak of the "bad breast." The child is a secondary identification figure. The solution of the conflict between the two women by the bone incident, and the solution by the bread, are somewhat of the nature of a *deus ex machina* solution.

STORY 13MF

13MF: This scene takes place in a small room of a tenement house. Very poor people . . . young—students. The betterment of the mind means so much to them. They have starved to go to the university. . . . Sometimes working at nights . . . so . . . they can afford to go to school in the day. They have known each other since childhood, and as they grew older, married and, having much in common, lived happily though precariously, sometimes not having enough for food, most of the time dressed very poorly. This winter was very cold . . . the girl's coat was very thin . . . and somehow she must have caught a cold. . . . The boy, her young husband, finds her in bed shivering. . . . "What's the matter?" he asks. "Guess I caught a bit of a chill," she answers. He feels her brow and she is very hot! He becomes alarmed and says, "I'll go get a doctor!" . . . "I'll be all right, don't bother." . . . He sits by her side, and talks to her, to keep her company . . . besides, he has no money for a doctor! After a while he notices that she hasn't said anything for quite some time . . . he shakes her, but she is unconscious . . . he becomes frantic, and runs out to find some doctor, but the doctor down the street is not in his office . . . and he runs back to the room. The girl has pushed the covers partly off of her, in her fever, and her full round breasts are exposed . . . he leans down to talk to her . . . he sees . . . she is not breathing . . . ! So quickly life goes . . . he doesn't know how long he has been sitting by the small bed . . . he gets up . . . and calls the police . . . ! Heartbroken . . . he is determined . . . "To hell with education! Money is what counts! If we had had money . . . she wouldn't have died!". . . He leaves school . . . goes into the world . . . amasses a fortune after a time . . . but, he has not peace of mind . . . money can't buy that!

Descriptive theme	Interpretive theme	Diagnostic level
A poor starving girl dies because husband cannot afford a doctor.	If one is poor, one has to let one's wife die,	Feels deprived orally. Aggression against wife. Projection.
He calls police.	calls the police.	Unconscious guilt feelings.
Heartbroken, he makes much money without peace of mind.	makes much money, is disturbed.	Need for acquisition (money), for security. Guilt.

Clinical notes

Again the acquisitive needs, denied in the first story, come out here strongly, very often feelings of material deprivation stand for a feeling of being deprived of love. In this story reference to starvation clearly refers to oral deprivation.

The unconscious guilt feelings over unconscious aggression are demonstrated by his calling the police.

STORY 17BM

17BM: The boy or young man on the rope is a gymnast . . . takes great pride in his muscles and ability. . . . Today some girls came in to see the men working out . . . and this particular boy was doing everything to appear the hero and strong man in their eyes . . . not that he cared particularly to meet the girls . . . it's just that he wanted them to see that he is the best around. While he is doing all this showing off . . . a small, thin chap with glasses . . . and a portfolio joins the girls, and they all turn eyes on the muscular young man. He smiles to himself and he takes a running leap at the hanging rope and shinnies up like Tarzan, and starts doing all sorts of difficult feats, one-arm planches, dislocations, and so on, for about five minutes, and then he looks at the group that were watching him, and sees that they (the girls) are laughing at the little fellow, who is trying to lift a huge weight . . . and being very funny about it. The muscular one comes down the rope, watching as he descends. "Why should they choose to look and laugh with the skinny, scholarly chap, when I was being so sensational!!"

Descriptive theme	*Interpretive theme*	*Diagnostic level*
A young man with great pride in his muscles and ability shows off to girls to impress them as being best.	If one shows off with great pride in one's body, it is narcissistic more than heterosexual.	Great body narcissism; exhibitionism. Little heterosexual interest.
At the same time a thin scholarly fellow makes them laugh, and the muscular one feels the other is stealing the show.	The girls may prefer a funny scholarly chap.	Homosexual competitiveness. Great stress on being thought entertaining. Feeling of inadequacy.

Clinical notes

This story probably reflects a double identification, in that inquiry revealed that the subject thinks of himself both as muscular and, on the other hand, as too little. The other stories, too, show his need to be considered scholarly. His actual appearance was that of a small, inoffensive man, whereas he was a professional athlete. This theme is also related to competition with a brother three years older and has much to do with the patient's homosexual competitiveness with other men rather than genuine heterosexual interest. This man sees people primarily as an audience. His only object cathexis is an anaclitic one. The laughter which the second identification figure arouses was one of the patient's most important conscious needs (getting the laughs).

STORY 18BM

18BM: His wife always said . . . "You can't step on peoples' toes . . . and not expect to get hurt yourself!" And he would answer, "If telling the truth . . . if honesty is stepping on peoples' toes, then I damn well am going to step on plenty of toes!"

This afternoon . . . during the lunch hour in the factory . . . he had a bunch of the workers gathered round him . . . and was explaining to them . . . the way the economic system worked. How they . . . the workers were browbeaten . . . how the people with money . . . made more money by making them work like slaves . . . for little more than slave money. That the worker had no chance for security in his old age . . . working conditions weren't even good. . . . Look at the way they had accidents, because the power machines didn't have protection screens around them . . . the bad lighting, etc. . . . etc. . . . One of the foremen overheard this and went to the boss' office . . . and told what he had heard.

That night, as he was walking down the dark street that led to his house . . . a car drove alongside, and some men jumped out . . . something hit him on the head . . . he was dazed by the blow . . . then he was hustled into the car . . . driven out to the country and beaten up. It was four o'clock in the morning by the time he got home . . . sick and sore in his body. . . . He knew why he was beaten up. . . .

The next day, although it was an effort for him to go to work . . . he went . . . his face all swollen . . . his body sore and wracked with pain. . . . His fellows started asking him questions . . . and he said . . . "You all know me. I have no enemies. I think I am well liked . . . yet last night coming from work . . . I was set upon by some thugs . . . thoroughly beaten . . . and apparently left for dead. It couldn't have been thieves . . . because they didn't try to take anything from me . . . and they kept shouting as they were kicking and punching me . . . 'This oughta teach you to keep your mouth shut . . . you lousy communist!' . . . You see, it was for what I have been speaking to you about that I was beat up! . . . I must of said some very true things for them to try and shut me up . . . !" The workers asked . . . "What are we going to do?" . . . and he answered . . . "What they have done to ME, is not of great importance . . . but, WHY they have done it is! So, we must organize . . . a union . . . and force them to our demands!"

The workers organized . . . and started making small demands at first . . . until they forced the bosses into making their shop . . . clean . . . safe . . . and better wages. This showed the way . . . and very soon the other shops followed . . . and at least now, the workers live like humans. . . .

Descriptive theme	*Interpretive theme*	*Diagnostic level*
A man tells workers they are being abused, even though his wife says this might lead to harm to himself.	If one is verbally aggressive against authority against a female's advice	Need for verbal aggression. Sees female figure (mother?) as being against aggression against authority.
Someone informs on him and he is severely beaten.	one is severely harmed by agents of the authority	Authority is seen as depriving (inviting aggression—masochism). Severe guilt feelings.
Thereupon he leads the men to organize a union.	but then leads men to successful modified counteraggression.	Socially acceptable aggression permissible (after self-punishment).

Clinical notes

The female figure is certainly unexpectedly introduced here. The exploiting authority is probably an image of the parents. The whole story shows the subject's problem with aggression, his turning it against himself, and his ability to express it only in a modified form after he has been punished.

CHAPTER V

SOME CLINICAL AND OTHER SPECIAL PROBLEMS OF THE T.A.T.

A. On Diagnostic Groups

AMBITIOUS AS WE ARE TO DO AS MUCH AS POSSIBLE WITH OUR projective techniques, it is as yet hardly customary to talk very much about their limitations. Nevertheless, they all have some shortcomings, of course, and the better we test the limits, the better able we will be to use them. The problem of the relationship of the latent data to overt behavior constitutes one possible difficulty (Chapter I). But this is only one limitation. Having had occasion to study about 30 patients who had been given projective tests, either in psychoanalysis or in prolonged psychoanalytic psychotherapy, I have had a chance to learn about a number of these problems. Although all projective tests have shortcomings, I will confine myself to the T.A.T.

Although the T.A.T. has been very useful and illuminating in all the cases I have studied, in a number of them the major problems of the patient did not appear in the T.A.T. For instance, the entire analysis of one male patient of 20 centered to an unusual degree around one focal sadomasochistic fantasy. That fantasy existed when the patient was five years old, with him in the passive role. He was healthy enough to switch to a more active, masculine role by the time he was twelve, but the fantasy was in essence the same (instead of being kidnaped, he became the kidnaper). In the course of nearly three years of four or five weekly sessions we managed to identify the most detailed features of the fantasy; various pictorial aspects could be identified with specific places, dates, and occurrences of several years of his life. This fantasy had layers like the trunk of a tree. Nevertheless, nothing suggestive of this fantasy occurs in this man's T.A.T!

The analysis, of course, did not merely consist of the analysis of one fantasy. On the contrary, the fantasy was pieced together only in the midst of all sorts of other more or less relevant material. And the T.A.T., of course, showed his anxieties, and that he used avoidance as a main defense mechanism; this very fact led to the suspicion, on first studying the T.A.T., that there must be more there than appeared in the stories.

It may be that the mechanism of demise is particularly pernicious to securing projective data. This is, of course, the mechanism of choice in manics, and therefore my examples come primarily from that group, although not exclusively. (The above-mentioned patient had a character disorder, and all the patients referred to here were seen in private practice while they were carrying on gainful activities and were certainly not frankly psychotic.)

When the mechanism of avoidance is used, the T.A.T. material may be long and apparently very rich, yet it will defy analysis. This is, of course, the experience with any form of output of manics or hypomanics. Fortunately at least one story usually turns out to contain the real core, while the others have such an overgrowth of defense that it requires very special pains and an awareness of the centrifugal nature of the material to be able to use it. With manics and other predominantly oral character disorders, the most useful story usually turns out to be the one told to picture 11. The theme of devouring, which this Boecklin picture suggests, contains precisely the stimulus this group responds to.

The defenses revealed by the T.A.T. are identical with those appearing in free associations and in dreams. Those patients who give the most frustrating T.A.T. stories may spend hours on seemingly irrelevant material and recount long, involved dreams more suitable for Hollywood scenarios than for analysis.

It is a fact, then, that, by and large, T.A.T. records do not always permit one to identify the presenting clinical symptoms. In the records of two pronouncedly agoraphobic women there is nothing to indicate manifest agoraphobia; in the records of three severely anorexic women there is nothing that shows the presenting problem of anorexia.

This is purely a matter of methodological interest, part of the problem of the relationship of the overt to the latent. I see no reason why one should need the T.A.T. to identify a clinical syndrome; ask the patient—she will be glad to tell you that she is agoraphobic or anorexic.

However, the T.A.T. was very useful in all these cases in reflecting the underlying dynamics. It showed the ambivalence, the exhibitionism, and the fear of aggression in the agoraphobes, as well as the figures the aggression was directed against. A posteriori, one could identify all the component parts that belonged to the picture. An exception may be the quantitative aspects; as in dreams and fantasies, it is difficult to appraise the strength of the variables involved, and it would be difficult to predict whether they are strong enough to turn up as manifest syndrome formation. With a study of defenses, however, this is not impossible. There have been a number of records, particularly of the C.A.T., where I could successfully predict anorexia as a clinical syndrome, although at times only a detailed consideration of the defenses permitted me to differentiate between overeating and anorexia.

These observations of mine are entirely in agreement with the excellent theoretical formulations which Sargent presents in her pyramid of diagnostic inference (Figs. 2 and 3)* [294]; she states that after a consideration of the raw data of the tests comes a level of generalization; then a second inferential level of theo-

---

* Figures 2 and 3 are reproduced, by permission, from Sargent, H.: *The Insight Test,* New York, Grune & Statton, 1953.

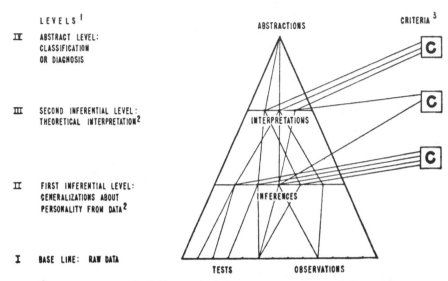

FIG. 2. Pyramid of diagnostic inference, reasoning, and abstraction.

[1] Level I. Test scores, patterns, scatter, quantitative and qualitative signs (perceptual distortions, peculiar associations, content, over- or underresponse, etc.).

Level II. Identifying characteristics: overalert, compliant, rigid, naive, anxious, disoriented, etc.

Level III. Postulated mechanisms and processes such as projection, repression, regression, denial, isolation, introjection, etc.

Level IV. Categories such as neurosis, psychosis, schizophrenia, hysteria, obsessive-compulsive; "good" or "poor" candidates for profession, employment, etc.

[2] Intrinsic validity established by convergence of independent judgments.

[3] External validity established by pre- or postdiction of events or conditions from tests and observations checked against criteria (C). Sample criteria: life history, course of illness, progress in therapy, vocational adjustment, experimental behavior, etc.

retical interpretation; and only then a third (abstract) inference as to the classificatory diagnosis. She demonstrates the overlapping of the two levels of inference for two (or more) diagnostic labels.

I realized long ago how well the identifying features of psychodynamics and character structure can be revealed in the T.A.T. when I gave it to patients in analysis and found a high level of agreement; often the analysts found that the T.A.T. was able to throw light on features which had not yet become entirely clear in analysis.

Murray first used this method of comparing T.A.T.'s with analyses; as far as I know, both his attempt and mine were nonsystematic (mine was interrupted by the war). However, Ethel Tumen Kardiner [188] has carried out a systematic study along these lines and has found statistical corroboration for the T.A.T.'s ability in this regard.

Within limits, one can often make statements about the diagnostic group to which a patient belongs. Although it has been pointed out before that I do not believe that the main strength or function of the T.A.T. lies in its ability to diagnose specific nosological groups, it can be of use for such diagnostic indica-

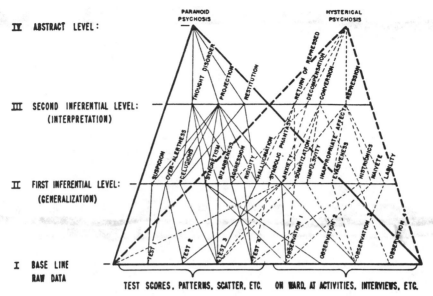

FIG. 3. Overlapping diagnostic pyramids. Solid lines represent, for one case, the derivation of inference from raw data, interpretation from inference patterns, and abstraction from interpretations subsumed under the finally selected label. Dotted lines represent the same sequence for a second case. Note that a single first-level inference (e.g., anxiety) may be based on data from several tests and/or observations and that a single test score may lead to more than one inference (e.g., test 3, perhaps the Rorschach). The interpretation that projective defenses are operating derives from not one but several inferred characteristics. Likewise, the diagnosis of paranoid schizophrenia or hysterical psychosis depends on a combination of theoretical interpretations or conceptualized processes.

tions. If I give a few stories as examples below, I do so with misgivings, since I firmly believe that the pattern of a number of stories is most important, and dislike giving single stories as evidence of any trend. The space available makes it undesirable to reproduce whole T.A.T. protocols; therefore I am making a minimal use of this unhappy compromise of picking out specific stories, and I caution the reader against it.

Not infrequently one will notice that *obsessive-compulsives* give their attention to small details in the pictures, and they will often respond with more than one story to a picture. We may also find that the storyteller stays distant and expresses sarcastic attitudes toward the hero, remaining emotionally isolated himself. In *hysterics and hypomanics,* on the other hand, we find a great deal of affect and a lively identification with the hero.

In *manifest homosexuals* I have noticed a tendency toward frequent manifest homosexual references and a recurrent shift of identification not only from males to females but also within one sex. The result is that these stories are rather difficult to score.

Manics will often indicate strong tendencies of oral incorporation; very many references to food and getting things may appear (although this is, of course, not pathognomonic at all). Again, in *depressed patients,* suicidal themes, a depressed

overall mood, and self-depreciation, along with other signs of a very strong
superego, may be apparent.

Below is the story of a manic-depressive girl in remission, illustrating the oral
tendencies with three references to eating in a brief story. The picture (11)
frequently elicits reference to food; stories of attack are often integrated with this
theme:

> This picture takes place in Texas about 5000 years from now. Civilization is extinct. An atom bomb
> has killed everyone, and the whole earth is beginning again. The remains of civilization are the
> Spanish arch in the right lower corner. On the top are a few birds looking for *food*. There's a mountain
> on the left side, and from a cave a sort of snake-bodied, duck-footed animal is wiggling out. He's going
> to strike the birds, *eat* them, and then go merrily on his way looking for more *food*.

In the T.A.T. stories of *psychopaths,* one usually finds little punishment for any
aggressive act engaged in by the hero in the story, evidence of a weakly integrated
superego (see stories of Streicher, Section B of this chapter).

There are other cases where we would like to be able to make real inferences,
for instance, if the potentiality (or actuality in the past) of antisocial acts exists,
and we wish to help predict future behavior. One such case occurred when I was
asked to help determine whether or not a young boy should be released from an
institution. He had killed a small child, apparently in some sexual excitement.
Institutionalized, he was a model inmate on a behavioral level—bland, noncommittal, and inaccessible to psychotherapy. At the time of commitment and again
when he came up for disposition at the end of a year, he was given the T.A.T. and
other tests by the staff for help in understanding his problems. When none of the
tests threw any light on the psychodynamics of the crime, he was referred to me
for the administration of a T.A.T. under the influence of intravenous Amytal
Sodium. After the intravenous administration of 7½ gr. of Amytal Sodium and
1½ gr. of Nembutal orally, a marked psychomotor effect of the drugs was noted:
general relaxation, drowsiness, slurring of speech, and occasionally such lack of
motor control and sleepiness that the T.A.T. cards dropped out of his hands.
Despite the action of the drugs, the boy gave 15 stories which in no single
instance revealed any *primary* pathological evidence in the theme itself that
would have permitted one to pick out his T.A.T. as belonging to a noticeably
disturbed person.

However, although it was impossible from his T.A.T. stories to predict his
actual behavior, small breakthroughs of original impulses came to light. For
instance, he made one slip of the tongue in the following story to picture 8BM:

> These two boys have gone out hunting. They shot a lot of boys—I mean, animals, and decided to
> split up to get more pheasants. They agreed to meet at 8:30 at night to count the game and to go
> home. This boy was standing in the bushes. Twenty feet from him he heard something move. He goes
> to look at what he caught and finds his friend and rushes him to the doctor. The doctor says the boy
> will be all right, and in the end the boy gets OK and forgives him for what he did.

The slip betrays the apparently original aggressive impulse which becomes
absorbed in a perfectly acceptable hunting story, then breaks through again in the
boy's injury. An inquiry into the small detail of 8:30 at night revealed that that

was the time for lights out at the institution and strongly suggested that it was at this time that his fantasies were permitted to emerge. Similarly, he started his story to picture 1 by saying:

This boy does not like to practice his trumpet—I mean he likes to play his violin.

He changes a negative response immediately to a positive one. The story he gave to picture 15 is as follows:

An undertaker; he is very sad because he is putting to rest all these people. He goes out one night and looks with remorse at all the work he has done. He tries to find out how he can undo his work. He can do nothing about it.

In this story, the undertaker behaves as if he had killed all the people he buried, revealing the original aggressive impulse only by what would otherwise be incongruent guilt feelings.

There are other T.A.T.'s of murderers which present similar problems. A woman who had previously attempted to kill her sleeping children by stabbing told the following story to 3BM*:

Is this a girl? I think it's a girl; she seems to be crying; leaning against a bed. At her feet I think there's a gun. Well, it looks as though she had planned to use the gun and instead of doing so had fallen asleep. (?) Probably planned to shoot someone with it. (?) Well, a neighbor perhaps that she didn't like. (?) No one would know that but herself—can't imagine what reason you'd have for it except disliking them, maybe. I don't think anything will happen. She'll have changed her mind by the time she's more rested.

Although, like all this woman's stories, the content is innocuous in that nothing actually occurs, and it would be impossible to make any concrete predictions as to her behavior, certain things do emerge. The effect in this story is grossly inappropriate: a girl who had planned to shoot someone falls asleep instead. An active impulse is easily replaced by a passive one. There appears to be no particularly strong reason for the planned shooting of the neighbor except a vaguely expressed dislike.

The story she tells to 13MF is in some ways reminiscent of those of the boy murderer:

There's a picture of a young lady in bed and a man standing with his arms across his eyes; seems to be walking away from the bed. Seems to me the lady has died and he is remorseful; seems he is in a shock state of remorse over her death. (?) Nothing to indicate it wasn't from natural causes. (?) Husband; he'll have to go on alone.

Although the woman in the picture died from natural causes, yet the husband is in a "shock state of remorse" over her death. (This resembles the undertaker in the previous story who is remorseful over the people he has buried.) In this story, there seems to be a clearer aggressive impulse and its denial.

---

* Courtesy of Miss B. Guttman, of the Psychology Department, Queens General Hospital, N. Y.

Psychiatric Differentiation

Although attempts at psychiatric differentiation with use of the T.A.T. have been unsatisfactory in general, a good deal of recent work has supported my contention that various diagnostic groups differ clearly in certain of their ways of responding to thematic stimuli. In a study of psychoneurotics, Foulds [125] found that hysterics started stories more quickly than depressives and told longer stories at a quicker pace. Depressives produced more illness themes to picture 3GF than hysterics, who produced more themes involving quarrels. Davison [102] has described differences among certain diagnostic groups in terms of the kinds of interaction described in their stories. He concluded that anxiety reactives produced a significantly greater number of themes of "man moving toward man, the depressive reactives of man moving toward woman, the hebephrenic schizophrenics of man moving against man, and the catatonic schizophrenics of no relationship between man and woman."

Norma Aaron [1] was able to determine several personality differences between asthmatic, allergic, and normal children using T.A.T. responses. Some of the obtained differences were: asthmatics showed significantly more hostility than normals on a measure of hostility relating to card 3; asthmatics showed significantly more disturbance with the parent of opposite sex than did normals, but none with the parent of the same sex; asthmatics and allergics both indicated general feelings of loneliness and rejection by the parents significantly more than did normals.

Theoretical stress on the role of power concerns underlying paranoid symptomatology led Wolowitz and Shorkey [354] to study power themes in the T.A.T. stories of paranoid schizophrenics and other psychiatric patients. Paranoids' stories contained significantly more power imagery than those of the nonparanoids. Subdividing the nonparanoids into different diagnostic categories, it was found that paranoids were most highly differentiated, in terms of a greater number of power themes, from patients classified as anxiety reactions, psychophysiological reactions, and nonparanoid schizophrenics.

Karon's [190] hypothesis, drawn from clinical experience, that mothers of schizophrenics are unable to meet the needs of their children and use the children to meet their own needs by manipulating their behavior, has been analyzed by means of the T.A.T. Mitchell [237] has demonstrated that mothers of schizophrenic children can be differentiated significantly from mothers of normal children on the basis of T.A.T. responses. The criteria used for the successful differentiation supported Karon's [190] hypothesis; if there was an interaction between a dominant and dependent individual and the dominant individual did not meet the specified needs of the dependent individual or met his own needs at the expense of the dependent individual, the story was scored pathogenic. Most mothers of schizophrenic children received higher pathogenic scores than control mothers.

The T.A.T. with Schizophrenics

Contrary to findings by Rapaport [271], and in partial agreement with Eron's report [109], it is my experience that schizophrenia cannot easily be diagnosed as such from the T.A.T. I am speaking here of the latent schizophrenics one sees as they come to private offices. Rapaport's signs probably hold true primarily for hospitalized schizophrenics, where there is such manifest pathology that one would hardly need a T.A.T. to make the diagnosis. However, in a considerable percentage even of latent schizophrenics one *may* find ample indications of the severe disturbance in the T.A.T. stories. These indications may be either stories of bizarre content which did not appear in ordinary communications, such as John Doe's reference to "reading without eyes" in his story to picture 1 in Chapter IV, or very blatant symbolic expressions suggesting a closeness of the unconscious to conscious awareness far beyond the ordinary. Thought disturbances may become apparent in T.A.T. stories when they are not discernible in conversation or in interviews. Certain "signs" may also be considered as suggestive, but not conclusive, indicators, for instance, reference to deadness, e.g., with regard to the violin in story 1, and ruins and destruction in story 11. This type of response suggests a reflection of intrapsychic consciousness of lack of affect severe enough to be consistent with the diagnosis of schizophrenia.

One may, however, find these signs or any of the criteria mentioned above in the records of adolescents or artists who are not schizophrenic insofar as one can determine. Below are good examples of stories given by a latent schizophrenic artist who was referred for somatic complaints. After fairly short-term psychotherapy, this man has been able to lead a happy and productive life for the past seven years. Since he is an artist, the grossly bizarre nature of his stories was influenced by his lack of conventionality and, possibly, a somewhat tongue in cheek attitude.

Here is his story to picture 7BM, which he entitled, "Don't Kiss Me Any More":

Papa, your moustache, with its horrid, dirty color, feels unpleasant against my cheek when you kiss me. In fact, I feel uncomfortable when you come too near. Why don't you embrace a bush, it has the same texture? And don't give me your old philosopher's look, your philosophy is not objective enough, it's only based upon your own shortcomings and frustration, which all hark back to the fact that you were abnormally kind to your mother.

And so Papa takes the son's advice and goes in the backyard to a bush, but finds that it is his own father.

Following is his story to picture 11:

Liberatus has just flown from the womb which hangs lazily on the castle ramparts, swinging in the breeze. He dashes over the bridge pursued by three horrible mammoth turkeys, with beaks lined with alligator teeth. The bridge expanse between them crumbles, dashing the turkeys against the rocks below. Temporarily safe, he looks back at the womb and it now appears as a tremendous tongue with four webbed feet. But his safety is temporary, for his supposed refuge ahead is the City, gleaming not from the sun but from heavy phosphorus powder, which having been put layer on layer on the outside of the building, appears sponge-like, and when viewed closely is not glamorous but dusty and deadish. The heroic view of the city from this distance is indeed deceptive.

The subject reported many dreams just like this story.
His story to picture 12M follows:

The son with his sensuous upper lip drawn up, his feet languidly held apart, and his hand close to his genitals, seems to be in the midst of a very pleasant dream. The old man motions and chants, believing he has induced this dream and sleepy state. As the old man turns, one sees that he has no facial features. He wants the young man to awaken now, so he can suck some of his youth from him, vampirish or something like that. The old man feels that then perhaps he will have a face again. But when the young man finally gets up, he kicks the old man down and walks away.

An absence of facial features is another schizophrenic sign.
Story 13MF:

The young woman stands nude on the model stand. But she is without detail, no facial features, no teats, no fingernails. The artist first paints small circles on her breasts of a very beautiful color, a wonderful coral, like the color in some shells he brought from Acapulco. But as he paints in more details she becomes less, rather than more, lifelike and finally falls down flat as if she were an unsupported mannequin. The artist feels very tired and sick in the stomach; all this work for nothing. He goes out into the streets and sees all his fellow mannequins mechanically moving about.

An indication of emotional impoverishment consistent with schizophrenia might be seen in the "mechanically moving about."
Story 17BM:

Mike Jensen is climbing the thousand-foot rope that leads though he does not know it, to hell. He pauses on his ascent in the arena, as he notices a woman sitting in the second balcony, feet wide apart. Why is man always attracted to frustrating glimpses of women's thighs and hairy organs, when women happen to be a bit indecorous in the way they sit? Needless frustrations, must train oneself not to be diverted by such things; the only worthwhile thing is the whole salami.
So upward he goes again, but he slips when he unexpectedly comes to some thorns interwoven in the rope. And as he slips down the rope at a terrific speed, he is split in half; as he lands in the sawdust of the arena, he appears as two sides of a cow, newly delivered to the butcher, and waiting to be put in the icebox.
But some people like warm meat; and just as spectators break from the bleachers to uproot the football goals, many people with grotesque ape-like faces rush to rip at the red-purple meat.

The utter cruelty and bizarreness are again very suggestive and a strong indication of a schizophrenic process.
An example of thought disturbances in the T.A.T. of another latent schizophrenic is the following story to 17BM:

The man is climbing up the rope. There is a crowd chasing him. He is viewing something. Might be looking out to sea. Looking for a boat to come in. He'd be one of the men to bring in the cargo. He's alongside of the building. People are chasing him because he is on the side of a building. He is in a hurry—he is in a funny position. People are mad at him—has no clothes on. Walking around the streets naked. He is some character in history. Brutus. He wouldn't be looking for a boat after all—just fleeing from the crowd. They are after him. He took their money—he wants to get rich all of a sudden and retire. He gets away—does not look worried. Gets on top of the building. Gets on the road and gets away. He has no money with him—so he gets away somehow without the money.

In this story one may see some incoherence, some non sequiturs: "People are chasing him because he is on the side of the building."
Another example of a schizophrenic who, in the course of time, made a serious suicidal attempt, may be seen in the following stories:
Story 1:

. . . Broken violin . . . sick boy . . . unhappy boy . . . lonely boy . . . Outcome should be successful . . . could be competent violinist. . . . May I ask, is there a time on this? (None) . . .

(*What led up to?*) Well, he may have lost his mother—or his father. . . . Either of which may have been violinists. . . . Is that enough? . . . The alternate is—suicide. . . . That's a problem which he will have to face himself.

Story 3BM:

(Long initial pause) It appears like—appears that this picture represents—a deformed person—possibly a hunchback . . . depressed and—contemplating what to do about his dilemma. . . . As in the first picture, this problem is unresolved. I mean by that—it could be successful in that an adjustment can be made to his deformity . . . or . . . the alternate course of action. (Returns picture.) (*Which would be?*) Suicide.

The "broken violin" and the "deformed hunchback" suggest extreme disturbances of self-image. The mention of suicide in a relatively inappropriate context forecasts the future development.

Adolescents

The T.A.T. stories of adolescents are often the most rewarding in illustrating classical oedipal conflicts, e.g., the following story of a 13 year old boy to picture 5:

(Long pause) I am trying to figure the thing out. Well, she could be either calling a member of the family or investigating a noise she's heard in this room. The light's on. Looks to me like she's showing a little bit of the element of surprise. She's surprised. A little bit of fright mingled in with this. Surprise and fright mingled in. As if maybe she heard a burglar downstairs in the house. The way it's drawn she's tensed up in a way. As if ready for sudden action. Might be that there's a burglar in the house. She's calling somebody in the house. She could be calling one of the children or her husband. Or she heard this noise, came downstairs, found this burglar in the house. Doesn't quite know what to do. Been taken by surprise. Doesn't know whether the burglar will kill her or not—like most people who own their own homes, and burglars enter. Don't know whether the burglar will kill you or not. Most burglars carry guns or a blackjack to knock you out. Burglar overpowers her and takes valuables, or her husband comes down and overpowers the burglar.

In saying, "She could be calling one of the children or her husband," he really asks whether he or the father would be the rescuer of the mother; also either the father or he could probably be the burglar. Judging by associations to the story in the last two lines, we have a choice of his being the burglar and taking the valuables or the father coming down and overpowering him. This story represents variations on the classical rescue fantasies. It also illustrates the most frequent dynamics behind burglar fears, and makes use of the classical symbolism of robbery of valuables from a woman as a representation of sexual drives.

Similarly, story 11 of another adolescent boy of 18 shows the paranoid-like fear of the father figure who has always "bested him":

. . . Some surrealistic painter's idea of a fleeing individual chased by a number of goblin-like monsters led on by another person, possibly it's—a—sna—possible escape of this man being chased will be of no avail. He's just going on and on into an everlasting nightmare. . . . By the appearance of the . . . Man's touch has been around here . . . through the bridge, road. Must be a nightmare, then, of some human—because in the dream man's influence has shown itself in the bridge and the road. Possibly the dreamer is seeing himself chased into an eternity that there was no hope to escape from.

Perhaps he was just fooling himself that getting away from these things for a while would make him safe. I suppose he hasn't given up life or thoughts of a better life because he hasn't given up running away from these evil things. Maybe the man behind these ghoul-like things is a person he fears or hates—*some* strong emotion between him and that man. Feels that he's been persecuted all his life by this man and has spent his whole life running away. Possibly this man driving the beasts has bested him in business deals or in the choice of a mate . . . he's always had the upper hand. On the other hand, it may be his own reflection on himself that he—during his life has persecuted some individual and—a—is repenting or seeing himself as a chased individual sees himself. The man whose mind is reflected in being the pursuer, he may because of his dastardly deeds be a washout or disintegrate because he feels sorry for the other man. And the other man, after seeing himself in actual life being treated the same way he is, in his dreams, probably finally gave up trying to escape some relationship that will never end; just continue on till he dies; just gave up all hope.

Another case of an adolescent girl [60] permits us to demonstrate the value of the T.A.T. for studying small developmental changes in a personality. A 16½ year old girl was seen in a social agency and given a T.A.T., a Wechsler-Bellevue Intelligence Test, the Goodenough Drawing Test, and the Bender-Gestalt Test. At that time, the girl was found to be an essentially normal adolescent with a compliant attitude toward a mother seen as benevolent, though somewhat domineering.

Eight months later the girl returned to the social agency because of a minor emotional problem. At that time, a psychiatric interview substantiated the impressions gained from the tests named above. However, as the girl had suffered quite a traumatic experience since the administration of the tests, a second T.A.T. was administered by a different examiner to ascertain whether there were any new dynamic developments. It was noted in the psychiatric interview that the girl now described the mother as somewhat more domineering—which description may have had some basis in fact, related to the mother's entering into the menopause.

The first and second T.A.T.'s were compared; they were then shown to two psychiatrists—independently—and to three classes on the T.A.T. which I was conducting. These classes contained 110 students, most of whom had acquired a Ph.D. and many of whom were practicing clinical psychologists. In all cases, the two T.A.T. records were shown for blind comparison; the judges were told that these were T.A.T. records of the same person, given on two different occasions. They were not told which test was given when, nor what happened in between. The results were unanimous; the second record was identified as having been given later and was thought by the judges to have been administered after psychotherapy. They pointed out changes in the direction of maturation in the second record.

It must be emphasized that the subject had not received any psychotherapy and that the changes noted by the judges confirmed our personal impression of this girl's spontaneous emotional growth over a critical eight months' period, as reflected in the difference in the two T.A.T. records. The slight emotional disturbance for which the girl returned to the agency seems to have been incident to this developmental process and disappeared promptly.

Following are four stories from each of the two T.A.T.'s administered, which are representative of the changes discussed.

Picture 1, boy with violin:

First record of T.A.T. See a boy at the fiddle; doesn't look very happy; seems to be sad. Don't think he wants to play fiddle, though mother must want him to. I think mother wants him to for his education; wants him some day to be a violinist, but he doesn't want to by looks of this.

Second record of T.A.T. This is a boy looking at a violin. There is a sheet of music. He is thinking if he can play or not. I imagine he likes to play. He asked his mother for a violin and is thinking about it now. He played and became great. He looks very interested in it.

In the first record we see the hero compliant to the mother, unwillingly and unhappily. In the second record there is an independent striving, interest, the mother seen as giving. The tone is happier, though self-criticism has entered in.

Picture 14, silhouette at window:

First record. Picture of fellow looking at stars or moon; must be thinking of someone he loves, or perhaps his mother; likes to be with her; seems lonesome; might be far away from home somewhere. That's all.

Second record. This is a boy looking out of a window. It's dark out. He is looking at the stars and sky. He is thinking of his future; of opening up a business—or what he's going to do. He is thinking of his girl and home, and is peaceful. Maybe he got what he wanted, a happy life today, a happy home.

The first record shows dependence on mother, longing and lonesomeness. The second record shows a very similar story, but the hero is peaceful, planning for the future, with independence and heterosexual gratification (even though the hero is still a male).

Picture 17GF, girl on bridge.

First record. This picture looks as if by the river and men are working there. Girl leaning over bridge and she must be dreaming that someday her boy friend, off to war, and someday he would come home. That's about all. (*What sort of girl is she?*) Looks to be nice, sits home and waits, wouldn't go out with other fellows; she must love him very much.

Second record. This is a river scene, down South. I'd say a girl is on a bridge. It's a nice day and men are working. She's dreaming; looking out on water.* Must have someone on seas—husband, or boy friend and she's longing to have him near her and see him again, to have him safe. He comes home and she sees him once more and they're happy.

Again, the two stories are extremely similar. But in the first record it all stays on the fantasy level, and there is no resolution. In the second record a happy solution of the same problem is permitted on the reality level.

Picture 20, man by lamp post:

First record. Man by a light; seems to be waiting for someone; seems to be impatient; seems to be waiting for fiancée and they can't see each other. Waiting for another man. The reason he may not be able to see his fiancée, for mother forbids it. (*Why?*) She may not like him and so they have to meet on corners. (*Why doesn't the mother like him?*) Bad disposition or different faith. (*How does the girl feel about this?*) Girl likes him very much and doesn't care what the mother says, but she doesn't want to hurt mother so sees him on the side. (*What is the outcome?*) In the end, she realizes that he is bad for her and listens to her mother.

---

* Any reference to water or fire in T.A.T. (or C.A.T.) stories suggests a history of enuresis. Empirically this correlation has thus far been 100 per cent in cases where inquiry was possible.

Second record. He is waiting for his girl to come down. She is someone he loves. Her mother may not approve of him and they have to meet outside. They love each other deeply. They meet on street corners. In the end her mother realizes that they love each other and grants their wish that they want to be married. Her mother disapproves of him because he might be of a different faith, might not have job, or be of a different class than she.

In the first record, mother is seen as a barrier to the hero's sociosexual adjustment and the girl complies with her mother's wishes, which she identifies with her own advantage. In the second record, the mother is still seen as disapproving but her approval is no longer essential for the hero, who is more autonomous now, and, by implication, more attached to the heterosexual object than to the mother. Here, the mother subsequently grants her approval, and the subject has thus achieved a synthesis.

B. The Influence of Contemporary Events on T.A.T. Stories

Some of my earlier experiments dealt with artificially introducing aggression in subjects by provoking them or giving them posthypnotic orders to feel aggressive. Thereafter, when these subjects were asked to give stories to the T.A.T. pictures, it became apparent that they would project some of the aggression into the stories. Split-half comparisons between five stories told under these circumstances and five stories told without induced aggression, however, showed that the main personality characteristics persisted despite the artificial situation that was introduced. To a large extent the subjects would differ in their manner of handling the problem of aggression, expressing it either as extra-aggression or intra-aggression, or reacting with guilt feelings, etc. On another occasion in a similar manner I studied depressive feelings and joyfulness induced by means of hypnosis. Again, the effect on the T.A.T. stories was such as to leave the essential personality structure intact [20].

In an experiment by Coleman [93], an attempt was made to gauge the effects of a pleasurable, optimistic movie on the T.A.T. stories of children. Of all the stories obtained from the 37 children tested both before and after the movie showing, only one story (out of a total of 370) seemed clearly to reflect the content of the film.

A grim real-life situation provided us with another more reliable opportunity to study the effect of current experience on T.A.T. stories. Julius Streicher and Alfred Rosenberg were given T.A.T.'s in Nuremberg prison at the time of their trials. The tests were given in German and then translated as carefully as possible.* Both men were in prison at the time, after the failure of what to them was a life's work, awaiting a nearly certain death at the gallows. Since their T.A.T.'s have no specific outstanding merit in and by themselves, for the sake of brevity only a few illustrative stories will be presented from each record.

---

* The tests were given by Dr. G. M. Gilbert, in his official capacity as Army Prison Psychologist at Nuremberg; he reported on his experiences elsewhere [142]. The author is greatly indebted to Dr. Gilbert for making these T.A.T. records available to him.

*Streicher**

Julius Streicher probably deserved more than any other top-ranking Nazi the clinical diagnosis of psychopathy (in the sense of a person with an undeveloped superego). His newspaper, *Der Stuermer,* was full of perverse, pornographic literature and pictures. He pulled out men's beards and engaged personally in whippings and other expressions of sadism and uninhibited impulses. His intelligence was the lowest of all the Nazis tested at Nuremberg. Below are presented four of his T.A.T. stories.

3BM: Kurt Heinz is the only son of the manufacturer Grundher. Just as the proverb says, "one child is a misfortune," so it turned out to be in this case. All of Kurt Heinz's wishes were fulfilled both by his father and his mother. There was nothing denied him. He was both Mama's and Papa's boy— but an unfortunate child. Although his father told him: "Kurt Heinz, never take the revolver I have in my night table," the spoiled child did what he had secretly decided to do. While the father and mother were going walking, he took the revolver out of the bedroom, and said to his friend Lothar: "Stand against the wall, I'll put an apple on your head and I'll play William Tell. Stand against the wall. You will see, nothing will happen. I'll shoot the apple off your head." Kurt Heinz suddenly realizes the consequences of disobedience. Greatly disturbed and repentant, he waits for the return of his parents with the determination to tell his father: "Father, you were right when you warned me. I have learned enough from this moment to last me a lifetime. Father, I promise you, you will never have any more trouble with me."

4: He is an artist. His model is sitting half naked on the sofa. Suddenly, the door opens and his girl friend surprises him in his studio, having just returned from a vacation and surprised him in this intimate episode in the studio. "Why do you do this to me?" she says to him. "Didn't you promise to think only of me, when I left you? Didn't you say, when you kissed me good-by, that I am the only girl in your heart? Speak, why do you turn away? Can't you look me in the eye any more?" His eyes turned far away and he said: " I did not want to be unfaithful to you; I fought against it—but some demon in me caused me to forget for a moment—only for a moment. We'll talk about this later. Go now. Leave me alone with the girl. I'll talk to her and explain how this came about and why it had to be this way." After the model left, the young painter knocked on the door of the adjoining room and said: "Now we can talk." He looked at her with a penetrating look, as if to say, "We don't have to talk—you understood me when you left." She gave him both hands, and said to him, "My dear friend, I feel that I have not lost you. You are alive in me, and will always be in me. Your love excuses the moment you forgot me." (Now let loose and tell me what you really think.) Of course, she is a mulatto; the artist is a fine type, with bright eyes and blond hair, is surprised by his mulatto lover at the moment that a blonde, blue-eyed Nordic girl came to pose for him. The mulatto makes accusations that he is two-timing her with the blonde. He is silent—if he were to talk he would say, "I loved you only with lust. There is blood in you which prevents me from possessing your soul. Blood attracts blood. My true love belongs to the blonde girl, with whom I wanted to enjoy this hour."

5: The woman opens the door and says to her snoring husband: "Come on, the food is on the table." But the man says: "As long as I am eating, please stay in the kitchen, because when I see that face of yours I lose my appetite."

8BM: There was a duel. The two men had fought over a woman. Two doctors are busy trying to get the bullet out of the wounded one's body. The victor turns away from the operation and looks thoughtfully into the distance. He knows that he was the guilty one and his bullet had apparently killed an innocent man. He is thinking about it—self-accusations about the injustice of fate in this duel. He says with bitterness: "It's a terrible thing that I, the guilty one, am victorious, and the innocent one, who had a right to kill me, had to lose his life."

---

* Reprinted by permission of the *Journal of Projective Techniques.*

Streicher's story to picture 3BM shows the hero engaged in a forbidden aggressive act—wounding his friend with a pistol. Although the hero repents verbally, the story is without regard for the wounded victim, and without actual punishment for the aggressive hero. In this the theme differs markedly from similar stories of neurotics or well-adjusted people, who may express various forms of retribution or remorse; the hero might be punished by the parents, by the police or court, or might be considering committing suicide, and might think of a variety of ways of apologizing and attempting to console the victim.

Story 8BM shows a similar theme: Against the background of an oedipal theme, the hero appears guilty and yet, in the duel, is permitted to kill the innocent man without punishment or consequence except some very superficial verbalization in the form of a monologue. We have found in past experience [30] that the relationship between a crime committed in the stories of the T.A.T. and the punishment meted out to the guilty one by the subject is an excellent measure of the strength of the superego. The more severe the punishment in relation to the crime, the more severe a superego we deal with, and vice versa. In the case of Streicher, we can certainly say that the punishment is much less than to be expected by any civilized mores and thus can conclude that he hardly suffered from a severely controlling superego.

Similarly, in stories 4 and 5 we can observe the aggressive, unkind, primitive attitude toward women and the utter lack of guilt feelings; he uses a glib rationalization for his unfaithfulness by ascribing it to some demon within him—a not infrequent mechanism in young children (particularly postencephalitic ones). His attitude toward women in story 4 leaves room for speculation about his possibly identifying Jews with them—seeing them as an inferior race—and its ultimate relationship to his feeling about his mother, but this is outside our present frame of reference.

Rosenberg

Alfred Rosenberg was the original theoretician, or rather, the mythologist, of the Nazi party, of Aryanism and racialism. He emphasized the cultural values of early Germanism, urged a return to the pre-Christian religious cults, and a love for unadulterated nature. In conflict with other Nazi leaders, he fell into disgrace years before the final debacle. Below are seven of his T.A.T. stories.

3BM: This is a woman who has had little happiness in her life and had no pleasure in her work. She has fallen in love with an adventurer, full of fantastic hopes. She clung to this last hope of her womanly existence and sacrificed all her savings to him. When the lover began to notice that her money was becoming exhausted, he began to desert her until she finally realized one day that he had left her completely. When she realized this, her last hope was lost and she just collapsed. This moment is represented in the picture. It shows a woman who is not beautifully built, with ugly hands and fingernails, crying on the sofa. She is middle-aged and has no further hopes.

7BM: In a popular restaurant, a carefree young man gets acquainted with a man of the world. The old man sees a new victim in the young man. He introduces the young man into a circle of young adventurers and adventuresses. In the course of time the young man drinks and gambles his fortune away so that he finally must tell the old man that he is no longer in a position to continue this wild life.

At this moment the friendship of the old man ceases and he considers whether to leave him for good or to advise him to get money by underhanded means. The picture shows the scheming old man and the disillusioned young man at this moment.

9BM: An adventurous youth gets tired of his home. The peaceful existence in his mother's home has become boring. He decides to go bumming and see life in the raw. On the way home he runs into a vagabond party. A Negro who has run away from his boss and other similar characters are looking for jobs with little work and good pay. The young man joins this trio; they do some work on farms along the way and the young man notices that each time they leave a place they take something with them. But that was not what he left his home for. He finally decides that adventuring doesn't have to be combined with stealing and such things. On a hot afternoon, all four lie down on the grass for a rest. . . . The three tramps fall asleep and our young man now has time to look them over. He decides that they are rather brutal company with whom he could not live very long. He gets up slowly as they lie there snoring and decides to look for better company for his adventurous spirit.

10: A loving mother notices how her daughter has become gradually estranged from her. All her admonitions to be careful in her selection of friends are laughingly rejected. The estrangement between mother and daughter becomes greater and greater. The daughter trusts herself entirely to her lover and ignores all warnings from her mother. One day the daughter realizes that her friend has left town without saying a word. She learns from her friend that he does not intend to return but has left for a foreign country. Betrayed in all her hopes, she returns to her mother. The latter receives her with understanding and love. This is the moment of the expression of motherly love, with an attempt to show that the daughter intends to be more careful in the future.

12M: In a little town there lived an old man who had all kinds of mysterious magnetic and telepathic powers. It was said that he could often, though not always, produce cures by this means. One day he is asked for help by a worried mother. She tells him of her son who has recently become somewhat mentally disturbed. He suffered from attacks of mental depression. Little incidents appear to him like the persecution of bitter enemies and he has become quite sick and desperate. The old man follows the woman to her son. He sits at his bed, listens to the young man's stories, and then strokes him gently on the temples. At the same time he explains all these incidents in a calm manner and in a short time the boy falls asleep. The next day he wakes up refreshed and after some further visits the anxiety actually disappears and he can again associate freely with his friends.

17BM: The acrobat is pulling himself up for his trapeze act. At the other side of the circus he sees an old colleague doing a new stunt. He holds still for a while and watches this new stunt. His attitude is half wonder and half jealousy. He grasps his rope more tightly and says to himself, after watching a while, that he could never perform such a stunt with all his strength. Thus depressed, he climbs down again and refuses to perform any stunts that day.

19. A schoolboy had many friends who were artistically talented. One was musical; another had written some stories. And so the boy was also inspired to take up some form of art. He tried painting. Since he could not succeed in spite of all efforts, he took lessons from a well-known painter, in order to be able to compete with his friends. He pursued this study with great interest and, just as his friends indulged in fantasy on the piano, he wanted to make pictorial compositions. He painted clouds and waves. But when he finished a painting like that and showed it to his friends, he got only a storm of laughter. It was evident that, without talent, even painting was a book with seven seals. That was probably the story of the man who painted this picture.

In story 3BM Rosenberg identifies with a girl who has fallen in love with an adventurer who promptly deserts the girl and leaves her depressed.

Story 10 is a repetition of this theme, with the one addition that the mother is left by a hapless girl who, however, returns to the understanding maternal care after having been left by the faithless man. Story 7BM is only a slight variation of the theme in that a young man comes under the spell of a ruthless adventurer who is about to desert the youngster as soon as he has been fully exploited. In story 9BM the hero leaves what is specified as his *mother's* home, for bad company, with which he soon becomes disenchanted.

In these stories it appears that Rosenberg identifies himself with a girl, or a young man, seduced and exploited and betrayed by a figure which one must strongly suspect of representing Hitler himself. Aside from the feminine-homosexual relationship of Rosenberg to Hitler, which these stories suggest, it becomes apparent that our subject had a strong mother fixation. A tone of depression and hopelessness can be noted throughout all responses. The bad company which the hero gets into in 9BM probably represents the Nazi party, for the plundering and brutality of which our subject expressed belated disdain.

Story 12M again shows the general tone of depression, with awareness of a mental disturbance in the hero, and a wishful ending. This is the only story in which a male figure is seen as benign; it must be pointed out, though, that even here the male is helpful only through the instrumentality and care of the mother. Story 17BM also shows hopelessness and depression in a competition that may well refer to the higher star of Joseph Goebbels. Story 19 speaks of a young man who tries to learn from a well-known painter in vain. It is most likely a repetition of the themes of the earlier stories, Hitler being the house painter and erstwhile illustrator of picture postcards who achieved quite some notoriety. The bitter criticism, at the same time, against the unsuccessful painter we may surmise to be directed against Hitler himself, in a not unusual condensation of the theme and the main identification figures.

Streicher appeared in the T.A.T. as a man of great physical and verbal aggressiveness and with a primitively lustful and despising attitude toward women. At the same time he showed an absence of superego functioning consistent with the diagnosis of psychopathy. Rosenberg appeared markedly depressed. He seems to have had a passive homosexual attachment to Hitler, identifying himself twice as a girl in this relationship. He also reveals a strong fixation on his mother.

Both men were in jail, expecting to be hanged, with all their desires and hopes doomed. Even so, our brief and simple analysis of their T.A.T. records shows widely differing personalities despite the overwhelming contemporary situational factors to which both were equally exposed at the time of the administration of the T.A.T. The stories not published are consistent with this statement except for the fact that some depressive overtones also appear in some stories of Streicher, although mostly as superficial religious speculations.

These T.A.T.'s, then, we believe, throw some light on the much-discussed point of the possible invalidating influence of contemporary situational factors on the overall validity of the T.A.T. While the current mood of depression enters into the stories of both men, there is nevertheless evidence to show that clearly different personalities emerge; the essential character structure revealed is consistent with the historically known facts about these two men, and may be taken to represent the more stable, permanent, and significant features of their makeup. Thus, the influence of contemporary situational factors does not seem to affect the validity of the T.A.T. as a method of clearly demonstrating the essential dynamics of personality. Furthermore, these two T.A.T. records confirm previous work [23] which showed that such current experiences as experimentally provoked anger or depression [20, 31] did not disadvantageously affect the fundamental validity of the personality structure revealed in the T.A.T.

The Problem of Overt and Latent Needs in the T.A.T. *

The interpreter of T.A.T. stories is frequently presented with the necessity of deciding whether or not a need expressed pertains strictly to the fantasy level or might be expressed in reality, for example, the need for aggression or for achievement. The psychologist should have available a maximum of clinical and biographical data about the patient. It must be kept in mind that the clinical situation is not one concerned with testing the validity of the instrument. Problems of the validity of the T.A.T. are dealt with in experiments and must be decided there. If one has sufficient information on the patient, then the T.A.T. stories must be seen as complementary to the behavioral data obtained. For example, if the subject is unduly shy and retiring and the stories are full of aggression and guilt feelings, the dynamic implications are obvious.

On the other hand, there are certain indications from intratest situations which permit us to make assumptions about the manifest or latent needs expressed in the T.A.T. For instance, in stories of achievement it is extremely important to notice whether they follow the *deus ex machina* mechanism or are actually accomplished piece by piece, suggesting much more that they correspond to a behavioral need for achievement.

It was R. N. Sanford who pointed out some important rules concerning the relationship between fantasy needs and behavioral needs. He suggested that there are certain needs that are usually high in fantasy and low in behavior, namely, those needs which are usually prohibited and inhibited by cultural pressure from overt manifestation. These are mainly the needs of acquisition, aggression, autonomy, and sexual activity, the wish to be taken care of, and the need for harm avoidance, the last two suffering more cultural repression in men. On the other hand, some needs may find little manifest expression in fantasy but may find much expression in manifest behavior because of reality demands, such as the need for order, for avoiding social blame, for learning. Again, there is a class of needs which may be high both in fantasy and in behavior, indicating that, while these needs are permitted and encouraged socially, they may yet be sufficiently frustrated to need particular gratification on the fantasy level. To these belong especially the needs for achievement, for friendship, and for dominance.

The study of the defenses as a means of linking the latent and the manifest is of signal importance (see Chapters I and VII). Again, it must be emphasized that the T.A.T. should be used to complement behavioral data; only in specific instances is it necessary or desirable to use the T.A.T. for the prediction of overt behavior. For these cases—personnel studies, appraisal of suicidal tendencies, or likelihood of overt extra-aggression—the internal evidence of drive versus defense must be weighted apart from manifest behavior.

---

* See Chapter I, Section A.

CHAPTER VI

THE STUDY OF CHARACTER
AND DEFENSES
IN THE T.A.T.

THE WORD CHARACTER IN THE ENGLISH LANGUAGE CAN BE roughly equated with moral traits: one speaks of a good character and a bad character, and of "character witnesses" (who testify to one's good moral character). The word *Character* in German is not exactly identical with but roughly corresponds to the American usage of the term personality.

However, in American psychoanalysis, psychiatry, and psychology, the term character neurosis is generally accepted and does not clearly relate either to character or neurosis. A character neurosis is a disorder of which the afflicted is usually unaware, although it is apparent to persons in his environment. It consists of character traits which are ego syntonic for the person having them. They usually cause him no complaint or concern, and are often the object of pride and affection on the part of their owner. However, by directly bringing him into conflict or unpleasant contact with environmental forces, they may produce hardship and discomfort. Probably the most frequently mentioned subspecialty of this disorder is the obsessive-compulsive character neurosis in which a person isolates his emotions very well (too well), is apparently unaffected by what goes on around him or manages to appear well controlled and smooth, and is often thought of as machine-like in efficiency, orderliness, lack of spontaneity and real warmth, etc.

The diagnostic counterpart of a character neurosis is the psychoneurosis, in which the person suffers from subjective symptoms which appear more or less ego alien. It has become axiomatic that there is scarcely a psychoneurosis without some character neurosis, and that there is hardly a character neurosis which does not show some psychoneurotic features under pressure or under some psychoanalytic scrutiny. Nevertheless, the distinction is a very useful one, although it may be only quantitative.

Having neurotic character traits can probably most easily be conceptualized as a syndrome of defenses functioning well enough to avoid direct and open drive conflict at the cost of impoverishment of other ego functions. The impoverished ego functions may be those of spontaneity (e.g., in the case of obsessive rigidity) or those of reality testing (as in the case of extensive rationalizations, such as are involved in systematic political, ethnic, or scientific bias) or in the inability to learn from past experiences, as in the "success neurosis," which we will want to discuss further below.

The justification for this discussion of psychopathology lies in the fact that the T.A.T. may be an excellent means for the analysis of such character problems. Not infrequently a single story may clearly set forth the central theme of a person's life—an often pernicious theme and one of which the one afflicted may be entirely unconscious.

The following story told to picture 1 clearly illustrates such a pernicious theme:

At the age of 9 Karl was intrigued by the wonderful tones of his father's violin. Whenever Karl's father played. Karl would watch and listen and dream. After one such performance Karl's father asked him to put the violin back in its case. Karl was placing the violin on the table when he just sat back and stared at the instrument. It was at this moment that Karl realized that he must be a violinist like his father. Staring at the violin Karl suddenly closed his eyes and dreamed, as most children do, of some years later, when he would stand on a pedestal in the Great Palace of Vienna. It was his premiere as a soloist with a great orchestra. He was shaking, nervous, and afraid, yet intent. Intent on fulfilling his ambition. The noise of the impatient audience, the shouting of the stage hands in the adjustment of props and lights, the tuning of the various instruments, all helped to create his nervousness. Then, without further delay, the curtain opened, the audience became dead silent, the conductor knocked his baton repeatedly on the stand, raised it a final time, and on the drop Karl began to play. A sweet Viennese waltz, combined with the pleasures of his heart and soul, poured from his violin. The music ended, the audience rose to its feet and acclaimed Karl as a great interpreter of his country's music. The music of his father. Taking the customary bow in recognition of his appreciation, Karl suddenly fell from the pedestal. He never awoke from his dream, you see, Karl was dead. The shock of visualizing such a success was too much for his ailing heart to bear. Thus, the music world lost a promising musician because of a violin, an ambition, and a dream.

Freud coined a term, "Schicksalsneurose," which can only be poorly translated as "fate neurosis." It is sometimes spoken of as a success neurosis, with a more limited meaning. I prefer to call it the "Schlemiehl syndrome"; a person who has this is a person for whom everything seems to go wrong, through no apparent fault of his own—fate always seems to play him a dirty trick. The term success neurosis is more properly reserved for those cases where the attainment of success produces anxiety, depression, and other symptoms. Both disorders have in common a deep masochistic disturbance.

The story quoted above can probably be easily analyzed for its main features by anyone conversant with psychopathology: Karl tries to fiddle as well as his father. When he permits himself this attainment, even in a dream, he dies for it. We must view this as a theme of competition with the father (probably on an oedipal level) and the punishment commensurate with the crime of wanting to replace the father.

This story, unfortunately, was brought to me by one of my students, so that the clinical information was limited to start with, and I have been unable to follow it up as I would have liked. The main contention of my blind diagnosis was corroborated, however, that this person did suffer from repeated uncanny failures in his life. I would venture to guess that the main content of this person's character neurosis is almost entirely accounted for in this story.

A case where I can be on more certain ground is one of a former patient of mine. The following story was told to picture 11:

> Two men have come to kill the dragon. When the dragon appears, spouting flames that light up the area, one man flees in terror, while the other, equally afraid, hides from the terrifying animal by turning away from it but is unable to flee.
>
> This dragon has been the scourge of a country, devastating the land by scorching it with his breath whenever it walks abroad. Two strangers who visit this country are told of this danger to the community and volunteer to kill this menace.
>
> The man who has remained behind finds soon that the heat and light disappear and turning around comes face to face with the dragon, who no longer is terrifying. The dragon speaks of his loneliness because all run from him. He wants to be able to have contact with people but realizes they are frightened of him. He is very happy that this man has stayed and asks what it is that makes everyone run from him. The man tells him of the destruction the dragon leaves behind him. The dragon then understands this but also knows that his breathing flame is a part of him that he does not know how to change. He promises that he will not in the future wander around as he has done but remain hidden in the rocks where he will not do injury, and the man returns to the village to tell the people what happened. The people run him out. They are divided between those who do not believe him and those who believe him but blame him for not having taken this opportunity to kill the dragon, since they are sure the dragon will not keep his promise. However, the dragon does, and as the community again is able in time to build up its wealth, the people make pilgrimages to the mountain to leave thank-you offerings to the dragon.

It is most regrettable that Alfred Adler had to renounce all of psychoanalysis in order to feel that his contribution was secure; it is equally regrettable that psychoanalysis has not adopted some of his terms, e.g., "style of life." I believe that many character neuroses can most easily be described in terms of a defensive style of life, geared to neurotic goals, and blindly repetitive. For instance, in the case of the story quoted above, the patient clearly identified with the would-be monster who really wanted to be loved and appreciated. The patient felt monstrous inside because of his hostility. Orally deprived, the patient had often described himself as feeling like a puppy—inappropriately overfriendly to strangers, yet at the same time holding himself aloof from any real emotional involvement. He often antagonized people deeply without being aware of it and left himself open to being hurt by his expectation of being loved by everyone. In the story he is not only the monster but also the victim (who wants to be) befriended by the monster. Such a style of life finally led to enough realistic repercussions to bring him into treatment.

A different problem is depicted in the stories of a brilliant young scientist who suffered conflicts between his allegiance to the ways of his parents and new ideas (superimposed on earlier conflicts). This is his story to picture 1:

> A youngster has been called in from play by his mother to practice his violin lessons. He is annoyed and sulking over it. He is thinking of all the activities he would prefer to be carrying on. But he is a talented and sensitive child. Soon he will get over his annoyance and will take the instrument into his hands and practice. He will begin to enjoy his lessons.

This story shows a conflict between autonomy and compliance which is resolved in favor of compliance. The most significant aspect of this story is that the compliance becomes ego syntonic: he will begin to enjoy his lessons.

The other stories show that this process of psychoneurosis into character neurosis was not quite successful. Following is his story to picture 3BM:

The peasant boy has just been told by his father that he may not go to the big city to study sculpting and carving. He is needed to help on the farm. The family is poor and cannot pay for hired labor. The boy has gone into his own room and, unable to control himself, leans against his cot and weeps. His carving knife lies on the floor. But in time he will forget and accommodate himself to the limited ways and aspirations of the peasant. The weight of frustration will make him somewhat irritable, impatient, dulled, unaspiring, and uninspiring.

To picture 9BM he tells the following:

Four hoboes relaxing. They have just finished their improvised lunch, prior to which they had relaxed, prior to which they had breakfasted, prior to which they relaxed. On completing their noon nap, they will be on their way, planning the evening meal so that they may again relax. They have accepted tedium as their lot and made peace with it. Tedium is the lot of so many of us; we differ only in that we have not reconciled to it. Within us weighs heavily the hope and the longing for end and purpose.

And to picture 14:

He has spent several pained and fruitless hours twisting and turning in his bed, dissecting in his mind the two choices before him. Shall he hold onto the security of his present job, whose future is uncertain, or leap into the uncertainty of the present in the hope of achieving a greater certainty in the future? How difficult he finds it to renounce! He leaves his bed, goes to the window, and looks out among the pinpoints that dot, and the houses silhouetted against, the gradually lightening sky—as though they would offer him some aid in resolving his dilemma. He will return to his bed, his choice unmade, and will find a solution in his dreams.

These stories show the unresolved conflict, the intrapsychic awareness of the deadening process of repression and emotional isolation: tedium, dulled, uninspiring. Only irritability and impatience remain as a semblance of emotion, in what otherwise could best be characterized by Myerson's term, anhedonia. This anhedonia, this absence of any pleasurable sensation, is frequently the outcome of gross emotional impoverishment under the impact of obsessive-compulsive defenses, somewhat equivalent to a mild depression. The process as depicted in the T.A.T. is incomplete. Had it gone on to its completion, the person would probably become somewhat peculiar, mild-mannered, gentle, and living up to one-tenth of his potential.

This study of the character really involves a study of the defenses. The study of the defenses is so intimately connected with the problems of personality that this topic had to be discussed extensively in the elaboration of the ego psychology of projective techniques and again in discussing the relationship of the overt to the latent. If this subject matter is once more taken up here for its own sake, it is because a strictly clinical discussion should be presented in its own context: this aspect of apperception is relatively the newest, least is known about it, and it is probably the most important.

According to Fenichel [117], ego defenses may be divided into successful defenses, which bring about a cessation of that which is warded off, and unsuccessful defenses, which necessitate a repetition or perpetuation of the warding-off process to prevent the eruption of the warded-off impulses. Sublimation is a successful, not a pathogenic defense. It is not characterized by a specific mechanism and is thus not very easily discernible in T.A.T. stories.

Denial is an exceedingly common defense. The tendency to deny painful sensations and facts is as old as the feeling of pain itself. The ability to deny unpleasant parts of reality is frequent both in children and in adults, and we find many instances of this defense mechanism in T.A.T. stories.

One patient, in response to picture 2, described the woman ordinarily seen as pregnant as "slim, thin, and well-proportioned." His mother's pregnancy with a younger sibling had played an important role, and pregnancy fantasies were at the root of his anxieties. Here he simply denies the existence of pregnancy.

Denial of one's own aggressive impulses is another very frequent defense. The following story was told to picture 18GF by a woman who had attempted to kill her children:

> Looks like a mother holding a child at the foot of a staircase; might have been that the child fell down the staircase and the mother picked him up to see if he's hurt; looking him over very anxiously but I don't think he's hurt. The mother will be much relieved. (?) Tripped.

As was mentioned in an earlier chapter, this picture is usually seen as a woman attempting to choke another. The subject who told the above story identified with the older (maternal) figure but felt compelled to deny any element of aggression in the situation.

Projection is one of the most archaic of the defense mechanisms. It belongs to that early stage in which everything pleasurable is experienced as belonging to the ego, while everything painful is experienced as being nonego.

In one sense, of course, the T.A.T. deals entirely with projection, and some degree of this particular defense mechanism is to be seen in every T.A.T. story. However, in certain stories this element is particularly strong. When figures are introduced which are not in the pictures, this element can be said to be at work. Or in a story such as the following (to picture 13MF) and previously told in Chapter IV. The dynamic content (apparently killing the girl and directing the aggression against her) suggests the use of projection by this subject. (The fact that he seems partially aware of his own guilt feeling does not obviate the use of projection.) It is as if he might say, "True, it's my fault, but it's hers even more!":

> This is a young man who is going to the local university . . . a student. . . . He is very moralistic . . . that is, very virtuous . . . having a highly developed sense of what is right and what is wrong. He is also very religious. . . . He has been brought up very strictly and believes that one of the greatest sins that man can commit is to have sexual intercourse with a woman out of wedlock. . . . One evening, at a party, for some unknown reason, having taken too many drinks and feeling slightly lightheaded, he became very intimate with one of the girls present. He . . . his animal instincts came to the fore and he abandoned all his ideas of virtue, etc. He took this woman up to his room and went to bed with her. The next morning, after becoming sober and having regained his virtuous sense . . . or whatever you want to call it . . . he looked over and saw this woman beside him in utter nakedness. He was filled with anger, and wild . . . let's see (murmurs to himself) . . . and bitter passion at what he had done. A profound hatred swelled up in his chest for this woman that lay next to him. He ordered . . . she by this time had become awake . . . and he ordered her to leave his room. . . . She, not understanding what had brought this attitude of his about, believed that he was joking, and refused to leave in a jocular manner. . . . This man could think of nothing but to clear himself of this sin he had committed . . . cleanse himself of this sin. . . . And as this woman lay there laughing, and being overcome with his guilt, he seized her by the throat and strangled her. . . . Rising from the bed, and putting on his clothes, he became . . . he realized his predicament. He not only had committed a sin . . . a moral sin . . . but he had committed a greater sin by taking her life. . . . He

gazed down as she lay there at her statuesque stillness and was filled with remorse. Remembering a few days earlier . . . that a few days earlier he had bought a bottle of iodine, and which was now in the cabinet of the washroom, he went there and gulped down its contents (laughs) and consequently died. That was the end of that. . . . I just said that he strangled her because she was laying in bed next to him, and that was the easiest thing he could have done, by reaching over and grasping her neck.

Repression is a relatively less archaic mechanism, a derivative of denial. It consists of an unconsciously purposeful forgetting or not becoming aware of internal impulses or external events which usually represent possible temptations or punishments for, or mere allusions to, objectionable instinctual demands. The purposeful exclusion of these facts from consciousness is intended to hinder their real effects as well as the pain on becoming aware of them. Sometimes certain facts are remembered as such, but their connections, their significance, their emotional value, are repressed.

There are many neurotic attitudes that are obvious attempts to deny or to repress some impulse, or to defend the person against some instinctual danger. They are cramped and rigid attitudes, hindering the expression of contrary impulses, which sometimes nevertheless break through in various ways. The original opposite attitudes still exist in the unconscious; these secondary, conscious attitudes are called *reaction formations.* assuming opposite position

Both the conscious and the original, unconscious attitude are apparent in the following story told to picture 17BM:

> The man shown here is a circus performer and has been one for many years. His ambition has always been to be a solo performer instead of part of a trapeze trio. Until now he has not had the opportunity. In tonight's performance he will save a fellow trouper from a serious accident and as a reward for his bravery will be given the chance to do his act alone.

In this story, the act of bravery, saving the fellow trouper, is the reaction formation, or disguise, for the unconscious aggressive wishes against this person. It is somewhat reminiscent of the overprotective mother who constantly fusses over her child to hide from herself her basic (unconscious) lack of acceptance of the child.

Undoing is related to reaction formation. In reaction formation, an attitude is taken that contradicts the original one; in undoing, one more step is taken. Something positive is done which, actually or magically, is the opposite of something which, again actually or in imagination, has been done before. This mechanism can be most clearly observed in certain compulsive symptoms that are made up of two actions, the second of which is a direct reversal of the first. For example, a patient must first turn on the gas jet and then turn it off again.

Obsessive elaboration is not uncommon in the stories of obsessive-compulsive patients. The following story was told to picture 13MF*:

> A man and woman who may be in a bedroom or living room with a cot. She may have been ill and had been put to bed. The man may have seen to her wants or he may be a doctor who had been with her for a long time, especially through the night, and is now very tired. The woman may be sleeping or

---

* This story has already been quoted in Chapter IV, but I am repeating it here because it is such an excellent example of obsessive elaboration.

resting or may have died, and the man, her husband or doctor, has just gone through a long siege or, if the woman is his wife who died, he shows sorrow, or if she is just sick he shows fear and is tired. It may be that homicide has been committed and the man shows remorse and realization of the gravity of his act. Or there may have been cohabitation, the woman undraped in bed, the man having dressed. Also, a husband getting up early in the morning to go to work, not quite awake, while his wife is still asleep.

In this case we have at least four stories showing a progression from a relatively innocuous apperception to breakthrough of plainly homicidal thoughts. whether cohabitation is a further progression to an even worse crime in the mind of the subject or whether it constitutes a renewed vigor of defenses which culminates in the utterly innocuous domestic scene could not be ascertained.

Another mechanism of defense prevalent in compulsion neuroses is *isolation*. Here the patient has not forgotten his pathogenic traumata, but has lost trace of their connections and their emotional significance. The most important special case of this defense mechanism is the isolation of an idea from the emotional cathexis that originally was connected with it. The patient remains calm while discussing the most exciting events.

The following story, told to picture 2, is an excellent example of isolation:

> Very interesting picture. Is it a painting of some sort? The first idea that comes into my head is terribly Hollywoodish. (*The idea, not the picture.*) A man and a wife who work a farm and she looks as if her parents and forebears have also worked a farm. The girl in the foreground is the daughter who doesn't want to work the farm but who wants to lead a more intellectual life away from the burdens of the farm. The parents resent this. They seem to ignore her. She looks as if she's leaving them after an unsuccessful argument or discussion as to whether she's doing the right thing or not. I have no doubt she will leave them. The part where she's standing in the picture seems very rocky—whereas where the parents are standing seems very well worn. So we might say that her path may be uphill and that may be causing some of her parents' dissent. Well, the parents will continue in their way of life and the girl will continue on her rocky road and the way it always happens in Hollywood is that the girl always makes something of herself. (*How does it happen outside of Hollywood?*) It can be either way, but that's because I really don't care.

The last few words of the story—"I really don't care"—is the credo of the isolater. By this defense mechanism he has managed to detach himself from all his feelings. This detachment is also inherent in his opening words: "Very interesting picture." The whole story has a cold, detached, intellectualized feeling tone common to stories of subjects who use the mechanism of isolation. Isolation and overintellectualization usually go together. In fact, the normal prototype of isolation is the process of rational, logical thinking, which actually consists of the elimination of affective associations in the interest of objectivity. Compulsion neurotics, in their isolation activities, behave like caricatures of normal thinkers.

Whenever a person meets frustration, there is a tendency for him to long for earlier periods in his life when his experiences were more pleasant, and for earlier types of satisfaction that were more complete. The intensity of this tendency increases with two factors which are closely interrelated: the degree of hesitancy with which the individual accepts newer modes of satisfaction, and the degree to which he is fixated to earlier types. However, very intense and sudden disappointments and dangers may provoke *regressions* even in individuals without strong fixations.

Regression is much more common in children than in adults who are not psychotic, since the precondition for the use of regression as a mechanism of defense is a weakness of the ego organization. The following story was told by a 9 year old boy in response to story 3 of the C.A.T.:

Well, this lion is troubled by mice. He's sitting there and doesn't know what to do about the mice. He's tried everything, so he calls the exterminator and the exterminator says, "The only thing to do is to blow the mice out," but the lion says, I've tried that and lost three houses." "Why not make traps?" "But the mice have certain things that disconnect the traps and they always get the cheese." "Why not try poison, then?" "But that's impossible because the mice know it's poison and they'll never come out." Finally the lion decides he will move to Florida, but when he gets there he sees now . . . he's being troubled by worms coming through the floor. So finally he says, "I'll go back and live in the jungle where I belong."

This little boy was troubled by his younger sibling. First he tried aggression, then aggression with the help of someone else (the therapist), then withdrawal (moving to Florida), and when that didn't help either, he regressed to infantile habits (the jungle).

The mechanism of *displacement* is employed when the anxiety aroused by a certain situation, person, etc., is displaced onto something else. There can be displacement of affect as well as displacement of object. In T.A.T. stories, this defense reveals itself by the use of far-distant times and places and by ascribing problems to people other than the hero, as well as by changing the nature of the anxiety.

One subject, of Jewish-American stock, began his story to picture 4 as follows:

This seems to be taking place in some isolated place. Maybe a South Sea Island.

The same subject started his story to picture 2 by saying:

This girl, about 19 years old, would probably be named Olga, of Ukranian parentage and stock.

Coping

A concept broader than the one of defense is the concept of coping. It offers a useful way of viewing the evaluation of the T.A.T. (and C.A.T. and S.A.T.). Being asked to tell stories to the pictures is to perform a task. How does the subject go about coping with this task? How does she respond behaviorally? Is she confused, frightened, negativistic? Does the story constitute a good coping effort? Does the subject achieve closure? Are there different ways in which closure is being achieved? Is the first attempt at a story the most successful and the following two increasingly disorganized by uncontrolled drives? Or is it the other way around and the stories show improved coping effort suggesting a potential of dealing with problems which were found overtaxing initially. In a broad sense all of human behavior including dreams, neurotic and psychotic symptoms and "normal" behavior, can be usefully viewed as attempts at coping.

CHAPTER VII

THE USE OF THE T.A.T. IN PSYCHOTHERAPY

A. Special Therapeutic Uses of the T.A.T.*

TEST RESPONSES ARE FORMS OF BEHAVIOR OF THE PATIENT, LIKE any other forms of behavior except that the responses are made to standard stimuli and thus permit controlled comparisons from one person to another. Furthermore, the content which appears in psychological tests may demonstrate fantasies and psychodynamics which even a skilled psychoanalyst will not anticipate or suspect after many months of psychoanalysis. Many years ago a training analyst permitted me to administer the T.A.T. to a patient of his who volunteered to participate in the investigation. The analyst agreed that the T.A.T. pictures brought out important features that had not become clear during almost a year of psychoanalysis. Ethel Tumen Kardiner in an unpublished study [189] was able to demonstrate experimentally with the cooperation of a number of psychoanalysts and their patients that the T.A.T. could successfully illustrate the psychodynamics which had become clear only after prolonged analysis. From the standpoint of planning treatment it is useful to obtain as much advance information as possible.

The T.A.T. is of particular value as a vehicle of the psychotherapeutic process itself, especially in cases where therapy must of necessity be short term, in emergency situations (self-endangering or extremely crippling depressions, or acute anxiety), or in social agency settings, clinics, etc.

The type of patient encountered in any of the above situations is frequently quite naive about psychotherapy and entirely unaccustomed to the thought processes involved in it. He considers his complaints to be organic or environmentally caused, since he is quite unused to any degree of objective introspection.

In such cases, one very important use of the T.A.T. is *to help the patient to gain some "distance" from himself* and to establish the *psychotherapeutic attitude*. An adolescent may come, for instance, completely isolating all feeling, intellectualiz-

---

* The T.A.T. may be especially useful in Emergency Psychotherapy and Brief Psychotherapy (see additional references; Bellak and Small, 1965).

ing, and—in essence—saying that he is coming only because his mother wants him to. After he has produced T.A.T. stories, I ask him what he thinks of them. He often replies that these are stories about the pictures and have nothing to do with him. My first step, then, is to tell him that I have heard very many stories about these pictures and that his responses differ from others I have heard before. To illustrate this to him I proceed to give him a number of themes, quite different from his own, to several pictures. This fact of being different often makes a strong impression; the entering wedge has been supplied. *Part of his behavior has become ego alien instead of ego syntonic.*

We can now proceed to wonder *why* his stories are the way they are rather than the way some other people's stories are. I may choose some very contrasting stories to tell him. For instance, our emotionally isolating adolescent may have told stories which actually show a good deal of despair and anxiety. I may read someone else's less disturbed stories (if this seems necessary) and ask him what the difference is between his stories and the others. Now *insight* may slowly emerge, and he may say that his stories show some unhappiness. I may then ask why that should be. If necessary, I may point out the specific circumstances of unhappiness in the stories—namely, loneliness, fear of failure and incompetence, etc. I prefer to hand the patient several of his own stories and ask him to play psychiatrist and tell me what they seem to have in common. This way the patient may actually learn to look for common denominators in his behavior, and the process of *working through* may be started. By asking the patient to tell me whatever else the stories bring to his mind, many a naive and even unintelligent patient may be introduced to the concept of *free association.*

Often a central problem can be approached in this way, which might otherwise be almost unapproachable except in very long-term therapy. For instance, an ex-tuberculous patient was referred to me in a social agency. He was well recovered but still retained considerable secondary gains from his past illness. It was extremely urgent that he help to support his family again. He had been in the theater, and many of his difficulties stemmed from the fact that he still wanted to pursue a theatrical career rather than a presumably steadier and more attainable means of livelihood. He was to some degree aware of the unreasonableness of his attitude, but felt unable to react differently—his heart was only in the theater.

Among a number of instructive T.A.T. stories, the one to 17BM proved most useful for the occupational problem. The patient's story was as follows (the italics in this and other stories are my own):

A circus performer on a rope. There is a security on the rope that indicates that he has had much practice. He does not seem young though his physical appearance is that of a young man. There is a kind of satisfaction on his face which makes me believe that his work is his greatest satisfaction. He knows he's good at this, if nothing else. *He enjoys doing this spectacular work, for at other times he is lonely and passes unnoticed. To hear the audience marvel at his dexterity is compensation for his personal unhappiness.*

In associating to this story, the patient related that he had always liked to be admired. As a boy he felt very much overshadowed by a somewhat older and very brilliant sister. Slowly it emerged that he was a very good singer. His family came to marvel at his voice, and he was the center of the party when he sang. He finally felt less in the shadow. Then one day his voice started changing and his claim to admiration and love vanished, which caused him to be most depressed. Not long thereafter he had occasion to participate in a school theatrical production, and thus the transition was made to a theatrical ambition and new approbation.

Now we could discuss things. Here we had the dynamic core of his obsession with a profession he could not afford to follow. We could discuss his feelings of loneliness and inferiority, which he felt were assuaged when he was in the limelight. Naturally, no miracles were achieved; the T.A.T. is not a magic wand. All the principles of psychotherapy must be observed. But this story served as a starting point for two or three sessions which helped the man change enough to find gainful employment and maintain it. For the two succeeding years he was a steady supporter of his family for the first time in his life.

All test data may be useful when tied in to interpretations by the therapist. When one patient discussed the difficulties with which his wife threatened him, it facilitated matters greatly to show him his Figure Drawing Test, in which he had depicted the figure of the woman as a powerful Amazon while the male figure was much smaller and weaker. On seeing the pictures, he was struck by the fact that he tended to see women as stronger and himself as weak.

In another case a Rorschach response was useful after many months of psychotherapy, when the patient described her feelings of compliance: she had to do everything to please others; she lacked a feeling of identity, always fitting herself into a role consonant with what the environment demanded of her. A "dressmaker's dummy," who will wear any clothes and comply inanimately, was the Rorschach response describing her feelings.

In a patient who uses isolation as a main defense and who maintains an attitude of false unconcern, one may find it expedient to point out the recurrence of a hopeless, depressed tone and content in the stories.

For instance, the 16 year old male whose story 2 was mentioned in Chapter VI also told the following stories.

3BM:

Looks like a female in *great despair.* just had a great tragedy befall her. Gadget at her knee seems to be a collapsed knife or keys or something like that. The *tragedy* could be anything. Dead parents, or husband—running away—or a horrible misfortune like that. She does seem to be a little deformed. (*Author's note:* Self-image—deformed, crippled, etc.) Can't put my finger on it but—could be a deformed person pondering and weeping over her misfortune. I see less in this picture than in most of the others.

This is followed by a story to picture 13B:

Some perspective there. Looks as though the picture were taken from the top of the door. Seems to be a rather recent picture, of the past 75 years. Modern dungarees. He wouldn't be a pioneer. House is put together with nails; a kind of Tobacco Road. Boy is just staring at this photographer, who is a very unusual, a very new thing in his life. Seems to be looking at him with a little wonder, apprehension, tiny bit of fear. At first hand, I would have said he was a Kentucky mountaineer but the fact that the cabin seems to be in a dusty, sandy place—so—dust bowl, Oklahoma. The house is handmade, very old. The interior of the house seems to be *very dark and that would be the most revealing thing about him. And that's rather obscure.* The family is *very, very poor.* He is *jealous, envious* of the big owners and bankers that come around to check up on the sharecroppers' lives. Probably sees very few people like himself. Works with his father—will hold the same position as his father *without ever having a chance to have enjoyed himself.* Multitude of brothers and sisters just like himself, though. Doesn't look like he's too happy a child in the picture. Seems to stem from his *bewilderment* and his environment, which isn't a very enjoyable picture. The *lack of anything about him* seems to show that he's very alone or very . . . (pause) . . . empty.

In story 2, the hero will have an uphill fight on a rocky path. In 3BM the hero is in great despair and deformed, and in 13B the hero belongs to the suppressed and underprivileged. Yet this boy presented a manifestly bland personal picture, denying any need for help and psychotherapy (for which his parents had referred him). The stories, of course, offer a *wealth of other material* which, in due course, one may come to utilize as well (see Chapter VI).

In the case of another patient who was referred for scholastic difficulties in college, the opening story immediately reveals how he compares himself unfavorably with his successful parents, on the one hand, and the conflict between immediate enjoyment and investment in work for the future on the other hand. To picture 1 the patient said:

George's *family is talented.* His father and mother both have played before royalty. George is now eight years old and has been taking violin lessons for nearly a year. Today, after George has completed his practice session, he is reflecting on the months he has spent with his music *while his friends have been enjoying themselves* with less intellectual pursuits. *He is wondering if he will benefit enough* from the coming years of study to make it worthwhile. He has been told that he is very talented and, after all, his environment is ideal. Perhaps he will become a virtuoso comparable to his idols. His young mind unable to look any further into the future, George puts his violin in its case with reverence. He will now go out in the sunshine and *tomorrow* he will practice with renewed vigor.

Another patient, a 52 year old man, gave the following story to picture 1:

The violin belongs to the boy's father. Now his father is dead. The boy is thinking of the times his father invited some other musicians in for a home concert as he often did. His mother played the piano and all the friends brought their instruments—a flute, a cello, an oboe, a French horn. They would play far into the night—but the boy would listen from his bed and seek to catch the clear strains of the violin played by his father. One night the party was most gay—they played waltz tunes from Vienna and Hungarian dances. The boy heard the laughter and gay talk between pieces. Then they played the most beautiful waltz of all—the Blue Danube. In the final beautiful movement as the waltz neared its climax the boy heard the string on his father's violin break. Then all the playing stopped and the boy heard no sound—then a wail, low and prolonged, from his mother. He rushed down from his room. When the string broke, his father's heart had stopped. He was dead.

This story probably reflects a biographical detail of listening to "the parents making music"—presumably overhearing an intercourse scene. The boy feels isolated and competitive. Intercourse is probably conceived of as dangerous on the one hand, and on the other hand the father's death represents a wish and leaves the boy the inheritor of the violin. The T.A.T. was given some time after psychotherapy had started and probably reflects some transference phenomena. I refer particularly to the Viennese music, which is probably a reference to the therapist.

These examples may illustrate the direct use of one psychological test, the T.A.T., as a vehicle for communication from patient to doctor as a basis for insight for both, and as providing a pattern for interpretation and working through, providing economy in all these processes in cases where economy is indicated, for external or internal reasons.

Another therapeutic function of the T.A.T. has been noted by Holzberg [170]. He has conceptualized resistance to change in psychotherapy in terms of the patient's anxiety about adaptive regression. Holzberg's point is that projective techniques, such as the T.A.T., can play a significant role in overcoming such anxiety so that therapy can commence or continue. He regards the projective test experience as providing a chance to experience adaptive regression; thus, such test experience can overcome resistance to treatment by permitting the patient to practice regression under controlled conditions. Resistance in two patients noted by Holzberg was diminished in this way.

B. The Systematic Use of the T.A.T. in Relation to the Basic Steps of Psychotherapy

In psychoanalytic therapy one can speak *schematically* of four basic processes (which often overlap and coexist):

Communication. The patient communicates with the analyst by means of free associations.* Through these the analyst learns of the patient's behavior in a great many situations and finds a number of common denominators in the patient's behavioral patterns. The T.A.T. responses may serve as such communication.

Interpretation. When the analyst has become acquainted with a number of life situations of the patient, he may perceive a certain common denominator in the behavioral patterns and point it out to the patient in such doses as seem to him to be suitable at various times.

1. Horizontal study: The therapist may find a common denominator among the behavior patterns and interpersonal relationships of the patient's contemporary life situation, and we may speak of this process as a horizontal study of patterns.

2. Vertical study: Sooner or later it will be possible to trace, by free association or otherwise, the historical development of these patterns in the life history of the patient, leading to a more or less definitely defined early set. We may speak of this part of the therapeutic investigation as the vertical study of life patterns. Frequently it is necessary to point out both the vertical and the horizontal common denominators of the patient's current behavior in order to lead to a solution of his problems.

3. Relationship to the therapist: As a special case of current life situations of the horizontal pattern in its relation to the earlier historical ones, the relationship to the therapist may be discussed specifically in what is known in psychoanalysis as *analysis of the transference situation.*

Interpretation, then, means that the therapist points out to the patient the common denominators in his behavioral patterns, horizontally, vertically, and in special relation to the therapist. In all three instances the therapist finds that the patient suffers from apperceptive distortions of life situations. Interpretation

---

* This is not the only means of communication. The patient imparts information also by posture, facial expression, etc.

really consists in pointing out the *common denominators of the apperceptive distortions* and, in certain cases, in demonstrating the relationships of earlier life situations to percept memories in which these apperceptive distortions arose. The process involves the analysis of the present complex apperception into the parts that came to constitute the whole.

A brief example may be helpful here. The patient may have come with the presenting problem of vague anxiety attacks. It may develop that these apparently puzzling attacks occur typically when the patient is in contact with a strict authority figure who produces hostility in him. After this horizontal pattern has appeared, at one time or another a vertical one may also be found: the patient had a more or less specific relationship to his father (as becomes clear in the T.A.T., for instance) who originally produced these feelings of hostility in him with resulting anxiety. Further study will reveal a whole history of relationships to similar authorities prior to the current situation, and a similar attitude will be expressed to the therapist.

Insight. Insight development is the next step in the therapeutic process. The term insight is abused almost as much as the term psychotherapy itself. Frequently the term insight is used to mean simply that the patient is aware of being mentally ill. This is most often used in the discussion of psychotics, usually implying no more than just that. In the context of dynamic psychotherapy, insight must have this specific meaning—*the patient's ability to see the relationship between a given symptom and the previously unconscious apperceptive distortions underlying his symptoms.* More strictly speaking, we define insight as the patient's apperception (i.e., meaningful perception) of the common denominators of his behavior as pointed out by the therapist. The problem is seen in a new light and handled differently from then on.

This process may be analyzed into two parts:

1. Intellectual insight: The patient can see the interrelationship of his different horizontal and vertical patterns; he can see them as special cases of a general class or, in Gestalt language, he learns by insight and experiences closure. The pieces of isolated happenings become a memory whole, and a repatterning and relearning takes place.

2. Emotional insight: The patient reproduces the affect pertaining to the intellectual insight—relief, anxiety, guilt, happiness, etc.

If the intellectual insight alone is produced, limited or no therapeutic result may be achieved because emotional repatterning is an essential of the therapeutic process, be it conceived of as a regular libidinal-metapsychologic process or as a learning process in conventional academic psychological terms. The affect must be part of the Gestalt of a therapeutic experience.

Working through. The next step in therapy consists of the working through of the new insight:

1. Intellectually: The patient now applies what he has learned to pertain to a few situations, as pointed out by the therapist, to a number of other situations to which the same general denominator applies. If it has been pointed out that a pattern of apperceptive distortion exists as applying to the patient's present employer, his teacher, his analyst, and his father, he may now remember situations

involving an uncle, a superior officer in the army, an elder brother, or others as having been reacted to similarly.

2. Therapeutically (emotionally): In the therapeutic situation, the patient must experience the above with affect, and also reproduce the affect in relation to the therapist, and work them through.

3. Behaviorally: Outside the therapeutic session the patient goes on meeting the situations discussed and new ones similar to the ones scrutinized. While in real situations, he is aware of the insight recently gained. Under the influence of his new "mental set" he reacts differently to a progressive extent to these situations in the corrective direction suggested by the analysis of the situation. New problems arising are reanalyzed and the problem is worked out by persistent adjustment and readjustment between mental set and reality.

While the process of insight and the purely intellectual aspects of working through are best understood in terms of perceptual learning theory, the therapeutic and behavioral working through are actually best seen as a matter of conditioning and reconditioning, as well as a problem in which trial and error and reward and punishment lead to the final best result.

The T.A.T. is an excellent, tailor-made way of studying both the horizontal and the genetic patterns which are revealed, particularly by the more psychologically naive subjects, without their awareness of the implications of their stories. Valuable insight and cooperation are frequently gained when the patient discovers, to his surprise, that he has unwittingly reproduced some of his most important problems.

Combs [94] has demonstrated that there is an abundance of autobiographical material revealed in the T.A.T. which should enable the therapist to study some of the vertical patterns in the subject's behavior.

For the clinical use of the T.A.T. in psychiatric practice, one may either take down the stories oneself or use recording devices. In this situation we have found it advantageous to have the patient *write down the stories himself,* either in the office or at home. It will quickly appear to any therapist at all conversant with dynamics that the T.A.T. practically always mirrors some or all of the basic problems, conflicts, and sentiments of the subject. Thus it can be used not only by the therapist for his own insight into the patient's dynamics, but can also be given to the patient for him to work on, in the same way as any of his other productions.

To summarize:

1. The T.A.T. can be used as a vehicle with any kind of psychotherapy. It is especially indicated in brief psychoanalytic psychotherapy because it reveals the situations which need discussing; one may select those pictures which are most apt to bring out the problems of a specific patient where time is of the essence for external or internal reasons.

2. The T.A.T. may be a useful vehicle when the patient has a special difficulty in free associating or in communicating generally because of lack of familiarity with the psychotherapeutic process, inhibitions, specific resistances (when protracted resistance is not analytically useful), etc.

When using the T.A.T. in the actual psychotherapeutic session, it is well to wait for a time at the beginning of the session before presenting the story or stories to the patient. During that time one may find out if there is anything more acute and specific the patient may have on his mind which is more urgent than the material in the T.A.T. If there is nothing acute, and particularly if the patient has difficulty in starting or quickly runs out of material, it is time to take up the T.A.T.

It is expedient to stop the interpretations of the T.A.T. material some time before the end of the session, so that the patient may still have an opportunity either to bring up more distantly related material that was evoked, or to discuss current problems which he did not remember before.

The technique of analyzing and interpreting the stories for the patient varies. There should be two copies of each story. The method of choice in handling each story is to let the patient read it and elaborate on it if he can, then to discuss it and free associate to it. After all associations have been made, the therapist steps in and discusses all the material again, with analysis and interpretations as indicated.

One or several stories may thus be taken up during each session, and therapy proceeds according to patterns revealed in the T.A.T. stories.

Another method is to use the stories only when the patient has difficulty in free associating or when one or several of the stories contain the same pattern currently revealed by the patient's associations. Again, the patient should be allowed to read a copy of his productions. Often he will see the pattern of his own accord and be able to interpret the story and his revelations, thus acquiring insight in the most desirable manner. If he fails to do this, the therapist can try to help him do so or analyze and interpret the material for him.

In handling the T.A.T. stories, the therapist should consider the material as he would a *dream* or *fantasy* and analyze it on that basis. The story and its analysis may be presented to the patient as though it were his dream or fantasy, or it may be taken up as an almost direct statement of biographical material or emotional content connected to behavior patterns.

The T.A.T. is helpful in facilitating the establishment of the "psychotherapeutic attitude"; many patients find it hard to relate data of any value. In psychotherapy we are, in essence, asking the patient to stand off and observe himself, to report to us what he observes, and to collaborate with us with a part of his self. This is a difficult task, especially for the less sophisticated subjects.

When we ask the subject to read over his own stories, the naive patient may say that he simply described the pictures. We can then tell him of other stories and interpretations that have been given to the same pictures. This usually has a marked effect on the person: it may introduce to him for the first time the *subjectivity* of his thought processes, and he may now be more willing and able to stand off and observe them. This process may be facilitated if, on rereading his stories, the subject is spontaneously impressed by how much of the content refers to himself, or if we have occasion to *point out certain repetitive patterns* to him.

The use of the T.A.T. does not obviate the fact that all the principles of careful psychotherapy must be observed: one should start with the more acceptable aspects, not upset the patient unduly, not interpret things which the patient is not ready for, etc. No one inexperienced with psychotherapy generally should use the T.A.T. in therapy either!

C. Use of the T.A.T. in Group Psychotherapy Programs

Brief mention should be made of observations which have indicated the useful-ness of the T.A.T. in selection of group therapy candidates and in evaluating behavior in group therapy programs. Ullmann [328] has noted that significant correlations were obtained in his investigation between T.A.T. scores of neuro-psychiatric patients and group therapy scale predictions, as well as between T.A.T. scores and a hospital status criterion. The fact that T.A.T. cards are concerned with interpersonal relationships apparently affords the best explana-tion for their suitability as a potential method of selecting group therapy patients. Fairweather et al. [114] have employed the T.A.T. to compare the relative effec-tiveness of psychotherapeutic programs. The test diagnosis interaction was signifi-cant; group therapy and control groups indicated more positive T.A.T. changes for nonpsychotics than for psychotics, and individual therapy was superior in terms of T.A.T. change when given to long-term psychotics. The ability of the T.A.T. to describe patients' behavior in psychotherapy has thus received some validation; the test can be used by the psychotherapist as one measure of evalua-tion of the patient's progress.

D. Diagnostic Aspects in Relation to Therapy*

Psychological tests have much the same relationship to psychotherapy as clini-cal pathological tests and x-rays have to general medicine. Like the medical man, the psychotherapist should have a basic knowledge of testing procedures in order to be able to request the *appropriate* one, and should understand the basic mean-ing well enough to be able to integrate the test results with the additional data. As in general medicine, the therapist should not blindly rely upon the test results, nor should he expect from them an exact diagnostic answer to every problem. It is the clinician's job to make a careful clinical evaluation and to integrate all the factors. No test can be a substitute for clinical knowledge and acumen. It is inappropriate for the psychotherapist to expect an answer to all his problems from the psychologist, and for the psychologist to offer definitive statements without knowing the clinical situation. When I play the role of psychologist, I prefer to offer my data as "consistent with" such and such a disorder, i.e., "This patient's record is consistent with a sadomasochistic character disorder."

Psychological tests may be helpful in diagnosis, if diagnosis does not imply simply attaching labels to a patient, but rather implies gauging liabilities and assets; if diagnosis involves therapeutic planning and prognostication, the great significance of the tests is obvious.

If I restrict myself to the projective personality tests, then it seems to me that they can be divided into two kinds: those concerned essentially with testing formal quantitative aspects (which I increasingly believe indicate primarily de-grees of ego strength), and those which reveal content (dynamics).

---

* Diagnostic aspects have been discussed throughout the book. Here we merely wish to emphasize a few considerations with regard to therapy.

Of the first category, the Rorschach is the main representative; of the second, the T.A.T. It should be kept in mind that this division is somewhat arbitrary, in that the Rorschach may elicit some indications of interpersonal relations and the T.A.T. may offer some ego strength indicators.

From the standpoint of therapy, the quantitative indicators may permit one to gauge the amount of strain and stress to which a patient may be safely exposed by interpretations and transference tensions; the content tests supply the substance of the personality itself, like dreams and fantasies made to order.

The quantitative indicators are predicated upon the probing of subsemantic levels, by studying neuromuscular expressions (as in figure drawing) or perceptual patterns (as in the Rorschach). Thus they may reveal motivations which are unconscious in the sense of never having had any verbal representations. A breakthrough of aggressive impulses due to a brain defect may often be covered up verbally while it will manifest itself myoneurally (e.g., in a drawing). The content tests reveal particularly well matters that are unconscious in the psychoanalytic sense.

More detailed principles of classification of what is usually subsumed under projective tests might be helpful for the clinical selection of proper tests for therapeutic purposes. These suggestions will indicate only the *primary* useful aspects of certain tests and will not ignore the fact that each test contributes on several levels.

I believe that one may group available techniques under five headings:

1. Methods based upon the study of *content:* The T.A.T., C.A.T., and S.A.T.
2. Study of *expressive, perceptual, structural* aspects: Mira, Mosaic, Rorschach, and graphology.
3. *Gestalt functions:* Bender-Gestalt, Mosaic, Rorschach.
4. *Body-image or self-image:* Figure Drawing, T.A.T., Rorschach.
5. *Methods of preference:* Szondi.

It is apparent that all five organismic aspects enter into every one of the projective methods, although in varying degrees. One might keep these categories in mind for the selection of techniques for each individual problem of diagnosis and therapy—either for the purpose of arranging a rounded battery or for selecting the one test for a specific clinical need. One might use these five variables for a systematic inquiry into the test results of any one technique.

A more general classification scheme, relevant to the choice of tests for therapeutic purposes, derives from the "levels hypothesis" which has generally been interpreted as meaning that the less the structure of the test, the deeper the level of personality being tapped. For example, Stone and Dellis [315] found that the Wechsler-Bellevue, Forer Sentence Completion Test, T.A.T., Rorschach, and Draw-A-Person Test reached successively lower, or more primitive, impulse control systems in their subjects. In a similar vein, Theiner [323] has noted greater frequency of acceptable needs expressed in response to a relatively structured test (Rotter Incomplete Sentence Test), and greater frequency of unacceptable needs on the T.A.T. (less structured).

Again, it is feasible that this "levels" principle can be used either toward the selection of a specific test in order to obtain specific kinds of information or toward the selection of several tests to secure a more global picture of the individual.

E. Some Contraindications to the Use of Psychological Tests

A brief statement is in order concerning *contraindications for psychological tests,* for whatever purpose they may be used. Meyer [235] has published a paper on this topic. He is particularly concerned with the effect of the prospect of testing upon the patient (in terms of keeping or breaking appointments) and with how testing affects the continuation of therapy. By examining extensive clinical records, he finds that testing does not generally have an adverse effect. However, he suggests seven contraindications to testing in order to avoid disturbing consequences: (1) acute psychosis, incipient psychosis, or acute anxiety states; (2) extreme difficulty in establishing relationships (where adjustment to an additional person would be an undue burden); (3) any likelihood that the patient will interpret referral for testing as disinterest on the part of the therapist; (4) likelihood that referral will be interpreted as evidence of incompetence of the therapist; (5) a specific fear of "test" situations in life and a tendency to run away from them; (6) the possibility that testing material might stimulate more material than seems desirable at the time (incipient psychosis?); (7) any indication that the therapeutic situation at the time of referral seems to make testing inadvisable, whereas it might be advisable at a later, more suitable date. These points seem to comprise the most careful consideration published thus far on the entire subject of the testing situation from the point of view of the patient-therapist relationship.

I have frequently used the test myself with patients in acute anxiety states and severe depressions without any untoward effects. In all cases judgment must be used, and if extra precautions are taken to create a nontraumatic atmosphere, tests may still be very useful; in fact, in many acute conditions, when the patient is otherwise unable to profit by communications, the tests may be easier for him to deal with and may focus on the very core of the problems.

CHAPTER VIII

REVIEW OF LITERATURE RELEVANT TO THE INTERPRETATION OF THE T.A.T.

A. Stimulus Value of the T.A.T.

IT HAS LONG BEEN RECOGNIZED THAT, IN ORDER TO PROPERLY interpret thematic responses, it is of primary importance to take into account the influence of the stimulus itself in determining the response. Goldfried and Zax [146] have investigated this area and concluded that in evaluating T.A.T. themes it is necessary to make interpretations only with regard to the stimulus value of the specific card. They obtained ratings of all the T.A.T. cards on 10 bipolar adjectival scales, such as happy-sad. The ratings indicated that the cards vary a good deal as to their ambiguity, that is, the number of scales that consistently describe the picture. It was also observed that the stimulus properties of some cards are such that it is likely they will "pull" negatively toned stories. Specifically, it was found that for certain cards (e.g., 2, 5) the stimulus pull is weak enough to assume that the story reflects the inner state of the subject; on the other hand, for pictures such as 4 and 13MF, the stimulus properties of the card are likely to be more responsible for the resultant story than are the subject's inner needs.

A few other studies have been reported which investigated the effect of stimulus properties on the expression of specific needs or personality variables. Lubin [220] tested the effects of T.A.T. cards whose stimulus properties elicit the expression of either sex or aggression. The significant effect of the stimulus properties of cards on sexual and aggressive expression was interpreted as indicating that certain dimensions [186] of the T.A.T. response are determined by stimulus configurations. Murstein [248] studied the projection of hostility on the T.A.T. as a function of stimulus, background, and personality variables. The stimulus properties of the cards used accounted for more than half of the total variance. Murstein concluded that the results provide evidence that the stimulus is definitely the most important determinant of the content of a T.A.T. response.

Another possible way in which the stimulus properties may influence responses has been investigated in studies which have dealt with the effects of similarity between the subject and certain characteristics of the T.A.T. figures. Weisskopf-Joelson and Money [342] hypothesized that physical similarity between the subject and the central T.A.T. figure would affect the amount of projection, but their findings indicated that increasing similarity did not yield statistically significant increases in either amount of projection or in the diagnostic value of the stimuli. Thompson [324], using the Negro T.A.T. that he devised, found that blacks produced more when the T.A.T. used blacks than they did with the traditional T.A.T. Other research, though, has questioned this result (Korchin et al. [203]; Riess et al. [276]). Weisskopf [338] has refuted Murray's [245] hypothesis that males project more when the central figure is male rather than female. Finally, Weisskopf and Dunlevy [340] found no effect on amount of projection when pictures of physically normal, obese, and crippled figures were shown to the respective subject groups. Weisskopf-Joelson and Money [342], after reviewing these findings, suggested that differences in the similarity dimension may cause qualitative changes in projection rather than quantitative, and specifically that decreasing similarity should lead to increased projection of ego alien materials.

Hunt and Smith [175] studied the constraining effects upon responses to thematic projective material of structural elements involving shared cultural meanings. It was hypothesized that patterns like those depicted in the T.A.T. are likely to include a variety of cultural and subcultural symbols which can act so as to evoke responses mediated by shared cultural meanings and given independently of any effects of individual personality. By comparing a modified T.A.T. card with the original, it was shown that variations in component features of the cards produced notable differences in sociocultural classifications that were likely to affect their use, e.g., differences in the subject's perceptions.

B. Sample Variables

Illustrative examples of the possible influences of certain sample variables upon thematic responses are contained in the following studies. Sex differences in fantasy patterns have been found by May [227], who deduced from clinically oriented studies the types of sequences to be expected in men's and in women's fantasies. In women's fantasy, it was hypothesized that there would be reflected the sequence in feminine masochism: suffering followed by joy, failure followed by success. Fantasies of men were expected to reflect the pattern of ascension followed by descension, the syndrome of the male's attempt at ascension and later fear of falling. These hypotheses were strongly supported by May's study with the T.A.T. in that, in terms of sequence of action and feeling, women's stories showed movement from more "negative" emotion and experience to more "positive" emotion and experience, whereas with men this direction of movement was reversed. Men tended to see any decline or fall as total and final, while the possibility of resurgence was implicit in the female pattern. A second finding was that stories written by women tended to include, more often than those of men, phenomena such as dreams, fantasy, and prayer, elements which signify that women are more likely to tolerate, and make use of, shifts in level of psychic functioning.

Tooley [326] examined the expressive styles of three age groups of women, adolescents, late adolescents (18–22 years), and adults, as reflected in T.A.T. themes, in order to obtain a description of the defensive and adaptive modes peculiar to late adolescence. Themes written for card 2, which has shown its relevance to late adolescent problems (Henry [162]), and card 18GF, chosen to maximize affective arousal so that defensive techniques could be seen, were judged according to the criteria of "flamboyant," "impersonal," and "constricted." Late adolescents were judged to be flamboyant in writing style significantly less often than the other two age groups, and impersonal significantly more often. The expressive style of late adolescents was described as moderate in emotional tone and heavily characterized by intellectualizing defenses, a style which facilitates the handling of developmental tasks of late adolescence and which indicates a defensive structure specific to that developmental period. This kind of study points to the potential usefulness of the T.A.T. in studying developmental differences.

Rubin [288] compared the T.A.T. stories of two I.Q. groups, seventh and eighth grade girls of high I.Q. (M=124), and seventh- and eighth-grade girls of low I.Q. (M=78). With respect to data uncorrected for the effects of verbal productivity or socioeconomic status, there was a tendency for the high I.Q. group to use more achievement, dominance, and affiliation themes in their stories than the low I.Q. group; there was no difference between the two groups in number of rejection, seclusion, or dependency themes expressed; and the high I.Q. group used a greater total number of themes in their stories. In general, differences in the incidence of specific themes or total number of themes did exist between the two groups, but such differences were found to be associated with either verbal productivity, socioeconomic status, or both. When the effects of socioeconomic status were held constant, differences continued between the measures of achievement and dominance themes in the two groups, although differences on the measures of affiliation and total number of themes disappeared. One of the findings is contrary to past research done by Rosen [279] and by Veroff et al. [330], both of whom found that incidence of achievement themes in T.A.T. stories is related to socioeconomic status. The present findings indicate that the incidence of achievement themes is more closely related to I.Q. than to socioeconomic status.

Thematic expression has been found to vary along the dimensions of so many variables, it is not surprising to learn that thematic drive expression has been studied in relation to different occupational groups. Levine [211] compared the T.A.T. performances of mathematicians, creative writers, and physicians by means of Pine's [261] system for rating amount, integration, and directness of drive expression, and also in terms of expression of affect. Writers were most expressive, followed by mathematicians and then physicians. Mathematicians tended toward relatively high use of direct, socialized forms of drive content, whereas physicians were characterized by indirect, disguised forms more than the other groups. These emphases appeared to serve defensive and integrative functions. Writers showed no emphasis on either direct or indirect expression. Intergroup differences that were obtained indicated the existence of relationships between occupations and characteristic patterns of regulating drives and affects. The study also demonstrated the reliability of Pine's system, which evidently taps dimensions of personality not necessarily relevant to psychopathology but which reflect characterological differences significant in major life adaptations.

The studies that have been concerned with possible race differences in thematic responses have led to somewhat less than definitive conclusions, mainly because of variations in the number and kind of related variables that have been experimentally controlled, and in the type of differences being evaluated. Mussen [252] compared the T.A.T. responses of black and white lower class boys and found that blacks perceived the general environment as more hostile. Aggression expressed by blacks was more verbal and less physical, blacks expressed less need for achievement and fewer themes of accomplishment, and whites suffered more feelings of rejection in personal relationships, particularly in the case of the mother. Mussen concluded that many differences exist among the black and white cultures not attributable to differences in class structure. Megaree's [230] conclusions about this problem area were somewhat different, although he was concerned more with personality differences than cultural ones, as manifested in the T.A.T. He compared the scores of lower-class white and black male juvenile delinquents on the T.A.T. and two other projective tests and found no differences on T.A.T. scores. The two groups had been matched on I.Q. It was noted that these results were consistent with those of other studies previously reported in the literature which also matched black and white samples on I.Q.; earlier studies which had not matched I.Q.'s reported more projective test differences. For example, Veroff et al. [330] did not match for I.Q. and found a high proportion of significant differences. Megaree's concluding opinion was that projective test differences should not be used to make inferences about basic racial personality structure unless careful matching on other variables has been achieved. The present study indicates that white norms are applicable to black subjects of equivalent I.Q. in custodial settings.

Johnson and Sikes [182] investigated subcultural differences in thematic responses. They compared the T.A.T. responses of black, Mexican-American, and Anglo male psychiatric patients, whose ages, educational backgrounds, and occupational levels were quite similar. Diagnostically, the subgroups were almost equal. Using themes of achievement on card 1 as the measure of achievement concern, a tendency was found for Mexican-American and black groups to show more achievement. These themes also included the subcategory of frustration, which appeared more often in black and Mexican-American stories than in Anglo. Large differences were found for the family unity dimension as shown in card 2 themes. The Mexican-American group had the most consistent view of the family as unified, whereas the blacks were lowest in this category. Responses to the mother-son card (6BM) showed significant differences. For Mexican-Americans, the scene was one of a son leaving his mother, both viewed as being sad, while blacks tended to see the mother as rejecting and a situation of conflict. The father-son card elicited significant differences also, with blacks and Anglos responding similarly, and Mexican-Americans seeing a father giving his son advice and the son taking it. Johnson and Sikes concluded that it may be in the measurement of the relative strengths of interpersonal identifications that projective tests can be most useful in the formulation of culture and personality theories.

C. Aggression and Hostility

Much recent research has dealt with the dimensions of aggression and hostility as they are manifested in T.A.T. responses. The following studies illustrate some of the many variables which have been studied in relation to this problem area. James and Mosher [180] emphasized the relevance of the stimulus situation, and in their study related thematic aggression, which was elicited by thematic stimuli of high and low stimulus relevance, to the aggressive behavior of a group of Boy Scouts. Thematic aggression to high pull cards was related significantly to physically aggressive behavior, but thematic aggression to low pull cards was not. There was no relationship between self-reported hostility-guilt and fighting behavior; nor was any relationship obtained between hostility-guilt and thematic aggression elicited by cards of high stimulus relevance. Hostility-guilt was significantly negatively correlated with aggressive stories told to cards with little aggressive stimulus relevance. It was hypothesized that, when pictures are not suggestive of aggression, perhaps only people who are low in guilt over hostility are able to accept the responsibility for producing aggressive themes. The relationships obtained between thematic aggression and fighting behavior in adolescent boys support Kagan's [186] position. Kagan has stated that "unambiguous pictures are the best stimuli for yielding indicants of behavioral aggression." The results of the present study imply that to maximize prediction from thematic cards one must use stimuli that are quite similar to the relevant behavior.

Megaree [231] studied hostility on the T.A.T. as a function of defensive inhibition and the stimulus situation. He hypothesized that there would be significant differences in the aggressive imagery of inhibited and uninhibited subjects when T.A.T. cards or instructions strongly suggested an aggressive response, but not when experimental conditions did not suggest hostile themes. The following findings held true for women but not for male subjects: less inhibited people had higher hostility scores than the more inhibited; instructions to give hostile stories resulted in higher hostility scores than did neutral instructions; the higher the aggressive pull of the cards, the higher were the obtained hostility scores; and finally, the major hypothesis, noted above, was confirmed, but for women only. Partial support was thus found for the hypothesis that variations in aggressive imagery in response to stimulus conditions that are likely to elicit aggression reflect differences in inhibition level. Since the present study used group administration, the obtained sex difference could be an artefact of sex differences in response to group T.A.T.'s such as were found by Lindzey and Silverman [219].

Reznikoff and Dollin [275] investigated the concept that persons rated high on a social desirability (S.D.) scale would avoid expression of aggression on the

T.A.T., which the authors considered socially undesirable. Subjects were grouped according to their Edwards S.D. scale score and given T.A.T. cards which were later scored for overt, covert, and total hostility. S.D. groups could not be differentiated with regard to mean score on any hostility variables, although significant differences were obtained for all variables with regard to stimulus pull of the cards. Further analysis did indicate that high S.D. subjects were more likely than others to use covert hostility rather than overt. This is consistent with the idea that people with high S.D. are not likely to express aggressive feelings directly. It is Murstein's [250] opinion that personality sets like S.D. do not really affect the themes obtained with strongly structured cards such as compose the T.A.T.

Hafner and Kaplan [151] conducted a methodologically sound hostility content analysis of the Rorschach and T.A.T. and compared the hostility dimension on the two tests. The constructed scales were applied to the Rorschach and T.A.T. protocols of a group of psychiatric patients. For the Rorschach, correlations between overt and weighted scale scores, covert and weighted scale scores, and overt and covert scales were all positive and significant. The same results were obtained for the T.A.T. hostility scales except that the correlation between overt and covert scales was significantly negative. Correlations between the Rorschach and T.A.T. weighted scale scores, overt scale scores, and covert scale scores were all nonsignificant. Since for the T.A.T. overt and covert scale scores were highly related to weighted scores, but not to the same degree as for the Rorschach, and since T.A.T. overt and covert scale scores were negatively related as well, it was concluded that the T.A.T. was more sensitive to individual differences in regard to the overt-covert dimension of hostility than was the Rorschach. An interesting study was conducted by Winter et al. [352] using the Hafner-Kaplan scoring system [150]. T.A.T. stories were produced conjointly by three-member families: 50 families with normal children (Nor), 44 with emotionally maladjusted (Mal), 16 with schizophrenic (Scz), and 16 with delinquent children (Del). The Nor and Scz groups produced stories low both in weighted hostility and overt hostility, stories of Mal groups were high in both variables, and the Del families scored high in weighted hostility but close to the normals in overt hostility. The deviation of the Scz families' responses from the kind expected from clinical experience led the authors to suggest that their hostility is either so far removed from the level of explicit expression that it is conveyed in highly subtle ways or that the families avoid expression of emotional antagonism. No hypotheses were proposed in explanation of the unexpected responses from the Del groups. It was deduced, in general, that the basic value systems of the Mal, Del, and Scz groups are equally abnormal but that the mode of expression of hostility differs. In addition to the information about the expression of hostility contributed by this study, it should be noted that research such as this can result in effective use of the family T.A.T. as a diagnostic instrument as well as effective use of the T.A.T. in assessing family pathology.

With regard to the question of the relationship between simple T.A.T. aggression and overt aggression, Murstein [250] has concluded that there is little correspondence between the two with typical samples of adults, adolescents, and children. On the other hand, he stated that for both adults and children, persons with histories of overt hostility are relatively easily differentiated by thematic aggression. The following studies are representative of those which have been conducted using the T.A.T. with subjects who have such "histories of overt hostility." Stone [314] studied army prisoners who had committed nonviolent crimes, or deserted, or murdered, or intended to kill someone. The assaultive group projected significantly more hostility than the combined nonassaultive groups in their T.A.T. responses. Purcell [269] classified army trainees into three groups varying in antisocial behavior. Of the 15 comparisons made between any two of the three groups, 12 indicated highly significant differences. Antisocial men responded with more aggression themes than other groups, and their hostility expression was more direct. Punishment depicted was often of the external kind, while nonantisocial people manifested more frequent internal punishment than external.

Mussen and Naylor [253] were inspired in their research by Sanford et al.'s [293] finding that expression of high aggressive needs in the T.A.T. was correlated with low overt aggression, with a middle-class sample. Mussen and Naylor predicted that with lower-class subjects, high fantasy aggression would be overtly expressed, since in lower-class environments aggressive behavior is not punished. They tested preadolescent and adolescent delinquent lower-class boys with the T.A.T., and found that, among these boys, those who manifested high aggressive needs on the T.A.T. showed more aggressive behavior than those with low fantasy aggressive needs. A second result was that boys who showed much punishment press relative to aggressive needs in their stories showed less overt aggression than those who had low punishment press relative to aggressive needs. This relationship was less marked than the first was. Third, when high expression of aggressive needs was paired with a low ratio of anticipation of punishment to aggressive needs, a high amount of overt aggression was generally found, and vice versa. This study was offered as evidence of the validity of T.A.T. inferences concerning aggressive needs, although the conclusions were limited to the social class and age levels studied. Finally, a study which confirmed Mussen and Naylor's [253] general finding but whose scope was somewhat broader was conducted by Weissman [344]. Four matched groups of adolescents participated; they were identified as (1) aggressive acting-out institutionalized subjects, (2) less aggressive acting-out institutionalized subjects, (3) non-acting-out high school boys, and (4) aggressive acting-out high school boys. T.A.T. stories were compared on several hypothesized dimensions deemed relevant to aggressive acting-out behavior. The following three dimensions manifested significant and consistent differences: (1) Number of aggressive stories. This dimension was viewed as most likely to be useful as an indicator of aggressive overt behavior when groups being compared are distinctly different with respect to aggression. Weissman suggested that T.A.T. fantasies of aggressive adolescents, when compared to adults', are more closely related to characteristic behavioral patterns than to conflicts resulting from artificially induced drive states, such as reported by other studies. (2) Aggressive stories to cards not usually associated with aggression. Aggressive boys were more likely to tell aggressive stories to nonaggressive cards than were nonaggressive subjects. (3) Reaction time, which was the single best predictor of aggressive overt behavior for all groups.

D. Motivation and Apperception

The effects of several needs on the content of thematic stories, and the conditions which appear to determine whether or not these needs will be manifested in subjects' responses, have become the focal point of interest for many investigators. The previous review of literature that has dealt with aggression represents only one area within the more general field that will presently be surveyed. The achievement motive has been extensively studied by McClelland et al. [229]. They have determined that the occurrence of achievement in a thematic story is a joint function of three variables: (1) cues in the everyday environment and in the relatively autonomous thought processes of the individual, (2) specific cues introduced through the experiment, and (3) controllable cues in the specific picture. According to McClelland, when achievement imagery is part of the thematic story, it can be concluded that the individual is motivated to achieve and not indicating wish-fulfilling fantasy. McArthur [228] reexamined the effects of need achievement on the content of T.A.T. stories and hypothesized that self-projection accounts for all such effects. This hypothesis inherently questioned the list of eight effects of increasing the subject's need achievement which had previously been proposed by McClelland, who had considered four possibilities as to the description of the relationship between the subjects and the traits of the characters in his story. These were self-projection, contrast projection, complementary projection, and instrumental projection. McArthur stated that four of McClelland's proposed effects (more mastery tales, hero states need for mastery, hero wishes for mastery, and more mastery images) should hold true, while the other four (failure by the hero, actions to overcome failure, press hostile to mastery, and anxiety about mastery) merely represent artefacts of McClelland's design. This hypothesis was tested against a group of academic over-achievers, and the results suggested that the concept of self-projection does explain most of the achievement content of T.A.T. stories.

An interesting study was conducted by Orso [259], in which he compared the effects of achievement and affiliation arousal on the need for achievement. As determined from T.A.T. responses, it was found that male nAch scores were not significantly affected by achievement or affiliation arousal, whereas female nAch scores increased significantly after affiliation arousal and decreased significantly after achievement arousal. These sex differences were discussed in terms of differences between the male and female roles in our society insofar as there are discrepant meanings of achievement for men and for women.

Of two studies which sought to provide an index of the strength of the affiliation motive in T.A.T. stories, the earlier one (Shipley and Veroff [302]) used "separation imagery" as the criterion for designating affiliation-related stories. The results did not differentiate between aroused and control conditions. The scoring procedures used by Atkinson et al. [15] represent a more general definition of affiliation than those used in the earlier study, in which the definition of affiliation imagery was limited to separation anxiety. In the study by Atkinson et al., affiliation imagery was scored when the story indicated concern in one or more of the characters over establishing, maintaining, or restoring a positive affective relationship with another person. Affiliation motive arousal in some subjects was achieved by administering a sociometric test to them before the T.A.T. The low motivation control condition was a college classroom. The success of the scoring system and of the method of motive arousal was indicated by the significant difference obtained between the two conditions for their median n affiliation scores.

The relationships between the need for dependency and the T.A.T. and interview measures of dependent behavior were investigated by Fitzgerald [123]. He based his research on Rotter's formula [285], that need potential is a function of freedom of movement (FM) and need value (NV). Fitzgerald hypothesized that projective responses represent symbolic ways of obtaining gratification, and that frequency of response would be greatest when FM was low and NV high, thus creating a conflict situation. The finding was that projection of dependency on the T.A.T. was significantly related to conflict but not related to interview ratings of dependency. It was inferred that, at least for dependency, the T.A.T. is not a direct medium for the expression of need but is instead related to ego functions, e.g., conflict.

Thematic sexual responses have been investigated in relation to experimentally induced drive and inhibition. Clark [92] found that men shown pictures of nude women projected less sexual imagery than controls, whereas Strizver [318], in a comparable study demonstrating the influence of drive upon apperception, found that arousal increased sexual imagery. The factor which seems to have determined these conflicting results is that Clark's upper-class subjects were probably more inhibited than the lower-class subjects who participated in Strizver's study. Thematic responses to some degree depend upon the individual's personal evaluation of the situation.

The research conducted by Davids and DeVault [101] explicitly investigated the relations between personality and perception that were implicitly suggested in the two previously described studies. The T.A.T. and Draw-A-Person Test (D.A.P.T.) were included in a battery of psychological tests given to pregnant women. The sample was subdivided into a "normal" group and an "abnormal" group on the basis of hospital records of childbirth experiences. As predicted, a significantly greater proportion of women in the normal group perceived pregnant women in the T.A.T., particularly a pregnant woman in card 2, and drew female pictures on the D.A.P.T. Davids and DeVault noted that the finding in regard to selective perception in response to T.A.T. stimuli is relevant to the area known as "personality and perception," in which concern is directed to the influences of motivational factors on selection in perceptual organization. In the present study, working with a real life condition with specific physiological correlates, definite relations between motivation and perception were obtained. Compared to many women who have taken the T.A.T., the pregnant women in this study manifested a much greater likelihood of selectively perceiving pregnant women in the stimuli.

Dana's [97] report on thematic techniques in clinical use dealt with a good deal of the research that has employed thematic techniques to assess human needs, specifically, achievement, affiliation, hostility, sex, and power. A model was provided which designated the following research areas as relevant to clinical practice: card cue value, subject variables, examiner variables, and arousal conditions.

These four kinds of variables interact and affect the expression of any need in thematic content.

Cue value. Crude sortings of thematic stimuli for degrees of card pull for any one need have been frequent. While criteria for achievement cards of high and low cue value have been established, cue content for achievement should also be varied for similarity to work experience (Veroff et al. [331]), race (Cowan and Goldberg [95]), and sex (Veroff et al. [333]). Low cue-value pictures (Veroff et al. [330]) and early use of low cue-value stimuli are valid need measures, while high cue-value pictures may measure guilt, at least for sex and hostility (Epstein [107]). Murstein [249] has suggested the use of medium or low cue-value cards following strong arousal by instructions. Such cards are clear in regard to identification of hero but ambiguous as to what is happening in the picture.

Subject variables. Dana identified these two major classes: (1) relatively permanent conditions that directly affect the intensity of need states, such as sex, race, religion, social class, education, intelligence, values, parental conditions, and family behaviors, and (2) transitory internal states that influence the expression of need states, generally by inhibition of scores (anxiety, conflict, defenses, guilt, and self-concept conditions). Not all the conditions of either class have the same effects across need states. The following data are relevant to the first class of variables. The sex of the subject is more relevant to *n* Ach than to *n* Aff. Whenever there is a differential definition by sex of what constitutes any need state, the thematic stimuli and arousal conditions must be varied in accord. Normative data from a sample of both sexes for *n* Ach, *n* Aff, and *n* Power have shown the contributions of age, education, family income, occupation, and race (Veroff et al. [330]) although subject variables had only limited effects. Rosen [280] showed the interactive effects on *n* Ach of social class, family size, birth order, and age of mother. Nuttall [256] determined that although race (black) is relevant to nAch scores, the geographic region of childhood experience has as large an influence. It has also been demonstrated that religion influences *n* Ach, with Jews, Catholics, and Protestants, respectively, obtaining decreasing scores in a national sample (Veroff et al. [332]). One finding relevant to the second class of subject conditions was that, for *n* Ach, all measures showed that anxiety or conflict over fears of possible failure served to inhibit or distort achievement scores (Sampson [290]).

Examiner variables. Bernstein [67] has shown that the sheer presence of an examiner and individual differences between examiners influence the expression of affect on the T.A.T. Broverman et al. [78] have pointed out that there are definite differences, at least for *n* Ach, between individual and group administration due to the more immediate influence of the examiner on individual administrations. Sexual imagery and *n* Sex scores are also affected by examiners or social settings (Martin [225]). In conclusion, Dana suggested that future research relevant to clinical assessment should include these issues: (a) simultaneous measurement of needs, (b) assessment of anxiety and conflict relative to each need by independent indices and/or by intraindividual comparison of need scores from neutral and aroused conditions, (c) control of both classes of subject conditions, (d) recognition of examiner influences, and (e) consensus on methods for measuring needs.

CHAPTER IX

THE APPLICATION OF THEMATIC ANALYSIS TO LITERARY PRODUCTS

PATHOGRAPHIES OF A PSYCHOANALYTIC NATURE, ALTHOUGH OF-ten persuasive clinically, nonetheless have troubled those concerned with the rigors of methodology. A suspicion of *post hoc, ergo propter hoc* reasoning has not been easily dispelled.

One way of analyzing literary products in a more reliable manner is to use our T.A.T.-type of analysis. In this case, the artistic product serves as the primary data from which inferences about the personality of the writer are made with the help of the same outline that we used for T.A.T. stories.

We have touched before on some of the differences between the creative process under ordinary circumstances and in response to T.A.T. or C.A.T. cards (see Chapter I). We mentioned the difference in mental set, among other things. The creative end product in the case of a published literary effort and a T.A.T. story also vary widely, of course. The published story may be the result of innumerable rewritings and editing (from that standpoint, a writer's first draft would be the best source for analysis of his personality). Also, part of the writer's frame of reference is adaptive to the audience he wants to reach, the market he wants to sell to. He may have developed a style adaptively and to a considerable extent consciously. He may even have made a concentrated effort to keep content referring to him personally out of his story.

Despite all these differences and caveats to be kept in mind, the end product, unless vitally affected by other than the author, is a product of his personality, albeit modified by a variety of adaptive ego mechanisms. This product therefore basically lends itself to analysis as a personal document just as T.A.T. stories do, except that one has to allow for special complexities and possible difficulties in arriving at correct inferences with regard to unconscious motivation. (Incidentally, the analysis of political documents and speeches with regard to the personality of the author is also possible and may be extremely valuable in the future *if* the caveats about ghostwriters, editors, etc., are remembered.) Among writers, some always write essentially about themselves, and every story is their own story. Others attempt to keep themselves out and supposedly "think up" stories totally unrelated to their own experience. Nevertheless, their product—in terms of choice of content and with regard to expressive and cognitive style, aside from its susceptibility to study by content analysis in the sense of counting the frequency of words, noun-verb ratio, etc.—remains uniquely theirs and therefore lends itself in principle to an analysis of their personality [183].

Somerset Maugham's stories fall somewhere between the two extremes of direct biography and self-exclusion. Manifestly, source material comes from all over the world, Europe, Russia, the Far East. However, Maugham's personality shines through all of them.

Thirty of Maugham's stories were selected randomly from two volumes, picked by the present author's then six year old daughter and by their numerical characteristics—1, 2, 11, 12, 21, 22 [226]. I think that even the very statistically minded, if they knew Maugham, would not object to this simple procedure of selection. It will become quite clear that the themes and characteristics which become manifest in the selected stories have a great similarity to most of the rest of Maugham's writings, including his major work, *Of Human Bondage,* which is considered to be in large part autobiographical.

A. Somerset Maugham—Analysis of the Stories*

The first story, luckily enough, is "Rain"—luckily, because it is particularly widely known both as a movie as well as the original short story.

"Rain"

Descriptive theme. A zealous missionary, driven by great religious fervor, has always resisted the ordinary feelings of compassion, sex, and fear in his desire to rise above them for the sake of a stern religious morality. When he meets Sadie Thompson, a prostitute, he feels compelled to interfere with her activities in his efforts to save her soul (at the cost of great misery and actual danger to her). However, he finds himself increasingly attracted to her (note his dream of breast-like mountains, his remaining with her later and later into the night) and ultimately makes a sexual advance. He kills himself in consequence.

Interpretive theme. If emotions are very strong, especially sexual desire, and one tries to control them while in intense contact with a woman, control may be destroyed as well as oneself.

Diagnostic level. Presence of strong drives, aggressive and sexual. Attempted defenses are denial, repression, rationalization, withdrawal, and reaction formation. Adaptively tries to deal with his conflict by becoming a missionary. Fears loss of control over drives, especially sexual drive. Fears destruction by women. Concern about self-destruction; suicidal ideas are present.

These bald statements leave out many subtleties of the story. Let me plead

---

* Sections A-C are reprinted from [38] by permission.

again the need for economy. However, even though briefly, I must point out a few of the other features. The theme of the missionary is not the only one. He is not the only hero; Sadie Thompson is another.

Descriptive theme. A prostitute is reduced to a fearful clinging wreck by a zealous missionary bent on saving her soul, but she rises contemptuously when his moral principles collapse and ordinary lust shows through.

Interpretive theme. If a lustful woman meets a zealously moral man, she is reduced to weakness, but she recovers her strength if the man appears prey to lust.

Diagnostic level. Woman is seen as lustful, seductive. Moral man is seen as strong. Man unable to control his desires is seen as contemptible by woman. Control is very important; its loss is contemptible.

Another subtheme is concerned with Dr. Macphail. One must consider him another identification figure for the author (of course, Maugham projects some of his own sentiments on all the figures). Let me simply remark that the doctor appears compassionate but tries to remain uninvolved to avoid the discomfiture of too much emotion. He tries to accept with passivity the missionary, his own wife, and the world around him but finds himself uneasy. He engages in action in a desultory way (and with a good deal of conflict) only when he feels he can no longer avoid doing so.

The minor female characters in the story appear as controlling, either by their aggressive attitudes or by their moralistic ones. In fact, the most repetitive concern seems to be with emotions that could overcome one, especially with regard to women who tend to control.

Let me anticipate some broader inferences here by pointing out that the waitress, Mildred, in *Of Human Bondage* is not too different from Sadie Thompson in her effect on the protagonist. Nor is the principal character, Philip, himself a doctor, too different from Dr. Macphail. It is common knowledge that Maugham was a medical school graduate.

"The Fall of Edward Barnard"

In a general sense, one might describe this story as a not so gentle mockery of American culture, especially as seen through the bourgeois pretensions of wealthy women and their effect on men.

Descriptive theme. Edward Barnard is a traditional and upstanding young Chicagoan. Just as soon as he saves enough money from his work in Tahiti, he plans to return home and marry the beautiful, cultured, controlling, and ambitious Isabel. However, he comes to enjoy the easy and simple life of the islands, particularly the companionship of a half-caste girl. Unlike Isabel, she puts him at his ease.

Bateman Hunter, in love with Isabel, but friend to Edward also, is vaguely puzzled and distressed by Edward's change. He tries to persuade Edward to return home. When Edward renounces Isabel, Hunter himself returns to marry her. Isabel's dreams, as she embraces Hunter, are of business success, tea dances, and the look of distinction and solidity which horn-rimmed glasses will give her new fiancé.

Interpretive theme. If one is caught in the demands of petty bourgeois culture, as represented by controlling, ambitious women, one may find life much happier in an undemanding culture (which permits more passivity) and with simpler women (who are no threat and do not make one feel inferior). A selfless male friend helps out reliably.

Diagnostic level. An unease about cultural demands. Sees women of society as subtly controlling, demanding, ambitious. Sophisticated women of this kind produce feelings of unease, inferiority. Attempts solution of anxiety and conflict by withdrawal (geographic and psychological) and by turning to more primitive women and less demanding societies. Uses rationalization, emotional isolation, and withdrawal as defense. A male friend is seen as selfless and dependable. Since we know something of the author's actual life history, we can add that his travels to primitive countries were adaptive ways of dealing with his problems. Writing was another way of dealing with his conflicts. He described writing *Of Human Bondage* as a cathartic experience. His friendships with men were often lifelong, his heterosexual relations apparently either transitory or distant and tempestuous [183].

"The Yellow Streak"

Descriptive theme. Izzart, the handsome, English-educated son of a white father and half-caste mother, is constantly unnerved by the thought that someone will discover his mixed parentage. During a mission with Campion, a visitor to the Malayan jungle, the men are involved in a boating accident. Izzart is so intent on saving his own life that he ignores Campion's pleas for help. Miraculously, both men survive. Campion is publicly silent about Izzart's part in the near catastrophe but, triggered by Izzart's fear and guilt, makes it privately plain to him that he attributes his cowardice to the "yellow streak"—the "tainted" blood.

Interpretive theme. If a man is "tainted" by a (racially) inferior woman (mother), he fears his inferiority (the yellow streak) will emerge to his shame and peril. His fear that others will recognize this inferiority constantly haunts him.

Diagnostic level. Feels inferior. Projects his feelings of inferiority on others. Inferiority is blamed on a woman, specifically his mother. Woman is seen as something inferior as well as a source of embarrassment and shame. The main concern is one of controlling emotion, particularly fear.

"P & O"

Descriptive theme. Mrs. Hamlyn is returning alone to England from the tropics after 20 years of happy marriage. Her husband has fallen helplessly in love with another woman. She and her husband both viewed the intrusion of his new love as one would an illness—it is uncontrollable, and one must bow before it. On shipboard she meets the vital and forward-looking Mr. Gallagher, a retired planter, who is going home to begin a new life. Mr. Gallagher has left behind his native wife, after making what he considered generous financial provision for her. This wife, however, has become incensed and cast a spell upon him. When Mr. Gallagher sickens and dies on board, to the consternation of the ship's doctor, apparently as a result of this spell, Mrs. Hamlyn's own anger evaporates, and she feels great compassion for the love that, like an unrestrainable force (a spell), befell her husband.

Interpretive theme. If love befalls one, it is like a sickness against which one is defenseless. If one fights a (native) woman's love, she will kill one. It is best to bow to uncontrollable emotions.

Diagnostic level. Fear of emotion, particularly of heterosexual love. Fear of being overwhelmed by love (for woman). Fear of being killed by hate of woman. Defense used is emotional isolation and sublimation into compassion.

This story also involves the complexities of the caste system in British society, observations on emotional callousness, and the selfless relationship between simple men. Once again, a doctor (the ship's doctor—a sympathetic character) is cast into a hopeless conflict between passivity and activity.

"Mr. Harrington's Washing"

Descriptive theme. Mr. Harrington is the prototype of the proper Philadelphian. He has a strong set of morals and principles of behavior, which he takes with him into the upheaval of revolutionary Russia. There he comes in contact with Alexandra, "a mad Russian," who has had a powerful effect on all sorts of men and whom he significantly nicknames Delilah. Mediocre, resolute, stubborn, but rigidly sticking to his principles throughout, Harrington insists on getting his laundry before departing from unsafe Petrograd. Alexandra, who loyally accompanies him on this last mission, is attracted by a street crowd. Harrington, trailing behind her, is attacked and killed.

Interpretive theme. If one has a strong set of moral and behavioral patterns, one is helped through many difficult situations. But one may also be led into absurdity. If one gets tangled up with a woman, she is likely to cause one's misfortune and death even though her intentions are the best.

Diagnostic level. Conflict between conventional and less rigid behavior. Gentle mockery of bourgeois mind in unresolved conflict. Woman is seen as powerful and dangerous. Even when she means to be loyal and protective, she may be fatal.

"Footprints in the Jungle"

Descriptive theme. Bronson, a plantation man, takes Cartwright, temporarily down on his luck, into his home in order to lend him a helping hand. In time, Cartwright and Mrs. Bronson have a love affair, "swayed by turbulent passion." Although all three are basically decent people, Mrs. Bronson encourages her lover to kill her husband rather than risk discovery. The police chief learns of the crime, but there is insufficient evidence to bring the case to court. The new couple live on happily, since remorse for a crime does not seem to sit heavily if one can be absolutely sure one will not be found out.

Interpretive theme. If a woman comes between two men, she causes trouble and death. Sexual passion may be the motive for murder even though the people involved were, and remain, perfectly decent people. They may not even suffer remorse.

Diagnostic level. Sees women as causing trouble to men, as separating them, and as being fatal to them. There is the suggestion of an oedipal problem: one man must be killed for the other to get his woman. Passion is seen as overpowering, threatening to transcend control, specifically control of aggression. An unintegrated superego condones murderous aggression as an uncontrollable force.

"A Friend in Need"

Descriptive theme. A seemingly pleasant, kind, middle-class sort of man is approached by an irresponsible, happy-go-lucky acquaintance who is in desperate need of a job. The former casually sends him to his death by proposing to him a dangerous swimming feat as the price for a job—a job which in fact he doesn't have to offer at all.

Interpretive theme. If one is happy-go-lucky, one may be prey to the most incongruous hostilities of one's fellow man. This is probably due to disapproval and envy of an easy way of life and implied success with women.

Diagnostic level. Fear of and desire for drifting, passivity. Sees people as incongruously and often casually cruel. This ascription of cruelty may be associated with concern over their envy and disapproval of easygoing ways and of success with women. The latter are felt as dangerous. There is fear of helplessness, guilt over sexual desires, and passivity, and a great deal of cruelty is projected on others.

"A Romantic Young Lady"

Descriptive theme. The beautiful daughter of a duchess falls in love with a poor young man who returns her affection. Her mother disapproves and begs for help from a countess who employs him as mule driver to her valuable and showy team. When the young man is made to choose between his beloved and his glamorous job, he chooses the latter.

Interpretive theme. If a man has to choose between a woman and an esteemed job (with animals), he rather callously chooses the job.

Diagnostic level. A sarcastic, low esteem is expressed for women. "There is not a pair of mules in the whole of Spain to come up to ours . . . one can get a wife any day of the week, but a place like this is found only once in a lifetime. I should be a fool to throw it up for a woman" [226]. So says the young man.

A subtheme is also concerned with the fact that the duchess and countess, though rivals previously, get together in this adversity. The beautiful young woman is met many years later, settled down comfortably as the stout, flaunting widow of a diplomat.

"The Kite"

Descriptive theme. A young boy, in joint venture with his parents, learns to love flying kites. As he grows older, this becomes the guiding passion of his and their lives. He meets a girl of whom his mother disapproves and, against her wishes, marries. His marriage is unhappy, his wife interferes with his kite flying, and in anger he leaves her and returns to his parents. In retribution, his wife smashes his best kite. He retaliates angrily by choosing prison to the alternative of paying her support.

Interpretive theme. If a young man who has lived happily with his parents gets involved with a woman of whom they disapprove, the new woman may make him unhappy, interfere with his freedom, destroy the things he loves. Feels tremendous anger toward her.

> You see, I don't know a thing about flying a kite. Perhaps it gives him a sense of power as he watches it soaring towards the clouds and of mastery over the elements as he seems to bend the winds of heaven to his will. It may be that in some queer way he identifies himself with the kite flying so free and so high above him, and it's as if it were an escape from the monotony of life. It may be that in some dim, confused way it represents an ideal of freedom and adventure. And you know, when a man once gets bitten with the virus of the ideal not all the King's doctors and not all the King's surgeons can rid him of it [226].

This is what the narrator comments on the events he relates in the story.

Diagnostic level. Tends to see life with parents as peaceful in infantile (sexually?) gratifying way. Woman is seen as making one unhappy, controlling one's life, interfering with infantile phallic pleasures and with man's freedom. Woman is seen as undermining his power. Conflict between monotony and adventurous, whimsical diversion. Woman is seen as plainly castrating, evil, controlling, interfering with narcissistic (sexual?) pleasures.

"The Happy Couple"

Descriptive theme. An apparently insignificant couple, in love with each other and warmly devoted to their baby, are found to have been the onetime doctor and female companion to an old lady they killed. Her inheritance enabled them to be married. At their trial, the jury found them not guilty despite overwhelming evidence, supposedly because of the fact that they had not had sexual intercourse during their long premarital relationship. The woman had been willing to commit murder to marry the man she loved, but not to have an illicit love affair.

Interpretive theme. People are not what they seem. They may appear to be very decent people and yet commit murder. If people control their sexual desire, anything may be forgiven them. People are very strange. Sometimes one person must be disposed of for others to find happiness.

Diagnostic level. Suspicious of people, of their deceptive appearances, of their complex natures which may conceal murderous aggression. The problem is of reconciling aggression and conscience. Unintegrated superego. Sex appears more prohibitive than aggression. Oedipal problem. Sees people as odd.

It is interesting to compare this story with "Footprints in the Jungle." In both instances one meets a quiet, pleasant, unobtrusive middle-aged couple who have committed murder in order to live with one another. In both stories, the murderers escape punishment for their crimes and live happily (though somewhat furtively) ever after. Once again, in "The Happy Couple," a doctor is the protagonist and is under the sway of love for a woman.

B. Summary

*Unconscious Structure and Drives (1–3)**

The subject seems to have a continual struggle with aggressive and sexual drives. He feels strongly that their control is vital. Death follows loss of control. The character structure that has resulted from his attempts to deal with these problems is one of emotional isolation and detachment. He is an onlooker, peering in from the outside with considerable puzzlement and much suspicion of the barely repressed drives that lurk beneath the surface of his fellow men. And yet he is not without compassion. There seems to be a conflict between active participation in the demands of the world, especially those of bourgeois culture, and the giving in to passive desires, to the call of simpler living under more primitive circumstances. From the attempted resolution of this conflict arises the beachcomber, the wanderer, albeit in this case a highly sophisticated one. The self-image that results seems that of a mildly ineffective person who feels rather like a leaf in the wind and is not at all aware of his own strong emotions, especially of cruelty toward women.

Conception of the World (4)

Puzzling, demanding, to be faced with wary eyes, full of surprises and over-whelming situations.

Relationship to Others (5)

Urbane, mildly compassionate, warily expectant, but uninvolved manifestly; latent, strongly aggressive, hostile feelings toward women, projected onto them. Sometimes there is aggression toward men, though often men are seen as dependable if not affected by women.

Significant Conflicts (6)

Control versus lack of control of aggression and sex. Conflict between activity and passivity, between conformity and nonconformity, between identification as a man and as a woman.

Nature of Anxieties (7)

To be dominated, constrained, controlled, especially by women. To kill or be killed in triangular conflicts. To be embarrassed. To lose control of aggressive or sexual drives.

---

* Numbered headings correspond to those of the T.A.T. blank.

Main Defenses (8)

Reaction formation, emotional isolation, repression, and withdrawal from object relations. Extensive projection of aggression and sexual desires. Very superficial object relations.

Superego Structure (9)

An unintegrated superego; it is usually quite harsh, but occasionally, with a touch of cynicism or detachment, aggressive transgressions seem permissible, possibly more so than sexual ones.

Integration and Strength of Ego (10)

The well-constructed stories show an ego strong enough to attain some closure and to maintain control. However, control is attained at the cost of considerable emotional isolation, of constriction and stereotyping of experiences, and of tangential relations to people. The self-image is one of a good deal of ineffectualness, but identification with the role of an urbane, controlled Englishman serves adaptively to maintain adequate functioning, which is enhanced by a very high intelligence and vast experience with the world.

C. Final Report

The author seems to have a continuous struggle with aggressive and sexual drives, feeling strongly that their control is literally vital, as seen in the stories "Rain," "The Happy Couple," "Footprints in the Jungle."

The character structure which has resulted from his attempts to deal with these problems is one of some emotional isolation and detachment, an onlooker looking from the outside in, not without compassion, with considerable puzzlement and a good deal of suspicion of the barely repressed drives that might lurk under the surface in his fellow man, as seen through the eyes of Dr. Macphail in "Rain," the narrator in "Mr. Harrington's Washing," and in the plot of "A Friend in Need."

There seems to be a conflict between active participation in the demands of the world, especially of the bourgeois culture, and the giving in to passive desires, generally, and the call of simpler living under more primitive circumstances, specifically, as in "The Fall of Edward Barnard" and "A Friend in Need."

The self-image that results seems that of a mildly ineffective person who feels somewhat like a pebble pushed about by the tides, e.g., "The Fall of Edward Barnard" and Macphail in "Rain."

Women are seen as domineering and demanding, such as Isabel in "The Fall of Edward Barnard," the women in "Rain," the wife in "The Kite"; or as leading to disaster—Sadie Thompson, "Delilah" in "Mr. Harrington's Washing." Women are also often seen as causing a feeling of inadequacy either as Edward Barnard had in relation to Isabel or as in the case of Izzart's mother in "The Yellow

Streak." Apparently, the author uses his defenses so extensively that he is not aware of his own strong aggressive drives, projected especially on women.

The constant conflict between activity and passivity, conformity and noncon-formity, male and female identification can be seen all throughout the stories, with a fear of failure, of embarrassment and shame, a feeling of inadequacy constantly threatening to emerge.

When one is aware of some of the writer's life history, it becomes apparent that his defenses indeed necessitated a certain amount of constriction of his life to a rather restless, tangential relationship to people, traveling a good deal, almost by design an onlooker who participates only vicariously via his notebook in stories which, as seen in the sample examined, center on a relatively narrow range of themes. He was obviously able to function, nevertheless, by conforming with a character quite acceptable within the setting of the upper-crust Anglo-Saxon society—urbane, polished, knowledgeable, and, above all, not causing any diffi-culties by uncontrolled emotions. He was very sensitive and shy beneath this stiff-upper-lip front, and yet he was often involved in bloodcurdling and some-times cold-blooded cruelties, as in his work as an intelligence agent. His own account of his married life suggests something less than affectionate warmth.

One wonders if the attempt to control all emotion might be related to the fact that some critics have spoken of Maugham as a great craftsman rather than a great artist, feeling apparently that his stories lacked depth and were too neatly pack-aged. Could this same problem, especially in relation to women, also be related to his marital difficulties and to the fact that he wandered the earth so restlessly and aloof?

D. Discussion

The external features and the geographical settings of Maugham's stories vary a great deal. If one compares him, for instance, with Tennessee Williams, it is obvious that he is not constricted with regard to milieu. Williams almost always chooses the setting of the American South. Yet I believe that Maugham shares with Williams the constrictions of essential subject matter. Whether the adven-tures are in Malaya or India, Chicago or Petrograd, the theme and its treatment stay fairly constant. Control of the emotions, the difficulties people get them-selves into if they do not control them, and especially the dangers to men in their feelings for women are the leitmotifs that govern his work. A certain aloof compassion goes hand in hand with urbanity. Stylistically one always notes a form of prompt dispatch in the tightly organized plots. There is constriction here, a measure of stereotype, within the creative personality.

Freud, in his paper on the poet, mentioned perceptual selectivity with regard to the causal relationship between a writer's productions and his personality. In the case of Maugham, it seems that his stories are the result of such a selective viewing of life. They are the product of the forms of adaptation and defenses with which he tried to deal with his own life and his own emotional problems. We have some clues as to what these emotional problems might be. There are some suggestive relations among his feelings for women, the loss of his mother at an

early age, his aggression and his stammer, his personal shyness, his marital difficulties, and his restless wanderings. However, these conjectures with regard to
causal interrelations to the early life history are not of central concern to us and
could not progress beyond the usual state of loose guesses on the basis of limited
material. We are on safer ground if we limit ourselves to inferences covering the
relationship between literary production and the personality of the author.

One can speculate further: In what way can the kind of story analysis we have
done here contribute to the understanding and critical analysis of literature? The
systematic frame of reference for analysis of literary products may be generally
useful for any author's work. The range and depth of a literary piece are often at
the center of critical appraisal, and a T.A.T. type of analysis may well give a more
reliable account than the customary free-style appraisal. Perhaps one of the reasons for widely differing critiques may be, at least in part, the lack of any base line
of comparison.

The type of psychological analysis presented here may well throw some interesting light on the relationship between an author's personality and his work. I do
not know that such enlightenment would add anything to the values of literature,
but it might add some interesting facets to the story of man and his behavior.

CHAPTER X

OBJECT RELATIONS THEORY AND ASSESSMENT WITH THE T.A.T., C.A.T., AND S.A.T.

A. Perspectives on Object Relations Theory

P SYCHOANALYSIS IS IN MANY WAYS A PERCEPTUAL THEORY. MOST clearly, the concept of projection involves a perception, i.e., the structuring of some contemporary experience by apperceptions previously laid down (see pg. 24).

The "previously laid down" apperceptions are often also referred to as "structure"—K. Eissler said percepts become structure [106]. And of course, percepts of the important or "significant people" are the most important internalized images; those and the ones of self—originally the "body image" as described by Schilder [297], and later, more broadly, the series of "self images" one has.

Recently, Jacobson [179], Mahler [223], Kohut [200], and Kernberg [194] have elaborated upon "object relations theory." It has developed a life of its own, at times even seen in contrast to classical analysis.

Nevertheless, psychoanalysis was always an "object theory." Freud made that most concrete in his conception of the superego as being largely the result of internalized parental images expressing strictures and inhibitions. In the *Ego and the Id,* Freud [317] showed how the superego is formed out of internalized identifications primarily with the father for the oedipal-stage male child. And, in his paper on "Mourning and Melancholia," [316] Freud suggested that one of the ways we become able to work through a mourning reaction over the death of a loved one is to develop an "inner image" or "introject" of the lost object.

Melanie Klein, Fairbairn [113] and other members of the British school emphasized the importance of the earliest internalized objects. Klein [198], notably, developed a rather comprehensive picture of how a child gradually builds up inner images of family members that then make up the child's internal fantasies of what these and other people are like. These then influence how the child experiences and relates to other people in his actual daily life. For example, if the child has a father who is extremely aggressive, the child may tend to build up an inner image of father figures as extremely aggressive and frightening. Other men similar in age to the child's father, may then be experienced as if they were all as aggressive and frightening as the child's own father. Another example illustrated in Melanie Klein's clinical sessions with children is the way a child develops an inner fantasy of the parents' relationship to each other. This could be an image of a loving parental couple or of a couple who always fight and argue with each other. This interpersonal relationship of a parental pair is represented intrapsychically in the child's inner world.

Sandler and Rosenblatt [291] suggest the term "representational world" for the constellation of images of parents, siblings, relatives, and other significant individuals that exist in the child's internal, intrapsychic world. Another way of putting it is that the child's unconscious is not only made up of libidinal and aggressive drives and unconscious wishes. The unconscious is also made up of fantasy images of human beings that significantly influence the individual's everyday behavior.

The many different characters in the T.A.T. stories produced by an individual may, then, be viewed as a window into the variety of self and object representations that made up the individual's representational world. They are the cast of characters within the individual's experience of actual people from day-to-day.

The T.A.T. and its offspring, the C.A.T. and S.A.T., are suitable projective tests for the assessment of an individual's interpersonal and intrapersonal object relations. Since the individual is presented with a set of pictures of human beings or animals in social situations and asked to construct a fantasy story about each picture, the outcome of these tests provide rich material about the individual's ability to relate to others, his capacity for experiencing other people with an appreciation of their complexities, and the individual's *manner* of experiencing interpersonal relationships in his family, job situation, or circle of friendships. The T.A.T., C.A.T., and S.A.T. allow a deep view into the individual's level of interpersonal experiences, conflicts, and level of development and functioning.

B. An Analysis of Object Relations in the T.A.T.

Object Relations Approach to a T.A.T. Case

The following is an object relations interpretation of the T.A.T. protocol previously described on pages 83–95. This is the case of "John Doe," male, age 25, single. The method of analysis is similar to the basic approach previously outlined in which object relations is viewed as one of the ego functions [42, 46].

One of the functions of the ego is to internally represent in fantasy the individual's actual and imagined interpersonal experience. For T.A.T. analysis, the clinician begins by making an inventory of the cast of characters in each story with a note or two about the personality of each character, like the program notes one reads before seeing a play. The next step is to make an inventory of the interactions among the characters with a few notes characterizing the type of each interaction. It is then a simple step to write a short summary of the object relations in each story.

1: This child is sick in bed. He has been given sheet music to study, but instead of the music he has come across a novel that interests him more than the music. It is probably an adventure story. He evidently does not fear the chance that his parents will find him thus occupied as he seems quite at ease. He seems to be quite a studious type and perhaps regrets missing school, but he seems quite occupied with the adventure in the story. Adventure has something to do with ocean or water. He is not too happy, though not too sad. His eyes are somewhat blank—coincidence of reading a book without any eyes or knowing what is in the book without reading it. He disregards the music and falls asleep reading the book.

Cast of Characters	*Type of Personality*
Boy	Sick, withdrawn in bed, reads adventure novel instead of studying music, blank eyes, omnipotent (knows book's contents without having to read it)
Parents of boy	No details given
Classmates and teachers at school (Implied)	No details given

Social Interactions	*Type of Personality*
Boy is given music to study	Passive receptive object relation
Boy misses school	Object hunger evident
Boy reads novel about ocean or water (desire to regress to "womb," to mother as narcissistic gratifying object)	Passive receptive object relation

Summary

Sick, regressed, and passive-receptive self representation is given music to study, but instead withdraws into fantasy of regression to womb. Object representations seen as providing, but also as external superego figures to check up on him if he is practicing music. Story ends with regression to "womb" (ocean, water) resulting in merger with other (author of adventure novel) with symbiotic omniscience (ability to then know contents of book without reading it).

Sequence of story suggests withdrawing from reality-orientation of music study others gave him to work on into "womb" fantasy of psychotic level of merger of reading other's mind. Story suggests tendency to schizoid withdrawal from current reality of others as an adult (blank affect and inner fantasy life) and to regress to being a sick child or fetus, to be omnipotently cared for by the mother. Passive-aggressive anal level struggle for control seen in relation to parents, music, and school and statement of missing school are highest level of object relations noted. However, the fetal level of regression, somatization, idea of others attempting to control him, check up on him, and his knowing the book's contents without having to read it suggests a diagnosis of psychosis.

3BM: This is a girl in a cell and she has been jailed because she was found guilty of prostitution. She is in this position in the picture because she is very ashamed, not because of being arrested, because she is quite familiar with the police, but because of the fact that her picture and a newspaper write-up was being sensationally spread across the country. She knew that her sister, who was a nun, would suffer from it, and it made her feel very badly because she, at one time, had a chance and an opportunity to follow her elder sister's example but it was too late now. She grabs a concealed knife from under her blouse and stabs herself.

Casting of Characters	Type of Personality
Girl	"All bad," sexually promiscuous, jailed for prostitution, and ashamed of national publicity (desire for grandiose level of exhibitionism)
Police	Superego representation that jails—stops—her from id discharge.
Sister of girl (nun)	"All good," nun who suffers from problems of her sister

Social Interactions	Type of Interactions
Girl jailed by police with whom she is quite familiar	Police superego representation restricts and stops sexual drive discharge and exhibitionism of girl.
Girl's sister, the nun, suffers due to girl's badness	"All good" self representation suffers from threat of contamination by "all bad" self representation, so "all bad" presentation must be killed off by suicide of bad girl prostitute

Summary

Primitive splitting between "all bad" sexual representation of girl prostitute and "all good" sexless self representation of nun sister of girl. "All bad" self representation may seek grandiose level of exhibitionism, while "all good" self representation may suffer from such exposure and contamination. In order to preserve "all good" representation, solution offered is to kill off bad self by violent suicide. Since the patient is male, this could also be a homicidal desire to kill oedipal sexual mother, so as to preserve the needfulfilling "all good" mother of infancy or fetal period.

4: The girl in the picture is half-caste. She is in love with the man who is going to leave her and return to his wife. They have spent quite some time together in intimacy. She is pleading with him to stay with her or help figure some way to plan for the coming of the child she is going to bear. She is in poor circumstances financially, and he tells her she should make arrangements to conclude the birth and thus everything would iron out because he is definitely determined to leave as the affair in his mind is at an end. She is very broken up by it. She pleads for him to spend one more night, which he agrees to, and in the middle of the night she sets fire to the house, thus solving the problems of all concerned.

Cast of Characters	*Type of Personality*
Girl	Poor, desperate about abandonment by man friend, pleading, suicidal, and homicidal
Man friend of girl	No details given
Unborn child	No details given

Social Interactions	*Type of Interactions*
Girl pleading with man not to abandon her and her unborn child, so she kills all of them	Panicking at threat of abandonment, so aggressive impulses erupt (symbolized by fire) and killing
Man friend wants her to kill unborn child	Homicidal interaction
Fetus in womb	passive receptive object relation

Summary

Poor, desperate pregnant self panics at threat of abandonment by father of baby and kills self and others, which may express merger wish through shared death. Abortion and setting fire to all of them may represent a desire to rid self of demanding, dependent fetus self representation. Theme of fetus in womb is now stated directly, where it was only implied in Story #1.

Panic reaction to threat of abandonment, outbreak of homicidal and suicidal aggressive impulses, and regression to fetal or merged and fused state (united in death) further suggest primitive object relations with lack of self-object boundaries indicative of psychosis.

6BM: This is a scene in a play. The two characters are on the stage; one is a famous elderly actress, who has a son about the age of the young man appearing opposite her. The dialogue in the play has suddenly taken on a new meaning for her. She sees now that the play, which was written by her son, has an entirely different meaning in this scene in the picture. The boy is telling the mother that he has just committed a murder. She understands now that this was her son's way of conveying to her the terrifying fact that that is actually what had happened. In the play, as her son had written it, the climax comes when the mother calls the police. But the famous actress decides to put her own climax into action after the play is over. She calls her son and says, "The climax of your play will have to be changed." She says, "I think the audience will perfer this one," so here she draws a revolver and shoots him. (What kind of murder was it?) Oh, a girl. Motive primarily to do with sexual. She had been unfaithful.

Cast of Characters	Type of Personality
Famous elderly actress on stage	Exhibitionistic, homicidal (kills son to punish him for murder he committed)
Son of actress who wrote play about murder	Controls others (writes play they are in), homicidal, and is indirect (tells mother of his murder through his play she acts in)
Young man on stage same age as author of play	Twin fantasy? No details given
Police	No details given
Unfaithful girlfriend of play's author	Sexually unfaithful

Social Interactions	Type of Interactions
Actress feels son tells her of his crime indirectly and punishes him by killing	Manipulative and homicidal object relation (retaliatory)
Son writes play for mother and others to act in	Magically controls others
Young man in play	Passive, controlled by others
Girlfriend of play's author	Unfaithful to play's author

Summary

The idea of a scene in a play shows patient's desire for some distance from the primary process of earlier stories by isolation of affect defense. But this quickly breaks away, as author of play magically controls mother and others, is indirect (reappearance of passive-aggression of Story #1), and homicidal solution to girlfriend's being unfaithful to him (reappearance of homicidal retaliation for abandonment of Story #4). "All bad" manipulative son is punished by mother killing him (reappearance of attempt to rid self of "all bad" self representation by homicide as in Stories #3BM and 4).

The magical control of others, homicidal aggression, and suggestion of twin theme in young man actor, who plays author of play, again shows the primitive level of the patient's object relations. Again we see attempt to rid himself of the bad, sexual, and homicidal part of the self.

7BM: This would be a man and his son. The son is very depressed over his health. The father is telling him that as a young man he too had the same illness, and that it can be cured if the son has the will to cure it. The father tells the young man that he himself alone can cure it. The son believes that there is no hope, but replies that he will go away for a little while and think it over. The father replies, "You are not doing a favor to me by saying that. I am thinking about your getting well for the simple reason that you have a wife and children to support, and in the event of your being bedridden, the responsibility for your family will be put entirely upon your mother and me." The young man finally concludes that he will take his wife and family with him and try to make things go better in a healthier climate. (What kind of illness did he have?) T.B. (Did he get better?) No, I don't think he does. After a few years he dies and the children are old enough to support mother or perhaps he left insurance. Never contacted father again. No correspondence. After not having heard from each other for a long time, the old man dies and leaves the children a large estate. This is his way of having repented.

Cast of Characters	*Type of Personality*
Father of son	Father identifies with son's illness
Mother of son	Mother will resent taking care of son's family
Son	Son is depressed over health, feels helpless, withdraws to healthier climate
Son's wife	Dependent, needing support, but ends up supporting mother?
Son's children	Children dependent, needing support

Social Interactions	*Type of Interactions*
Father tells son he had same illness and son should cure himself, so father and mother won't have to support son's wife and children	Father overidentifies (Patient's merger fantasies?) and relates by *telling* son what to do. Controlling of son and rejecting of him.
Children need support and later they support mother	Children dependent, but later reverse roles

Summary

Continuation of themes of bedridden dependence, threats of rejection responded to by someone dying in this case through somatization, schizoid withdrawal (to go off and *think*), and withdrawal and regression to womb (go to healthier climate). Primitive level of object relations, although this story shows more depression (oral dependency, turning aggression against the self, somatization, and object loss) than psychosis. Since this is the last story reported, it may mean that the patient is only capable of pulling himself out of psychosis to a level of severe depression. Narcissistic grandiosity is seen in comment that son can only cure himself alone.

Overall object relations summary

The *main characters* in this man's T.A.T. stories are seen as sick, passive-aggressive, withdrawing, and regressively dependent (Stories #1 and 7BM) or as sexually promiscuous and suicidal (#'s 3BM, 4, and 6BM). The *secondary characters* are very similar to the main characters. They tend to be controlling and rejecting (Parents in #1, police in 3BM, boyfriend in 4, girlfriend in 6BM, and father and mother in 7BM), detached (sister in 3BM, father in 7BM), homicidal (mother in 6BM), or passive, withdrawing, and imitative (wife and children in 7BM).

The lack of much differentiation between the main and secondary characters suggests (1) lack of much self-object differentiation and (2) little evidence of development of repression. This is always important in object relations assessment on the *T.A.T.*—to look at the within group differences among the *main characters* and the differences between these two groups of story characters in order to get a clinical understanding of the level of self and object differentiation within the patient's internal representational world. The primitive splitting of the all good nun sister and all bad prostitute sister in #3BM further corroborates that the patient has not developed much differentiation between self and other beyond primitive splitting and that he tends to defend by primitive splitting, rather than with higher more oedipal level defenses, such as repression, ambivalence, and other related defenses.

Analysis of the *social interactions* show that this man's object relations are very primitive. There is very little directly stated social interaction among any of the characters in his stories (#1 and 3BM have the littlest interactions of all the stories). In #4, the only stated interaction is in the pregnant girl's pleading with the father of her unborn baby not to leave her to return to his wife and her action of setting fire to the house killing him, herself, and the unborn baby. This tendency to react to threat of abandonment with panic and impulsive homicidal and suicidal aggression is a pre-oedipal response to anxiety, rather than the response of signal anxiety in individuals who have reached the oedipal and higher levels of development.

6BM has directly stated interactions of the son telling his mother he committed a murder, which now shows sequentially how the patient will follow the previous firesetting murder. The mother responds by shooting him (she abandons him and punishes him for his murder by killing him). The directly stated interactions in 7BM are the father telling the son to cure himself without anyone else's help including that of the father and mother. The son withdraws to a healthier climate with his wife and children, but later he dies and later the father dies. This shows a controlling and abandoning interaction by the father and a withdrawing somatization response of the son. Parallel action is seen in the son and family withdrawing together to the healthier climate and the son and father later dying. Withdrawal and imitative action is normal for a pre-oedipal age child. But the somatization response to parental abandonment by dying again shows the severe level of this man's depression.

Failure of reality-testing is seen in "reading a book without any eyes" or knowing what is in the book without reading it in Story #1; the prostitute who cannot reform, be forgiven, and become a nun in #3BM; the idea that the son can control his mother's reaction to his crime by having her act this idea out in a play he wrote in 6BM; and the idea that only he alone by himself can cure his tuberculosis in 7BM. This man's level of reality-testing, therefore, is not as actively fluid, loose, and grossly distorted as in individuals in the midst of active psychosis. Instead, we find subtle, indirect evidence of failure of reality-testing and delusional thinking in the above examples characteristic of latent schizophrenia or a psychotic condition currently in some state of remission.

Discussion of Implications of Object Relations

In object relations theory, three areas are useful in determining whether this patient is actively psychotic:

1. The level of self-object differentiation. The self-object differentiation of primitive splitting is a more borderline level of psychopathology that is more developed than the delusionally fusing self-object lack of boundaries in actively psychotic conditions. Which is his level?
2. The level of reality-testing.
3. The level of acting out of sexual and aggressive impulses.

Clearly, in all these areas, this man's T.A.T. shows a psychotic condition. The lack of much difference between the main and secondary characters in his stories suggests little self-object differentiation and the reality-testing level shows delusional merger ideation. Finally, the level of acting out of sexual and aggressive impulses is extremely primitive with the imagery of prostitution, adultery, homicide, and suicide. The likelihood of acting out of these homicidal and suicidal ideations should be taken very seriously in treatment planning.

In sum, this is a man with a latent schizophrenic or psychotic depressive condition currently in remission with some presence of self-object differentiation and some reality-testing. However, his acting out potential of suicidal and homicidal impulses is at an extremely dangerous level, particularly since he believes others want to control him, abandon, and murder him. The patient definitely does not have a borderline disorder, since his self-object differentiation, reality-testing, and control of acting out impulsivity are not at the level of borderline patients. If the patient is not currently on a psychiatric inpatient service, on anti-psychotic medication, and under active suicide and homicide watch, these interventions should be immediately put into effect.

Conclusion

This case example demonstrates an object relations analysis of a T.A.T. protocol according to the approach of Kernberg [194] and Volkan [334]. We have attempted to emphasize the value of highlighting the cast of characters in the story with the type of personality of each character and of analyzing the types of social interactions among these story characters. The main characters can be viewed as the more conscious self, while the other, secondary characters can be viewed as the part of the self that is less available to immediate awareness. The presence of primitive splitting seen in characters in the same story of opposite qualities and the level of reality-testing can be investigated in order to determine the pathological level of these object relations in the T.A.T. protocol.

Since object relations stems from Freud's ego function approach, the reader will note the similarity of this object relations analysis of this T.A.T. protocol with the earlier analysis of this case in order to illustrate the congruity of these two approaches and the diagnostic agreement in interpretation of the T.A.T. in clinical practice.

CHAPTER XI

BORDERLINE AND NARCISSISTIC DISORDERS IN THE T.A.T., C.A.T., AND S.A.T.

A. Brief Overview of the Diagnostic Concept of Borderline and Narcissistic Disorders

TWO VERY POPULAR PSYCHIATRIC DIAGNOSES OF THE PAST DEcade are the narcissistic personality disorder intensively studied by Heinz Kohut [200, 201], and the borderline personality disorder intensively studied by Otto Kernberg [193, 195]. Other individuals made substantial contributions prior to, concurrent with, and subsequent to the contributions of Kohut and Kernberg. Their own prolific writings and those of a substantial number of disciples have aroused a great deal of interest [44, 45].

The significant factor in both diagnoses is the identification of a psychiatric disorder that is characteristically pre-oedipal, rather than an oedipal level neurotic disorder (obsessive-compulsive, hysterical, or phobic neurosis), but is possibly, except for brief episodes, not psychotic. Earlier, the term "borderline" referred to an individual at the border between psychotic and neurotic disorders. This could be a stable disposition or a labile one. It was Kernberg's contribution to insist that "borderline" designated a specific diagnostic entity with distinct criteria in terms of object relations and defenses and calling for specific therapeutic management.

Narcissistic pathology was also earlier thought of as referring to a psychotic patient's withdrawal into a fantasy world of his or her own without a realistic relationship to the needs, perceptions, and existence of other people. However, narcissistic features could also be seen in a neurotic individual as in someone who wants a circle of noncritical admirers or someone who marries a famous person. The dictionary defines narcissism as love of the self at the expense of love for others (as putting one's own needs above those of everyone else and a lack of empathy for, and sensitivity to other people's feelings). This latter definition is the key factor in narcissistic personality disorder. In Kohut's theory, the development of narcissism follows a timetable of its own, similar to and parallel with Freud's original libidinal developmental schedule. From this theory it derives propositions concerning the treatment of narcissistic personality.

Neither Kohut's nor Kernberg's concepts are generally accepted by psychoanalysts. The Kris study group [2] on borderline conditions at the N.Y. Psychoanalytic Institute did not find a circumscribed condition as defined by Kernberg and had doubts about the appropriateness and usefulness of his delineation. Psychoanalysis had usually accepted the coexistence of pre-oedipal and oedipal aspects in various admixtures and to varying degrees in virtually all neuroses and other conditions. Kohut's complex and rather idiosyncratic formulations have found similar critique. Nevertheless, the borderline concept as well as that of the narcissistic personality, without rigid definitions, have merit as heuristic hypotheses.

Diagnosis of psychotic process in psychological tests in general is well covered by Weiner [336]. Psychotic process on the T.A.T. is seen in the presence of direct sexual and aggressive themes, themes of persecution, characters magically transforming from one thing to another, themes of omnipotence, magical power, figures being part one thing and part another, juxtaposition of extremes (angels and devils, acts of murder and loving tenderness), ideas of reference (thinking one card is connected to another card previously given), disorientation and confusion as to person, place, and time, lack of clear body boundaries, and gross deviation from the stimulus. The more one sees these indicators on psychological tests, the greater the possibility that the individual is either actively psychotic, has a latent psychosis, or has psychotic features. The frequency of indicators helps decide the severity of the condition.

Another useful method was pioneered by Anna Freud [128]. Hers was a developmental approach to diagnosis, called the "Developmental Profile." The idea is to identify in the clinical material (social history, set of referring symptoms, therapy sessions, and psychological tests) the predominant level of development in the area of psychosexual phases (oral, anal, oedipal, latency, adolescence, etc.), aggression, interpersonal object relations, defense mechanisms, and other areas. A clinician who sees severely disturbed individuals for testing can begin with the item approach of looking for a large number of indicators of psychotic process and then consider a developmental diagnosis. Here the key question is whether the person tested is predominantly pre-oedipal (stuck on a level typical of a child from birth to age 3 years) or oedipal neurotic (three years and above).

B. Salient Indicators of Pre-Oedipal and Oedipal Level Functioning

The following features are characteristic pre-oedipal vs. oedipal diagnostic indicators:

1. Panic reaction when signal anxiety is appropriate.
2. Primitive splitting, rather than ambivalence.
3. Denial and splitting as defenses, rather than repression to fend off awareness.

4. Part-object experience and part-object perception, rather than whole-object experience and whole-object perception.

5. Unstable internal object or lack of internal object, rather than stable, internalized object constancy (the ability to hold in one's mind an image of another person independent of being in the other person's presence).

6. Superego is split between extreme punitive "all bad" and libidinal "all good" images, rather than being flexible, reasonable, appropriate, and in tune with society's ethical principles.

7. Affect states are extreme and "pure" forms of love, hate, fear, sadness, and joy, rather than a neutralized, modulated array of feelings and nuances of feelings in between.

8. Shame and humiliation is experienced rather than oedipal neurotic guilt.

9. Introjective/projective relatedness [334] of self-object relatedness [201], rather than identifactory relatedness or relating to others as independent, separate individuals.

10. Fragmentation and disintegration, rather than synthetic function (ability to organize experience and perception into integrated "Gestalt," or meaningful wholes).

11. Acting and reacting, rather than experiencing and acting with a presence of observing ego function (self-observation and self-monitoring).

12. Defenses of incorporation and introjection, rather than identification.

13. Immediate discharge of impulses in acting out, rather than delayed gratification.

T.A.T. indicators of the above characteristics of pre-oedipal versus oedipal developmental stages are the following:

Panic anxiety rather than signal anxiety can be seen in characters in a story engaging in sudden, wild, frenetic, or repetitive actions in the face of danger or threat. A monster threatens and a small animal simply jumps up and down, runs, screams, or does an action over and over on the C.A.T. Or the smaller animal may simply "freeze", immobilized and overwhelmed with fear. A signal approach would be to mention a danger in the future and an attempt to plan, prepare, and cope with the danger, as in calling for help, building a fort, hiding, or working out a trap. In the chapter on neuropsychological assessment, we give the example of a child who symbolized the need for signal function by the need for the story figures to have a fire alarm to call the firemen to put out a fire in the kitchen. (see page 223)

Primitive splitting rather than ambivalence is the key feature for borderline pathology according to Kernberg [194]. He defines primitive splitting as the keeping apart of extreme affects of love and hate, extreme impulses of aggression and libido, and extreme images of the self and of other people (called self and object representations) that are characterized as "all good loving" and "all bad hating." One sees T.A.T. characters that are either angels or devils, good guys or totally evil ones, without evidence of story figures who are somewhat good and somewhat bad, who have more than one side to their personalities. Volkan [334] speaks of such fantasies of borderline patients as being all in black and white, rather than in technicolor. Ambivalence is seen in the T.A.T. by such statements as "either this . . . or that." Splitting in narrative style would be something more like, "It's this. No, it is only that." The concept of splitting, its soundness, and its usefulness have however been widely questioned (especially Pruyser) [19].

Part-object rather than whole-object experience and perception is seen on the T.A.T. in splitting, as we discussed above, where there is not a development of characters that have a combination of different feelings, traits, and activities, but a juxtaposition of good vs. bad characters.

Object Constancy is seen in behavior when the toddler begins to be able to play alone, with the mother in the next room or having been left in the care of a babysitter. When the mother leaves, there is no longer the temper tantrum panic reaction to separation anxiety. The child can now realize that the mother still exists independent of the child's immediate perception of her. Prior to object constancy, the child experiences the separation as a death, "out of sight, out of mind." If the child doesn't see or hear his mother, then mother must be dead. Hence the extreme level of panic and the extreme tantrums. The lack of object constancy can therefore be seen in T.A.T. stories as a theme of separation anxiety, upset shown when one figure leaves another. Right after leaving home, for example, the next action is falling and getting hurt (as in C.A.T. story #2 where one part figure lets go of the rope and the child on the other side falls and gets hurt, symbolizing separation from the parent), getting attacked by a storm or by a threatening figure, or getting sick. Object constancy could be seen in characters who leave others, who leave home, and can plan, use strategy, and use defenses to handle the dangers that occur in the future. *Little Red Riding Hood* telling the wolf along her path through the woods that she is going to grandma's house is an example in story form of maintaining an image in one's mind of the mother figure in the face of separation and threat.

Pre-oedipal superego is seen in T.A.T. stories of extreme punishment for mild transgression, as when a character is jailed or killed because he urinated on the floor or falls down a cliff and dies because he just "didn't look where he was going." A more oedipal, neurotic, or normal level of superego exists when the punishment fits the particular crime. The child spills his food on C.A.T. story #1 and the mother asks him to clean it up and not spill the next time. Or one character calls the other a name and then apologizes for it. Pre-oedipal children do not usually think to say, "I'm sorry," because their punishment for a crime is much more extreme than that, they feel as if they should be or—are going to be—severely beaten for what they did. A mere apology is not in their scheme of things due to the lack of development of an oedipal level of the superego. Pre-oedipal superego is often split between this very primitive, punitive, extreme punishment for extreme and even very mild infractions and extremely, magically good, all-forgiving godlike features. The child violates a taboo, such as stealing the giant's belongings in *Jack and the Beanstalk* and the primitive superego punishment is seen in the giant trying to eat and/or kill Jack. The all-good superego is seen in the ending, where Jack has the giant's magical belongings to share safely alone with his mother "happily ever after."

Extreme affect states rather than neutralized, modulated affect states are seen in T.A.T. stories in the use of extreme affect words, such as "hate," "love," "devastated," or "ecstatic," predominantly, rather than a range of gradations of affect words, such as "somewhat saddened," "a little annoyed," "interested," "surprised but understanding," etc. This goes along with #2 above (use of primitive splitting rather than ambivalence) and #4 (part-object rather than whole-object experience and perception). *Shame and humiliation rather than guilt* is seen in stories where the antagonist ends up with his pants down in front of an audience, slipping on a banana peel, or publicly embarassed in some way. While guilt is seen in characters expressing remorse over actions that caused harm to others, expressing sorrow over a missed opportunity due to doing something reckless or stupid, or expressing self-criticism or self-recrimination for actions they feel interfered with the happiness of other people. Egocentrism versus role-taking ability is related here in that the pre-oedipal individual becomes more upset over shame and humiliation and seeks to avoid doing things that will humiliate himself, while the oedipal individual is more concerned about the feelings of others and more guilty over causing hardship to others.

Introjective/projective rather than identifactory relatedness is seen in very young children relating to the mother as if they are an extension of the mother and as if the mother is an extension of them. The infant acts as if the mother is only there to feed and comfort him or should smile and laugh when he smiles and laughs. The toddler, when angry with the parent, may project this anger onto the parent and imagine the parent is a monster furious with the toddler. The young child treats the parent as a self-object, then, rather than as a separate individual with independent needs. The parent is treated as both part of the self and part of the other, part self and part the parent. This is seen in the T.A.T. in frequent changes of a character's identity, sex, changes of pronoun from singular to plural and back to singular, and magic transformations from one thing to another. The theme of eating up another or being eaten up on C.A.T. stories represents this oral incorporative, introjective attempt to obliterate the independent existence of the self and the other as separate individuals. The idea of one figure "reading another's mind" or having the exact same thought as the other at the same time is another example of this kind of symbiotic oneness characteristic of pre-oedipal individuals. This is seen in emphasis on symmetry or seeing "twin" context on *Rorschach* and also on T.A.T. as the theme of twins.

Fragmentation rather than synthetic function is seen on T.A.T. in stories that are disjointed, aimless, and lacking in a sequential organization towards a logical ending. The story may begin about a little chicken eating and abruptly switch to a baby sleeping in its bed as in a free association without a clear connection between the two themes. *Acting rather than acting with self-observation* is seen on T.A.T. stories in which the characters simply do different things, while there is no attempt to reflect on meaning about the actions or the picture. The boy looks at the violin, tries to play it, then puts it down (on card #1) is an example of acting without self-observation. By contrast having the boy thinking about what he should play, how long he should practice, if his parent is happy with his practicing, or comments about whether the picture reminds the storyteller of some of his own feelings, etc., are examples of the observing function more characteristic of the oedipal level of development. Finally, *defenses of incorporation and introjection rather than identification* are seen in stories where a figure experiences a separation or loss and reacts by eating up the other, being eaten up by the other, or imagining one is seeing a ghost of the deceased, rather than dealing with loss by doing something similar to the deceased person's former activities, such as taking up an activity that used to be the hobby of the deceased. *Acting out versus delayed gratification* is seen in eating right away, screaming for something one wants, demanding something immediately, rather than waiting.

The above constellation of pre-oedipal characteristics can be illustrated in C.A.T. protocols of children of preschool age, who are still predominantly on a pre-oedipal level. The first protocol is that of a girl of 4½ years, whose father physically abused her:

C.A.T. Protocols Illustrating Pre-Oedipal and Oedipal Level Functioning

Card #1: There were three chickens pecking at the trees and then the tree falls down and then they'll have to get another tree.

Comment

Oral emphasis is stated (pecking the trees) and theme of impulsivity, fragmentation, and panic anxiety is suggested by the tree falling down, as if the child seeks oral supplies from the parent (symbolized by the tree) and the parent falls apart.

Card #2: A little, three little bears and they wanted to pull a rope to tie around a tree and then they tied another rope around a tree and then it will fall on the Daddy.

Comment

Some desire for body boundaries and for synthesis is perhaps symbolized by the pulling a rope around the tree (a boundary to hold the self together), but in the end the tree falls continuing the theme of impulsivity, fragmentation, and panic reactions of becoming helpless and overwhelmed in the face of stress, rather than being able to mobilize coping mechanisms. That the tree falls on the father may indicate her anger at the abusive father or express something about the parents "falling upon" each other in a sexual or aggressive manner that was frightening to the child, as if the world were falling down.

Card #3: A big, big, fat Daddy lion and he killed a baby. A baby and then nothing happened (She gets very excited and flings the card in the air).

Comment

Stuttering is a typical anxiety reaction in young children, which perhaps occurred in this child when presented the lion and mouse picture that is often associated by children as a father and child. The lion "kills the baby," which indicates extreme aggressive impulsivity coming from her life experience and also intensified from her pre-oedipal tendency to project some of her anger onto others, so that she sees the other as even more threatening and angry. Flinging the card is again a panic response of acting out and immediately discharging her impulses, rather than being able to verbalize her feelings or mobilize other defense and coping mechanisms.

Card #4: Once upon a time there was kangaroo's and they went in the forest and got lost. They went and then they got lost again.

Comment

Separation from the parents and loss is symbolized in this story, which states an oral level theme. Repetition in action is similar to the stuttering above, which indicates anxiety and acting out impulsivity, rather than acting with self-observation.

Card #5: Once upon a time there was a little crib and a baby. The baby wasn't sleeping, because it was his bedtime and he forgot to eat dinner.

Comment

Oral neediness is stated again indicating a pre-oedipal level of psychosexual development, rather than an oedipal level which would be expected from her current age of $4\frac{1}{2}$ years.

Card #6: Once upon a time there was a little bear, little bears, and they wanted to eat frogs and then the frogs got hungry and they went into their place to eat the bears. They wanted to, but they couldn't do it.

Comment

This is an excellent example of the self-object or introjective/projective relatedness typical of pre-oedipal level individuals. The larger figures (adults?) want to incorporate, merge with, fuse with, and introject the littler figures (children?) and the littler figures want to eat up and incorporate the larger figures (the frogs want to eat up the bears). Following the sequence of her C.A.T. stories shows that she attempts to defend against separation and loss by primitive oral incorporation fantasies (to eat up or be eaten by the other so that the two of them are joined together).

Card #7: That one! That's a funny one. I don't know. No story on that one.

Comment

This is a picture of the tiger attacking the monkey, which is first defended against by reversal of affect ("that's a funny one"), then denial ("I don't know"), and finally by avoidance and withdrawal ("No story on that one"). These are all typical pre-oedipal level ego defenses, as opposed to more oedipal and higher level defenses of repression, reaction formation, rationalization, or sublimation, etc.

Card #8: Nothing about that one either. . . . Once upon a time there were four little monkeys. They were standing and the mother monkey said to the father monkey one, "I would like to go outside and play with the baby monkeys." And then nothing else. The father one said yes.

Comment

She starts with denial, avoidance, and withdrawal, but then manages to relate a mundane, everyday type of story. This type of trivializing is again a defense away from letting oneself go in free association and personally meaningful fantasy. It is similar to concrete description of the pictures. It may suggest a denial of parental criticism (the picture shows the mother monkey pointing her finger towards the child monkey next to her) and a desire for the mother to nurture and play with her without the abusive restrictions she experiences from her father in reality. The pause at the beginning can indicate denial or blocking defenses.

Card #9: Once upon a time there was a little, a mommy rabbit, and she was so sad that nobody was home with her and then she cried.

Comment

The affect of sadness to loss is expressed directly.

Card #10: Once upon a time there was two doggies. The baby doggy had to go outside and he went right there—he went in the toilet. The end.

Comment

We see a further denial of parental criticism in the failure to report the action in the picture on the card of a parent or adult dog spanking a puppy on its knee. The use of the word "suddenly" is typical of pre-oedipal level thematic stories symbolizing the sudden outbreak of impulses, a panic reaction to stress. This story suggests the puppy first went to the bathroom where the puppy was when the suddenly had to go, which further expresses acting out impulsivity, rather than an ability to delay immediate gratification. But she then ends it with the puppy going to the bathroom in the appropriate place, a suggestion that she is able to move in the direction of oedipal level development.

C.A.T. *Summary*

This girl of $4\frac{1}{2}$ years should be within an oedipal, neurotic level of psychosocial development. Instead, the C.A.T. suggests that the life stress within the family (parental strife, father's physical abuse) contributed to her staying primarily at a pre-oedipal level more typical of a child of $1\frac{1}{2}$ to $2\frac{1}{2}$ years of age.

In terms of the pre-oedipal characteristics enumerated at the beginning of the chapter, her C.A.T. shows panic reaction rather than signal anxiety function (cards 1, 2, and 3 with falling trees and killing), impulsivity (cards 1, 2, 3, and 10 in stuttering, repeated actions, primitive actions, (use of "suddenly"), acting out rather than delayed gratification (#10 with the going to the bathroom right where one is rather than in the toilet), dependency (#2 with theme of rope tied to adult figure); themes of separation and loss (#'s 4 and 8), regression to oral neediness (#'s 1, 2, 5, 6 and 8); self-object relatedness rather than self and object independence (#6 with the figures eating each other up); direct pure affect (#'s 3 and 9); and pre-oedipal level defense mechanisms of denial (#'s 3, 7, and 8) reversal of affect (#7), avoidance and withdrawal (#7 and 8), and blocking (#8 with its pause).

The child might be diagnosed, then, as having an adjustment disorder with pre-oedipal fixation or regression secondary to the family stress and abuse.

Following is another typical pre-oedipal level C.A.T. story to card #3 in a boy of 5 years of age, who is hyperactive.

Card #3. I'm not touching that one! This once upon a time is about a big lion that's sitting in his chair alone. He got up, went outside, scared all the people, ate one people, and real scary! You know what made him friendly?—a magic ball.

Comment

He first defends by avoidance and withdrawal ("I'm not touching that one!"), then brings in the theme of oral incorporation (eating up people) and of panic anxiety (scaring everyone). Finally, he reaches for magical thinking in the magic ball that makes him friendly, which also suggests dependency upon the mother (perhaps symbolized by the round ball) and undoing (the scary one becomes magically friendly). This shows an ability in this child to respond to stress and anxiety with the mobilization of defenses, so this child is closer to an oedipal level of signal anxiety, rather than the predominantly pre-oedipal panic reaction to anxiety in the little girl of $4\frac{1}{2}$ years above. But this boy's defenses are still pre-oedipal level defenses, rather than oedipal or higher ones.

The following is a story of a neurotic level child of 5 years, which shows what we would expect to see in a C.A.T. when a child is no longer on a pre-oedipal level, but has reached the oedipal level and by age 5 years is already well on the way to resolving and working it through on an age-appropriate level:

Card #7. Oh God! this is really scary. . . . Ok, here I go. . . . Once upon a time there was a lion catching a monkey and the monkey was running away on his rope. Then he was climbing up the tree, and the lion was crying (he gestures a roar) like this, "Rhhhhh!" He sounded like my Dad laughin'. Every time I go "Whoo!" to my sister, she runs. She thinks it's a ghost, but it's only me. In the night, in the dark, I do it, when there's not the light.

Comment

He is able to verbalize his fear of this card with the picture of the tiger attacking the monkey, "This is really scary," which pre-oedipal level individuals often do not do. They step back from the card, turn it over, refuse to do a story, or express a story only of aggressive actions of chase and escape. This boy then does retreat first to the pre-oedipal defense of avoidance and withdrawal (the monkey running away), but then comes back with a superb example of the typical oedipal level defense of identification with the aggressor. The boy identifies the tiger (lion here) with his father's loud laughing (a reversal of affect or reaction formation defense) and then tells us that he identifies with the father's roaring in scaring his sister. The father scares him, so he scares his sister, which shows oedipal identification with a quality of the father and a tendency to deal with aggressive threat by turning passive-into-active and becoming the threatening one to others, rather than remaining the helpless, panicked, passive recipient of threat from larger adults.

C. Specific Indicators of Borderline Pathology

In this chapter, we can only provide an introduction to this developmental type of T.A.T. and C.A.T. The reader should also review chapters 4 and 6 in this text for further explanation. Abrams [3] and Sutton-Smith et al. [320] suggest further developmental analyses of narratives. What is important for this chapter is to first distinguish the T.A.T. or C.A.T. protocol from psychotic process by using the list of psychotic *indicators* we suggested at the beginning of this chapter and then move on to distinguish whether the protocol is predominantly pre-oedipal or predominantly oedipal or above in *developmental* level in ego functions, defenses, and object relations. If the protocol has numerous psychotic indicators and is predominantly pre-oedipal, a diagnosis of psychotic process is to be considered (along with psychotic indicators on the other projective tests). If there are only a few indicators of psychosis or no indicators of psychosis, but the protocol is predominantly pre-oedipal, then a diagnosis of borderline disorder could be considered (providing the patient is over 8 or 9 years of age and there are signs of borderline pathology on other psychological tests in the battery).

Borderline pathology is often identified with individuals whose level is predominantly pre-oedipal, but is not fundamentally psychotic. But one must also look for the following characteristics, as noted in the DSM-III [11]:

1. Impulsivity or unpredictability in spending, sex, gambling, substance abuse, shoplifting, overeating, physically damaging acts (at least two of these).
2. A pattern of unstable and intense interpersonal relationships with marked shifts of attitude, idealization, devaluation, manipulation (consistently using others for one's needs).
3. Inappropriate, intense anger or lack of control of anger seen often in frequent temper tantrums.
4. Identity disturbance manifested by uncertainty about several issues relating to identity, such as self-image, gender identity, long-term goals or career choice, friendship patterns, values, and loyalties.
5. Affective instability: marked shifts from normal mood to depression, irritability, or anxiety, usually lasting a few hours and only rarely more than a few days, with a return to normal mood.
6. Intolerance of being alone seen in frantic efforts to avoid being alone (desperate calls to the therapist on Fridays before the weekend loneliness), depressed when alone.
7. Physically self-damaging acts such as suicidal gestures, self-mutilation, recurrent accidents or physical figures. Also periodic use of drugs, alcohol and overeating in the same manner.
8. Chronic feelings of emptiness or boredom.

D. T.A.T. Protocol Illustrating Borderline Disorders with Some Psychotic-Like Features

Adult Case of Borderline Disorder with some Psychotic-like Features

The following T.A.T. is from a 30 year old woman, who had one hospitalization for a suicide gesture in which she took sleeping pills. This case nicely illustrates the presence of a few psychotic-like features within a developmental level that is predominantly pre-oedipal. Key characteristics of borderline disorder, as defined by DSM-III further substantiate the diagnostic impression that she is not fundamentally psychotic, but has a borderline disorder with mild psychotic-like features:

1: This little boy is, let me look closely. This is ambiguous. You'd have to be a genius to make what I'd like to about this picture. The boy is missing that, don't write that. Let's see. He just got this violin and he was told he had to play this musical instrument and he hates the violin. He just had a lesson and he's been practicing for hours and he's just taking a rest now, he hates the violin. I have two different endings—one's healthy and one's not. I don't know which one to go with. As he got older, one day he smashes that violin against the wall and broke it. Then another way of ending it, it is bothering him, so he practiced it so he could become a better player and he became a great violinist.

But there's a little piece down here which could be broken, so he's upset that his violin could be broken. Oh, no! That's because he doesn't know how to play it and he doesn't want to play it.

Comment

Primitive splitting is suggested by the juxtaposition of extremes—the "unhealthy ending" of smashing the violin against the wall and breaking it and the "healthy ending" of practicing and becoming a great violinist. In splitting, two opposite feelings or ideas are kept apart from each other. They could not be part of the same story, for example. So she makes two different endings. Splitting is also suggested by the juxtaposition of "genius" and the boy at the end who feels broken like the violin could be, "because he doesn't know how to play it (low self-esteem) and he doesn't want to play it (anal level oppositionalism)." Aggressive, angry impulsivity, grandiosity (great violinist, genius), and part-object perception ("little piece here") are borderline features.

2: Ah, this is the one I get stuck on, this picture. It doesn't make sense to me. Um, um . . . (pause) I'm much less anxious than I used to be when I talked about these pictures. This is a wierd picture. Um, ah (heaves a sigh). This daughter's going to school. She's, the bus is coming from the left, but she's looking toward the right. Her mother's standing up against the tree that doesn't belong in the picture, facing another direction. The brother is plowing the field beside a horse and they're all in different zones. Well, very soon after the girl leaves for school, the mother starts . . . what does the mother do? Um, the mother does work that she has to do in the house and the son plows and takes care of the animals and they have lunch.

Comment

Pre-oedipal, borderline characteristics are predominantly the sense of fragmentation, part-object, or splitting in the idea that the tree "doesn't belong in the
picture" and that each family member is in a "different zone" and the notable
separation anxiety, when presented with this picture of a girl appearing to be
leaving for school or coming back from school to the family on the farm. She gets
stuck, blocks, becomes vague, pauses, and heaves a sigh presumably at the idea of
the "daughter's going to school" (all indicators of high anxiety).

3: (. . . she sighs). This girl goes to school for, um, disturbed people and she's just there
now in the student common room, upset. Wait, I think there's scissors on the floor next to
her. (She puts the card down.) She's upset because everyone's out that night and she's the
only one there.
   She goes to sleep early, she talks to a teacher, and then shortly after that, she flips out
and leaves school. Could be a biography, but it's not. At the beginning, I was thinking she
was pregnant and she was thinking she had to get an abortion and then there's another one
where she kind of looks like a lesbian from the behind. I used to have pretty elaborate
stories on these.

Comment

Anxiety over separation is clear from the beginning hesitation, sighing, filler
sounds (ah, uh, um), and the content itself. The defenses of avoidance and withdrawal are noted in her putting the card down and the action in the story of
"going to sleep," which is also an oral regression. Panic and fragmentation then is
expressed in the next action of "flipping out," and "leaving school" is another
form of avoidance, withdrawal, and regression. The negation form of denial
comes in the statement, "Could be a biography (about herself), but it's not."
Having an abortion may also continue the theme of separation anxiety and the
idea of a "lesbian from the behind" expresses the possibility of sex-role identification confusion and identity disturbance often seen in borderline patients.

4: God!, these cards don't make much sense to me. (She holds the card up close.) This
woman's husband just got home from work and . . . he, I can't tell if he's happy. He looks
like he's rushing off to somewhere. He's going to run upstairs, because he heard that his
daughter fell out of a tree today and the wife's just trying to tell him that it's not that bad.
That she's sleeping, but he wants to rush right up there. They all come downstairs in an
hour at the end and eat dinner and the little girl's a lot better.

Comment

"The meaninglessness" of the cards may illustrate her use of denial (blocking
off immediate awareness) and possible splitting. Separation anxiety is suggested
by the idea of coming home and "can't tell if he's happy" juxtaposed with the
contrary idea that "He looks like he's rushing off to somewhere." Primitive
splitting may be present here with this co-existence of opposite feelings and
thoughts. The daughter's accident and sleeping after it show borderline features
of self-damaging acts, impulsivity, and depressive withdrawal.

6GF: Who makes up these pictures, anyway? . . . (pause) . . . This woman's sitting on the couch and her husband just came back behind her to ask her what drink she wanted for dinner. They're waiting for company to arrive. That's it. . . . Later on, the company comes, they have a nice time, and have one too many drinks and just get very intellectual and on and on. There's sort of a debate going on and then the company leaves. The company sort of staggers out, crawls, and that's the night.

Comment

Pause suggests anxiety and blocking. Acting out impulsivity is suggested by having "too many drinks," possible defensive intellectualization ("get very intellectual") and regression (crawling out). Some fragmentation of thoughts is evident by the fits and starts and disjointed ideas in the style of relating the story and in its overall narrative organization.

7GF: This mother's trying to talk to her daughter about, uh (long sigh) about her having to go into the hospital and her daughter's very upset. She can't even look at her and the daughter runs up to her room and spends the whole night there. She falls asleep, but the mother comes to say 'Goodnight' to make her feel better.

Comment

Theme of separation anxiety is repeated here (leaving the mother and going to the hospital), which is reacted to with defense of withdrawal (runs up to her room) and regression to sleep (falls asleep). But she only seems to feel better when separation is removed by the mother coming back to her.

8BM: How many are there? Well, ah, this boy is imagining what's happening behind him. These two men are cutting open his friend behind him. He often imagines things like that that scare him and sort of, he gets engrossed in these fantasies. He ruined the whole room. These men ruin the whole room. These men do it all. They shoot holes in the windows, knock out the walls, cut open this man's intestine. Take it out and leave him there and he's in pain. No anesthesia. These guys aren't doctors. This boy is just dreaming the whole thing up. It's just his fantasy. It didn't really happen. Well, he acts out sometimes and in drawings or what he writes. That's not me talking. I don't have thoughts like that, don't you think?

Comment

Acting out of aggressive impulses (ruining the whole room by shooting holes in walls, cutting open the man on the table) is defended against by displacement ("He ruined the room . . . these men ruin the room") and denial ("This boy is just dreaming the whole thing up. It's just his fantasy. It didn't really happen. . . . That's not me talking . . .") The primitive and intense aggression and the preoedipal level of defenses against it are typical identifying features of the borderline disorder.

10: I don't understand this picture. I don't, I can't tell if it's two women or a man and a woman. They almost look alike. Like twins. Ah (she sighs), I don't know. These women are twins (she puts the card out at arm's length) and they were usually very close to each other and here they're, they look very intimate with each other. Since they grew up as twins, they're always very physical with each other in a way, in a sisterly sense (she laughs embarassingly) and here they haven't seen each other, because the funeral of a friend brought them together.

Comment

Sex-role confusion and the theme of twins (self-object merger) are further examples of borderline disorder in this story. She also suggests the presence of primitive splitting in the juxtaposition of the theme of merger (twins and intimacy) with the opposite theme of death, loss, and separation (the funeral).

13MF: Ah, I don't like this one, either. They had a "one night stand" and they just picked each other up at a bar one night. Um, he's leaving after that, he has a hangover, and he's leaving. He's got all his clothes on. They never see each other again. He just leaves. Ah . . . I just thought of something else. She could be dead and he saw her and he's very upset. But why would she have no clothes on? Scratch that. Well, they weren't close before, but now he really cares about her, but she's dead.

Comment

Acting out impulsivity and the borderline experience of intense, short-lived interpersonal involvements are expressed in the idea of "one night stands," during which they meet, presumably have sexual relations, and "never see each other again"—an experience this patient has had frequently. Then she shifts the thought to extreme loss through death either because separation often feels like a total death to her (as in the previous story) or because her anger at separation stirs up extremely primitive and intense aggressive impulses. Denial is then evident in her desire to "scratch that."

Summary

The T.A.T. protocol reveals the key features of a borderline disorder with psychotic-like features with the frequency and primacy of primitive splitting (card #'s 1, 2, 10 and 13MF), denial (cards #'s 3, 4, 8BM, and 13MF), and separation anxiety (#'s 2, 3, 4, 6GF, 7GF, 10, and 13 MF). Tremendous aggression, impulsivity, high anxiety, avoidance, withdrawal, regression and blocking are further identifying features.

Sex-role confusion is seen on #3BM suggested by the lesbian themes and stated very directly on #10, where she is not sure if they are a man and a woman and then moves on to make them twins. The borderline patient is also at the border in ego boundaries, so that the self is experienced as part-self and part-other and others are experienced as part-other and part of the self. The borderline fuses, separates, and refuses, back-and-forth. The borderline lacks cohesion of the self or ego integration and has unstable boundaries between the self and others. Therefore, at points of stress, the borderline's self becomes further fragmented, further disintegrated, and further split into part-object and part-self representations and there is a further tendency to merge and fuse with need-fulfilling objects. Separation anxiety is a key issue causing panic outbursts in which the inappropriate level of intense anger and aggression may appear psychotic to others. The borderline may attempt to frantically merge with the separating love object, so that a family member or boyfriend or girlfriend of a borderline individual feels overwhelmed by this overbearing demandingness. However, the borderline is often as terrified of closeness as he or she is of separation. So when the borderline begins to feel merged and intimate, he may begin to feel threatened with loss of the self, panic, and abruptly reject the love object so desperately desired. Because of these two deep fears of separation and of merger, the borderline's interpersonal relations are overly intense resembling the turbulent storms of conflicting needs for dependence and independence of toddlers and of adolescents.

These abrupt swings between intimacy to the point of twinship and extreme isolation in themes of death are seen in this T.A.T. protocol as we read from one story to the next. The borderline's interpersonal relations are also overly intense, because of the extreme "pure" expression of affect. The anger is a pure, deep anger, as is the sadness or love. Affects are unneutralized, unmodulated by the nuances seen in higher functioning individuals. So others feel intensely drawn to, involved with, and also rejected by borderline individuals. These extreme mood and feeling states also swing from one extreme to the other, so they are in a deep, almost suicidal depression one hour or day, in ecstatic joy the next, and later apparently calm and normal. When calm and normal, they complain of emptiness and boredom, which is really due to the schizoid-like operation of the defense of primitive denial and primitive splitting (a clouding over of immediate awareness).

The borderline individual may abruptly turn to self-damaging behavior, such as accidents, gambling, alcohol, or drug abuse, as a frantic attempt to feel alive again (after the schizoid emptiness and boredom has come upon him) or to calm the stimulus overload through drugs or alcohol (after the stimulating aspects of these behaviors have made him start to feel too alive and potentially out-of-control and fragmented). Because of this primitive splitting, mood swings, and swings between the schizoid emptiness level of denial and stimulus overload, the borderline individual typically is not consolidated enough to be an addictive personality, but uses drugs, alcohol, gambling and the lot in a fragmented and an intermittent manner.

A continuing debate in the literature is over what is the key issue in borderline pathology. Some feel it is separation anxiety and the lack of appropriate reaction to anxiety, rather than having developed a signal function to anxiety. Some feel it is due to a fragmented, split, or "unintegrated" ego that needs to develop further towards integration [351]. Some feel it may be fundamentally influenced by organic factors, such as neuropsychological dysfunction in the area of perceptual, perceptual-motor, and motoric integration so that the individual has basic deficits in synthesizing functions and is thus prone to fragmentation and unorganized panic under stress. Others emphasize the predominant use of primitive splitting and related defenses, such as denial, idealization, devaluation, and projective identification, rather than repression and its related defenses of reaction formation, rationalization, intellectualization, and sublimation.

The reader will notice that these issues are the main characteristics of the pre-oedipal stage of development, which we listed at the beginning of this chapter. It is for that reason that Kernberg writes of the borderline disorder as the main disorder of pre-oedipally fixated individuals, who are not psychotic. He suggests that the disorder is due to a constitutional level of aggression that is higher than in normal individuals and to a failure to successfully resolve the rapprochement subphase of the separation-individuation process, when the child swings between intense separation and merger fears due to not having yet developed an inner image of the mother (object constancy). Narcissistic disorder and many other pre-oedipal disorders are, therefore, considered by Kernberg to be subtypes of borderline disorder, since he views the borderline disorder as the central pre-oedipal disorder.

Kohut [200], on the other hand, views narcissistic personality disorder as the central pre-oedipal disorder. Consequently, for him, the borderline disorder is a subset of the narcissistic personality disorder. The characteristics of narcissistic pathology are similar to borderline pathology—difficulty in forming and maintaining relationships, little empathy for others' needs and feelings, grandiosity in unrealistic schemes, exaggerated self-regard, constant demandingness for attention, inappropriate idealization of certain hero figures, and intense envy of others. Extreme almost paranoid-like anger is often expressed, when the narcissistic person feels rejected or even mildly criticized. Also, there is an emotional aloofness at times and a sense of entitlement as the individual feels "splendidly isolated" from the common needs of other people. Very few patients who would fit Kohut's criteria of narcissistic personality disorder present themselves for psychological evaluation. Consequently, we cannot at this time provide an example of a T.A.T. protocol from such a patient. One would expect, however, to see in narcissistic patients the pre-oedipal characteristics we have illustrated above, but without the predominant borderline features of impulsivity, extreme mood swings, and indicators of fragmentation in storytelling style and content. The narcissistic patient typically is better organized and more stable. Hopefully, further research will provide us with valuable insights into how narcissistic patients might express their fundamental psychodynamics on the T.A.T.

CHAPTER XII

THE T.A.T., C.A.T., AND S.A.T. IN NEUROPSYCHOLOGICAL ASSESSMENT

A. Some General Remarks on Neuropsychological Assessment

THE UTILITY OF THEMATIC APPERCEPTION TESTS IN THE AREA OF personality assessment has long been established. In recent years, clinicians have also increasingly recognized their occasional incidental usefulness in the diagnosis of certain brain disorders, localization of brain lesions, certain types of verbal language disorders, and learning disabilities. In this chapter, we will present an introduction to this quickly developing area and present a child and adult case to illustrate the use of C.A.T. and T.A.T. in the diagnosis of attention deficit disorder, a disorder that is both very prevalent in our school and patient population and is a good example of neuropsychological characteristics seen on thematic apperception tests.

In a popular text on neuropsychological diagnosis, Lezak [215] points out that, "Stories composed by brain injured patients possess the same response qualities that characterize organic Rorschach protocols." Following Piotrowski [262] and Foegel [215], Lezak lists the characteristics below:

Identifying Features of Neuropsychological Deficit in T.A.T. and C.A.T. Responses

1. Use of fewer words and ideas in relating stories Piotrowski [262] calls this low R (low number of Rorschach responses) for the Rorschach test).
2. Response times may be longer with several punctuating pauses (Piotrowski's T (response time) on Rorschach test).
3. Concrete description of the picture, rather than a free fantasy elaboration of one's own. Simple listing of items in the picture, such as table, chair, window, violin, etc. (Similar to Color Naming, Cn, on Rorschach).

215

4. Tendency to provide a story that is trite with few characters and little action [262] notes less *M* (less movement responses, M for Human Movement, FM for Animal Movement, and m for movement of inanimate objects).

5. Presence of confusion, misinterpretations of items in the pictures, and confusion in the story theme. (Similar to Piotrowski's finding a low Form (*F*) level in the majority of Rorschach responses of those neurologically compromised.)

6. Brain damaged patients tend to give few of the most common themes (few Popular (*P*) responses on Rorschach).

7. Perseveration of theme on several T.A.T. cards (Piotrowski's *Rpt* on Rorschach).

8. Automatic repetition of certain phrases or words (*AP* on Rorschach).

9. Inability to change an unsatisfactory response (*Imp* on Rorschach).

10. Expressions of self-doubt (*Plx* on Rorschach).

11. Inflexibility, concrete responses, catastrophic reactions, and difficulties in dealing with the picture as a whole.

To a lesser extent, individuals with the *Attention Deficit Disorder* (A.D.D.) or specific language influencing learning disabilities will also tend to show the above constellation of characteristics in C.A.T. and T.A.T. stories. As mentioned on page 49 (picture #1) failure to recognize the violin had long puzzled me. A study by Chamson [89] now supports my clinical hunch that this is one of the most reliable indicators of A.D.D. in the T.A.T. She compared 49 high school students classified as emotionally impaired. She administered the T.A.T. and visual contrast sensitivity tests. Fifteen percent of the ADD population failed to see the violin while none of the emotionally disturbed group misperceived it. The visual contrast sensitivity test yielded significant differences at the .01 level. This work strongly supports the clinical experience with the T.A.T.

To the above list, we can also add the following additional characteristics from our own clinical experience:

1. Failing to report an obvious object in a picture that tends to be salient and organizing to most individuals without neuropsychological disorders, such as not mentioning the violin in T.A.T. card #1. This contrasts with the more psychogenic selective inattention, such as a child not mentioning that the dog is "spanking" the puppy on C.A.T. card #10, because of a desire to deny this perception out of one's own psychological conflicts around being punished. The individual with neurological dysfunction misses salient objects due to a deficit in attention and perceptual discrimination capacity.

2. Tendency to report a stereotyped story one has heard, read in a book, or seen on television, such as trying to turn C.A.T. card #1 into "Goldilocks and the Three Bears" or C.A.T. card #3 into "Old King Cole" or relating a movie plot to T.A.T. cards. (Similar to exclusive use of Popular (*P*) responses on Rorschach).

3. Inability to stick with one central character throughout. Individual may shift the story from being about one character, then change it to revolve around someone else. Children with Attention Deficit Disorder (A.D.D.) tend to shift the C.A.T. story from being about a bear, to being about a lion, etc.,

change the sex of the hero (he, she, he, etc.), and frequently change pronouns from he, it, us, you, etc.). This is also found on Rorschach content responses and is similar to the shifting, distracted level of attention of these individuals in academic settings and in social interaction with others. Their minds seem to wander and not to focus and remain sustained.

4. Inability to develop a parallel plot ("Meanwhile, back at the ranch . . ."). The ability to do this requires keeping one idea in the back of one's mind, while relating another idea, and then coordinating the two ideas together in a logical, integrated manner. A high development of this is seen in Russian novels or in the so-called "family sagas" of popular American literature.

5. Tendency not to bring the story to an ending, to a logical conclusion. This is seen in A.D.D. children's tendency not to finish things they start in school, not to finish homework, etc., and in the tendency of adults with A.D.D. to frequently change jobs.

6. Breakthrough of primitive sexual and aggressive comments and ideas (Similar to direct mention of "blood" to the perception of red color or the naming of shapes as sexual objects on the Rorschach). Without a developed synthetic function, of coordinated, integrated perception, and of a level of organized repression, such individuals are very open to the sudden intrusion of very direct sexual and aggressive feelings and associations being immediately expressed. This is considered to be an ego function in psychoanalytic personality theory, which may also be influenced by physiological deficits in the capacity to form perceptions into meaningful gestalts mediated by the visual and brain functions.

7. Frequency of impulsive actions by characters in stories, which could also be described as characters engaged in acting out behavior, such as spitting, kicking, hitting, biting, urinating, defecating, etc.

8. Characters in story do not appear to plan, prepare, or anticipate in advance of action. They do not think before acting. There is an absence of asking someone for advice, looking at a map, or reading a book to prepare for a future action. Characters simply act and react.

9. Noticeable lack of a coordinated action sequence. The Fogel and Lezak list speaks of little action. Here we stress the absence of a chain of first one action, then another related action, then another, and on to a logical conclusion. Preschoolers typically give stories of one of two actions, elementary school children will provide a series of actions, and early adolescents may add a parallel action. Brain damaged individuals or those with A.D.D. or significant learning disabilities tend to give stories of no action, only a single action mentioned, or at the most two actions.

10. One character may be described as dependent on another, clinging to another, or calling for help. This is due to need of such individuals for another person as a monitor of their impulsivity and as a guide to do what they feel they cannot do. Psychoanalytic theory calls this a need for an auxiliary ego. Separation anxiety may be present for this similar need (for an auxiliary ego) as a "container" of the individual's own impulsivity as well as for basic dependency behavior encouraged by a parent or due to the individual modeling dependency after a parent who is dependent.

11. Characters in stories described as trying to learn, trying to do things, but failing to do so successfully may reflect some aspect of A.D.D. Adults on the T.A.T. card #1 may tell of a story about a boy trying to learn to play a violin, but after trying, he gives up, or fails to learn it. Within the stories, there may be an expression of a character having frequent accidents or falls, which is typical of A.D.D. individuals with hyperactivity and intense impulsivity. Another frequent theme within a story is getting lost and being lost, something they often experience in life when trying to follow directions for driving somewhere. This involves their difficulty in paying attention to the one who gave them directions, paying attention to the road, and spatial difficulties in discriminating left from right, up from down.

12. Relative absence of characters working together in groups in a story. Generally, the action involves one or two. This is like the phases of early childhood play starting with solitary play, going to parallel play or imitating play (one child imitates what another does), going to turn-taking (Tag), and moving up to Cowboys and Indians or Spacemen, etc. Individuals with serious neurophysiological deficits or disorders have difficulty organizing in groups, as they do planning in advance or even organizing their everyday routines.

13. Sudden outbursts of impulsivity in some individuals may be expressed in their thematic apperception stories as an action occurring quickly without warning. Children use the word "suddenly" or "all of a sudden" in their stories, while adults may have a character coming up from behind and startling another, as in Story #6GF.

14. Individuals with hyperactive impulsivity may symbolize their need for a "container" of their feelings of sudden outbursts, wild abandon, and restless energy by story themes of a character returning home to his or her "house," returning to "mother," or drawing a "boundary line," "frontier line," lines that protect and "bound" one group of people from another. The idea of keeping American Indians on a reservation or poverty-stricken minority people in ghettoes, or nuclear power plants in rural, unpopulated areas simply may symbolize a need to keep wild impulses localized, structured, and safely contained. Keeping the dead in coffins buried in the earth is another symbolization of the need for a container for fears in some individuals' projective stories.

15. Left-right orientation difficulty in some individuals may be expressed by tending to report an object on the right side of a C.A.T. or T.A.T. picture as being on the left side or vice versa.*

The first T.A.T. (Card #1) from an adult with significant A.D.D. shows some of these above characteristics:

Once upon a time there was a little boy about 8 years old looking at something. Looks like a picture. But while he was looking, he was wondering about the future, more or less contemplating what the future would be like for him. He pictured himself having a family

---

* The authors are indebted to Dr. Perry Faithorn of Larchmont, New York for this valuable observation.

like the one he was in and since he was happy now, he figured he would always be happy. He was waiting to eat dinner one night, that's when he was looking at the picture of himself, his sister, and parents, and his dog. And as he was looking, he was thinking how happy he was and visualizing he would have the same kind of family himself. And as he was drifting off, his mother called him and said dinner was ready, and this sudden burst of reality snapped him out of the thoughts he was having. Do you want to know my hidden thoughts? It reminds me of myself of when I was younger, dreams I had. But the mother calling is a good thing, snapping me into reality. Just being called for dinner is nothing bad in itself, but just a symbol of accepting reality.

Here we see the tendency to wander off in thought, to become distracted. His mother snaps him back to reality, but he totally missed the object of the violin, which is generally a most salient, organizing object for most individuals for T.A.T. Card #1. His mind drifts from the future to the past to the future, so that he is not grounded in the present reality. How often teachers describe such children as "in outer space," as never paying attention to what the teacher is trying to teach. While the story is long for an adult with A.D.D., we note that there are only two actions—looking at the picture and then hearing his mother call him to dinner. The action is not well coordinated and the subject fails to provide a logical ending to the story. There are few characters, only the boy and his mother, and the relationship seems to be one of dependency of the boy on the mother. The first action is really a description of the picture, which is repetitiously described for a long time until the second action of the mother calling him is introduced. There is very little action taking place in this T.A.T. story. Psychodynamically, we can speculate that while the mother of this adult may want to snap the individual into accepting reality and dealing better in the real world of everyday life, it is to come to dinner that is demanded, which could also express the mother's underlying desire to keep this adult dependent upon her. (This adult, over 34, lives at home.)

A.D.D. Child Case

Hyperactivity, impulsivity, and inattention in children has been widespread and was earlier described as "Minimal Brain Damage" or "Minimal Brain Dysfunction" (MBD). It is now referred to in the current *Diagnostic and Statistical Manual of Mental Disorders* of the American Psychiatry Association as "Attention Deficit Disorder" (A.D.D.), which is either "with hyperactivity" or "without hyperactivity." The typical symptoms are *inattention* (failing to finish things the person starts to do, seeming not to listen, becoming easily distracted, not concentrating on schoolwork or other tasks requiring sustained attention, and not sticking to a play activity); *impulsivity* (acting before thinking, shifting excessively from one activity to another, not organizing work, needing a lot of supervision or for the teacher to be right next to the child when working, frequently calling out in class, and difficulty awaiting one's turn in games and group situations); and *hyperactivity* (running about or climbing on things excessively, difficulty sitting still or fidgeting excessively, difficulty staying seated, moving about excessively during sleep, and being always "on the go" as if "driven by a motor").

Boys are 10 times more apt to have this disorder than girls. Psychological testing usually looks for significant difference between nonverbal, perceptual-motor tests and the verbal tests that are typically much higher. The Wechsler Performance Scale IQ is usually 10 or more points lower than the Verbal Scale IQ and the Bender Gestalt Test usually has numerous errors of shape rotation, shape distortion, perseveration, overlaps, figure integration, and size consistency difficulty. These are all signs of both spatial, visual problems, difficulty in integration of visual and motor functioning, inattention, and impulsivity. Spatial integration difficulty can also be seen on the *Rorschach* in the failure to provide many Whole (W) gestalt responses with good differentiation into many details (Hd, Ad, d). Typically, the responses are not whole-object, but part-object responses. The subject sees the inkblot not as a whole gestalt (W), but as a part (D). Color Naming (Cn) is both a sign of concrete description of the inkblot picture and a sign of impulsivity. Projective drawings also have few details, poor integration of the details into organized wholes, and may also have poor perspective. The C.A.T. and T.A.T. are highly useful in further corroborating the diagnosis of A.D.D. by looking for some of the 26 characteristics we listed at the beginning of the chapter.

C.A.T. Protocol Illustrating Attention Deficit Disorder

Lisa, aged 6 years 9 months, was referred for testing due to school adjustment difficulties and hyperactivity. She has a poor attention span, is frequently switching her seat in class, and functions below grade level. Among several tests administered, the C.A.T. revealed the following:

C.A.T. Protocol

1: Once upon a time there were three chicks eating porridge. *Anything else?* They were talking about their porridge, too. They said, "My porridge is too, too cold." (I repeat request for a "make pretend" story of her own, not something she heard, saw on TV, or read in a book). I don't have imagination. *Anything happen next in the story you started?* I don't know. Only how it goes in the story.

Comment

We see here lack of self-esteem in the comments, "I don't have imagination" and "I don't know." Tendency to give stereotype story she's heard or seen and tendency to describe in concrete terms only what is seen by her in the picture on the card are evident. Talking about their porridge suggests some ability to go beyond action itself and the idea of the porridge being too cold suggests feelings of being rejected or deprived.

2: I knew this one—"Goldilocks and the Three Bears." (I again explain the nature of the test, the direction to provide one's own fantasy from your own mind, your own imagination, a make-pretend story, pretend the picture you see is part of a bigger story you make up yourself, etc.). I can't think of anything. They're trying to, if somebody falls down the hill, the second one gets to win. They fall down the hill and they hurt theirself.

Comment

Again we see the tendency to provide a stereotype tale and perhaps difficulty paying attention to the direction I gave her, as A.D.D. children have difficulty paying attention to teachers in school. Low self-esteem is repeated in her comment "I can't think of anything." But then she does manage to elaborate a fantasy of her own, which brings in a theme of trying to do things and failing (also her experience in school) and the theme of accident proneness (falling and getting hurt). There is also the theme of a chain reaction, if one falls down, the second one gets to win (is she the older of two siblings wherein she feels the younger, second born gets to win when she fails?), but at the end "They fall down the hill and they hurt theirself." Presumably they all end falling down getting hurt. This could also suggest her perception of a divorce, since card #2 is often seen by children of separation and divorce as a struggle, a tug-of-war between the two parents in which the child is asked to take sides. If so, does Lisa feel that when one parent left, the other won custody, but they all ended up losing? These are questions that could be explored in psychotherapy or verified from the social history. The C.A.T., like a dream, provides a way for children to express their feelings about their lives and then a way for us to hypothesize about what their feelings and perceptions might be about their lives.

3: I don't know any of these. It's a lion, but I can't even talk about it. But he was make pretending he was Old King Cole . . . *What happens next?* I don't see Old King Cole on TV. I imagine it is on the TV. And he called for his pipe and his bowl to eat and three fiddlers. He has a cane, too. There's a mice in the wall. Nothing else in the wall, either. Flowers are on the rug, too. *Anything happen there?* I don't know. The mice is travelling around in the wall, putting his head out and back in, out and back in, back out and in again and again.

Comment

She again brings in a stereotyped story and describes the details of the picture before her. When she notices the mouse, she perseverates, the mouse coming out, going in, out, in over and over suggesting the perseverative, driven, repetitive actions typical of A.D.D. children in life and seen in their C.A.T. stories. It also suggests an approach/avoidance style with regard to fear of a potentially predatory larger animal that could attack the mouse if he stays out. Anxiety and fear also may stimulate the hyperactive, frenetic activity. Instead of being able to tolerate anxiety, she may engage in sudden, impulsive actions over and over in this driven, compulsive manner.

4: Two babies, one riding a bike and one in the mother's pouch. The mother's hopping with a picnic basket and pocket book and I see trees . . . *Next?* If she looks at her babies, lets go of her picnic basket, lets go of the baby in her pouch, all the food is going to be on the floor and cheese will be rotten. The baby lets go of the balloon and it flies away and the other one rides his bike and crashes into one of the trees there. The mother doesn't want that to happen.

Comment

She moves away from a beginning concrete description of the picture before her to provide some action and fantasy elaboration on the theme of letting go (separation of the mother from the children) and letting go of impulses (when the children are deprived of mother's holding and nurturance—food that drops and becomes rotten), the child crashes into a tree (aggressive assault on the tree with also potential for serious harm by hitting the tree). The fact that she places this letting go in the hypothetical and adds at the end, "The mother doesn't want that to happen," suggests a desire to monitor impulsivity and develop signal anxiety (the ability to anticipate danger in the future), rather than react to danger with sudden panic, frenetic action, primitive impulsive outbursts, and feelings of being totally helpless, totally overwhelmed.

5: A bed, two beds, floor, a lamp, windows, curtains are there. . . . *anything happen next?* The rain and the thunder and the lightning broke the window. Nothing else happened. It's making noise in the house by the rain and thunder and everything was wet and the crib was wet, too.

Comment

Beginning with concrete description of the visual scene in the picture on the card, she moves into a theme of being overwhelmed by external danger. The storm outside intrudes and breaks into the house and overwhelms everything. This is a typical theme in C.A.T. stories of A.D.D. children to experience the environment as impulsive and as dangerous as they feel their own feelings to be. On the one hand, this is an externalization of their own impulsivity onto the environment (they are not dangerously aggressive, it is the environment of the weather and big animals and adults that are aggressively threatening to them). On the other hand, this may also be part of their actual experience. They act impulsively and the parents aggressively act out, which is modeled by the child in the child's hyperactivity. Usually, it is an interaction between the two participants, parent and child, and the two domains of physiologically increased activity level and that of emotional anxiety, lack of signal function, and lack of adequate defenses. The theme of everything wet at night also suggests the possibility of this child having encopresis, which is often seen in A.D.D. children having very poor impulse control.

6: Two mother bears and one momma bear and the other father bear and the baby bear in the cave. They think it's winter. Then the wind blew in the cave and they got chilly . . . *Anything else happen?* They had to sleep cuddling together and all that stuff, 'cause it was cold together and all that stuff like I said before.

Comment

The environment overwhelms again, comes into their home, which is defended against here by dependent clinging. While the previous story shows no defense against being overwhelmed, this story shows a step forward with the defensive coping mechanism of using another person as an auxiliary ego to cling to and to help one with ego control over one's own impulsivity. Separation anxiety is usually intensified in A.D.D. children to some extent by the need for the adult figure as an auxiliary ego to monitor and control their impulsivity. It may also be increased due to the tendency of the parent to be somewhat rejecting of the A.D.D. child.

7: One tiger is chasing the monkey. A monkey got afraid. Then the monkey climbed up a tree. But the tiger catched him and killed him.

Comment

The fear of aggression from the environment continues in which the defensive reaction is the monkey climbing up a tree (the ego defense of avoidance or withdrawal symbolized by actively trying to escape external threat).

8: One Papa monkey, one momma monkey, and one grandma monkey with a baby monkey. And they lived in a house and then they put on the stove with food and they didn't know the stove was burning and they smelled the smoke. They had to hurry out of the house. They had to pull down the alarm; if they don't put on the alarm, the firemen will not know where the house or where the fire is. Always when you have a fire, always put on the alarm.

Comment

This is a marvelous story illustrating the attempt to develop a signal function in a child with a *moderate* level of A.D.D. The danger is the burning stove. They smell the smoke (a signal of fire). They run out of the house (the ego defense of avoidance/withdrawal expressed again). Then they put on the alarm for the firemen to put out the fire (perhaps symbolizing her dependency upon a parent when she feels impulsively aggressive). The child with *severe* A.D.D. would not be able to create a C.A.T. story such as this with the ego defenses and the symbolization of the need for signal function (the anticipation of danger and the ability to mobilize coping mechanisms to cope with it).

9: A crib, a door, windows. The family is next door to the baby. The next neighbors— that's the father and the mother. Then they had thunder and lightning broke the baby's window. Then the room got all wet on the floor and then the baby fell on the floor and hurt his head.

Comment

She begins with concrete description of the picture and then again brings in the theme of the environment coming into the house and making everything wet, which leads to the baby falling and getting hurt. Encopresis, falling out of bed, and being let go of by the holding mother or father are all suggested in this story. The only defense is the statement that the parents are next door to the baby, so it may be that this is how she feels when separated or threatened with separation from one or both of the parents. She falls apart and is overwhelmed and lets go of her own impulses. This may also be why it is more scary for her at night, when she is sleeping by herself away from proximity to the auxiliary ego parent.

10: Two dogs, one the momma and the papa died and there was a little puppy. Then the puppy, he had to vomit. And he stopped the vomitting; then the momma was standing up. Then the momma flushed the toilet and that's the end of this one.

Comment

Note that she used the word "mother" before in story #4 and now she regresses to the more infantile word "momma" for the parent in the story. Since the picture shows a bathroom scene, it may be that she has anxiety around the bathroom perhaps related to some enuresis suggested by the previous stories of flooding by water. This anxiety is responded to, then, by the ego defense of regression, going back to acting like a much younger child as if to say "I'm just a baby, so how can I help myself?" The desire to externalize bad feelings is suggested by the child vomitting. The mother then flushing the toilet shows the ego defense of undoing, but it is the auxiliary ego adult that does the undoing not the child figure himself.

Summary of C.A.T.

The C.A.T. suggests Lisa has fears of dangers in the environment, of storms, of attacking animals, fear of the dark at night, separation fear, anxiety about falling and getting hurt, fear of fire, and perhaps anxiety over the need for approval (the bathroom story #10). To cope with these fears and anxieties, she uses defenses of dependent clinging, avoidance/withdrawal, denial ("I don't know" comments), regression to more infantile behavior, repetitive, ritualized action (motor intensity), and acting out of impulses (immediate discharge of anxiety in action that is maladaptive, rather than adaptive). She tends to give concrete descriptions of the picture or to provide a stereotypic story she has heard or seen, rather than freely elaborate a fantasy story of her own. The stories are short without much fantasy elaboration, but she shows an ability to go beyond the visual data before her (which is another reason she is of moderate A.D.D., rather than severe). There is a tendency not to finish stories similar to the tendency in schoolwork of A.D.D. children to become distracted, not to stick with things, and not to finish what they started. But a few stories are given endings again suggesting a moderate rather than severe A.D.D. syndrome.

As with children with a severe A.D.D., many of Lisa's C.A.T. stories show smaller figures totally overwhelmed by storms or by larger threatening figures without much evidence of any attempt to cope with these dangers, without really doing anything to counteract these dangers. Then there are a few stories in which the smaller figure either tries to run away, climb a tree, or go back in his hole (which are indicators of the ego defense of avoidance/withdrawal) or the smaller figures regress to infantile, dependent clinging to a more powerful adult figure (defenses of regression and dependent clinging).

The acting out in Lisa's stories rarely seems to be used defensively to counteract threat, but rather seems to be largely an intensification of her hyperactivity. Similarly, the use of ritualization or preservation is sometimes thought of as an ego defense, as it is part of undoing (doing and undoing over and over, for example), but here it again seems to be for the most part an intensification of her driven, compulsive hyperactivity symptom. The final instance of her having a moderate, rather than severe A.D.D. and of moving in the direction of neurotic (higher ego structure) are the two stories suggesting the beginning development of signal function. These are the stories about what could happen if the mother lets go of food and of the baby in her pouch (#4) and the family that puts on the alarm to call the firemen to put out the fire from the burning stove (#8). A hallmark of the borderline child is the absence of signal function. Anxiety and fear leads them to total panic, fragmentation of the self structure, and impulsive acting out—often psychotic-like. The neurotic child, however, can deal with anxiety and danger as a signal to mobilize ego defenses and coping mechanisms. Lisa not only shows the ability to use ego defenses of denial, avoidance, withdrawal, regression, dependent clinging, perseveration/ritualization, and some defensive acting out, she has also symbolized the idea of signal function in two stories, which may also be an example of the observing ego function.

T.A.T. Protocol Illustrating Attention Deficit Disorder

T.A.T. Protocol

Julie Sand, 24 years old, has suffered from a long history of dyslexia (reading problems), dyscalculia (arithmetic problems), and other school problems since her early childhood. Ms. Sand reported that she had a short attention span, was hyperactive, had difficulty sitting still, had physical coordination difficulties, and visual focusing difficulties from her early childhood onwards through high school. This resulted in slow learning, feeling that she was "stupid" in some areas and "clumsy," and extreme headaches. Frequent earaches and inner ear infections further complicated her social and academic adjustment in her early years. By third grade, the school psychologist felt she might be depressed because of her lack of reading ability, intense headaches, frequent falling, lack of close friends, stubborn behavior, and outbursts of bulliness.

Ritalin was tried for a while between the ages of 9 and 12 years, she remembers, which resulted in some improvement in the above difficulties. Her early flair for vocabulary, for expressing complex issues, and for relating to adults when at her father's place of business, etc., provided a very confusing contrast to her and her parents (and probably also to her teachers) to the above learning disabilities syndrome. It was unclear why such a talented, indeed gifted and precocious child, could have such major school learning difficulties. An intelligence test given towards the end of elementary school showed around 139 IQ in the Verbal area, hence her parents were informed that she should be getting straight A's. The conclusion tended to be that all her problems were emotional, that she was just lazy, unmotivated, and uninterested. Valium was started, which she feels she became addicted to by 14 years of age. The school and behavior problems persisted, so that she ended up quitting high school.

Ms. Sand continued to do well in sales work, but has had a very erratic work history involving frequent job changes, mood swings from manicky and restless overactivity to withdrawal and depressive states often with suicidal ideation. In the attempt to get some release from these feelings of low self-esteem, labile mood swings, some explosive temper outbursts, restlessness, depression, feelings of scatteredness or lack of integration, and frequently intense anxiety, Ms. Sand increasingly attempted to self-medicate herself with barbituates, diet pills, and marihuana. However, Ms. Sand reports that these drugs have little effect and that she feels that she has a high threshold for being affected by medication or drugs of almost any kind. She feels more prone to feelings of depression at night, becomes extremely agitated and hyperexcited during activities of social interaction, such as car auctions, and often experiences her mind racing with numerous fast moving thought patterns in the evening, all of which she often attempts to "quiet" with drugs, but experiences little relief.

Recently, Ms. Sand has been attending a college, majoring in business administration and political science. Her parents have emphasized the value of gaining a marketable skill, such as computer programming or some other technical skill, and Ms. Sand is not sure she could manage such type of work due to her early history of learning disabilities, her restlessness, and pattern of changing jobs. She also feels that she may be capable of working towards a career that would capitalize more on her high verbal skills, such as in sales, politics, law, creative arts involving writing, advertising, or public relations work.

Ms. Sand has also been feeling very depressed, had suicidal thoughts and has contacted a psychiatrist wondering if she should go into a hospital or if she should have a neurological work-up to determine if there could be some organic basis for her continued academic and social difficulties and unhappiness. Psychological testing was, therefore, requested in order to assist in the identification of these difficulties and to help Ms. Sand in her vocational decision-making at present.

1: Looks like he was practicing and just stopped with something. He laid his violin down and his music and he's looking at it. Looks like he's just trying to figure out how to do that, right? Something's not jogging. He's just staring at the music and trying to figure out how the music goes, so he can play it that way. Looks like he's saying, "This just doesn't sound right. How can this be?" Either that or he just doesn't want to practice. You won't be a great violinist. I remember my sister had to practice the piano. She'd just sit there and look at the music. So you got two stories out of that one.

Comment

Here we have the theme of trying to play or learn the violin, not going it successfully, and wanting to withdraw and give up trying. She appears confused about the plot, should it be this or that? She asks the tester for approval at one point. The tendency to wander off with inattention is stated, "He's just staring at the music . . ." Then she switched central characters to bring in her sister, but realizes, "So you got two stories out of that one." This suggests the shifting of attention from one character to another. The story lacks a real ending.

2: Hmmm . . . (long pause). This reminds me of an old farm family. Probably their daughter and she's holding books and seeing that's her way out of the fields. Those are her parents. Her parents are dressed in farm clothes and she is not, maybe she's in college and this is her way out. She looks like it's her reason, her way out. Looks like a far away look in her face, different dimensions than they are and she can feel it and see it. The books are the way out.

Comment

Punctuating pause is seen. She stays close to a concrete description of the picture. She does not go beyond the visual information given by the picture. No action is stated, except holding books and looking with a far away look in her eyes. The latter aspect restates the tendency of the mind to wander off in inattention, without specific focus. No ending is given. A personal dynamic or defensive withdrawal is suggested by the far away look at the theme of finding a "way out" of the farm life of her parents.

3BM: Hmm. (Pause) This looks like she's got an anxiety attack or a depression attack and she's just gone limp. Keys are on the floor. Either they're crying or giving up for the moment. She's tired of it all. Like why ever more move, why pick up the car keys, and start going through everything again. Something activated some kind of emotional trauma and how it would end? I, it would end in many ways. It could pick up with the keys and go on, but if it's serious enough, she could take a bottle of pills and end it. It reminds me of being tired of it all. Either tired or go and get undressed and go back to bed and start all over again.

Comment

Confusion is seen in the plot probably related to depressive feelings she has within her. Depressive anxiety, in other words, intensifies the A.D.D. characteristic of lack of focus, shifting theme, confusion of theme, inability to finish plot with an ending. The breakthrough of primitive impulses appears to be just about to occur, in this story perhaps the suicidal impulse of taking pills. Defensive withdrawal and turning aggression against the self are present in this idea of taking pills to end her struggle.

4: This looks like it should be at a 1930 movie. Um, there's a bad tragedy, something's wrong and she's asking him not to go, to stay, and he's going. So she's trying to hold onto him to reason with him. I think it was the type of fury that you see in many men, "Bam Bam!, I'll do it anyway!" (gestures angry movements in the air). It looks like there's anger in his eyes and she just looks like she's pleading with him to reason with him, and he's just about going to turn and go and she's going to end up crying. He goes off and has a big fight.

Comment

Breakthrough of primitive aggressive impulse is clear in this story, perhaps a turning outwards of what she turned inwards on the last story. The man has fury "Bam Bam!" and she gestures angry movements in the air. The female figure clings to him bringing out a dependent clinging similar to A.D.D. individuals. The story has a sequence of action and an ending, which suggests a mild-to-moderate rather than a severe level of A.D.D.

6GF: It's an old Gary Cooper movie. He's come up behind her, startled her, and he may be saying something that got her off guard, maybe he caught her doing something or he's lecturing her and she's saying, "What the hell do you want?" Or she looks like she's a little stunned and taken aback and he looks like he's demonstrative, authoritative, like he thinks he's just giving advice and she should be taking it and looks half out of it and about to say, "*You* do it that way!"

Comment

The sudden outbreak of impulsivity is stated in the idea of the man startling the woman from behind, a typical theme of this card in A.D.D. individuals. The swearing also suggests impulsivity. Again she "looks half out of it," further stating the wandering mind of inattention. Depressive, passive, dependent withdrawal tendencies is a theme in this story.

7GF: Ah. . . . (pause). The mother is reading a story to her daughter, again from back in the 30s or 40s time, like an old Jewish mother or Italian mother, and the young girl's just going off and she's the character in the story her mother's reading and she's holding a doll and kind of limp. She's listening to her mother, but she's kind of far off and her eyes are just (gestures) kind of going. She has a far away look also on her face. She's not turned towards her mother, listening and her mind is wandering. She's there, her spirit's in the story. Either that or she's thinking I want to go out to play.

Comment

Punctuating pause is seen. The girl listens, but her mind is wandering (a marked symptom of the A.D.D. syndrome). The withdrawal is present in mind wandering, in the idea of wanting to go out to play, and in the reference to long ago in time (the 30s or 40s). References to earlier times are examples of the defense of regression as well, another frequent theme in this woman's T.A.T. stories.

8BM: Oooooh! (She puts the card down near the floor next to her side). It reminds me of what I would think of someone who's returned from war and would have to think back. Paramedics. It's a flashback. Seeing someone lying on a table, doctor cutting him, another person holding a light, and the guy on the table, and yet he's all dressed up in suit. It looks like he's not part of the picture, like it's a flashback for him. What gives me that impression is the way the light comes into his head. It makes it seem like he's definitely separate from the scene and the vagueness of the scene makes it again seem like it's a flashback kind of thing.

Comment

Defensive avoidance and withdrawal is evident in putting the card down near her side (nonverbal proximity, distancing, biting, hitting, or other behavior with the T.A.T. cards always need to be noted as they usually corroborate the content analysis of the stories, as is evident with this woman). She withdraws further by regressing in time ("It's a flashback"). Inattention is again restated in her separating the boy from the scene. She mainly describes the picture giving only one action of "doctors cutting him" and not providing an ending.

9GF: This, I don't like this. The one girl is running away from something. Either she had a fight with her boyfriend or somebody assaulted her, something scared her and she's running away from it. I think it's like this other girl looks like she's sitting behind a tree, I don't know if she's trying to hear or not. . . . But she overhears and sees her running and she doesn't do anything to help her. She's hiding behind the tree just watching the other girl run, like she was eavesdropping, maybe not purposely, but was a witness to whatever has upset the other one.

Comment

Punctuating pauses, self doubt, concrete description of the picture without fantasy elaboration of her own, and shifting aspects of the theme of confusion ("either this or that . . .") are A.D.D. characteristics in this story. A defensive withdrawal or avoidance (hiding behind a tree) is also noted.

10: It shows love, compassion. The other person on the right needs that physical reassurance and the other person seems to be kissing her on the forehead saying it will be allright with compassion. It's sensitive and yet her mother has darkened out, part of her forehead, her facial features are (gestures vagueness). But it looks like she's holding on or learning. That's about it.

Comment

Some dependency is stated, the concrete description of the picture, the few words, and the single action (kissing and reassuring) are notable. Depressive theme of the "mother darkened out" is suggested, as well as the A.D.D. symptom of part-object or vague visual perception.

12M: . . . (Pause). It reminds me of a priest giving last rites. . . . The priest wouldn't be leaning with a foot on the bed (pause) . . . It's really, I don't know. It's a weird picture. It could be an old man looking physically decrepit looking at a physically well boy and looking over him and thinking why isn't he like that. It's hard to tell if he's dead or alive. His legs are crossed, so he's alive, not dead. Either that or the priest. A very old man. It looks like his hand is closed and he's giving last rites or he has closed his eyes.

Comment

Punctuating pauses, the breakthrough of primitive impulses, self-doubt expressions ("I don't know"), confusion of plot ("either that or . . ."), and mind wandering (?) suggested by the eyes closed are further statements of A.D.D. characteristics in this T.A.T. story.

13MF: Hmmm! This could be many things. Either he just strangled her or she's laying there dead *or* they've just made love and she's laying there and he's just gotten up and gotten dressed. But it looks like he's sad, so he may have just done her in and he looks distraught in a way. But I prefer it was that they've just made love, but it looks like it was more violent. Like he's saying, "What have I done?," and turning away from it. The abuse a woman has to go through whether she's alive or dead.

Comment

Breakthrough of primitive aggressive and sexual impulse is very clear on this card with references to strangling, laying dead, making love, something "violent." Guilt and defensive withdrawal are displaced onto the man figure, as she displaced the learning disability with the music lesson onto her sister on card #1. Defensive passivity is expressed in regards to the female in this story, who lays there dead and who has to go through abuse "whether she's alive or dead." She manages to go a little beyond the description of the picture, which again shows the mild-to-moderate rather than severe A.D.D., but she fails to provide a sequence to a logical ending for the story.

Conclusion

It is clear from the pattern analysis of Ms. Sand's psychological tests that there is a strong neurological underpinning to her academic, social, and emotional problems, which has recently been described as a general learning disability or Attention Deficit Disorder (A.D.D.) syndrome [43, 47]. This leads her into vulnerability to sensory overload, to desires to withdraw, restlessness, and to job changes.

Diagnostic impression is, therefore, of Attention Deficit Disorder with depressive and obsessive features.

CHAPTER XIII

THE C.A.T.*

A. Nature and Purpose of the Test

T HE CHILDREN'S APPERCEPTION TEST (C.A.T.)† IS A PROJECTIVE method or, as we prefer to call it, an apperceptive method of investigating personality by studying the dynamic meaningfulness of individual differences in the perception of standard stimuli.

The test is a direct descendant of the T.A.T., although it does not compete with or substitute for it. Unsurpassed as we believe the T.A.T. to be for adult personality investigation, it is nevertheless relatively unsuited for young children to the same degree that the C.A.T. is unsuited for adults. Ideally, we should like to see the C.A.T. used for children from three to 10, Symonds' Picture Story Test used for adolescents, and the T.A.T. used for adolescents and adults.

The C.A.T. was designed to facilitate understanding of a child's relationship to important figures and drives. The pictures (Fig. 4) were designed to elicit responses to feeding problems specifically, and to oral problems generally; to investigate problems of sibling rivalry; to illuminate the attitude toward parental figures and the way in which these figures are apperceived; to learn about the child's relationship to the parents as a couple—technically referred to as the oedipal complex and its culmination in the primal scene, namely, the child's fantasies about seeing the parents in bed together. Related to this, we wish to elicit the

---

* L. Bellak and S. S. Bellak, C. P. S. Inc., P. O. Box 83, Larchmont, New York, 1948. The test is also published in French by the Centre de Psychologie Appliquée Paris, France; in Italian by the Organizzazioni Speciali, Florence, Italy; in English for the British Empire by the Australian Council for Educational Research, Hawthorn, Victoria. Australia; in German by Verlag für Psychologie, Göttingen, Germany; in Spanish by Editoriale Paídos, Buenos Aires, Argentina; and in Portuguese by Mestre Jou, São Paulo. Brazil. An adaptation for India has been devised by Uma Chowdhury, with the help of B. S. Guha and L. Bellak, published by Manasayan, New Delhi, India, and the test has also been published in Japan.

† The original C.A.T., consisting of 10 plates depicting animals in various situations, was published in 1949. It was followed in 1952 by the Children's Apperception Test, Supplement (C.A.T.-S.), and in 1965 the Children's Apperception Test, Human (C.A.T.-H.), was published, consisting of an exact substitution of human figures for the original animal ones. Most of the remarks in this chapter refer to all three versions of the test. A few of them refer to the original C.A.T.—for convenience's sake, sometimes designated as C.A.T.-A. For a discussion of the C.A.T.-H. and the C.A.T.-S., see Chapters XIV and XVI respectively.

1

2

3

4

5

FIG. 4. Pictures for use with the C.A.T.

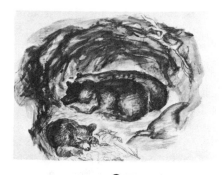

6

7

8

9

10

FIG. 4 (*cont.*)

child's fantasies about aggression, intra- and extra-, about acceptance by the adult world, and about his fear of being lonely at night with a possible relation to masturbation, toilet behavior, and the parents' handling of and response to it. We wish to learn about the child's structure, defenses, and his dynamic way of reacting to, and handling, his problems of growth.

This test, similar to the T.A.T., is primarily concerned with the *content* of productions. An analysis of apperceptive behavior is usually concerned with *what* one sees and thinks in distinction to an examination of expressive behavior, which is concerned with *how* one sees and thinks. We have previously discussed this relationship of adaptive, expressive, and apperceptive aspects of psychological productions in the previous section on the T.A.T., in which I pointed out that the Rorschach is primarily a study of the formal organization of expressive factors. As such, it is better qualified to facilitate diagnosis, if this term is taken to mean identifying a given person with a nosological entity as set forth in an official manual on diagnosis. On the other hand, the C.A.T., like the T.A.T., is better able to reveal the dynamics of interpersonal relationships, of drive constellations, and the nature of defenses against them.

Thus, I believe that the C.A.T. may be clinically useful in determining what dynamic factors might be related to a child's behavior in a group, in school, or in kindergarten, or to events at home. The C.A.T. may be profitable in the hands of the psychoanalyst, the psychiatrist, the psychologist, the social worker, and the teacher, as well as the psychologically trained pediatrician. It may be used directly in therapy as a play technique. After the original responses have been given, one may wish to go over them with the child in the form of play and make appropriate interpretations.

Furthermore, the C.A.T. should lend itself particularly well to much-needed longitudinal research studies on child development; if the C.A.T. were administered to children at half-year intervals from the third year on, we might learn a good deal about the developmental fate of a number of psychological problems thus far studied only in psychoanalytic investigations or other cross-sectional studies. The latter are, by necessity, reconstructions and inferences which need further confirmation and/or elaboration. In research studies and in clinical use alike it should be helpful that the C.A.T. is relatively culture-free. Since we deal with animal pictures, the test can be used equally well with white, black, and other groups of children—except, of course, those groups who might be unfamiliar with some of the inanimate objects pictured, such as bicycles, etc.

Lack of familiarity with the animals depicted does not seem to constitute a problem, since the children simply substitute animals with which they are familiar.

B. History of the C.A.T. and the C.A.T.-H.

The original idea of the C.A.T. came about as a result of a discussion, between Ernst Kris and me, of theoretical problems of projection and the T.A.T. Dr. Kris*

---

* I am extremely grateful to the late Dr. Ernst Kris for having provided the stimulus and inspiration for our own work.

pointed out that we could expect children to identify themselves much more readily with animals than with persons, a fact we have known ever since Freud wrote his story of little Hans in "The Phobia of a Five Year Old." After thinking the whole problem over for nearly a year, I specified a number of situations fundamental to children which might conceivably be expected to expose the dynamic workings of a child's problems. It seemed that the T.A.T., a wonderful instrument for adults, could not entirely fulfill the needs with young children, and similarly Symonds could not recommend his Picture Story Test for use prior to adolescence. Theoretically, we had reason to assume that animals might be preferred identification figures from three years up to possibly 10, and thus we set out to create, pictorially, situations vital to this age range.

Violet Lamont, a professional illustrator of children's books, agreed to draw the pictures according to our suggestions, adding a few of her own liking. She presented us with 18 pictures, some of somewhat anthropomorphized nature, some entirely in animal fashion. These we had photostated, used some sets ourselves, and distributed others to a number of psychologists working with small children. I had known the majority of these psychologists in connection with my T.A.T. courses and therefore knew that they had an acquaintance with projective procedures and their use. They were good enough to use the original pictures of the C.A.T. and to send us protocols with additional information about the subjects' background, etc., as well as their own impressions of the problems of the test.

On the above basis, and on the basis of our own experience with records, we reduced the number of cards from 18 to the 10 most useful ones and developed the data described herein.

During the last 15 years a number of studies have focused on a comparison of the relative merits of animal versus human figures. Despite the limitations of the studies purporting to show that human figures in the C.A.T. setting may have more stimulus value than the animal figures, it was decided to develop a human version for use in certain specific situations.*

Among the studies reviewed, those of Budoff [82] and especially of Weisskopf-Joelson and Foster [343] suggest that some children seem to do better with animal stimuli, and some with human stimuli, and that these preferences may be associated with specific personality variables, for instance, children having difficulty with producing responses seemed to do better with animal figures. Future exploration of relative preferences of some personality types, the relationship of defensive patterns, age, I.Q., and psychopathology is likely to be much more fruitful than the mechanical either/or propositions of many previous studies.

Another important reason for providing a human equivalent to the C.A.T. was found in the clinical fact that sometimes children between seven and 10, especially if their I.Q.'s were high, would consider animal stimuli beneath their intellectual dignity. Needless to say, many found them "childish" for purely defensive reasons. Nevertheless, it was felt that a human version would lend itself especially well to an upward extension of the usefulness of the C.A.T. and go further towards closing an age gap between the applicability of the C.A.T. and the T.A.T.

---

* The material from the following line to Section C is reprinted from [55] by permission.

The changing of the animal figures to human figures presented a number of difficult problems. In fact, this process highlighted many of the advantages of the original choice of animals with regard to figures which were rather ambiguous as to age, sex, and many cultural attributes.

Three different artists tried their skill in portraying the regular C.A.T. in human form (C.A.T.-H), following the instruction of myself and Sonya Sorel Bellak—recreating the pictures of the C.A.T. as human presented varying degrees of difficulty. (See Fig. 7, Chapter XIV, for the final version of the C.A.T.-H. figures.)

In picture 1, for instance, the adult on the left was clothed in a shapeless garment which could be a male or female in pajamas and robe. The hairdo and facial expression can at best be described as not necessarily of either sex. About as much can be said for the children's figures.

In picture 2, the adult human figure on the right was initially turned more sideways to avoid the problem of breasts, or their lack, as a defining characteristic, but we finally decided to reproduce this figure in the same position as the bear in the original. We experimented with a variety of garments and hairdos before arriving at the present version.

In picture 3, the lion was meant to be a father figure and was always seen that way, so we faced no problem of disguise of the sex of the figure. However, the representation of the mouse in a semblance of the relationship to the lion that was often ascribed to it by children was a difficult matter. There is simply no way in which a child could elicit stories either of outwitting the lion by disappearing into its hole (possibly with the lion bumping his head in pursuit), or of any version of the fable of the mouse helping the lion. However, the child was given a somewhat mischievous facial expression, and a child so inclined might still produce stories of similar nature, by giving help to a man who needs a cane to walk, or by interpreting the shadow near the left knee as an object suitable for mischief.

Picture 4 presented relatively few problems except for the absence of tails, of course, and the fact that an infant in arms is not quite the same as an infant in the maternal pouch, alas.

Picture 5, with the anthropomorphic situation in the original, presented little difficulty.

Picture 6, however, was a different story. If one is interested in what Murray has called *press claustrum,* there just is no substitute for a cave. To preserve some of the possible stimulus value of the outdoor situation (in primitivity, in romance, in fear of animals, and the wild), the tent-like nature of the structure was emphasized by introducing the new feature of trees. Undoubtedly responses taking off from the story of the three bears will hardly continue to play a role.

Picture 7 was a real challenge. Fears of being devoured needed to be given a stimulus resembling the tiger threat. The grasping, evil-toothed, genii-like figure, supplemented by a steaming kettle (as seen in cartoons about cannibals), was introduced for that purpose. The way the child is depicted might result in chances of escape roughly equivalent to those of the monkey in the original.

Picture 8 presented the by now familiar problem of sexual identity. However, the adult figures were nearly always identified as female with the possible exception of the extreme left figure. Therefore, this one was dressed in alacks, rather than a dress, giving it still some ambiguity, at least in most of the American subcultures.

Picture 9, with its anthropomorphic setting and lack of determining characteristics, presented no adaptational problem.

Picture 10, however, was redrawn many times until we finally arrived at a version relatively ill-defined with regard to sex and still leaving the most frequent two choices available—being dried and cared for, or being spanked. In order to maintain more ambiguity, the child's face is seen in profile rather than full face, as the dog is seen in the original.

There is little doubt that the degree of ambiguity of the sex of the figures in the C.A.T.-H. will vary much more with different cultures and subcultures than the original animal figures. One of the reasons for choosing the animals at the time had been their relative freedom from cultural determinants, at least within the western world (the furniture in some of the original C.A.T. pictures was redrawn in the Indian, Fig. 5, and the Japanese, Fig. 6, versions). However, in those instances in which the C.A.T.-H is preferred from the start, the advantages determining the choice will presumably outweigh the disadvantages of less ambiguity.

C. Theory of the C.A.T.

The theoretical considerations of the C.A.T. and the C.A.T. Supplement, presented later, do not differ basically from the theoretical problems and the frame of reference previously discussed for the T.A.T. However, there is one additional aspect to be considered in the C.A.T. and the C.A.T.-S.—the use of animals as stimuli. As has been noted earlier, on the basis of psychoanalytic experience with children it was expected that children would identify more readily with animal than human figures. This assumption was predicated on the fact that emotional relationships to animals are easier for children to handle, and that animals are usually smaller than adult humans and are "underdogs" like children. Animals play a prominent role in children's phobias and as identification figures in children's dreams; on a conscious level, they figure importantly as children's friends. The primitivity of animal drives of oral and anal nature also increase animals' symbolic proximity for children. From the technical standpoint of a projective test, it could also be assumed that the animals would offer some manifest disguise: aggressive and other negative sentiments could more easily be ascribed to a lion than to a human father figure, and the child's own unacceptable wishes could be more easily ascribed to the less transparent identification figure, as compared to human children.

The use of animals as identification figures by psychotics and in primitive cultures also tended to support the expectation of a high stimulus value for children. Furthermore, clinical experience with the Rorschach has empirically established the high animal per cent and, even more striking, the relative absence of human figures in the Rorschach records of children, particularly with the younger age groups.

These theoretical expectations have been bolstered by an experiment made by

1

2

3

4

5

FIG. 5. Indian adaptation of the C.A.T. by Uma Chowdhury, assisted by B. S. Guha and L. Bellak.

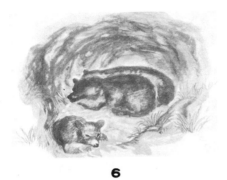

6

7

9

10

Fig. 5 (*cont.*)

1

2

3

4

5

FIG. 6. Japanese adaptation of the C.A.T. by Samiko Marui.

6

7

8

9

10

FIG. 6 (*cont.*)

Bills [70], who tested 48 school children both with T.A.T. cards and with 10 pictures of animals engaged in various activities. Since his experiment was a preliminary investigation, Bills confined himself to comparing, in the two sets of stories, only word count, refusals, description, and coherency. He found that almost all the children told considerably longer stories to the animal pictures and that all the children seemed to find the task easier. One animal card was rejected as compared to 18 T.A.T. cards. Two of the children rejected the entire test when first presented with the T.A.T. cards; none of the children rejected the test when the animal cards were presented first.

Vuyk [335] has also reported work with the C.A.T. indicating that animals as stimuli produced richer stories than were obtained with the use of human figures with children.

There is a good deal of literature in support of the theory that children identify more readily with animals. Goldfarb [145] expressed marked interest in the animal fantasy of children and found a close connection between the psychodynamics of the individual child and the kind of animal which predominated in the child's fantasy. Blum and Hunt [73] believe in the superiority of animal over human figures because the latter might be "too close to home," and that the use of animal figures overcomes the child's resistance. Bender and Rapaport [649] support this concept on the basis of clinical experience. Olney [258] found that over 75 per cent of children's picture books contained animal characters, while Spiegelman et al [309] report that animals appear in 50 per cent of all Sunday comic strips.

Biersdorf and Marcuse [69] used six of the C.A.T. cards and had the same artist design six corresponding cards, substituting human figures for the animals. Otherwise the two sets of cards were similar, though not identical. Some unnecessary differences (e.g., only one figure in the crib in picture 5, the kangaroo being carried in the arms rather than the pouch in 4, ambiguity removed in 1 where the figure is obviously female, etc.) make the results quite questionable. In administering the two sets of cards to 30 first-grade children ranging in age from approximately six to eight years, they found no significant differences in the two sets of stories. However, it is extremely likely from empirical evidence with the Rorschach and in psychoanalytic practice that animal stimuli and animal identification figures may be of greater value with the younger children than with children of six to eight and older.

Furthermore, the usefulness of the C.A.T. does not depend upon whether or not animal pictures produce better or only equally good stories. The C.A.T. and C.A.T.-S. pictures were carefully selected to elicit themes relevant to children's growth and emotional problems. There is considerable evidence thus far that the C.A.T. is clinically useful, and the question of animal versus human stimulus will probably remain a more or less theoretical issue.

D. On Some Differences between C.A.T. and T.A.T. Responses

By virtue of the fact that the subjects of the C.A.T. are children below 10, certain systematic differences exist between their responses and those of adults to the T.A.T. Specific differences from year to year, both in formal characteristics of language and thought processes, and dynamic differences in terms of psychoanalytic theory, are yet to be investigated.

By and large, stories to the C.A.T. and C.A.T.-S. are shorter and less complex than those of adults to the T.A.T. Very frequently, particularly in three and four year olds, the responses do not occur in clear-cut themes. Haphazard, sometimes descriptive remarks may be made to one or another of the pictures, and rejections are not infrequent. However, it should be emphasized that the majority of children, even in the younger age group, do tell proper stories, if not to all the pictures, at least to some.

The structure of children's stories is naturally poorer than those of adults. What would be considered a thought disturbance of major proportions in an adult is merely a reflection of appropriate immaturity in a child. If one is inexperienced with children's fantasies one must be careful not to be misled by seemingly pathological productions. It must be kept in mind that what would have to be considered schizophrenic in an adult simply corresponds to an appropriate developmental expression in a child.

Symbolisms, as reported by Freud, are much more abundant and much freer in children's stories than in those of normal adults. This of course parallels the nature of children's dreams. Simple wish fulfillment is quite frequently manifest.

Instead of revealing the entire character structure, C.A.T. stories may sometimes reflect transitory problems; developmental stages are shown, phases of socialization, of internalization of the superego, may clearly appear. Children often express a moral in their stories, when the internalization of mores and the superego formation become complex enough, beginning at around the age of six. In essence this is learning the "other side of the rule" as Susan Isaacs [177] calls a child's growing awareness of "Do unto others as you would have others do unto you." Our observations of the finer features of internalization are consistent with Van Ophuijsen's teaching—that, in essence, obsessive-compulsive neurosis first appears at the age of seven.

The observations of Piaget [260] concerning the language and thought processes of children are amply illustrated in C.A.T. stories. While concretisms, syncretisms, and animistic notions abound, the most striking aspect is usually the specificity of the children's productions. Characters are usually given proper names, and events are placed in specific locations at precise times. A large field for exploration exists in attempts to codify these maturational aspects to provide normative data for the clinician.

C.A.T. stories of preschool children are also likely to reflect differences in perceptual style among the children that are related to each child's reactions in the test situation. Moriarty and Murphy [240] have noted that the following devices are used in coping with the demands of the C.A.T. task: reduction in level of participation; resistance to further inquiry; positive efforts at problem solving; restructuring or reversing roles with the examiner; using a familiar story as a prop; being overprecise in small areas of the picture; the use of fantasy or magical processes; using humor; releasing tension through motor expressiveness; appealing for help from the examiner; using defensive maneuvers such as regression, denial, avoidance, projection, and sublimation.

E. Administration of the C.A.T.

In the administration of the C.A.T. account must be taken of the general problems of child testing. Good rapport must be established with the child. This will, in general, be considerably more difficult with the younger children as well as with the more disturbed ones. Whenever possible, the C.A.T. should be presented as a game, not as a test. In cases of children who are obviously aware that it is a test—whether from previous experience with such procedures or sophistication, etc.—it will be advisable to fully acknowledge this fact, but to explain most carefully that it is not a challenging kind of test in which the child must face approval, disapproval, competition, disciplinary action, etc. In other words, it is important for the administrator to convey positive attitudes to the child. Not only does this situation aid in the establishment of good rapport, but it also has other effects. Lyles [222] has found that positive attitudes, compared to negative or neutral ones, on the part of the examiner elicit increased productiveness and an increased inclination to adaptation in the child. Negative attitudes lead to an increase in anxiety and aggression.

For the actual instruction, it may be best to tell the child that we are going to engage in a game in which he has to tell a story about pictures; that he should tell what is going on, what the animals are doing now. At suitable points, the child may be asked what went on in the story before and what will happen later.

It will probably be found that much encouragement and prompting may be necessary; interruptions are permitted. One must be certain not to be suggestive in one's prompting. After all stories have been related, one may go over each of them asking for elaboration on specific points such as why somebody was given a certain name, proper names of places, ages, etc., and even questions regarding the particular type of outcome of a story. If a child's attention span does not permit this procedure, it would be well to attempt it at a date as soon after administration as possible.

Cain [87] suggests a supplementary "dream technique" for use on cards 5, 6, and 9 especially, where the characters are often seen as being asleep. In these instances, the examiner's final question is, "What did X dream?" Dreams that children report have been found to contain more unconscious material than the original theme, and to be based more on fantasy.

All side remarks and activities should be noted, in relation to the story being told. Blatt et al. [160] advise attending to physical activity, gestures, facial expressions, or posturing accompanying the responses; they view this "elaboration of the response" as equivalent to the adult's verbal productions.

Haworth [160] reviews all the relevant literature.

A difficult situation to deal with may arise if the child wants the examiner to tell a story; this is primarily a request to be given something rather than to have to give, and is best dealt with in that light. While it may help to explain that we want to hear what the particular child can make of the picture, it may be necessary to promise (and to adhere to it) to tell a story later, or to put off testing until one can ingratiate oneself with the child by a giving of one kind or another, then to resume again.

It is helpful to keep all the pictures out of sight except the one being dealt with, since the younger children have a tendency to play with all pictures at once, choosing them at random for storytelling. These pictures have been numbered and arranged in a particular sequence for particular reasons and should therefore be administered in the order indicated.

If, however, a child is particularly restless and one has some indication as to what problems his current disturbance may be related to, one may restrict the test to those few cards which are likely to illuminate those specific problems. Thus, a child who apparently has sibling rivalry problems might be given cards 1 and 4 particularly, etc.

F. Description of and Typical Responses to Pictures

Below, we present typical themes seen as responses to the various pictures.

Picture 1

Chicks seated around a table on which is a large bowl of food. Off to one side is a large chicken, dimly outlined.

Responses revolve around eating, being or not being sufficiently fed by either parent. Themes of sibling rivalry enter in around who gets more, who is well-behaved and not, etc. Food may be seen as a reward or, inversely, its withholding seen as punishment; general problems of orality are dealt with, i.e., satisfaction or frustration, feeding problems per se.

Picture 2

One bear pulling a rope on one side while another bear and a baby bear pull on the other side.

It is interesting to observe whether the baby here identifies the figure with whom he cooperates (if at all) as the father or the mother. It may be seen as a serious fight with accompanying fear of aggression, fulfillment of the child's own aggression or autonomy. More benignly, this picture may be seen as a game (tug-of-war, for example). Sometimes the rope itself may be a source of concern, i.e., breakage of the rope as a toy and fear of subsequent punishment, or again, purely as a symbol concerning masturbation with the rope breaking representing castration fears.

Picture 3

A lion with pipe and cane, sitting in a chair; in the lower right corner a little mouse appears in a hole.

This is usually seen as a father figure equipped with such symbols as pipe and cane. The latter may be seen either as an instrument of aggression or may be used to turn this paternal figure into an old, helpless figure of whom one need not be afraid. This is usually a defensive process. If the lion is seen as a strong paternal figure, it will be important to note whether he is a benign or a dangerous power.

The mouse is seen by many children as the identification figure. In such a case—by tricks and circumstance—the mouse may be turned into the more powerful one. On the other hand, it may be totally in the power of the lion. Some children identify themselves with the lion, and there will be subjects who will switch identification one or more times, giving evidence of confusion about role, conflict between compliance and autonomy, etc.

Picture 4

A kangaroo with a bonnet on her head, carrying a basket with a milk bottle; in her pouch is a baby kangaroo with a balloon; on a bicycle, a larger kangaroo child.

This usually elicits themes of sibling rivalry, or some concern with the origin of babies. In both cases, the relation to the mother is often an important feature. Sometimes a child who is an older sibling will identify himself with the pouch baby, thus indicating a wish to regress in order to be nearer to the mother. On the other hand, a child who is in reality the younger may identify himself with the older one, thus signifying his wish for independence and mastery. The basket may give rise to themes of feeding. A theme of flight from danger may also occasionally be introduced.

Picture 5

A darkened room with a large bed in the background; a crib in the foreground in which are two baby bears.

Productions concerning primal scene in all variations are common here; the child is concerned with what goes on between the parents in bed. These stories reflect a good deal of conjecture, observation, confusion, and emotional involvement on the part of the children. The two children in the crib lend themselves to themes of mutual manipulation and exploration between children.

Picture 6

A darkened cave with two dimly outlined bear figures in the background; a baby bear lying in the foreground.

This again is a picture eliciting primarily stories concerning primal scene. It is used in addition to picture 5 since practical experience has shown that 6 will enlarge frequently and greatly upon whatever was held back in response to the previous picture. Plain jealousy in this triangle situation will at times be reflected. Problems of masturbation at bedtime may appear in response to either 5 or 6.

Picture 7

A tiger with bared fangs and claws leaping at a monkey which is also leaping through the air.

Fears of aggression and manners of dealing with them are here exposed. The degree of anxiety in the child often becomes apparent. It may be so great as to lead to rejection of the picture, or the defenses may be good enough (or unrealistic enough) to turn it into an innocuous story. The monkey may even outsmart the tiger. The tails of the animals lend themselves easily to the projection of fears or wishes of castration.

Picture 8

Two adult monkeys sitting on a sofa drinking from tea cups. One adult monkey in foreground sitting on a hassock talking to a baby monkey.

Here one often sees the role in which the child places himself within the family constellation. His interpretation of the dominant (foreground) monkey as either a father or mother figure becomes significant in relation to his perception of it as a benign monkey or as an admonishing, inhibiting one. The tea cups will, on occasion, give rise to themes of orality again.

Picture 9

A darkened room seen through an open door from a lighted room. In the darkened room there is a child's bed in which a rabbit sits up looking through the door.

Themes of fear of darkness, of being left alone, desertion by parents, significant curiosity as to what goes on in the next room, are all common responses to this picture.

Picture 10

A baby dog lying across the knees of an adult dog; both figures with a minimum of expression in their features. The figures are set in the foreground of a bathroom.

This leads to stories of "crime and punishment," revealing something about the child's moral conceptions. There are frequent stories about toilet training as well as masturbation. Regressive trends will be more clearly revealed in this picture than in some others.

Haworth [160] notes that a blank card, an all black card, or a half-black and half-white card can be added. Her use of the half-and-half card has shown that it uncovers strong racial feelings in black children.

G. Influence of the Perceptual Aspects of the Stimulus on Responses

In the interpretation of thematic materials of children, it is important to remain aware of the perceptual inaccuracies which may exist for certain age groups and which may therefore affect the responses given. Boulanger-Balleyguier [75] has found shifts in common reactions to some of the C.A.T. stimuli in a group of children 3 to 7 years old. Some of her findings follow:

Card 3. The pipe is not recognized well enough by children below 6 years to be mentioned. Only after age 6 do themes of conflict between the lion and mouse appear frequently. The perpetual accuracy of young children with respect to small details is questioned. This card does not yield data about father-child relationships until both figures are perceived.

Card 4. Children under 6 don't recognize the animals as kangaroos, are not aware of the pouch, and often omit the baby figure. The card is not indicated for the study of sibling rivalry or birth themes.

Card 7. The common response is concerned with conflict. Nonperception of conflict on this card is significant for interpretive purposes.

Considering the high frequency of certain omissions for many of the stimuli and the regular decrease of such omissions with age, it is suggested that young children do not actually perceive these figures. Those omitted most often are either blurred or vague (hen on card 1, bear on card 6) or very small (mouse on card 3, baby on card 4). Where the incidence of omissions is different for boys and girls, or where the decline is not regular with age, the emotional significance of the omission is greater.

CHAPTER XIV

THE C.A.T.-H.

A. Development of the C.A.T.-H.

AFTER THE CREATION OF THE C.A.T. MANY STUDIES WERE RE-
ported which showed that some children responded better to
animal stimuli and others to human figures. Bellak and Bellak [52], partly in
response to this new evidence, therefore developed a human modification of the
C.A.T. (C.A.T.-H.). It was also believed that the human form would be more
adequate to the intellectual development of some children between the ages of 7
and 10, especially those with high I.Q.'s.

B. Review of Studies Comparing Animal versus Human Pictures

The following studies are representative of the kinds which were conducted in
the intervening period between the development of the C.A.T. and the creation
of the C.A.T.-H. with the purpose of comparing responses obtained with different samples of children on animal and human forms of the C.A.T.

Budoff [82] tested 4 year old preschoolers with C.A.T. cards and an analogous
human set. There were no statistically significant differences between picture sets
on measures of productivity, story level, and transcendence index, although the
general trend indicated higher scores for the human figures on story level and
transcendence index. It was hypothesized that, where responses to human figures
seemed especially threatening, animal figures elicited more productive stories
possibly due to the increase of psychological distance.

Biersdorf and Marcuse [69] tested first-grade children with animal and human
pictures. No significant differences were obtained on the following measures:
number of words, ideas, characters mentioned, characters introduced, and re-
sponse-time indices.

Armstrong [12] compared the responses of first, second, and third-grade children on five C.A.T. cards and a duplicate set with human figures. The mean I.Q.
for each grade of children was in the superior range. Significantly higher transcendence index scores were found for the human figures, in that more subjective,

personalized, and interpretive responses were obtained instead of mere description.

Boyd and Mandler [77] studied third-grade children's reactions to human and animal stories and pictures. It was found that animal stimuli led to a greater degree of expression of ego involvement, particularly as manifested in the projection of negative affects. On the other hand, it was reported that the more significant effect of human stories on the production of imaginative material did not corroborate the hypothesis of children's primary identification with animals.

A recent study using animal and human figures with children aged 5½ to 7 years was conducted by Weisskopf-Joelson and Foster [343]. It was found that the mean transcendence index scores for all stories to human pictures compared with all stories to animal pictures did not differ significantly. A more detailed analysis of the results indicated, though, that the group of children with the lowest transcendence index scores were more productive when responding to animal pictures, suggesting to the authors that low scorers are able to reveal themselves more easily when they believe that they are telling about animals rather than humans. It was inferred that personality differences among children are associated with greater productivity to either animal or human pictures, depending on the specific personality involved.

Bellak and Hurvich [55] have considered the evidence obtained from several reports in the literature (see Table 1) concerning the superiority of either the animal or the human pictures, and have noted that the two most influential factors responsible for the conflicting evidence have been variations among the studies in stimulus cards used and in outcome measures employed. The sets of human drawings used have generally not been characterized by the ambiguity of age or sex that is achieved with the animal figures. As far as outcome measures are concerned, dynamic evaluation of the responses has been infrequent.

C. Modification of the Pictures for Use in the C.A.T.-H.

The major difficulty in the creation of the human drawings for inclusion in the C.A.T.-H. derived from the effort to achieve at least some ambiguity with regard to some of the figures in terms of age, sex, and cultural attributes. Although the C.A.T.-H. figures are not as free from cultural determinants as are the original animal figures, the C.A.T.-H. has and will serve as a highly useful instrument for those purposes for which it was developed. The set of 10 pictures that were finally selected is shown in Fig. 7.

D. Studies with the C.A.T.-H.

Haworth [158] tested a clinic sample of children whose diagnoses ranged from neurotic difficulties to borderline psychoses with the C.A.T. and an experimental set of C.A.T.-H. provided by me. All stories were scored for specific defense mechanisms, as assessed by Haworth's "A Schedule of Adaptive Mechanisms in C.A.T. Responses" (Fig. 8) and for story content, assessed with the Haworth

TABLE 1. Studies of Animal vs. Human Figures*

Stimuli	Subjects	Response measures	Results	Ref.
10 T.A.T. cards vs. 10 chromatic pics of rabbits in various activities	48 M and F, 5 to 10, normal school children	Story length, card rejections	Animals—significantly longer stories, fewer card rejections	49
Same as Bills [70]	8 M and F, 3rd grade, normal school children	Comparison on 26 of Murray's manifest needs	Animals seen as easier for children; correlation from a 0.09 to +0.58 (3 stat. sig.)	50
6 C.A.T. cards (1, 2, 4, 5, 8, and 10) vs. comparable human set	30 M and F, 1st grade, normal school children	Number of words, ideas, characters mentioned, characters introduced, response-time indices	No significant differences	48
Same as Biersdorf and Marcuse [69]	28 M and F, 5.4 to 8.5, emotionally disturbed	Similar to Biersdorf and Marcuse [69], plus ratings of clinical usefulness	No significant differences; human judged more clinically useful	174
5 C.A.T. cards (1, 2, 4, 8, 10) vs. a comparable human set	60 M and F, 1st-3rd grade, I.Q. superior, normal school children	Story length, number of nouns, verbs, ego words, transcendence scores, and reaction time	Human significantly higher transcendence index; other measures no difference	6
C.A.T. vs. T.A.T.	75 M and F, 9-10.6, normal school children	Amount and kinds of feelings, themes, conflicts, and definite outcomes	Human—all response criteria significantly higher except number of words	169
2 stories (with animal or human characters), each followed by 2 pics of animals or humans in ambiguous action	96 M and F, mean age 8.5, mean I.Q. 101, normal school children	Story length, presence of original ideas, value judgments, punishment, reward, new themes, pronoun I, and formal features	Human for stimulus stories; animal for stimulus pics	56

* Reprinted from Bellak and Hurvich [55] by permission.

TABLE 1. Studies of Animal vs. Human Figures* *(cont.)*

Stimuli	Subjects	Response measures	Results	Ref.
Same as Biersdorf and Marcuse [69]	72 Japanese, M and F, 6 to 12, normal school children	Definite outcomes, expression of feelings	Human—more definite outcomes and more expression of feelings and significant conflicts	103
C.A.T. vs. comparable human set	28 German, 8-9, 2nd grade, normal	Story length, speed of verbalization, number of themes, reaction time	Human—superior on all the response measures	247
9 C.A.T. cards (6 omitted) vs. comparable human set	18 M and F, age 4, all I.Q.'s above 120, normal nursery school children	Productivity, story level, and transcendence index	No statistical difference; trend in favor of human	61
4 C.A.T. cards (3, 4, 9, 10) vs. comparable human set, color and black and white	40 M and F, 5.5 to 9, normal kindergarten	Transcendence index	No difference except by personality	277

* Reprinted from Bellak and Hurvich [55] by permission.
  See additional references.

C.A.T. Story Dynamics form (Table 2). No significant differences were obtained between the animal and human forms on the total number of categories receiving critically high scores. However, a difference was found, for this group of children, between the two sets of stimuli concerning the elicitation of certain defense mechanisms. The largest difference in critical score incidence was in the projection-introjection category, with the greater number of such scores on the animal form. Children were most consistent between forms in the Identification category. The story content analysis enabled a card by card comparison of the two versions. There was high agreement in the themes elicited by the two forms, although a greater degree of negative affect was expressed in responses to certain cards for the animal form.

    Card 1. Oral gratification is the main theme for both animal and human forms. For those subjects not using this response on both forms, the trend favors the animal form, while more oral deprivation is used on the human form. The adult is most often seen as the mother on both forms, with only a few responses of "shadow" or figure other than father (who is seen one-third as often as mother). Few punishment themes are reported on either form.

    Card 2. Predominantly seen as a game, rather than a fight, on both forms, with the pair most frequently seen as the winner, especially on the human card. The child is more often seen with either mother or father on the animal version and almost exclusively with a peer on the human form.

    Card 3. No outstanding use of either the adult attacking the child or the child helping the adult on either form. The large figure is seen as powerful (or as king) *only* on the animal form, and is more

1

2

3

4

5

FIG. 7. Pictures for use with the C.A.T.-H.

6

7

8

9

10

FIG. 7 (*cont.*)

A Schedule of Adaptive Mechanisms in CAT Responses

MARY R. HAWORTH, Ph.D.

Name ....Bd: .... Date: .... Age: ....

Critical Scores: ....

TOTALS	DEFENSE MECHANISMS

A. Reaction-formation (only one check per story)

.... 1. Exaggerated goodness or cleanliness
(A+ .... 2. Oppositional attitudes, rebellion, stubbornness
B=5) .... 3. Story tone opposed to picture content

B. Undoing and Ambivalence (only one check per story)

.... 1. Undoing
.... 2. Gives alternatives; balanced phrases (asleep—awake; hot—cold, etc.)
.... 3. Indecision by S or story character
.... 4. Restates (e.g., "that............, no this...........;" "he was going to, but............")

C. Isolation

.... 1. Detached attitude ("it couldn't happen," "it's a cartoon")
(6) .... 2. Literal ("it doesn't show, so I can't tell.")
.... 3. Comments on story or picture ("That is hard"; "I told a good one.")
.... 4. Laughs at card, exclamations
.... 5. Use of fairy-tale, comic-book, or "olden times" themes or characters
.... 6. Describes in detail, logical; "the end"; gives title to story
.... 7. Specific details, names or quotes ("four hours"; she said, "............")
.... 8. Character gets lost
.... 9. Character runs away due to anger
.... 10. S aligns with parent against "naughty" child character; disapproves child's actions

D. Repression and Denial

.... 1. Child character waits, controls self, conforms, is good, learned lesson
(5) .... 2. Accepts fate, didn't want it anyway
.... 3. Prolonged or remote punishments
.... 4. "It was just a dream"
.... 5. Forgets, or loses something
.... 6. Omits figures or objects from story (on #10 must omit mention of toilet *and* tub or washing)
.... 7. Omits usual story content
.... 8. No fantasy or story (describes card blandly)
.... 9. Refuses card

E. Deception

.... 1. Child superior to adult, laughs at adult, is smarter, tricks adult, sneaks, pretends, hides
(3) * from, steals from, peeks at or spies on adult (only one check per story)
.... 2. Adult tricks child, is not what appears to be (only one check per story)

F. Symbolization

.... 1. Children play in bed
(4) .... 2. See parents in bed (#5)
.... 3. Open window (#5, #9); Dig, or fall in, a hole
.... 4. Babies born
.... 5. Rope breaks (#2); chair or cane breaks (#3); balloon breaks (#4); tail pulled or bitten (#4, 7); crib broken (#9)
.... 6. Rain, river, water, storms, cold
.... 7. Fire, explosions, destruction
.... 8. Sticks, knives, guns
.... 9. Cuts, stings, injuries, actual killings (other than by eating)
.... 10. Oral deprivation

G. Projection and Introjection

.... 1. Attacker is attacked, "eat and be eaten"
(4) .... 2. Innocent one is eaten or attacked
.... 3. Child is active aggressor (bites, hits, throws; do not include verbal or teasing attacks)
.... 4. Characters blame others
.... 5. Others have secrets or make fun of somebody
:............... 6. S adds details, objects, characters, or oral themes
.... 7. Magic or magical powers

(* or 2, if both are E-2 responses)

Fig. 8. A Schedule of Adaptive Mechanisms in C.A.T. Responses, by Mary R. Haworth. Copyright C.P.S. Inc., Box 83, Larchmont, New York 10538.

PHOBIC, IMMATURE OR DISORGANIZED

H. *Fear and Anxiety*

....   1. Child hides from danger, runs away due to fear
(3)   ....   2. Fears outside forces (wind, ghosts, hunters, wild animals, monsters)
....   3. Dreams of danger
....   4. Parent dead, goes away, or doesn't want child
....   5. Slips of tongue by S

I. *Regression*

....   1. Much affect in telling story
(2)   ....   2. Personal references
....   3. Food spilled
....   4. Bed or pants wet, water splashed
....   5. Dirty, messing, smelly; person or object falls in toilet
....   6. Ghosts, witches, haunted house

J. *Controls weak or absent*

....   1. Bones, blood
(1)   ....   2. Poison
....   3. Clang or nonsense words
....   4. Perseveration of unusual content from a previous story
....   5. Tangential thinking, loose associations
....   6. Bizarre content

IDENTIFICATION

K. *Adequate, same-sex*

....   1. S identifies with same-sex parent or child character
(L=   ....   2. Child jealous of, scolded or punished by, same-sex parent
or >K)   ....   3. Child loves, or is helped by, parent of opposite sex

L. *Confused, or opposite-sex*

....   1. S identifies with opposite-sex parent or child character
....   2. Child fears, or is scolded or punished by, opposite-sex parent
....   3. Misrecognition by S of sex or species
....   4. Slips of tongue with respect to sex of figures

This checklist has been designed primarily as an aid in the qualitative evaluation of children's CAT stories; it can also be used to furnish a rough quantitative measure for making comparisons between subjects and groups. The Schedule provides a quick summary of the number and kinds of defenses employed as well as the content of items used most frequently. The categories are arranged as nearly as possible on a continuum from indicators of high control and constriction to suggestions of disorganization and loosening of ties to reality.

Directions for Scoring: In the blank preceding each item, indicate with a check mark (or the card number, for future reference) any occurrence of such a response. A story may be "scored" in several categories and, except where indicated, a story may receive checks on more than one item under any one category.

After all stories have been scored, record the total number of checks for each category in the blank provided. The number in parentheses under each of these blanks indicates the *minimum* number of checks regarded as a "critical score" for that category.

For the Identification measure, the equivalent of a critical score is secured by comparing the relative number of checks for categories K and L. If the sum of checks for L is equal to or exceeds the sum for K, identification is considered to be "confused" and contributes one unit to the total of critical scores.

The final quantitative measure consists of the number of categories receiving critical scores (and *not* the total number of checks for all categories).

On the basis of research findings,[*] five or more critical scores would indicate enough disturbance to warrant clinical intervention.

[*]Mary R. Haworth, Ph.D., A Schedule for the Analysis of CAT Responses, *Journal of Projective Techniques & Personality Assessment*, Vol. 27, 1963, No. 2, 181-184.

FIG. 8 *(cont.)*

TABLE 2. C.A.T. Story Dynamics

Name: Sex: Form: A or H

1. Oral gratification_____ Deprivation_____
   Adult is Father_____, Mother_____, Shadow_____ Other_____ *M & F_____
   Punishment theme_____

2. Game_____ Fight_____
   Winner: Pair_____ Single_____
   Child with: Parent of same sex_____ of opposite sex_____ Peer_____

3. Adult attacks or scolds child_____ Child helps adult_____
   Adult is king_____ old, tired, lonely, etc. _____
   Child teases or attacks adult_____

4. Picnic_____ Disaster, fire, etc. _____
   Bike runs over tail or leg_____

5. Parents in bed_____
   Children play in bed_____ Naughty_____ Sleep_____

6. Child runs away_____ *Camp (Hibernate)_____
   Attack from outside: feared_____ takes place_____

7. Child is: attacked_____gets away_____ turns on large fig. _____*Friends_____

8. Scolding, punishing_____ Child is helpful_____
   Mention of picture_____ Secret_____
   Male adult_____

9. Attack from outside: feared_____ takes place_____
   **Everyday event_____ Loneliness_____ *Naughty_____
   Parents in another rm._____ *Sleep_____ *Sick_____

10. Naughtiness relates to toilet_____other_____
    Punisher is same sex_____ opposite sex_____
    Continues naughtiness_____ learned lesson_____

Cards rejected:
Unusual stories:

---

* Haworth included forty-eight items on her original story dynamics form. Lawton added six items when she employed the list. Additions of Lawton are identified by an asterisk.

** This item was deleted by Lawton in her study.

Reprinted from [52] by permission.

often seen as old or tired on the human form. The child figure teases the adult *only* on the animal form.

Card 4. Most frequently seen as going to a picnic or to the store on both forms, and with very few disasters happening in either version. Only a very few instances on either card of the child running over the adult's heel with his bike.

Card 5. Children are seen as playing, sleeping (most often), or being naughty equally on both cards; parents are mentioned equally on both forms.

Card 6. There is no difference between cards in terms of the child running away, fearing attack, or an attack taking place; none of these themes were used frequently.

Card 7. The smaller figure is frequently seen as being attacked on both versions, but with somewhat greater incidence on the animal form. The child escapes equally often on both cards and only infrequently turns to retaliate against the larger figure.

Card 8. Scoldings occur with equal frequency with both cards, and the child is rarely seen as being helpful. The picture on the wall is mentioned more frequently on the human form, and secrets are reported more often on the animal card. Male figures were seen *only* on the animal form and were mentioned in 10 of the 22 stories.

Card 9. Attacks are only infrequently reported as being feared or as taking place on either card. Rather, a preponderance of everyday events are mentioned (especially to the human form), and the parents are occasionally reported as being in the next room. Themes of loneliness occurred more often on the human form.

Card 10. Toilet naughtiness was reported with fair frequency on both forms, but with somewhat more on the human. Punishing parents are seen about equally as being of the same or the opposite sex, but with a trend for more same-sex parents on the animal form and more opposite-sex parents on the human form. In only a very few cases does the child "learn a lesson," and this tends to happen more often on the human form.*

Lawton [206] conducted a study similar to Haworth's [158]. She tested school children with the C.A.T. and the same experimental set of the C.A.T.-H. used by Haworth [158] and scored each form for the presence of 10 defense mechanisms. Analysis of the data showed no significant agreement between the two forms in eliciting or not eliciting the four defense mechanisms: reaction formation, isolation, symbolization, and identification. The one major exception was the result for projection, which showed significant agreement between forms. Lawton also compared the protocols for both forms with the expected themes and found considerable agreement between forms with a few exceptions, the principal one being the finding of more negative reactions on the animal form. Most of these thematic differences were deemed capable of resolution by slight modifications in the pictures, and not indicative of a theoretical difference between the forms.

Porterfield [266] administered the C.A.T.-H. and the Bender-Gestalt Test to a group of black preschool stutterers and to similar age and ability groups of nonstuttering classmates (adaptive group) and nonstutterers characterized by behavior problems (maladaptive group). C.A.T.-H. protocols were evaluated with Haworth's "A Schedule of Adaptive Mechanisms in C.A.T. Responses," and it was found that the categories of repression-denial, symbolization, and projection-introjection differentiated stutterers from nonstutterers. Significant differences were obtained between stutterer and adaptive nonstutterer groups on the three dimensions, with the stutterer group attaining higher scores on repression-denial and symbolization. Whereas no significant differences were found between stutterer and maladaptive nonstutterer groups on the C.A.T.-H. dimensions, differ-

---

* Reprinted from [55] by permission.

ences were obtained between these groups on Bender-Gestalt scores, the latter group performing on a lower level. These last findings are indicative both of the lesser relevance of the C.A.T.-H. to overt behavior, and of the relation of adaptive mechanisms to covert behavior.

In their study of second grade girls, Neuringer and Livesay suggest that the C.A.T. and C.A.T.-H. are equivalent forms. Myler et al. agree, and find in addition that the C.A.T. and C.A.T.-H. were more useful for second grade girls than the T.A.T.

CHAPTER XV

INTERPRETATION OF THE C.A.T.

WHEN ONE APPROACHES THE INTERPRETATION OF AN APPER-ceptive method such as the C.A.T., it is best to keep some basic principles firmly in mind. The subject is asked to apperceive—that is, to meaningly interpret—a situation. The subject's interpretation of the stimulus in following our instruction to tell a story exceeds the minimal "objective" stimulus value. He does so, by necessity, in his own way, which must be a function of continually present psychological forces which at that moment manifest themselves in relation to the given stimulus material.

If one accepts a motivational continuity of the personality structure, one may use the following analogy for a testing procedure as well as psychotherapeutic free association. If a river is sampled at various relatively close intervals, the chemical analyses of the content will be highly similar. Any pailful will be representative of the total content. This procedure is commonly followed in public health assays.

Now, if a new tributary joins (as compared to a new situational factor in psychological sampling), it may of course add factors about which the assayer has to know in order to account for changes in content. A primary genetic theory of personality, like psychoanalysis, maintains that the main contents of the stream will remain the primary matrix, which, after a certain point, can only be modified by tributaries to a greater or lesser degree.

To leave the dangers of further analogies, we believe (and by now, ample experimental literature supports this belief) that interpretations of stimuli in our test material give us a valid sample of the subject's psychic continuum known as personality. Still in its formative stage, it is, of course, more changeable in childhood. We can learn about the motivational forces from the fact that any individual response is meaningful for that person; we can furthermore increase our insight by comparing one individual's responses to those of others. To that extent, we are' really studying individual differences and making inferences about a given subject by this comparison.

To facilitate the interpretation analysis of the C.A.T. we are suggesting the study of the 10 variables discussed below as they are shown on the Bellak T.A.T. Short Form and C.A.T. Blank.

A. Ten Variables

1. The Main Theme

To recapitulate: We are interested in what a child makes of our pictures and then we want to know *why* he responds with this particular story (or interpretation). Rather than judge by one story, we will be on safer ground if we can find a common denominator or trend in a number of stories. For example, if the main hero of several stories is hungry and resorts to stealing in order to satisfy himself, it is not unreasonable to conclude that this child is preoccupied with thoughts of not getting enough—food literally, or gratification generally—and, in his fantasy, wishes to take it away from others. Interpretation, then, is concerned with the finding of common denominators in behavioral patterns. In this sense we can speak of the theme of a story or of several stories. A theme may, of course, be more or less complex. We find that particularly in our younger subjects of three and four it is usually very simple. In the case of S. Q. (p. 243), one may simply say that the theme in the lion story is "I do not want any clothes, and wish to be dirty and behave like a small child, because then apparently one gets more affection." On the other hand, themes may be more complex, as in subject M.I.'s (p. 245) "I'm powerful and dangerous but in order to be liked and to live in peace with myself, I must give up my aggressive and acquisitive wishes." The theme in such a case is simply a restatement of the moral of the story. A story may have more than one theme, however, and themes may sometimes be complexly interrelated.

2. The Main Hero

A basic assumption behind our reasoning thus far has been, of course, that the story which our subject tells is, in essence, about himself. Since there can be a number of people in a story, it becomes necessary to state that we speak of the figure with which our subject mainly identifies himself as the hero. We will have to specify, for this purpose, some objective criteria for differentiating the hero from other figures, namely, that the hero is the figure about whom the story is woven primarily, that he resembles the subject most in age and sex, and that the story events are seen from the standpoint of the hero. While these statements hold true most of the time, they do not always do so. There may be more than one hero and our subject may identify with both, or first with one and then with another. There may be a deviation in that a subject may identify with a hero of a different sex; it is important to note such identifications. Sometimes an identification figure secondary in importance in a story may represent more deeply repressed unconscious attitudes of the subject. Probably the interests, wishes, deficiencies, gifts, and abilities with which the hero is invested are those which the subject possesses, wants to possess, or fears that he might have. It will be important to observe the adequacy of the hero, that is, his ability to deal with whatever circumstances may exist in a way considered adequate by the society to which he belongs. The adequacy of the hero serves as the best single measure of the ego strength, that is of the subject's own adequacy. An exception is, of course, the case of the story which is a blatant compensatory wish fulfillment. Careful scrutiny will usually reveal the real inadequacy. See for example, story 3 of subject M. I., in which the hero is a mighty lion, who, however, does not like his body and in the end can be happy only by giving up his omnipotence.

Self-image.   By self-image we mean the conception which the subject has of his body and of his entire self and social role. Schilder first described body image as the picture of one's own body in one's mind. In Case 3, M. I., for example (p. 245), tells us about his own body image in unusually overt terms when he says, "he didn't have a beautiful body," and then proceeds to tell us how he would like his body to be, what fantasy self-image he would like to have, namely, that of a big, powerful, all-possessing person.

3. Main Needs and Drives of the Hero

Behavioral needs of the hero (as in the story). The story behavior of the hero may have one of a variety of relationships to the storyteller. The needs expressed may correspond directly to the needs of the patient. These needs may be, at least in part, expressed behaviorally in real life, or they may be the direct opposite of real life expression and constitute the fantasy complement. In other words, very aggressive stories may be told sometimes by a very aggressive child, or by a rather meek, passive-aggressive one who has fantasies of aggression. At least to a certain extent the needs of the hero may not reflect so much the needs of the storyteller as they do the drive quality which he perceives in other figures. In other words, he may be describing the aggression feared from various objects or referring to idealized expectations, such as brilliance and fortitude, ascribed to significant figures in his life and only in part internalized in himself. In short, the behavioral needs of the hero expressed in the story have to be examined and understood in the light of all the varieties and vicissitudes of drive modification and subsumed under the broader concepts of projection or apperceptive distortion.

It is the difficult task of the interpreter to determine to what extent the manifest needs of the hero correspond to various constituents of the storyteller's personality, and in addition what the relationship of these constituents is to the narrator's manifest behavior. It is here that comparison with the actual clinical history is most useful and entirely appropriate under clinical circumstances (as distinct from a research setting). If a child is reported to be particularly shy, passive, and withdrawn and his C.A.T. stories overflow with aggression, the compensatory nature of the fantasy material is obvious. On the other hand, it must remain a goal of psychological science to develop more and more criteria for increasingly valid predictions—by relating the fantasy material to actual behavior and to discernible behavior patterns. The study of ego functions is particularly useful in this respect [57, 58]. The relationship of drives expressed within the story, together with their vicissitudes may often serve as one clue, that is, if the story sequence shows an initial aggressive response with this aggression becoming controlled by the end of the story, chances are that this is a person who does not translate fantasy or latent need into reality. This assumption may then be checked against available behavioral data. There are other criteria helpful in attempting predictions about what might be called "acting out." The high degree of detail and realism in the description of needs may suggest a direct likelihood of their expression in reality. Vaguely structured needs of the hero are less likely to be related to reality.

Figures, objects, or circumstances introduced.   A child who introduces weapons of one sort or another in a number of stories (even without using them in context) or who has food as an integral part (even without eating it) may be tentatively judged on such evidence as having a need for aggression or oral gratification respectively. And since the introduction of a figure or circumstance not pictorially represented is extremely significant, this should be noted, possibly by adding an exclamation mark to the analysis sheet. External circumstances such as injustice, severity, indifference, deprivation, and deception (included with the figures and objects introduced) help to indicate the nature of the world in which the child believes himself to be living.

Figures, objects, or circumstances omitted.   Similarly, if one or more figures in the picture are omitted or ignored in the story related, we must consider the possibility of dynamic significance. The simplest meaning is usually an expression of the wish that the figure or object were not there. This may mean plain hostility or that the figure or object is severely conflict arousing, possibly because of its positive value. Of course, this level of inference can only be tentative; at present we do not have a large enough sample of norms to provide expectations regarding objects themselves, introduced and/or omitted.

4. The Conception of the Environment (World)

This concept is, of course, a complex mixture of unconscious self-perception and apperceptive distortion of stimuli by memory images of the past. The more consistent a picture of the environment appearing in the C.A.T. stories, the more reason we have to consider it an important constituent of our subject's personality and a useful clue to his reactions in everyday life. Usually two or three descriptive terms will suffice, such as succorant, hostile, exploiting or exploitable, friendly, dangerous, etc.

Identification. It is important to note with whom the child identifies in the family, namely, which sibling, which parent, etc. It will also be most important to observe the role which each parent takes with regard to adequacy, and appropriateness, as an identification figure, for instance, whether a male child after the age of five identifies with the father, or an older brother, uncle, etc., rather than with say, the mother or a younger sister. While, of course, the process of identification will not have been completed until the end of puberty, the early history may be of great importance.

5. Figures Seen as . . .

Here we are interested in the way the child sees the figures around him and how he reacts to them. We know something about the quality of object relationships— symbiotic, anaclitic, oral dependent, ambivalent, etc., at different stages of development and in different personalities. However, in a broader scheme we may descriptively speak of supportive, competitive, and other relationships.

6. Significant Conflicts

When we study the significant conflicts, we not only want to know the nature of the conflicts but also the defenses which the child uses against anxiety engendered by these conflicts. Here we have an excellent opportunity to study the early character formation, and we may be able to derive ideas concerning prognosis.

There are those conflicts which all children experience as they grow from one phase to the next. Thus, beginning at about age 3, we ought not to be alarmed to find evidence of the oedipal struggle and defenses against the fantasied relationship. Some conflicts are part of normal growing up; others may have pathological significance.

7. Nature of Anxieties

The importance of determining the main anxieties of a child hardly needs emphasizing. Those related to physical harm, punishment, and the fear of lacking or losing love (disapproval) and of being deserted (loneliness, lack of support), are probably the most important. It will be valuable to note in the context the child's defenses against the fears which beset him. We will want to know the form the defense takes, whether it is flight, passivity, aggression, orality, acquisitiveness, renunciation, regression, etc.

8. Main Defenses against Conflicts and Fears

Stories should not be studied exclusively for drive content, but should, in addition, be examined for the defenses against these drives. Not infrequently such a study of defenses will actually offer more information in that the drives themselves may appear less clearly than the defenses against them; on the other hand, the defensive structure may be more closely related to manifest behavior of the child. By means of studying drives and defenses the C.A.T. often permits an appraisal of the character structure of the subject.

Aside from a search for the main defense mechanisms, it is also valuable to study the molar aspects of the stories. For instance, some subjects choose obsessive defenses against a picture of disturbing content. They may produce four or five themes, each very short and descriptive, manifestly different but dynamically similar. Sometimes a succession of themes to one and the same picture shows the subject's attempts to deal with a disturbing conflict; successive stories may become more and more innocuous, showing an increase in defensive operation.

The concept of defense has to be understood in an increasingly broader sense, best discussed recently by Lois Murphy—with her associates—in connection with coping, i.e., the person's general ability and mode of meeting external and internal stimuli. With the advance in ego psychology and a focus on the problems of adaptation, a study of these functions is likely to play an increasing role in the exploration of projective methods. We not only want to know the nature of the defensive maneuvers but also the success with which they are employed and/or rather the sacrifice such maneuvers demand from the functioning personality.

The concept of perceptual vigilance may be thought of in connection with projective methods. Various studies have suggested that not only is the defensive projective function of the ego increased in stress but also its cognitive acuity may be improved at the same time.

In the study of children's stories, it must be remembered that we view the nature and pathogenicity of defenses and other structural concepts in terms of age appropriateness. What may be quite normal at one age may be pathological at another age. In the absence of reliable data, not only in the projective literature but any literature at all, some very rough, fallible guidelines have to be adhered to.

9. Adequacy of Superego as Manifested by "Punishment" for "Crime"

The relationship of the chosen punishment to the nature of the offense gives us an insight into the severity of the superego; a psychopath's hero who murders may receive no punishment other than a slight suggestion that he may have learned a lesson for later life, while a neurotic may have stories in which the hero is accidentally or intentionally killed or mangled or dies of an illness following the slightest infraction or expression of aggression. On the other hand, a nonintegrated superego, sometimes too severe and sometimes too lenient, is also frequently met in neurotics. A formulation as to the circumstances under which a person's superego can be expected to be too severe, and under what other conditions it is likely to be too lenient, is, of course, related to the difficult problem of acting out. In addition, however, it is a generally valuable piece of information.

10. Integration of the Ego

This is, of course, an important variable to learn about, for in its many aspects it reveals the general level of functioning. To what extent is the child able to compromise between drives and the demands of reality on the one hand and the commands of his superego on the other? The adequacy of the hero in dealing with the problems the storyteller has confronted him with in the C.A.T. is an important aspect in this variable.

Here, we are interested also in formal characteristics. Is the subject able to tell appropriate stories which constitute a certain amount of cognizance of the stimuli, or does he leave the stimulus completely and tell a story with no manifest relation to the picture because he is not well enough, therefore, and too preoccupied with his own problems to perceive reality? Does he find comfort and salvation from anxiety stimulated by the test by giving very stereotyped responses, or is he well enough and intelligent enough to be creative and give more or less original stories? Having produced a plot, can he attain a solution of the conflicts in the story and within himself which is adequate, complete, and realistic; or do his thought processes become unstructured or even bizarre under the impact of the problem? Does he have the ability to go from a past background of the story to a future resolution? This will depend on the age of the child as well as on his unique personality.

These observations, together with the dynamic diagnosis which the content variables supply—thus facilitating possible classifications of the patient in one of the nosological categories—are the main contributions of the C.A.T.

From a formal standpoint, it is useful to consider that telling stories to the pictures is a task which the subject must perform. We may judge his adequacy and ego strength and other variables from the standpoint of his ability and way of meeting the task. Of course, the adequacy of the ego and its various functions has to be considered in relation to the specific age again. Consideration should be given to a variety of ego functions such as drive control (related to the story sequence and outcome), frustration tolerance (related to adequacy of hero), anxiety tolerance, perceptual and motor adequacy, and others.*

B. The Use of the Short Form T.A.T. and C.A.T. Blank

For the purpose of facilitating the analysis and recording of the stories, I designed the Short Form T.A.T. and C.A.T. Blank. I have found that a similar blank which I designed for the T.A.T. alone served as a useful frame of reference, particularly in the beginning of one's experience and even for the experienced worker when a record seems unusually valueless; in the event of ordinary physical and mental strain, or of one's own emotional blind spots, such a schema will yield much better results.

Stories can be recorded individually. On the summary page, we recommend briefly noting the main data culled from every story in order to gain an impression of the whole. The final report we recommend be written in such a way that the most salient facets of the personality, as they appear, are summed up in the first large paragraph. In the second large paragraph, each general statement made in the first should be briefly supported by concrete references to the stories and details appearing in them. Or each abstract statement may be immediately supported by reference to the concrete story content it is predicated upon.

C. Case Illustrations

The following three cases are presented in rank order of disturbance revealed. Each is an example of various specific disorders, although they all have certain features in common. They will be formally analyzed and interpreted in detail so that the reader may observe some of the subtler aspects of insight to be gained.

Case 1 has been selected for its relative freedom from pathology. It demonstrates the developmental process of internalization of authority and social learning or socialization. These stories are classically illustrative of the "statement of a moral" so often found in children's stories. This child does it explicitly; it is more often implicit. The moral is so strongly and repetitively stated and reaction formation is so prominent that one wonders if the child is in the early stages of an obsessive-compulsive character disorder. The tentative appearance of this ten-

---

* The 1974 revision of the C.A.T. manual discusses ego functions depicted on page 5 of the Short Form in a way similar to that of the Long Form for the T.A.T.

dency would have to be investigated more carefully in a study of the behavioral aspects of his life and in the light of all other available data.

It will be particularly useful to compare stories 3, 4, and especially 5 in the three cases presented. While all three reveal primal scene fears, they are apparently of differing intensities and are handled in different ways.

Case 1*

The following C.A.T. stories are of a boy 7 years and 9 months old. His I.Q. was 133 on Form L of the Stanford-Binet. His father is an artist described as easygoing and apparently well adjusted, while the mother, although also gifted, as well as warm and outgoing, appears somewhat more tense. There is a little sister four years younger.

John himself is an attractive youngster with considerable social poise and many friends. He is without specific difficulties except for the fact that his teachers report that he is somewhat troublesome in asking embarrassing questions, putting the teachers on the spot. At times when his mother has been engaged in activities that took her away from home, John has been demanding and irritable. His relationship to the sister is said to be protective.

---

* The author is indebted to the late Miss Sadi Oppenheim for her permission to use this case.

SHORT FORM

BELLAK T.A.T and C.A.T BLANK

For Recording and Analyzing Thematic Apperception Test and Children's Apperception Test

Name___John_____ Sex __M___ Age _7-9_ Date_____

Education_____Occupation_____ _____; (circle one) m. s. w. d.

Referred by_____Analysis by_____

After having obtained the stories analyze each story by using the variables on the left of Page 2. Not every story will furnish information regarding each variable: the variables are presented as a frame of reference to help avoid overlooking some dimension.

When all ten stories have been analyzed it is easy to check each variable from left to right for all ten stories and record an integrated summary on Page 4 under the appropriate headings. That way a final picture is obtained almost immediately.

Then, keeping Page 4 folded out, the Final Report: Diagnostic Impressions and Recommendations can be written on Page 1 by reference to Page 4. Page 5 gives available space for any other notations. The stories then can be stapled inside the blank against Page 5. For further instructions see *Manual for T.A.T. Interpretation*, Psychological Corporation, by Leopold Bellak or *Manual for the C.A.T.*, C.P.S. Inc., or *The T.A.T. and C.A.T. in Clinical Use*, 2nd edition, Grune & Stratton, 1971, N. Y. C. by Leopold Bellak;

FINAL REPORT: Diagnostic Impressions and Recommendations

These stories reveal a child of above average intelligence, verbally gifted, who is in the process of adjusting himself to the world, i.e., in the process of socialization and internalization of rules and regulations. This may be seen in the moral which sums up nearly every story. His main hero is a child striving for autonomy in stories 1 and 4, and a need for curiosity and participation in adult freedom of acquisition, sex, and general achievement in stories 6, 8, 9, and 10, where he variously wants to know what is going on at night, at adult parties, etc. However, his hero usually has to renounce his goals and learn that it is better to obey the parents' instructions not to go to the brook, as in story 1 (which one can fall into), not to be too anxious to get honey, as in story 6 (one gets stung), or not to ride a bicycle too wildly (or one falls off, as in story 4).
He clearly has oedipal feelings, excluding father from the bedroom in story 5, and engaging in classical competition with him in story 7, where the monkey fighting with the mighty lion has his tail cut off, and expresses his resignation in the succinct, "If you want to keep your tail long, you don't want to fool around with the lion." Similarly, he is scared of nocturnal animals harming him. He identifies with mother in story 2, helping her pull the rope because father is stronger, but on other occasions, such as in stories 4 and 10, sees her as somewhat punishing and restricting.
Much as he wants to be grown up, there is evidence in story 10 and possibly in story 4 that he may identify slightly regressively with the younger sister. He has a strong curiosity which is in the service of the defenses. He wants to know how to avoid possible harm or injury, for instance in story 3 where the lion has trouble because he doesn't know how to read, and sublimates his interest in magnifying glasses, fingerprints, etc.
His anxieties center around fear of physical harm, sometimes obviously of a castration nature, for instance, the monkey with his tail cut off, being stung by a bee, and the breaking rope. His conflicts are characterized by a strong superego winning out over his need for aggression, autonomy, and sexual curiosity, to a point where he may possibly develop into a somewhat obsessive-compulsive character with some lack of spontaneity and a tendency to overcompliance. Reaction formation will undoubtedly figure prominently in his makeup. However, note should be taken of the realistic and usually happy outcome of the stories, and the lack of any viciousness in the superego. The punishments are always mild and sometimes considerate - for instance, in story 8 where the parents wait until the company has gone to spank him.
There is considerable hope that the problem areas pointed out will become part of a sufficiently well-functioning character structure rather than a character disorder or psychoneurosis.

	Story No. 1	Story No. 2
1. Main Theme: (diagnostic level: if descriptive and interpretative levels are desired, use a scratch sheet or page 5)	Need for autonomy evidence of superego compliance to authority figures	Identifies with mother. Feels aggressive contest may lead to damage.
2. Main hero: age _7_ sex _M_ vocation_____ abilities _verbally gifted_ interests____ traits____ body image____ adequacy (√,√√,√√√) and/or self-image____	Children	Child helping mother
3. Main needs and drives of hero: a) behavioral needs of hero (as in story): ____ implying: ____ b) figures, objects, or circumstances *introduced*: ____ implying need for or to: ____ c) figures, objects or circumstances *omitted*: ____ implying need for or to: ____	Child who has to learn. Brook misfortune. Enuresis?	Breaking rope. Fear of damage due to aggression
4. Conception of environment (world) as: ____		
5. a) Parental figures (m___, f_√_) are seen as _restricting_ and subject's reaction to a is ____ b) Contemp. figures (m___, f___) are seen as ____ and subject's reaction to b is ____ c) Junior figures (m___, f_√_) are seen as ____ and subject's reaction to c is _protective_	Both parents seen as instructive and nurturant	Competitive
6. Significant conflicts: _strong superego winning out over need for aggression autonomy?, and sexual curiosity?_	Between superego and aggression	Between superego and aggression
7. Nature of anxieties: (√) of physical harm and/or punishment _√_ of disapproval ____ of lack or loss of love ____ of illness or injury ____ of being deserted ____ of deprivation ____ of being overpowered and helpless ____ of being devoured ____ other ____	Mild physical harm.	Fear of damage resulting from aggressive competition.
8. Main defenses against conflicts and fears: (√) repression____ reaction-formation _√_ regression____ denial____ introjection____ isolation____ undoing____ rationalization____ other _intellectualization_		
9. Adequacy of superego as manifested by "punishment" for "crime" being: ( ) appropriate _√_ inappropriate____ too severe (also indicated by immediacy of punishment)____ inconsistent____ too lenient____ also: _mild and considerate_ delayed initial response or pauses ____ stammer____ other manifestations of superego interference____		Too severe and immediate
10. Integration of the ego, manifesting itself in: (√,√√,√√√) Hero: adequate _√√_ inadequate____ outcome: happy _√√_ unhappy____ realistic____ unrealistic____ drive control ____ thought processes as revealed by plot being: (√,√√,√√√) Stereotyped____ original____ appropriate____ complete____ incomplete____ inappropriate____ syncretic____ concrete____ contaminated____ Intelligence _above average_ Maturational level _high_	Happy Realistic	Happy Realistic

2

Ego function assessment from CAT data:

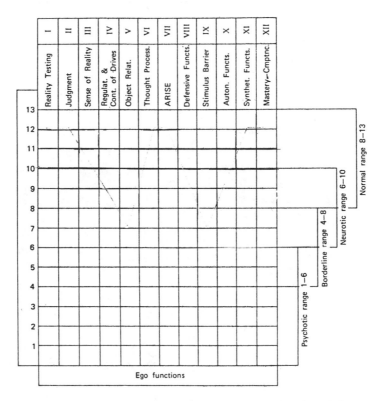

Ego functions observed during test administration:

273

Story No. 9	Story No. 10	SUMMARY
		1-3. Unconscious structure and drives of subject (based on variable 1-3)
Primal scene fears. Uses sleep and withdrawal as avoidance of anxiety.	Competition with adults. Compliance with maternal authority.	A need for autonomy, oedipal desires, aggression, and voyeurism are in conflict with a moderately severe, consistent ego syntonic superego.
Child	Small child	
	To be adult	
Night, mother, strange noises	Pot, fingerprints, magnifying glass	Result is adaptive striving and moderate anxiety - probably the part of developmental phase.
Implying curiosity concerning sexual events at night.	Implying need for regression, inquisitiveness	
		4. Conception of world: As firmly but fairly controlling and capable of being controlled by intelligent behavior.
	Mother seen as punishing, hostile, and domineering.	**5. Relationship to others:** The relationship to parental figures is somewhat ambivalent. Nothing emerges about peer relations.
Between superego and sexual desires	Between superego and autonomy	**6. Significant conflicts:** Between superego and oedipal desires, etc. (See #1)
Fear of physical harm or punishment.	Fear of disapproval	**7. Nature of anxieties:** Some fear of disapproval and castration.
Withdrawal		**8. Main defenses used:** Intellectualization, reaction-formation, healthy repression.
Too severe and immediate	Too severe and immediate	**9. Superego structure:** Consistent, somewhat too severe.
Unhappy Realistic	Unhappy Unrealistic?	**10. Integration and strength of ego:** Excellent integration, possible danger of somewhat obsessive formation later in life.

4

272

Story No. 3	Story No. 4	Story No. 5	Story No. 6	Story No. 7	Story No. 8
Need for intelligence and inquisitiveness as a form of protection against unpleasant surprises!	Need for autonomy. Compliance with maternal authority.	Fearful at night. Non-protective and scolding mother	Guilt feelings over oral acquisition	Has competitive aggressive feelings toward father. Afraid of father's strength. Castration anxiety	Feelings of competition with adults. Guilt feelings. Father seen as discreet
Adult lion	Disobedient child	Two children	Punished child	Monkey	Child
Needs to be informed.	Autonomy	For reassurance			
Crown, train, broken tracks, newspapers. Need to be grown up and adequate	Accident Compliance to avoid harm.	Bats, birds, and insects / Father To exclude father from bedroom.	Punisher Food	Pencil sharpener Need for preparedness	Food, dancing, magnifying glass Implying inquisitiveness
	Mother seen as instructive and nurturent	Mother seen as punishing and rejecting		Father seen as aggressive, competitive	Punishing Powerful Rejecting.
Activity – passivity	Autonomy – compliance	Fear of sexual desires	Between superego and acquisition	Between superego and aggression	Between superego and acquisition and sexual desires
Fear of inadequacy and surprise due to lack of information and attention.	Fear of physical harm.	Fear of physical harm and being overpowered and helpless	Fear of physical harm or punishment by phallic injury?	Fear of physical harm or punishment, illness, or injury. Being overpowered and helpless.	Fear of being excluded from adult society. Being found out by parents.
Too severe	Too severe and immediate		Too severe and immediate	Too severe? immediate	Just?
Happy Realistic	Happy Realistic	Unhappy Realistic	Unhappy Realistic	Unhappy Realistic	Unhappy Realistic

3

271

SUMMARY

Record of Main Theme (Diagnostic) and Other Main Data.

1. Need for autonomy; evidence of superego; compliance to authority figure; guilt feelings—superego. Conflicts: between superego and aggression and reacts with compliance, learning. Between autonomy and compliance. Some confusion of roles of mother and father.

2. Identifies with mother as the weaker one. Feels that aggressive contest may lead to damage. Fear of aggression? Fear of injury. Guilt feelings over aggression.

3. Need for intelligence and inquisitiveness as a form of protection against unpleasant surprises. Significant conflict: between activity and passivity.

4. Need for autonomy, aggression (riding fast). Guilt feelings. Compliance with maternal authority.

5. Fearful at night, probably related to primal scene noises. Mother seen as nonprotective and scolding. Probably suffers from a mild sleeping disturbance.

6. Guilt feelings over oral acquisition. Anxiety about physical harm—by phallic injury?

7. Has competitive aggressive feelings toward father. Afraid of father's strength. Castration anxiety. Need for preparedness.

8. Feelings of competition with adults. Need for oral acquisition. Guilt feelings. Superego. Sexual curiosity and guilt.

9. Strong interest in the primal scene. Primal scene fears. Uses sleep and withdrawal as an avoidance of anxiety.

10. Competition with the adults with regard to excretory functions. Strong superego. Mother seen as punishing. Anger at mother. Compliance with maternal authority. Self-image of younger child—regression.

STORY 1

Story 1: Something funny about this—chickens don't eat at a table—the chickens were eating their breakfast one morning and they went out and there they saw the rooster, and Mr. Rooster said, "How are you today?" And they said, "We're fine," and they wanted to go to the brook, but their mother said, "You shouldn't go to the brook, you might fall in." They said, "We won't." And they didn't obey their mother and they did go and they fell in and then they went to their mother and started crying and mother said, "I told you you shouldn't go," and they never did. The rooster is the mother; well, the rooster is the father, you could say the chicken then . . . (end of story.)

Descriptive theme	Interpretive theme	Diagnostic level
Chickens go to the brook against mother's warning	If one disobeys mother,	Need for autonomy;
and fall in,	one gets into trouble	evidence of superego;
and then go crying to mother and never did this again.	and obeys thereafter.	compliance to authority figure; guilt feelings—superego.

Clinical notes

This story shows a typical children's "moral"; note, however, that the calamity is minor and that punishment by the mother is absent save for simple repetition of the injunction. The only other point of interest is the indecision in the child's designation of the male and female roles to the rooster. If one had no data other than the stories, one would note this bit of possible significance and be on the lookout for a repetition in subsequent stories. As it happens, we do have a background on this child and we know that while both parents are benign, the father is particularly easygoing and that thus domestic management and decisions are relegated to the mother. Thus far, these observations are merely to be kept in mind without coming to any definite conclusions.

The introduction of water (especially getting accidentally wet) suggests the possibility of enuresis.

STORY 2

Story 2: One day a couple of bears met each other and they said—one bear had a rope, and they said, "Let's play tug-of-war." The baby bear was helping the mother bear because the father bear was the strongest, and the rope broke and then they had no more rope to play tug-of-war. They feel sorry.

Descriptive theme	Interpretive theme	Diagnostic level
When playing tug-of-war, the baby bear helps mother bear because father is stronger.	If mother and father are engaged in a contest, the hero helps mother because father is stronger.	Identifies with mother as the weaker one.

Descriptive theme	Interpretive theme	Diagnostic level
Then the rope broke and they had to stop playing	An aggressive contest can lead to damage	Feels that aggressive contest may lead to damage. Fear of aggression? Fear of injury.
and feel sorry.	and one feels sorry.	Guilt feelings over aggression.

Clinical notes

While the roles of father and mother were somewhat confused in story 1, here the father is clearly identified as the stronger one.

Again there is evidence of the existence of a superego without any excess of severity.

STORY 3

Story 3: Something wrong with this picture—the lion's not wearing the crown. Once there was a lion who was waiting for a train. He was a very nice-looking lion and he smoked a pipe and he had a cane and he waited but the train didn't come. All of a sudden he heard the train and it was on the other side, so he sat down again and he waited and waited and he sat there all day 'cause the train track was broken and the train didn't go through. He said, "I'm getting tired," and he got up and found out in the newspaper that the train track was broken, and so he went down into his house and took a long snooze on the chair like he is doing here, and then he had his supper and had to wait for his train till the next day. Darn old train. I'll make a moral for it: You can't tell if it's coming if you don't read.

Descriptive theme	Interpretive theme	Diagnostic level
A lion waits in vain all day for a train until he finds out that the track is broken and therefore has to wait another day.	Mishaps occur.	Fear of damage?
If one doesn't read, one can't tell what is coming.	If one is not intelligent and inquisitive, one may have trouble.	Need for intelligence and inquisitiveness as a form of protection against unpleasant surprises.

Clinical notes

Again a moral is expressed, making a virtue of the acquisition of learning.

In this boy's first story, the mention of "Something funny about this—chickens don't eat at table," was not significant by itself; however, in the above story there is a similar kind of expression in the first sentence, and we must begin to take note of the "stickler for actuality" quality and to look for any signs of repetitiveness in subsequent stories. The lion's not wearing a crown is certainly a threat of continuity through these first three stories: the indecision in story 1 over whether mother or father is the "rooster"; the definite relegation of superior strength to the father in story 2, with identification with the mother; and the reference in this last story to the lack of crown on the lion—crown being a literal expression of who's "king."

The reference to hearing the train and its appearance "on the other side" could be merely a biographical reference to the child's experience on some suburban railroad or city subway, and is not meaningful by itself. The reference to the broken track adds up with the broken rope in story 2 to at least a raising of the question of possible symbolic fear of genital harm. The history did reveal a recent increase in masturbation. Neither of these references suggests a problem of any clinical proportions. This may possibly be just a developmental factor related to the younger sister's being "different," may be related to his being a stickler for facts in these stories and correlate with the teachers' complaint of putting them on the spot, and suggests an aggressive or obsessive connotation.

STORY 4

Story 4: Once a mother kangaroo and her baby kangaroo went to the store. The baby kangaroo had a bicycle. There were three kangaroos. One was in the mother's pocket. The baby in the pocket was holding a balloon. The next day they went to the market again and when they were coming home the baby kangaroo said "I want to ride the bicycle very fast," and the mother said, "Don't ride fast or you'll fall off." But he didn't listen and fell off and mother said, "Serves you right." Whoever doesn't listen had a fall, the moral.

Descriptive theme	Interpretive theme	Diagnostic level
A little kangaroo wants to ride his bicycle fast		Need for autonomy; aggression (riding fast).
against mother's warning	If one doesn't listen to one's mother	
and promptly falls.	one gets into trouble.	Guilt feelings; compliance with maternal authority.

Clinical notes

At first only one child is mentioned, suggesting some sibling rivalry. While there may be some question as to whether the baby on the bicycle now refers to the baby sister or to himself, it is not unreasonable to assume that it probably refers more directly to the hero. The theme is really a repetition of story 1.

Here there is no mention at all of the food in the picture, and it is only casually referred to in story 1, whereas usually it is the theme. This may indicate little oral interest.

STORY 5

Story 5: What's in the bed? They look like bears to me but bears don't sleep in a cradle. Well, one night two bears went to sleep, two baby bears, and mother bear was sleeping right next to them, and they heard an owl and they got scared, and they woke the mother bear and she said, "That's just an owl." So the baby bears went to bed and they heard a bee, and they woke up again, and the mother said, "That's just a bee." And they heard a bat, and the mother said, "If you don't stop waking me up I'll have to sleep in another room." So the next morning the mother said, "What's the idea of making all that noise—you made more noise than the owl and the bat and the bee did." They felt scared. "I don't like sleeping." The babies stayed up all night looking out the window and mother was in another room.

Descriptive theme	Interpretive theme	Diagnostic level
Two children sleeping with their mother were scared repeatedly by noises at night.	If one hears noises at night, one wakes up scared.	Fearful at night, probably related to primal scene noises.
and woke the mother who finally threatened to sleep in another room, scolding them.	If one wakes mother, she is annoyed and threatens to leave one,	Mother seen as nonprotective and scolding.
The children are scared and don't like sleeping and stay up all night watching.	whereupon one doesn't like sleeping and stays up all night watchfully.	Probably suffers from a mild sleeping disturbance.

Clinical notes

The first sentence is a repetition of this child's characteristic literalness. It is very unusual for children to remark on the anthropomorphic aspects of the pictures. He did this in stories 1, 3, and 5, but not in stories 2 and 4. We should then take special cognizance of the kind of stories which evoke this characteristic and see what conclusions we may be justified in drawing. Thus far, we might tentatively say that stories 3 and 5 have one feature in common with reference to their calculated stimulus value: 3 is intended to arouse (among other things) phallic concern, whereas 5 is intended to elicit primal scene fears, and there is, of course, a close relation between the two. We might therefore say tentatively that when the boy is confronted with sexual considerations one of his defenses is to become concerned with "factual" and familiar realisms, or, on another level, we might say that a certain constriction sets in. Now we must ask ourselves why story 1 was prefaced in the same way when there is certainly nothing in the stimulus to cause sexual concern. To this one could only hazard a guess, and suppose that *any* anxiety-arousing situation, whether sexual, sibling rivalry, or whatever, provokes this special response in this boy. What can be considered anxiety producing in picture 1 can only be the fact that it is the *first* picture so that his frame of reference has not yet been sufficiently secured. For other children, of course, the picture more often has its emphasis on oral problems.

As to the primal scene per se, the main feature of his story is his omission of the usually seen second figure vaguely indicated in the large bed. Many children omit mention of figures altogether; some omit one parent or the other. We would expect this boy to omit the father, since it has become quite apparent that his relationship to his mother is stronger.

As to the specificity of the references to the various animal and insect noises, specificity is a characteristic of this child and he is merely being consistent. However, the animals he does mention, bats, birds, and insects, are phallic symbols not infrequently seen clinically as phobias. Children's fears of "noises in the night" very often refer to the sounds of the parents having intercourse.

The reference to "another room" is as yet obscure. Perhaps it is factually biographical; we do not know. In any case, when the mother does remove herself to another room on the following night, the babies' anxiety is apparently increased, since they stay up all night. All this tells us is that the subject does not benefit by closing his eyes to the bigger bed.

STORY 6

Story 6: One day two bears had a big supper and they felt so tired they couldn't even move from all the meal, so they fell asleep. Next morning when they woke up they went hunting for honey. The baby bear was first one to find it, and the baby bear looked in the honey tree hive and she grabbed some honey and the bees came zooming after her and she got stung on the nose, and she had a big bandage on her nose all night, and she went to sleep. Moral is: Don't hunt for honey if you don't want to get stung.

Descriptive theme	Interpretive theme	Diagnostic level
Bears are looking for honey and are stung on the nose. One shouldn't hunt for honey if one doesn't want to be hurt.	If one has (oral) acquisitive desires one may get hurt.	Guilt feelings over oral acquisition.

Clinical notes

Here again, as in story 4, one wonders if misbehavior is ascribed to the younger sibling, or the hero, or both. The child identifies again with the parent, moralizing as usual. There is the introduction of food in a stimulus where none appears. The child has omitted one figure that is present. This picture is generally perceived as comprising two large bears and one small one, which is actually the case. It is generally evocative of additional primal scene stories, either more intensely or less intensely described, because of its position in following up an earlier one, depending upon the particular child's modes of defense. The total omission of a more realistic mention of the figures involved, and the story of stealing forbidden food, can be tentatively considered as a most remote allusion to the sexual connotations of the story and is consistent with the child's strict sense of being "a good boy."

The nose as a choice of organ to be punished, having phallic significance, supports the notion of a sexual meaning to the story.

STORY 7

Story 7: The name of this story is "The Monkey and the Lion." One day the monkey was standing up on the tree and he saw a lion—I forgot, it was a tiger—for a moment, and the lion—the tiger is next to the king of beasts. "I want to show the lion that I could be next to the king of the beasts too. I'll fight the lion and win." (Monkey says this.) So the monkey sharpened up his nails with a pencil sharpener and tried to scratch the lion on the neck to kill him, but the lion jumped up and pushed him over and lion got the monkey by the tail, rather, the tiger, and the monkey had his tail shortened. And the moral is: If you want to keep your tail long, you don't want to fool around with the lion.

Descriptive theme	Interpretive theme	Diagnostic level
A monkey tries to compete with a lion	If one competes with authority figures	Has competitive aggressive feelings toward father.
but the lion overpowers him and cuts his tail off.	one gets hurt—cut down to size.	Afraid of father's strength. Castration anxiety.

Clinical notes

This story is classic in its demonstration of castration. It is so clearly stated that explanation or interpretation would be redundant. However, two additional items are also worthy of notice. First, the consistent specificity in the phrase, "The monkey sharpened his nails with a *pencil sharpener.*" Second, it is interesting that while the picture clearly shows the tiger attacking the monkey, the boy makes no mention of this fact and starts with an expression of his desire to show the tiger that he, the monkey, can also be "next to the king of beasts"—not quite the king. The earlier confusion between lion and tiger is quite clear and is also consistent with the subject's insistence on facts being facts. He knows that the lion is the king of beasts. The aggressive figure of the tiger urges him to acknowledge the unarguable superiority of the "king" (father). He makes his peace with the discrepancy with which he is faced (tigers are not lions) by admitting him the second most important position—next to the king—and then prepares to prove that he can compete with a secondary superiority. But he is merely paying lip service (as he has done all along with his moralizing) and is defeated.

Story 5, where the stimulus-implied father figure is omitted, corroborates the reflection of the sexual competition seen in this story.

STORY 8

Story 8: Once a monkey had a party and he invited a lot of people, but the little boy had to go to sleep because it was late, but the little boy didn't want to. He said, "I want to stay up for the party too," a dancing party and ice cream, and the father said no. But the monkey stayed up in his room and listened to the party and when they went dancing he snuck some ice cream, and his father, when he went to the ice cream with a magnifying glass, saw the monkey had had it so he called the mother in. But the monkey didn't come and pretended to be asleep but the father shook him. "What is the idea of stealing the ice cream?" Because of the company he didn't spank him, but the next day he did. No moral!

Descriptive theme	Interpretive theme	Diagnostic level
The parents had guests in. The child wanted to participate	If one wants to do things which the adults do	Feelings of competition with adults.
and have some ice cream	and permits oneself oral acquisition.	Need for oral acquisition.
against father's orders. Father discovers this and spanks him privately.	one is discovered by father and punished privately.	Guilt feelings. Superego. Father seen as discreet.

Clinical notes

Again, oral acquisition seems forbidden, possibly more than is quite reasonable, since ice cream is usually permitted to children, but again, as in the honey story (6), oral acquisition is associated with the prerogatives of the adults and their (sexual) dancing preoccupations.

The mother being called in emphasizes her role as the authority figure. The punishing being postponed until there are no strange witnesses suggests a level of discreet discourse in the family.

STORY 9

Story 9: Once there was a little bunny. He went out with his mother, and his name was Bunny Cottontail, and he always used to sing a song about himself: "Here comes Bunny Cottontail hoppin' down the bunny bunny trail, hippety hop." That night he stayed up, he wanted to stay up, he wanted to see what it was like in the nighttime and he heard strange noises and he got scared and from then on he never stayed up because he didn't want to get scared. And the moral is: Stay asleep if you don't want to get scared.

Descriptive theme	Interpretive theme	Diagnostic level
A little bunny wants to stay up to see what happens at night	If one wants to find out what is going on at night,	Strong interest in the primal scene.
and is scared by strange noises	one may hear frightening noises	Primal scene fears.
and chooses to stay asleep to avoid anxiety.	and renounce one's curiosity and choose flight into sleep.	Uses sleep and withdrawal as an avoidance of anxiety.

Clinical notes

This story is a direct supplement and counterpart to story 5. This time he chooses denial and avoidance as a way of dealing with the anxiety, which is strong though not overwhelming in story 5. The chances are that his defensive behavior in the present story presents the behavioral status consistent with the strong defenses in this child.

STORY 10

Story 10: One day a baby dog—his mother bought him a little pot that little dogs are supposed to make in but the little dog didn't want to make it in there. He said, "I want to make it in the big toilet." But his mother said not to or he'll get a spanking. But he didn't obey her and he did go on the big toilet and he got spanked the next day 'cause she found out somehow (took a magnifying glass and saw fingerprints). Then he got a spanking and he was crying and he promised never to do it again. It hurted him very much, the spanking, 'cause he was such a little baby, he felt mad to his mother.

Descriptive theme	Interpretive theme	Diagnostic level
A little dog wants to use the grown-up toilet, not his little one.	If one is little and one wants to use the big toilet (instead of the little one)	Competition with adults with regard to excretory functions.
His mother forbade it, but he did it against her orders	against mother's orders,	
and got spanked and cried and was angry and hurt	one is found out and spanked, is hurt and angry at mother	Strong superego. Mother seen as punishing. Anger at mother.
and promised never to do it again.	and promises to be good.	Compliance with maternal authority.

Clinical notes

The feature emerging most strongly here is the use of baby talk as an identification with the baby. That this regression takes place in response to a picture evoking images of excretory functions is particularly neat. Obviously the boy identifies strongly with his younger sibling, for the first time in any of these stories, and empathizes with the baby quite thoroughly. He also acknowledges that spanking hurts little babies (more than older children?). Perhaps he is recalling his own earlier experiences with toilet training and the identification is with himself. Certainly he has never been this sympathetic to his sibling before. It is interesting also, although it tells us nothing conclusive, that he feels that babies can feel angry with their mothers. He has not previously expressed any anger toward punishing figures in his other stories.

Case 2

The second case is that of an 8 year old boy whose C.A.T. was analyzed blindly in the course of a class on projective techniques. The C.A.T. record was obtained by the late Dr. Bela Mittelman, to whom I am very grateful, both for the record and for permission to use the case of the little boy who was a psychoanalytic patient of his. As it happens, I did not become familiar with the clinical data until four or five years after the initial interpretation of the C.A.T., which is presented here. While such a blind method is not recommended, it happened to have been a part of a teaching program.

The clinical facts are as follows: This 8 year old boy was brought for psychoanalytic treatment because he had suffered from eczema since his fifth month of life. He had been restless and cranky since the age of 2½ years, when he sustained a severe burn of the right thigh. He had been doing poor work in school and was a disciplinary problem because of minor but continuous infractions of rules, such as talking, giggling, and fighting. He was unpopular with the children, got into frequent scraps, and threw stones or hit them.

His behavior toward his brother, 13 months his junior, became very aggressive after his mother became more affectionate towards the younger one, about a year before. He frequently refused food, and he would not bathe himself or wash or clean his face, hands, or teeth unless there were constant reminders from his mother.

The mother had given him little intimate contact, adhered strictly to a feeding schedule, and was generally excitable. The child's hands had been tied for several weeks to prevent his scratching (when he was 2 and was hospitalized). The father and mother were divorced when the child was in the fifth month of analysis. The father is described as close to the children but less assertive than the mother. The parental divorce is reported to have renewed his mistrust of the world and endangered anew his confidence in the analyst's ability to help him (he had stoutly maintained that what he needed and expected was physical treatment). He saw the world as full of hostile forces and suffered an increase in his oedipal conflict and in his fear of retribution from his father.

It is easy to correlate the facts unearthed in the C.A.T. with the psychodynamics consistent with the boy's history: The feeling of hostility and hopelessness consequent to his traumatic infancy appears clinically and in the C.A.T., and so does his secondary regression to dirtiness and the jungle and his anger toward mother and brother. No sleeping disorder was reported clinically, and I do not know whether this means that it did not exist or whether it was minor enough to be lost in the multitude of complaints.

It must be remembered that projective techniques may point up problems which are not clinically manifest (see p. 133) but which may become so, under stress or when therapy interferes with the defenses; I have frequently seen this, e.g., in relation to impotence inferred correctly from Rorschach signs in adult male patients several months before they really become impotent in the course of psychoanalytic treatment. Also, curiously enough, I had no inkling of the eczema from the C.A.T. record. This coincides with observations that the T.A.T. may present a complete personality picture without permitting one to infer the chief complaint. All the component parts of the psychodynamics (of eczema, in this case) are present (lack of oral gratification, hostility due to very disturbed early mother-child relationship) but no specific reference to or indication of a skin disorder. Theoretically, this is a problem in need of further investigation. Practically, it is simple enough to see the skin disorder or elicit other chief complaints as part of the history taking; indication of this disorder need not be expected from the projective methods.

SHORT FORM

BELLAK T. A.T and C. A.T BLANK

For Recording and Analyzing Thematic Apperception Test and Children's Apperception Test

Name_____ Sex __M__ Age __8__ Date_____

(circle one)

Education_____ Occupation_____ ; m. s. w. d.

Referred by_____ Analysis by_____

After having obtained the stories analyze each story by using the variables on the left of Page 2. Not every story will furnish information regarding each variable: the variables are presented as a frame of reference to help avoid overlooking some dimension.

When all ten stories have been analyzed it is easy to check each variable from left to right for all ten stories and record an integrated summary on Page 4 under the appropriate headings. That way a final picture is obtained almost immediately.

Then, keeping Page 4 folded out, the Final Report: Diagnostic Impressions and Recommendations can be written on Page 1 by reference to Page 4. Page 5 gives available space for any other notations. The stories then can be stapled inside the blank against Page 5. For further instructions see *Manual for T.A.T. Interpretation*, Psychological Corporation, by Leopold Bellak or *Manual for the C.A.T.*, C.P.S. Inc., or *The T.A.T. and C.A.T. in Clinical Use*, 2nd edition, Grune & Stratton, 1971, N. Y. C. by Leopold Bellak;

FINAL REPORT: Diagnostic Impressions and Recommendations

This report is predicated only on the four stories analyzed in detail. In these stories our patient seems preoccupied particularly with the problem of aggression and counteraggression. Most of the aggression seems to be directed toward the younger brother, as for instance story 3, where the brother appears as vermin which the patient tries to exterminate, or in story 9, where rabbits (brother) are being hunted. In these two stories, as well as in story 8, which shows aggression toward the mother, the aggression seems to be of a very explosive, superficially strongly controlled nature. Because of an extremely severe though not integrated superego, the hostile wishes are usually turned into violent intra-aggression, and our patient himself comes to harm. The brother is seen as a nuisance and the mother as a braggart and somewhat coercive. The father figure does not emerge clearly in these stories except possibly as an accomplice and helper in story 9.

The patient perceives himself as rather helpless in coping with his problems and uses withdrawal and regression as defensive measures, as for instance in story 3, where he returns to the jungle, or in story 6, where he sees himself as troubled, suggesting that he suffers from insomnia because of nocturnal fears (probably concerning primal scene noises).

The treatment situation and transference relationship are reflected in story 3 and in story 6, where the boy seems to see the therapist as a fellow-conspirator against the brother (exterminator of the vermin), who is as useless as the carpenter called in to do away with the nocturnal disturbances. In fact, in the latter story, there is a suggestion that he conceives of therapy as a further unloosing of anxiety, and wishes to leave.

In summary, one may say that this is a fairly neurotic child with severe problems in his relationship to his younger sibling and to his mother, an inability to handle his repressed explosive hostility, and a potentiality for sleeping disturbances.

Copyright 1955
Leopold Bellak, M.A., M.D.

Published by
C.P.S. Inc.
P.O. Box 83
Larchmont, N.Y. 10538

Printed in U.S.A.

	Story No. 1	Story No. 2
1. Main Theme: (diagnostic level: if descriptive and interpretative levels are desired, use a scratch sheet or page 5)		

2. Main hero: age _8_ sex _M_ vocation _____ abilities _____
interests _____ traits _____ body image _rather helpless_
adequacy (√,√√,√√√) and/or self-image _____

3. Main needs and drives of hero:
a) behavioral needs of hero (as in story): _____
implying: _____
b) figures, objects, or circumstances *introduced*: _____

implying need for or to: _____

c) figures, objects or circumstances *omitted*: _____

implying need for or to: _____

4. Conception of environment (world) as: _full of hostile forces_

5. a) Parental figures (m ____, f ✓) are seen as _braggart_
and subject's reaction to a is _____
b) Contemp. figures (m ✓, f ____) are seen as _Therapist seen_
and subject's reaction to b is _as fellow conspirator_
c) Junior figures (m ✓, f ____) are seen as _nuisance_
and subject's reaction to c is _____

6. Significant conflicts: _between superego and_
aggression and counter aggression

7. Nature of anxieties: (√)
of physical harm and/or punishment ___✓___
of disapproval _____
of lack or loss of love _____ of illness or injury _____
of being deserted ___✓___ of deprivation _____
of being overpowered and helpless ___✓___
of being devoured _____ other _____

8. Main defenses against conflicts and fears: (√)
repression ___✓___ reaction-formation _____
regression ___✓___ denial _____ introjection _____
isolation _____ undoing _____
rationalization _____ other _withdrawal_

9. Adequacy of superego as manifested by "punishment" for "crime" being: ( )
appropriate _____ inappropriate _____
too severe (also indicated by immediacy of punishment) ___✓___
inconsistent _____ too lenient _____
also: _____
delayed initial response or pauses _____
stammer _____ other manifestations of superego interference _____

10. Integration of the ego, manifesting itself in: (√.√√.√√√)
Hero: adequate _____ inadequate ___✓✓___
outcome: happy _____ unhappy _____
realistic _____ unrealistic _____
drive control _____
thought processes as revealed by plot being: (√, √√, √√√)
Stereotyped _____ original _____ appropriate _____
complete _____ incomplete _____ inappropriate _____
syncretic _____ concrete _____ contaminated _____
Intelligence _____
Maturational level _____

2

Ego function assessment from TAT data:

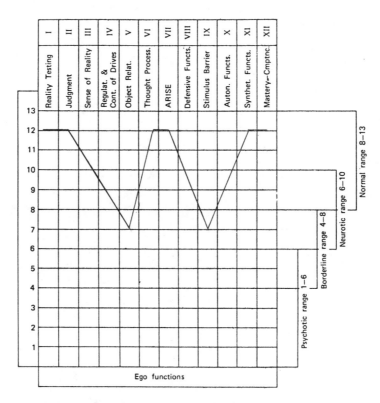

(From Bellak, Hurvich, & Gediman, *Ego functions in schizophrenics, neurotics, and normals.* Copyright © 1973, by C. P. S., Inc. Reprinted by permission of John Wiley & Sons, Inc.)

Ego functions observed during test administration:

Story No. 9	Story No. 10	SUMMARY
		1-3. Unconscious structure and drives of subject (based on variable 1-3)
Aggression towards brother seen as dirty. Severe superego and intra-aggression		Aggression is felt generally and specifically against mother and brother. Feels helpless against their annoyance, ridden by nocturnal anxiety especially, and rather guilty over his nearly murderous anger.
Male child		
Aggression. Intra-aggression		
Hunters, father, squirrels, dynamite		
Implying need for aggression		
		4. Conception of world: As dangerous, annoying. He is nearly helpless against it.
		5. Relationship to others: Father and therapist are seen as friends but rather helpless. Mother is seen as coercive braggart, and younger sibling as a nuisance.
Between superego and aggression		6. Significant conflicts: Between superego and aggression.
		7. Nature of anxieties: Of being coerced, annoyed, frightened at night.
Displacement Projection?		8. Main defenses used: Resignation. Displacement. Projection. Regression.
Severe		9. Superego structure: Inconsistent. Too little and too severe.
wishful unhappy. unrealistic		10. Integration and strength of ego: Not very well able to deal with aggression or the world around him.

4

Story No. 3	Story No. 4	Story No. 5	Story No. 6	Story No. 7	Story No. 8
Subject feels troubled by and unsuccessful in aggression toward small sibling.			Night noises are troubling subject. Hopes expert will do away with trouble		Mother seen as coercive. Subject resents mother's pleasure. Angry feelings toward mother.
Adult, male lion			Very troubled child		Male child
To get rid of vermin.					Manifest compliance
worms exterminator, traps, poison, jungle, Florida			Carpenter, Noise Falling Rocks		Explosion. Crooks
Implying need for aggression, withdrawal, regression			One adult parent. Anxiety over night noise. Wants something done about them.		Father. Implying aggressive wishes toward mother and exclusion of father
Father seen as friendly and powerless.					Mother seen as domineering, exhibitionistic
Between superego and aggression					Between superego and aggression
Of being ineffective, defenseless, and helpless			Anxiety at night concerning noises.		
Resignation					Manifest compliance
			None		None
Realistic and unhappy.			Realistic and unhappy.		Wishful and unrealistic.

3

287

SUMMARY

Record of Main Theme (Diagnostic) and Other Main Data.

1.

2.

3. Subject feels troubled by small sibling. Feels unsuccessful in aggression toward sibling; subject tries to enlist help of someone, probably therapist, whose role he sees as helping do away with sibling. Therapist considered useless. Sibling seen as outsmarting subject. He sees his extra-aggression as boomerang. He attempts withdrawal (or other modes of behavior), finds these measures useless, regresses to more primitive behavior. Conflict between superego and aggression, reacts with intra-aggression.

4.

5.

6. Night noises are troubling subject: primal scene disturbances? Subject hopes expert will do away with these troubles. Subject disturbed by therapist to a greater degree than by the primal noises, and refuses help of therapist.

7.

8. Mother seen as coercive, child complies manifestly. Subject resents mother's pleasure in house, considers her a braggart. Subject feels explosive anger in himself and wants to destroy mother's pleasure. Angry feelings against mother. Exclusion of father. Conflict between superego and aggression, reacts with manifest compliance.

9. Strong need for aggression toward brother. Severe superego. Severe intra-aggression. Anal character?

10.

STORY 3

Story 3: Well, this lion is troubled by mice, and he's sitting there and doesn't know what to do about the mice. He's tried everything, so he calls the exterminator, and the exterminator says, "The only thing to do is to blow the mice out." But the lion says, "I've tried that and lost three houses." "Why not make traps?" "But the mice have certain things that disconnect the traps and they always get the cheese." "Why not try poison, then?" "But that's impossible because the mice know it's poison and they'll never come out." Finally the lion decides he will move to Florida, but when he gets there he sees now . . . he's being troubled by worms coming through the floor. So finally he says, "I'll go back and live in the jungle where I belong."

Descriptive theme	Interpretive theme	Diagnostic level
A lion is troubled by mice;	If one is troubled by small things,	Subject feels troubled by small sibling.
has tried everything;	and one tries in vain to be rid of them,	Feels unsuccessful in aggression toward sibling.
calls in an exterminator	one calls in powerful (lethal) helper	Subject tries to enlist help of someone, probably therapist, whose role he sees as helping do away with sibling.
who makes suggestions already tried and found unless and/or harmful to oneself.	who makes suggestions already found useless (because one is outsmarted) or harmful to oneself.	Therapist is considered useless. Sibling is seen as outsmarting subject. He sees his extra-aggression as boomerang.
Then the lion decides to move away,	Thereupon one moves to a new field,	He attempts withdrawal (or other modes of behavior).
only to be troubled by worms,	only to be troubled by little things there too,	Finds these measures useless.
and finally returns to the jungle where he feels he belongs.	and finally regresses to more primitive conditions.	Regresses to more primitive forms of behavior.

Clinical notes

In this story the mice and the worms probably represent the younger sibling. The story is particularly interesting since we can see elements of the transference relationship. This child sees his psychotherapist in the role of an exterminator (who should exterminate the brother as a way of helping the patient). Apparently, however, he is thus far dissatisfied with the psychotherapist, feeling that therapy does not offer him any better solutions than he had already tried; for instance, permitting himself some extra-aggression seems to have boomeranged. His return to the jungle implies not only regression but also withdrawal. Inasmuch as this withdrawal is the result of a difficult reality situation, we are probably justified in thinking of it as secondary withdrawal, more comparable to a phobic situation (rather than of a primary withdrawal of object cathexis, as is seen in narcissistic disorders). However, the indications are not quite clear, and skin conditions are frequently consistent with severely narcissistic disorders.

STORY 6

Story 6: They're in the cave and they've been very disturbed by falling rock. And the bear goes to the bear carpenter and says, "Now you be sure no more rocks fall from my cave; my baby is very troubled." The bear carpenter comes and goes bang, bang. Later, he goes bang, bang every night. Finally the baby says, "This keeps me awake more than the falling rocks. Never mind."

Descriptive theme	*Interpretive theme*	*Diagnostic level*
Bears are in a cave and are disturbed by falling rock.	If one is troubled by falling rock noises in the night,	Night noises are troubling subject: primal scene disturbances?
Mamma bear asks bear carpenter to end this situation.	one enlists aid of carpenter	Subject hopes expert will do away with these troubles.
Bear makes noise himself.	who makes noises also,	Subject is disturbed by therapist
Baby is more disturbed by carpenter's noise (at night) than by falling rock	more troublesome than falling rock;	to a greater degree than by the primal noises,
and says, never mind.	one tells the carpenter to forget it—never mind helping.	and refuses help of therapist.

Clinical notes

Here we have a clear reference to noises in the night which are generally of a primal scene nature. The fact that the bear carpenter goes "bang, bang" confirms the nature of the disturbance and adds to it the possibility that the noises are inner ones of the subject's, as well as the usual environmental ones. The child is saying "The doctor disturbs me more than my family; I'll ask him to leave me alone after all." (The cure is worse than the disease.) We could then say about the therapy situation that the child is resisting because the treatment is too disturbing to him.

STORY 8

Story 8: Well, mother monkey and baby monkey are having company. Grandma and uncle come, and there's a picture of grandma monkey hanging on the ceiling. Mamma monkey says, "Now mind your manners, child, we're going to have a lot of company today." And the child says, "All right." Grandma monkey says, "What a beautiful house you have." And the mother is a big bragger. She says, "Oh yes, I have a beautiful house, and you should see my kitchen. It's so nice; everything is so nice." Just then a few crooks who were outside blew up the house, and the mother never bragged again.

Descriptive theme	Interpretive theme	Diagnostic level
Mother and baby are having company: grandma and uncle.	If one is having company,	
Mamma monkey tells baby to behave and baby agrees.	mamma wants one to behave and one does.	Mother seen as coercive, child complies manifestly.
Grandma compliments mother on beauty of house and mamma brags.	Grandma compliments mamma on beauty of house, and mamma brags.	Subject resents mother's pleasure in house, considers her a braggart.
Crooks outside then blow up house,	Crooks blow up house,	Subject feels explosive anger in himself and wants to destroy mother's pleasure.
and mother never brags again.	and mother never brags again.	Angry feelings against mother.

Clinical notes

This story again reflects the social level in the child's home. We have had glimpses on other occasions—the mention of Florida, and the ease with which this child procures paid professional help (the exterminator and the carpenter)—and now we get a realistic picture of the polite company manners observed in the home and the child's negative conception of his mother. The explosion already mentioned in story 3 again indicates the strong aggressive feelings bottled up in this child, here clearly directed to the mother.

On the one hand, we see a very strict superego which makes him comply manifestly; on the other hand, he permits himself rather vicious retribution when the house and, presumably, mother and the company (but perhaps himself too) are blown up. This is a good example of lack of integration of the superego constituting at the same time too much and too little control.

STORY 9

Story 9: My brother likes rabbits but I hate them, and I like squirrels but he hates them. I'll make up a bad story about him—I hate him! Rabbits are very troublesome; they smell a lot. Well, a rabbit is lying in bed and papa rabbit says, "I've heard that hunters are on the trail." The baby says, "Well, I have a smart idea. Since those hunters like to hunt, we'll give them something to hunt." And the father says, "What?" And the baby says, "Fetch me a lot of pillows." And they draw a lot of rabbits and they look real, and in each rabbit is a piece of dynamite; so when the hunters come they shoot at the rabbit and those hunters flew into China and said, "I'm never going rabbit hunting again."

Descriptive theme	*Interpretive theme*	*Diagnostic level*
My brother likes rabbits but I hate them. I like squirrels but he hates them. I'll make up a bad story about him; I hate him.	Temperamental differences with brother.	Aggression toward brother.
Rabbits are a nuisance; they smell a lot.	Brother is a nuisance, smelly.	Aggression toward brother, seen as dirty.
There are hunters, and the child fools them and punishes them by putting dynamite into rabbit decoys, and the hunters are blown all the way to China when they try to shoot the rabbits. They say they'll never hunt rabbits again.	If one wants to kill, one is killed oneself.	Strong need for aggression. Severe superego. Severe intra-aggression.

Clinical notes

This is a very complex story. At first the difference in sentiments between the brothers and their dislike of each other is clearly set forth. The sentence, "I'll make up a bad story about him—I hate him" may either refer manifestly to the rabbit in the picture or to the brother, although dynamically there is probably no difference. Under the impact of his emotions, this story is less well structured in that there is a transition from the stimulus of a picture of a rabbit in bed to hunters. Apparently the direct expression of aggression against the brother is interfered with and instead of the real rabbit he uses decoys. The next twist of the story brings about a switch of identification figures, where the hunters are being punished for their aggression. This is probably where the intra-aggression again appears; as in story 3, the aggressor himself gets into trouble and forswears aggression forever.

The complaint about the rabbits being not only troublesome but also smelling a lot may on the one hand refer to the younger brother's original lack of toilet training; on the other hand, preoccupation with smells may point toward an anal character structure in our patient.

Case 3*

Kenneth was 8 years and 5 months old at the time of testing, with an I.Q. of 89 on the Stanford-Binet. Entered in a parochial school before he was 5 years old, he proved to be so severe a behavior problem that the sisters refused to keep him. Things were no better in public school, where he proved to be an academic problem as well, in his inability to learn to read.

Kenneth is tall for his age, thin, and undernourished. He wears glasses. The mother appears to be a heavy, ignorant, placid woman who does not want her placidity disturbed. She apparently rejects Kenneth, preferring the younger child, a girl about 4 years old. The father, high-strung and unstable, expects his son to be perfect, and believes that perfection in children is attained by beating them. He also openly shows his preference for the younger child.

The boy's behavior at school is markedly aggressive; he has assaulted several children quite severely, stole from the girls' pocketbooks, removed articles from the teacher's desk, is constantly noisy and restless.

Kenneth does not come home for lunch as the other children do—his mother finds it too much trouble to fix lunch for him.

Kenneth loses bladder control by night or day and soils himself occasionally at school.

---

* I am indebted to Miss Greta Freyd for permission to use this case, and for the above data on Kenneth.

SHORT FORM

BELLAK T.A.T and C.A.T BLANK

For Recording and Analyzing Thematic Apperception Test and Children's Apperception Test

Name_____Kenneth_____Sex__M__Age_8.5_Date_____

                                                                    (circle one)

Education_____Occupation_____ _____; m. s. w. d.

Referred by_____Analysis by_____

       After having obtained the stories analyze each story by using the variables on the left of Page 2. Not every story will furnish information regarding each variable: the variables are presented as a frame of reference to help avoid overlooking some dimension.

       When all ten stories have been analyzed it is easy to check each variable from left to right for all ten stories and record an integrated summary on Page 4 under the appropriate headings. That way a final picture is obtained almost immediately.

       Then, keeping Page 4 folded out, the Final Report: Diagnostic Impressions and Recommendations can be written on Page 1 by reference to Page 4. Page 5 gives available space for any other notations. The stories then can be stapled inside the blank against Page 5. For further instructions see *Manual for T.A.T. Interpretation*, Psychological Corporation, by Leopold Bellak or *Manual for the C.A.T.*, C.P.S. Inc., or *The T.A.T. and C.A.T. in Clinical Use*, 2nd edition, Grune & Stratton, 1971, N. Y. C. by Leopold Bellak;

FINAL REPORT: Diagnostic Impressions and Recommendations

       These are stories of an exceedingly disturbed boy, as can be seen from the first story to the last. The themes deal throughout with deprivation and bizarre, diffuse, all-around hostility and destructiveness, particularly in stories 4 and 5. The hero as an identification figure is either a rat or a ghost, and the vile object of deadly aggression by incorporation (story 6). The father is seen as unremittingly aggressive, the mother mostly as depriving and punishing, as for instance in stories 1 and 10. The subject shows a great deal of hostility toward her when he specifies that she is put in the garbage pail head down in story 5 and has her head hurt repeatedly in story 4, as well as toward his baby sister.

       The superego, though vicious in its intra-aggression, as in stories 6 and 9, is also inconsistent. There is no evidence of any successful defenses.

       Although some degree of magical thinking is not unusual in children of this age level, story 6, which deals with the poisoned bones which are able to kill merely by contact, transcends the bounds of expectancy for this age. The malevolence and omnipotence which this child ascribes to himself are distinctly pathological.

       There are two suggestions in the stories that this child is probably enuretic: the matches which are introduced into story 8 and the running water in story 10.

       In view of the general lack of structure of the stories, the lack of control and tendency to bizarreness, the oral features of devouring, being devoured, and going to sleep (Lewin's oral triad), it is very likely that this boy will develop into an adult psychotic with schizophrenic and manic-depressive features.

	Story No. 1	Story No. 2
1. **Main Theme:** (diagnostic level: if descriptive and interpretative levels are desired, use a scratch sheet or page 5)	Mother seen as depriving children of basic needs and responding to crying.	Child and mother seen as aligned against father not powerful enough (wishful?) Subject finally feels
2. **Main hero:** age _Child_ sex _m_ vocation_____ abilities_____ interests_____ traits_____ body image_____ adequacy (√,√√,√√√) and/or self-image _rejected_	Child	Child
3. **Main needs and drives of hero:** a) behavioral needs of hero (as in story): _____ implying: _____ b) figures, objects, or circumstances *introduced*: _____ implying need for or to: _____ c) figures, objects or circumstances *omitted*: _____ implying need for or to: _____	Food Crying Appeal by crying	Falling down fear of weakness
4. **Conception of environment (world) as:** _____	Depriving	Aggressive
5. a) Parental figures (m_____, f_____) are seen as _father, aggressive and mother depriving and punishing_ and subject's reaction to a is _____ b) Contemp. figures (m_____, f_____) are seen as _____ and subject's reaction to b is _____ c) Junior figures (m_____, f_____) are seen as _____ and subject's reaction to c is _____	Mother seen as hostile, acquisitive and rejecting	Father- aggressive Mother- passive
6. **Significant conflicts:** _____	None	Between superego and aggression
7. **Nature of anxieties:** (√) of physical harm and/or punishment _____ of disapproval _____ of lack or loss of love _____ of illness or injury _____ of being deserted _____ of deprivation √ of being overpowered and helpless _____ of being devoured √ other _____	Deprivation. lack or loss of love.	
8. **Main defenses against conflicts and fears:** (√) repression_____ reaction-formation_____ regression_____ denial_____ introjection_____ isolation_____ undoing_____ rationalization_____ other_____		
9. **Adequacy of superego as manifested by "punishment" for "crime" being:** ( ) appropriate_____ inappropriate_____ too severe (also indicated by immediacy of punishment) √ inconsistent_____ too lenient_____ also:_____ delayed initial response or pauses _____ stammer_____ other manifestations of superego interference_____		
10. **Integration of the ego, manifesting itself in:** (√,√√,√√√) Hero: adequate_____ inadequate √√√ outcome: happy_____ unhappy √√√ realistic_____ unrealistic √√√ drive control_____ thought processes as revealed by plot being: (√, √√, √√√) Stereotyped_____ original_____ appropriate_____ complete_____ incomplete_____ inappropriate_____ syncretic_____ concrete_____ contaminated_____ Intelligence_____ Maturational level _low_	Happy; realistic; wishful	Realistic Unhappy

2

Ego function assessment from TAT data:

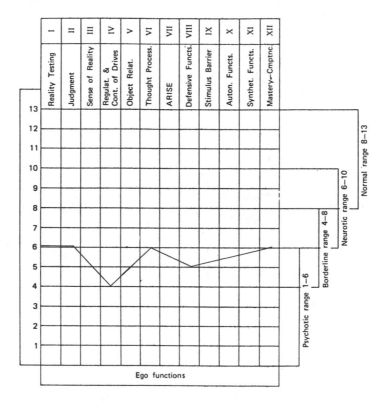

Ego functions observed during test administration:

Story No. 9	Story No. 10	SUMMARY
		1-3. Unconscious structure and drives of subject (based on variable 1-3)
Extreme aggression against mother, father, and younger sibling and great intra-aggression	Sees mother as coercive. Fear of bath. Identifies food and love. Associates food and bed.	Strong, primitive, oral, devouring needs, with generalized great and nearly bizarre aggression.
Ghost	Child	
Aggression		Urethral fixation (fire, water), with anal as well as acquisitive desires.
Cops, electric chair	Food, tub, running water	
Entire stimulus implying punishment, perseveration of intra-psychic stimuli	Implying oral needs. Urethral preoccupation	
concerned with aggression Dangerous	Hostile	**4. Conception of world:** As depriving, dirty, hostile, dangerous, devouring.
	Mother seen as aggressive and nurturant	**5. Relationship to others:** Full of wild aggression and afraid of theirs.
		6. Significant conflicts: Full of uncontrolled aggression.
Physical harm and punishment	Physical harm and punishment	**7. Nature of anxieties:** Some conflict over aggression.
Between superego and aggression	Between autonomy and compliance	**8. Main defenses used:** Inadequate defenses throughout.
	Too severe	**9. Superego structure:** Inadequate.
Unhappy Unrealistic	Happy Wishful	**10. Integration and strength of ego:** Poor in nearly every respect.

Story No. 3	Story No. 4	Story No. 5	Story No. 6	Story No. 7	Story No. 8
Subject feels small and in danger. Fear of being devoured by father. Withdraws rapidly into small dark place. Uses 'tricks' for indirect aggression against father.	Tremendous need for aggression toward mother. Enuresis.	Fear of his own aggressive wishes and of aggression against him at night.	Oral incorporation and aggression in the night.	Oral incorporation and aggression. Wants to supplant King. Notions of grandeur.	Sees great-grandmother as domineering mother telling on him to father. Enuresis.
Rat	Child	Ghost		Monkey and lion	Child
For aggression	For aggression	Aggression			
Mouse seen as rat. Feels dirty, aggressive		Ghost, rats, garbage pail. Preoccupation with dirt. Bizarreness	Lion. Poisoned bones	People, clothes. King	Birthday cake matches, lit candles
			Fear of father. Fear of death. Tremendous aggression	Acquisition. Desire to be King.	Urethral complex
Depriving	Full of aggression	Devouring	Bizarre	Devouring	Oral
Father seen as aggressive and hostile			Father seen as hostile and powerful	Father seen as hostile, powerful and aggressive.	Mother seen as domineering, hostile and untrustworthy
None					
Being devoured.		Nocturnal fears.	Being devoured, overpowered, and helpless	Being devoured, overpowered, and helpless.	
	None	None		None	
Happy Wishful	Wishful	Wishful ✓✓ Bizarre ✓✓✓	Unhappy ✓✓✓ Bizarre ✓✓✓	Wishful ✓✓✓ Unrealistic ✓✓✓	Wishful Happy

3

299

SUMMARY

Record of Main Theme (Diagnostic) and Other Main Data.

1. Mother seen as depriving children of basic needs, food (love). Patient feels unhappy. Mother seen as responding to crying. Subject feels especially deprived in relation to others (sister? mother?). Subject clearly identifies with deprived child in stimulus (chick minus bib).
2. Child and mother are aligned against father. Father doesn't quite manage (wishful?). Contest is between father and child alone? (Mother is no help or hindrance.) Subject finally feels defeated (without ever acknowledging that father wins; mother has a completely passive role in this story, but somewhat allied with child). Fear of being weak.
3. Subject feels small and in danger. Fear of being devoured by father. Subject withdraws rapidly into small dark place; uses tricks for indirect aggression against father. Poor self-image.
4. Tremendous need for aggression towards mother, some of it possibly sexually fused (crashing into her). Tremendous hostility manifesting itself in destruction of objects, including food, which he probably identifies with mother. Urethral problems.
5. Fear of his own aggressive wishes and of aggression against him at night. Identifies mother with dirt, garbage. Strong oral-incorporative wishes and fears (if ghost is the father). Bizarre story. Nocturnal fears.
6. Again subject expresses oral incorporation and aggression, this time in the night. Aggression against sibling or self. Since mother has previously been described as a repulsive figure, one might assume she is the one now described. Father and mother seen as wanting to revenge themselves upon the evildoer and are poisoned by the bones, which are more powerful than they; that is, our subject is so inherently evil and omnipotent that he is able to kill the parents merely by contact. Sibling (or self) suffers same fate. Bizarre story.
7. Repetition of oral aggression and incorporation. Identity of hero not clear. Perserveration of theme to extent of leaving stimulus. Assumes garb of king (father), wanting to supplant him after vanquishing him, and going further to notions of grandeur.
8. Sees great-grandmother as a domineering figure. Sees mother as "telling on him" to father (and thereupon?) he goes to get supplies and makes himself useful. Feels forced into servitude. Matches suggest urethral complex.
9. Extreme aggression against the mother, the younger sibling, the father, and great intra-aggression. Ignores stimulus entirely in perseveration of intra-psychic stimuli concerned with aggression.
10. Sees mother as coercive, punishing. Regressive resistance and fear of bath. Intra-aggression (flight *into* tub). Identifies food and love. Associates food and bed. Running water shows urethral preoccupation.

STORY 1

Story 1: She's going to eat the food up (pointing to big one), then the little ones won't have any. Then they're going to start crying. Then she's going to make some more . . . *(prompted)*. The mother will give him some food when it's cooked (pointing to chick without bib). *(Prompted)* . . . They all had their food already—all the others.

Descriptive theme	Interpretive theme	Diagnostic level
The mother will eat all the food, depriving the little ones.	If there is food, the mother eats it all up,	Mother seen as depriving children of basic needs, food (love).
They will cry.	and children cry.	Patient feels unhappy.
She will relent and make more and give bibless chick food.	Mother relents and cooks more for one,	Mother seen as responding to crying.
All the others already had some.	the others having already received theirs.	Subject feels especially deprived in relation to others (sister? mother?). Subject clearly identifies with deprived child in stimulus (chick minus bib).

Clinical notes

The first story already suggests an atmosphere of deprivation and unhappiness, the subject feeling especially neglected.

STORY 2

Story 2: The daddy bear is trying to pull the rope away from the mamma and the baby bear. The father bear wants to win, and the little one wants to win. The father pulls and pulls and can't get it away. So the baby is losing. *(Prompted)* . . . The baby will fall down. *(Prompted)* . . . The mamma will fall down too.

Descriptive theme	Interpretive theme	Diagnostic level
A papa bear is trying to take a rope away from the mamma and the baby.	If there is a contest between papa and mamma and baby,	Child and mother are aligned against father.
Father and baby are trying to win. Father can't succeed.	father tries but can't win.	Father seen as not powerful enough (wishful?).
Baby can't succeed. Baby loses.	Baby is losing.	Contest is between father and child alone? (mother is no help or hindrance).

Descriptive theme	Interpretive theme	Diagnostic level
Falls down, as does mamma.		Subject finally feels defeated (without ever acknowledging that father wins. Mother has a completely passive role in this story, but somewhat allied with child.)

Clinical notes

There are some inconsistencies in this story. Even though the father cannot get his way; in the next sentence the subject states that the baby is losing.

STORY 3

Story 3: (Sits up straight, big smug grin) The lion is waiting for the rat to come out of the hole so he can eat him up—eat him for his dinner. He's resting. The rat is coming out. The lion don't know the rat is coming out. *(Prompted)* . . . The lion will chase the rat, and the rat will run into the hole, and the lion will run into the wall and get a bump on his head (big smile).

Descriptive theme	Interpretive theme	Diagnostic level
A lion is biding his time awaiting the rat's emergence from his hole, whereupon	If one is small,	Subject feel small and in danger.
the lion intends to eat the rat for his dinner.	one is in danger of being eaten by big ones.	Fear of being devoured by father.
The rat outsmarts the lion,	One runs back into hole and escapes big ones,	Subject withdraws rapidly into small dark place,
and the lion is punished by a bump on the head from the wall of the rat's hole.	and the big one is hurt himself.	uses tricks for indirect aggression against father.

Clinical notes

This story continues the struggle between the father and the boy. This time the boy wishfully outwits the father. It must be considered significant that he identifies himself with a rat rather than the little mouse that is usually seen. The rat constitutes a more aggressive, more dangerous, and, at the same time, a socially much less acceptable, dirty self-image.

The theme of devouring is worth noting but may not be given too much pathological significance here since the stimulus tends to suggest this theme.

However, we will see that the theme recurs in later stories in a much more clearly pathological form.

STORY 4

Story 4: (Big smile at examiner) He's going to crash right into the mamma with his bike. The mamma will get hurt. Then he's going to run over her. The balloon will bust and he'll run over the milk and stuff and they'll spill all over the place. . . . Then she'll get up and run into the tree 'cause her hat's over her head and she can't see and she'll get a bump on her head again.

Descriptive theme	Interpretive theme	Diagnostic level
The boy will crash into the mother with his bike and hurt her, then run over her in addition; will break balloon, spill milk and food all over. Mother will run into tree because hat is binding her and will bump her head again.	If one gets a chance, one hurts mother repeatedly; one also breaks and spills things.	Tremendous need for aggression toward mother, some of it possibly sexually fused (crashing into her). Tremendous hostility manifesting itself in destruction of objects, including food. Enuresis (spilled fluid).

Clinical notes

Judging by the smile at the examiner, subject feels happy at releasing aggression, of which he apparently cannot get enough. If this story is compared with the one told to the same picture in case 1, the severe pathology in the present case is dramatically revealed. The way he destroys the food suggests that the food itself is a frequent source of frustration, probably also identified with the mother.

STORY 5

Story 5: The mamma bear is under the covers so she's afraid there might be a ghost around the house. The baby sticks its head out and screams. Then the rats came out under the bed and pushed the bed up near the window. The ghost puts its hand in and grabs the mamma bear and puts the mamma in the garbage pail, with her head first, and then the ghost takes the baby bears and takes them home and eats them. Then the ghost goes to bed—he's too full.

Descriptive theme	Interpretive theme	Diagnostic level
A mamma is under bed covers afraid of ghost around house. Baby is screaming in fear. Rats come out from under bed, are strong enough to push bed near window where	If one is in bed, there are rats and a ghost to threaten one.	Fear of his own aggressive wishes and of aggression against him at night.

Descriptive theme	Interpretive theme	Diagnostic level
ghost can get at the mother and dispose of her in garbage pail, head first.	Rats and ghost put mother in garbage pail, head first.	Identifies mother with dirt, garbage.
Ghost eats babies, goes to bed too full.	Ghost eats babies, goes to bed too full.	Strong oral-incorporative wishes and fears (if ghost is the father).

Clinical notes

This must be considered a rather bizarre story even for an 8½ year old boy. We seem to deal with multiple identification in this story, in that the rat in story 3 suggests that the rats in the present story who are so hostile to the mother also represent the subject. Probably the ghost is also an identification figure, further disguised for defensive displacement from consciousness.

The tremendous amount of hostility again becomes apparent in his refinement of detail, specifying, "with her head first." Probably the baby bears are here identified with the baby sister, if the ghost is our hero; but the possibility of another shift of identification, where the aggressor also becomes the victim, cannot be excluded. This story suggests an extreme of nocturnal anxiety, among other things, by a projection of his own aggressive impulses. Again, incorporation plays a clearly pathological role. This theme is illustrative of Bertram Lewin's [214] oral triad: the wish to devour, to be devoured, and to sleep. This suggests that the subject is likely to develop a severe affective disorder of a manic-depressive nature. Hand in hand with the bizarreness of the story, one would be inclined to predict that this boy might well go on to an adult psychosis which may at first appear of a manic-depressive variety and later become a schizophrenic disorder with affective features (schizoaffective disorder.)

STORY 6

Story 6: The baby bear's asleep in a cave and the lion's going to come in and eat him up. The lion came in and took the baby bear far away in the forest and ate him up and left the bones there. Then the lion came and took the other baby bear and took him to the forest and ate him up and left the bones there too. There's one there, asleep and fat. The father woke up and saw the two babies gone and he saw the bones walking around and he jumped on the bones and they died 'cause they were poison bones. Just the father and mother jumped. The bones came near the baby and he died and the bones died too. (Note: Questioning caused resentment, but examiner is certain that the "they died" referred to father and mother.)

Descriptive theme	Interpretive theme	Diagnostic level
A baby bear asleep in a cave is going to be eaten by a lion except for the bones.	If one is asleep, a lion comes and takes one away into forest and eats one, leaving only bones.	Again subject expresses oral incorporation and aggression, this time in the night.

Descriptive theme	Interpretive theme	Diagnostic level
The lion eats other baby bear in same way.	Lion returns for other baby, meting out same fate.	sibling or self this time being devoured.
One figure is fat and asleep in cave.	One figure is asleep and fat.	Since mother has previously been described as a repulsive figure, one might assume she is the one now described.
Father awakens, sees bones walking around, jumps on bones.	Father awakens, perceives children missing and bones walking around, and wishes to destroy them— mother does this too.	Father and mother are seen as wanting to revenge themselves upon the evildoer,
Father and mother both jump (and die?) because bones are poison.		and are poisoned by the bones, which are more powerful than- they, that is, our subject is so inherently evil and omnipotent that he is able to kill the parents merely by contact.
Bones approach baby, who also dies.	Bones approach baby, who also dies merely by the contact.	Sibling (or self) suffers same fate.

Clinical notes

This must also be considered a rather bizarre story even for the subject's age level, in view of the fact that it is a very unusual story to this or any other C.A.T. picture and so little suggested in its details by the stimulus. In a continuation of the theme of oral incorporation, the father figure is again seen as orally aggressive, although the latter part of the story shows some defensive switching with the father in a somewhat protective role; at the same time, the father is a victim, as are the mother and the baby sister. Earlier in the story our hero himself also has to die. In other words, we deal with an abundance and diffusion of hostility and aggression and intra-aggression.

The walking bones are probably the most bizarre feature of the story, the idea of poison occurring often enough in children without clear-cut or serious pathological implications, connoting fears of orally incorporating harmful objects related both to the mother's milk and fantasies of oral impregnation.

STORY 7

Story 7: A lion is chasing a monkey and the monkey is climbing up the tree and the lion breaks down the tree. The monkey jumps to the next tree and the lion grabs him by the tail and eats him up and only the bones are left. Then the tiger goes to one of the houses and eats the people and takes the clothes and said (voice pitched high and dramatic), "I'm the greatest king in the whole jungle." The end.

Descriptive theme	Interpretive theme	Diagnostic level
A lion chasing a monkey catches him by the tail and eats him up.	If a lion chases a monkey, he catches him and eats him up.	Repetition of oral aggression and incorporation. Identity of hero not yet clear.
The lion (tiger) goes to a house and eats the people,	Lion (tiger) goes to a house and eats the people,	Perseveration of theme to extent of leaving the stimulus (introduces people not existing in picture).
and takes the clothes of a king who was there, puts them on, and proclaims himself the greatest king in the whole jungle.	takes the clothes of a king and puts them on, proclaiming himself the greatest king in the whole jungle.	Assumes the garb of the king (father), wanting to supplant him after vanquishing him, and going further to notions of grandeur in being the *greatest* king in the *whole* jungle (the usual phrase being king of the jungle).

Clinical notes

Here we see a further perseveration of the theme of eating up people (or animals) with a reference to remaining bones. Again, this is mainly directed against the father figure (king) and all father figures (greatest king) in the whole jungle—a wild and primitive place in which this boy seems really to be living. The references to bones, particularly as in story 6 (poisoned bones of malevolent power) is the kind of literal organic concept seen in the Rorschach and in Figure Drawing responses also, and consistent with psychosis.

STORY 8

Story 8: They're having a party. The mother bear's grandma says, "You go get the lunch." He don't want to. The mamma tells secrets to the father about the baby and he don't like it. He got breakfast, dinner, and lunch and went out to get candles for the birthday cake. It was his birthday, and he got matches too and lighted the candles and blew them out. Then he cut the cake for the grandma, mother, and father. Then he ate and went to bed and the grandma went home and to bed.

Descriptive theme	*Interpretive theme*	*Diagnostic level*
There is a party and mother's grandma says, "Go get the lunch." He doesn't want to,	If there is a party, great-grandma asks him to get lunch. He doesn't want to.	Sees great-grandmother as a domineering figure.
but mother tells secrets to father about the baby and he doesn't like it.	But mother tells secrets to father which he doesn't like.	Sees mother as "telling on him" to father;
He gets breakfast, dinner and lunch and goes to get candles for his birthday cake (and matches). Lights candles, blows them out, serves cake to grandma, mother, father. Eats some himself,	He gets a great deal to eat, there is fire,	(and thereupon?) he goes to get supplies and makes himself useful. Feels forced into servitude, into passivity. Enuresis (reference to fire).
goes to bed. Grandma goes home to bed.	and he goes to bed.	

Clinical notes

This story appears extremely innocuous after the previous ones. The introduction of matches to light the candles suggests the possibility of a urethral complex, since fire, as well as water, has this diagnostic significance in T.A.T. and C.A.T. stories.

STORY 9

Story 9: The mamma bear came out of bed and made supper for the baby. The baby's looking and the mamma's dead, and the ghost came in and killed the baby. The papa came in and saw it and he took a bottle out. The ghost saw it and shot the father. Then the cops came and saw it and sent the ghost to the electric chair.

Descriptive theme	*Interpretive theme*	*Diagnostic level*
Mother makes supper for the baby and dies,	If mother dies	Extreme aggression against the mother,
and a ghost comes and kills the baby	and the baby dies	the younger sibling,
and later the father.	and father dies,	and the father,
And then the cops kill the ghost.	the ghost dies.	and great intra-aggression.

Clinical notes

This is a very disturbed story. It does not consider the stimulus at all, and diffuse, uncontrolled hostility abounds.

STORY 10

Story 10: The little doggie don't want to get hit. He's crying 'cause he don't want to get in the tub. The mother sits down and hits and hits and he barks and barks. He starts to run away into the tub. He turns the water on and takes a bath and she'll pet him and give him dessert, breakfast, and dinner, and supper, and pet him and put him to bed.

Descriptive theme	*Interpretive theme*	*Diagnostic level*
A doggie doesn't want to get hit and is crying because he doesn't want to have a bath. Mother hits him and he barks (cries).	If one doesn't want to take a bath, one gets hit by mother, cries,	Sees mother as coercive, punishing. Regressive resistance and fear of bath. Water suggests urethral problems.
He runs away—into the tub and takes a bath	and runs into tub,	Intra-aggression (flight *into* tub).
and is rewarded by being given a great deal of food and being personally put to bed by her.	and is rewarded by much food and personal attention (again, the very meaning of love to him).	Identifies food and love. Associates food and bed.

Clinical notes

In this story the hostile and fearful relationship between mother and child clearly emerges. Remarkable is his running into the tub. Food obviously plays a tremendous role in gratification. While it is only reasonable to point out that children generally go to bed after having eaten, the frequent association of the two in this subject's stories suggests that it is also part of the oral triad.

Postscript to Case 3

Kenneth was never known to me personally. The C.A.T. record and other information printed in toto above was kindly made available by Miss Freyd, when she took a course in the C.A.T. with me.

As an afterthought, having brought the rest of this book up to date, it occurred to me to try to check on the dire prognosis, so I got in touch with Miss Freyd, whom I had not seen in many years. It is due to her strenuous efforts to trace this boy's subsequent career that the following tragic history can be made available.

Kenneth moved from his hometown. After a few years, a social worker from the new domicile requested information on him because at about age 13 he assaulted his sister sexually, threatened to kill her if she told anyone, and when discovered in the act by his mother at one time almost strangled the mother. The father, who previously had told the school's social worker to mind her own business, that he knew how to handle the boy, then told the social worker she should take care of him—"he is all yours."

Ken was then sent to a state school. He ran away several times. At some later time, according to a relative, he seemed to adjust better for several years, worked, got married, and had a daughter. After about three years of marriage, he met another young woman who became pregnant by him. Meeting her in a park near his childhood home, he strangled her to death. He was executed at age 28, just about 20 years after taking the test reported here.

The C.A.T. report that he was an exceedingly disturbed boy was hardly overstated. Extreme aggression and hostility are noted throughout. The report failed to predict overt mayhem, though that fact was obvious from the behavioral report. What the C.A.T. supplies is the bizarreness of the aggression and the general severe pathology. It has been impossible to obtain institutional records to ascertain whether a psychosis was diagnosed at any point. The crime Ken was executed for certainly sounds like a direct repetition of his earlier tendencies to choke someone to death, and most likely was the result of sudden loss of control rather than premeditation. This makes the sentence a puzzling one. It is unlikely that any amount of therapy at that late date would really have made him a safe person to have around, but at the same time it is very unlikely that he could have been a person of sound mind who was aware of the consequences of his act while engaged in it. It is probably a reflection on the nature of our criminal justice that this man was executed rather than hospitalized.

This whole story underlines points I have made elsewhere [50]: that it is not only necessary to screen children psychologically at school entrance, but also to have the legal right to insist upon treatment, removal from a pathological home, and/or treatment of the parents, if necessary without their voluntary consent. Like the mother of Lee Harvey Oswald, this boy's father rejected professional help until it was clearly too late. Society can ill afford the burden of criminal psychosis, nor is it fair to innocent children to insist upon their parents' right to mistreat and cripple them.

D. Further Examples

Below, we present a number of parts of more sample records to illustrate a variety of responses to the C.A.T. They are not particularly selected for success, but rather in order to show difficulties and subtleties of interpretation.

Case 1

S. Q., aged 3 years, 11 months, male, black, poor socioeconomic situation. Subject was easily approached in nursery with an offer to help him dress for out-of-doors period. Later brought cut cheek to be cared for and accepted offer to play game (C.A.T.). Seemed a little indecisive about going out or coming with examiner. Short period observed in outdoor playground showed him to feel ill at ease, although not shy. Three stories of his record will be presented.

Picture 2: Bear, kitty cat, and rope man . . . A big, big bear . . . and he gets *so big*. *(What is he doing?)* He came to visit the people.

Picture 3: A pipe man that lives in the house. He's taking his clothes off. *(Why?)* Because he has no clothes. He threw all his clothes away. He don't want no clothes (singsong). No pants, no socks, no shoes. *(What does he want?)* He wants to have a lot of hair around him. *(What's he doing?)* He's sitting in a dirty chair with no clothes on.

Picture 9: Bunny rabbit. You see this bunny? He's in his bed. And the other bunny rabbit is way upstairs. He took the stuff and come home and said he may put another bunny up the house. He ran upstairs and come right back down *(singsong)* and the father bear come out from basement (dark left corner) and saw a rabbit—run upstairs—go upstairs to your bed!

Story 2 is certainly a very meager one. All that attracts attention is, "the big bear who got so big"—which by itself surely barely deserves any speculation. Story 3, however, demonstrates repeatedly that the subject rejects the clothing, wants to "sit in a dirty chair with no clothes on." This would indicate a wish to regress to an earlier stage. Still, we have no idea why. Then, in picture 9, the most manifest clue is contained in the fact that the bunny "may put another bunny up the house." This definitely sounds as though the subject is preoccupied with another baby coming into the house. Those psychoanalytically trained will be able to see a symbolic restatement of this thought in the running upstairs and the father bear coming out from the basement coupled with an apparent memory of being told to go to bed perhaps in connection with some sexual activity. Our assumption now may find some corroboration in the brief reference in story 2, "the big bear who got so big," which may refer to the mother's pregnancy. Then we can understand his regressive pattern in story 3 in relation to the arrival of the rival. These were the conclusions we arrived at on blind analysis of these stories.

A check with data from the social worker showed that it was not actually a sibling, but a little cousin that had arrived in the home. Since the aunt and the rival (her son) lived in the same household with the subject, the psychological significance was the same. The kindergarten teacher was replete with confirmation of the subject's behavioral problems. We had occasion to consider further the subject's statement that the hero "wants to have a lot of hair around him." The inference one could make is that he has compared himself to the father and wants to have hair on the chest and in the pubic area also. Outstanding among the behavioral problems as reported by the teacher was the fact that the subject explored his little girl playmates with a great deal of interest.

This record can serve as an example of relatively poor returns in a small child wherein each story by itself is quite disappointing unless and until one can bring each story in meaningful relation to the others. Nevertheless, the usefulness of the C.A.T., in this case, becomes quite clear. The teacher and social worker knew that he was a behavioral problem with excessive sexual interest in little girls. Our test relates his behavioral difficulties to rivalry with a sibling-like figure, and a preoccupation with procreation. Having established these relationships, it should be relatively simple to discuss this with the child apropos of his stories: that he must be angry about the new arrival; must wonder where babies come from, etc.

At the same time, the social worker might attempt to decrease his sexual stimulation by whatever means the circumstances might permit, and instruct the mother about handling him.

Case 2

K. S., aged 6 years, 4 months, female, white, upper middle class socioeconomic situation. We are presenting only the response to picture 3. In this, the lion becomes the father figure for this very bright girl, and the oedipal situation is clearly revealed.

> This will be a good one. King Lion, that's what I'll call it. Now, I guess I'll make a name for these, O.K.? There was a lion and he said to the king: "I have heard your stories and I hear you are very tired and you are looking for another lion to put in your place." This I don't want you to write—I just want to tell you (to examiner). You see, the other lion was the king of all the lions and was getting tired, so she said to the other lion, "If you will do all these hard tasks, if you can do them all, you will become king. The first task is that you must go and find a princess—a queen—no, a princess, to marry. If you don't find one who will be right for you—off with your head." "Ah!" thought this lion, "if I could only find my dear, dear daughter." Because he was a king of the lions also, but he never mentioned it, see. "Now, I can go and look for my daughter." This I just want to tell you, but don't write it.

The story was then considered finished but the subject took it up again, later:

> Now I don't want you to write this one, I just want to tell you about it. The king wanted to find his daughter. He had sent her out to seek the world and so he called her up at the first place she was supposed to be and they told him she had left. Then he called at the second place she was supposed to be and she wasn't there either. So he called her at the third hotel and they got her on the phone and she said she would be right there—in four minutes and they were married and then they played a joke on the other king. You know, this king was really the king of the lions but hadn't told anyone. So now they went before the other king and he said, "What are you doing here? Get out of here!" But they said they were married and that this king was the real king; so the other king had to go away.

Unabashed by cultural taboos as yet, the king (father) marries his daughter though some of the story becomes quite confused. There is clear evidence of identification—switching, as well. There is some subliminal awareness of the forbiddenness of it all in the fact that the little girl asks the examiner not to write the story down.* Aside from the dynamic aspects, the concreteness and specificity of the childish thought processes deserve note: "*in four minutes* and they were married."

Case 3

M. I., aged 10 years, 4 months, white, male, poor socioeconomic situation. We are presenting the following story to picture 3 to demonstrate how extensive and rife with material a response may be.

---

* Investigation revealed beyond doubt that this little girl was in marked conflict and rivalry with her mother.

Once upon a time there was a lion who lived in the forest. He was very mad and he didn't like anybody but himself, and he was very proud of himself and he didn't like no one but himself, and everyone was afraid of him because he was very strong and he could break anything, like trees that were 60 or 70 feet high and three feet thick, and he just pushed them like rope and they were nothing. One day, he thought that he was going to hypnotize all the people and animals so that he could rule over them. First, he went to one of the homes of the fox and he looked at them and looked at them until they were hypnotized and the whole family came running to him. Then he went to the chipmunks' place; he hypnotized their whole family and all the chipmunks that were around. He lived in a great big home and he had everything he wanted. After he hypnotized everybody and he had a great big chair and a nice pipe and he had a storage room full of tobacco and he had a dungeon and he had another one full of canes; but there was one thing he didn't have—he didn't have a beautiful body. He wanted to have yellow hair—yellow and brown together, blue eyes and his hair combed out nice and straight. He wanted all of his things shiny and he didn't have enough people to polish his canes and things. The next day he went into the forest again and he didn't see anyone, so he kept walking until he came to a big city and he did not see anyone there because it was dark, not even a light was shining, so he kept on walking until he came to a big, big castle. He was very jealous of it because it had a great big steeple and on the top was a great big diamond that he wanted and there was also a great big courtyard; on the other end was another part of the castle that had three steeples; a great big one in the middle and a smaller one on each side and they all had diamonds on them; and on the door there was a big ruby and the other door on the other side had one, too—a blue ruby and he was so jealous that he was running around in circles. And he roared very loud and it reflected on all the building around and it hit him in his ears and he got quiet because it hurt him. He had never known how strong his voice was. Then he was sneaking up into the castle, then he got near the door and he saw a bell and he didn't know what it was, so he pressed it and it made so much noise it scared him; then a little while no one answered it, so he saw the door knob and he opened it and saw that it was pitch black, so he was walking around in circles and finally he hit something—so he fell down, and found it was a door, so he opened it and found there was a bed with a beautiful princess on the bed and he saw it and he didn't like to see her having a good time when he wasn't, so he went over and gulped her down in one mouthful and after he was walking and when he got back to his castle he felt very funny. So he sat down and was thinking and got very mad at himself cause it was the girl—she was a very good girl and she loved everybody—and he went over to his place where he had lots and lots of food; so he got chickens, pigs (animals that were already killed) all food that the animals liked and then he went to another room and got wood. Then he was getting all the wood and food and everybody was watching him—even the mouse in the house. Then he went in another storage and he got tons and tons of cheese and made a big hole and the mouse made his home in the cheese. He was very hungry cause he was very thin and by the time he finished he couldn't get back in his hole. Then the lion went outside and gave everyone everything and he was very happy. The next day everyone liked him but he still didn't like himself because he forgot to unhypnotize beavers so he went over and unhypnotized the beavers and everybody liked him.

M. I. identifies himself with the lion in a story that is apparently to a large extent a wish-fulfilling fantasy. Frequently, however, self-criticism and awareness of self-deficiency stand side by side, with overcompensation. "He didn't like anybody but himself and he was very proud of himself and everybody was afraid of him and he could break anything like . . ." Then, after equipping himself with a beautiful home and a nice pipe, he suddenly shows us that he feels his body is inadequate. This is followed by a symbolic story of jealousy of a "great, big steeple" . . . "with two smaller ones on each side," probably a symbolic representation of a big genital. Subsequently, he finds a beautiful princess in bed. He then gives us a perfectly primitive oral fantasy of acquisition (probably of the mother): "he gulps the princess down in one mouthful." Having committed this crime, he shows us his conscience (superego) as a form of reaction formation to his drives. He procures tons of food for all the animals including the mouse and "gave everyone everything . . . then he was very happy." In the course of this story, he makes certain, in a parenthetical remark, that all the chickens and pigs, which he is now feeding to the other animals, were already dead. That is, he lets us know that he did not commit any further killing. Later, he finds the reward for renunciation of his acquisitive and aggressive drives in being liked by everyone, that is, we clearly find a picture of socialization. He still disapproves of himself until he recalls and undoes his earliest act and unhypnotizes the beavers.

This is the story of an apparently fairly disturbed child who feels that his body is inadequate, who has strong acquisitive and aggressive drives which he considers very evil, and who is developing an excessive superego to deal with these drives. The severity of the disorder and the full extent of it became clearer in a number of other stories which we do not need to reproduce here. Examination of the reality situation revealed that this child lived in a very disturbed home, the father having deserted, and the mother being suspected of gross promiscuity. The boy actually was physically undersized and frequently did not have enough to eat. This latter information highlights his (the lion's) dissatisfaction with his body and his great need for acquisition and oral incorporation.

This story and several others of this subject show an excellent vocabulary, and an organizing ability consistent with intelligence considerably higher than average. The C.A.T. proves most helpful in this respect since formal intelligence testing has resulted in an I.Q. of only 103. The C.A.T. shows us that his true intellectual level must be considerably higher and that probably the emotional disturbance of this child is responsible for his poor functioning.

E. Special Clinical Problems

Below we present a few highlights of special problems.

The following stories* are those of a boy of 7 years, 11 months, whose mother has been separated from his father since the boy was 4 years old. He was referred for consultation because he never defended himself when attacked by other children. He frequently asked his mother to get married and wants her to have a baby.

His first story is an excellent illustration of his pregnancy fantasies concerning oral incorporation and birth from the stomach by bursting. Also apparent is a fear of being devoured.

Story 1: Once upon a time there were three little chickens. All of a sudden they saw a ghost rooster. All got scared. The ghost rooster said, "I want to eat you," and they all threw their mush in his face and the rooster threw the bowls back at them, and they ran and called the papa rooster. And the ghost said, "I'd like to eat you." "Gobble, gobble, gobble." said the turkey, "I'll eat you, ghost rooster," and he chopped off his head. And the ghost turned into a man and he turned on the chickens and said, "Ah, nice chickens to eat," and they chopped off the man's head and he turned into a chicken and ate the mush until it was all gone and mush went into his stomach and came out through his eyes, and he ate more mush and more mush from the bowl but the bowl was magic and mush bowl kept giving

---

* I am indebted to Dr. C. Lealtad for permission to reproduce these stories.

more mush. Suddenly it gave sugar and more sugar, then fruit and fruit and fruit, and he ate it all and ate and ate and ate. And suddenly his stomach popped and he changed into a prince.

Story 3 shows a repetition of the theme in the eating of the tail and the cane. It also illustrates his preoccupation with the role of the phallus and castration.

Story 3: Once there was a lion, and he was king of the lions. "I'm getting so old a mouse could eat me up—guess I'll smoke my pipe." A little mouse was looking and he said, "Guess I'll try it." and he sneaked up and began eating a little of his tail and a little of his mane. But it was tough. And then he came up and tried eating a little of his cane and the cane popped. And the old lion sent for other lions to get the mouse, and another cane. But the mouse ran into the hole and one lion ran after him and ran in flat and his nose came out of the hole square. And the mouse said, "Hee, hee, hee," saw he had a new cane, and he gnawed and gnawed and gnawed and tried and tried and tried, but this cane was steel and he could only make teeth marks. And the lion walked and walked and walked and met an old man, and he said, "May I have your cane?" And took his cane. And then he met a bachelor, and he said, "May I have your pipe?" And the lion said, "Yes, you may. I can get another." And then he walked and walked and walked to the barber shop. And the barber said, "Can I have your mane to make wigs?" And he said, "Sure, cut all you want—I can grow more hair." Barber then cut mane and the mane grew and grew and grew and he stepped on his mane and tripped and fell and then the mouse killed him.

Story 5 explicitly reveals this child's pregnancy fantasies when he says that the stomach got so high and then burst open. The wish for the baby is actually expressed here.

Story 5: There was a little baby and father and mother and a crib with one baby. Every night they sat down and said a prayer, "How we wish we had two babies." And said maybe at Christmas maybe we'll get a baby. One night they looked in and saw two babies. "Oh, it must be a magic cradle. Oh, no. Make another wish for a flounder." The husband caught a giant flounder and opened him and ate him. "Here's another giant flounder—maybe the babies would like to eat it all themselves." The babies' stomach almost burst—stomach growled. Stomach got so high, couldn't get the cover over them. "Oh, I don't know what I should do." The stomach weighed over fifty pounds—then bang! There was lots of noise and the stomach burst open and the mother and father fell in and said. "What is this—a firecracker?" Other baby's stomach went up and stomach opened and it died. Maybe if we eat flounder and ate and ate and ate and ate—then they fell flat and everything goes BOOM and everything splits—even the earth split.

Story 6 repeats the theme, showing that any part of the body can be used in pregnancy fantasies, in this case the nose, whereas it is the mouth in story 7.

Story 6: Once there were two bears and they slept all day and all night, and if they hear of work they say. "We'll do it tomorrow." Would you like to eat tomorrow? Then they got hungrier and hungrier. Then they ate dirt. "Oh, what can we eat? Poison ivy?" Then they began scratching. Then papa bear said. "I know what to eat, honey from the pear tree." But there were bees and hornets who stung him, and he said. "Ouch!" And his nose got bigger and bigger and finally his nose broke open. Then two bulls came running out and ran into his stomach and there was noise louder than an atom bomb and he died. And he shouldn't have said, "We'll do it tomorrow."

Stort 7: Once there was a tiger and he ate everything in sight—lucky his paws were not in sight. Tarzan ran into the tree and a cheetah ran behind him. Tarzan jumped on him and the tiger said, "Try to kill me." Tarzan said, "I will. Don't eat everything in sight." The tiger ran to eat a tree one day and the tree fell and honey ran out. And the bees swooped into his mouth and into his stomach and the tiger tried to roar but all he could say was a buzzing sound from the bees. He got Tarzan to open his stomach but the lion fell dead. Tarzan saw him alive again and he said, "I'll never eat a person again, only honey." But he had not learned his lesson from the bees. So he reached for honey and the bee said, "I'll sting." The tiger screamed and fell back and the monkey tickled him in the stomach. The bees took the honey back but the tiger growled and the bees came down but ran back because they did not like to be in the tiger's stomach. Then the queen bee said, "I'll show him my beauty." She came down but the tiger ate her. Then the whole squad swarmed into his mouth and he chewed them. Then a big hornet came in and stung him on the tongue but his fangs chewed him. But one day the tiger ate poison ivy and died.

Story 7 also shows suggestions that the child takes the passive role ("Try to kill me"), that he has tremendous incorporative needs; he is invariably being visually overstimulated (the queen bee showing her beauty, and the tickling).

The next case, a 5 year old boy,* was actually referred to a medical clinic for chronic constipation for which he had been receiving enemas, laxatives, and an emphasis on eating foods that would promote intestinal activity. When the physical findings were entirely negative, he was referred to the Mental Hygiene Clinic.

The C.A.T. stories show that the child is concerned with fantasies of pregnancy, that is, conception and delivery. He is afraid that dangerous, explosive poisons get into him in stories 1 and 8, although the rabbit in story 9 and the mouse in stories 3 and 6 are also being eaten. The monkey in story 7 and the puppy in story 10 are also being devoured. On the other hand, the open window in stories 9 and 10 is connected with danger, suggesting that this little boy associates body openings with the entrance of danger. Story 1 also suggests that bowel movements are associated with exploding—probably a fantasy of giving birth by explosion.

The constipation started $2\frac{1}{2}$ to three years before at a time when his mother had been pregnant with a baby girl who died a few weeks after birth. It seems likely that medical help for the constipation was precipitated by an exacerbation of his condition, since at the time of his examination another baby sister was born. The patient shared his parents' bedroom at the time of both pregnancies.

A recent dream that the boy related was as follows: "I was in a car and it drove over the side into the river. My daddy was driving us across the bridge and my mommy and I were sitting in the back seat. It crashed into the water." This dream also suggests a concern with the parental relations and injury that might come to him as well as to his mother.

While playing after the administration of the C.A.T., he devoted himself to loading and piling blocks into trucks which he hauled across the floor, unloaded and piled up again, making such statements as, "Boy, I sure have got a heavy load this time!" This play too suggests the concern with carrying a burden with which he probably equates both pregnancy and feces inside him.

Story 1: What is they eating—poison. They would eat poison and they'd explode. Their heads would bust on the ceiling. (*What's that?*) It's a big old rooster standing and talking. (*Where did the poison come from?*) They bought the poison and thought it was cereal.

Story 2: I know what's going to happen. The rope's gonna break and they're gonna go ker-plonk on their seats. The little bear will go ker-plonk and the daddy'll fall on the baby. The mommy will fall on her seat. It's the mommy's rope and she doesn't want the daddy to pull on it.

---

* I am indebted to Miss J. Schoellkopf for permission to reproduce these stories.

Story 3: I know what's gonna happen. The mouse is going to come out of the hole. The lion is gonna eat the mouse. The lion is smoking a cigar with a cane. He should be smoking a pipe. (*Why did the mouse come out?*) Mouse doesn't know lion is there!

Story 4: I know what's gonna happen. The little mouse is going to run right under the kangaroo's legs and knock the mother down. She's carrying the purse, baby, and basket. He wants to get the baby out of there so he knocks her out and gets in.

Story 5: Where's the baby? Where's the mommy and daddy? Where's their beds? Something must have happened. He threw the baby and mommy and daddy out and then he had the whole house to himself.

Story 6: I know what's gonna happen. Mouse (baby bear) is sleeping in big bear's cage. In the morning the bears will see the mouse and eat him up.

Story 7: I know what this is gonna be. Lion is going to eat the monkey because the monkey's dropping from the trees. The lion doesn't like the monkey because monkeys eat lion's dads up. Baby tiger is gonna get the monkey.

Story 8: I know what's gonna happen. They're drinking poison. They think it's coffee. It's the mommy and daddy. Relation and little boy are talking. (*Who put the poison in?*) Cowboy didn't like monkeys eating up lion dads.

Story 9: I know what's gonna happen. If the lion came in the rabbit will get eaten up. The window is open. (*What does the rabbit dream?*) He dreams he's upside down; then the lion can't get him.

Story 10: Nothing's gonna happen! (emphatically). (*It looks like something is happening.*) There's a window open and if the lions come, they will eat up the puppy. (*What's happening right now?*) Dog petting little dog because he likes him.

F. Illustration of Longitudinal Clinical Data*

Following are shown, side by side, the responses of a boy who at the time of first testing was 6 years, 10 months, and at the time of the second testing 8 years, 5 months. Timothy was originally referred to the school psychologist because he was extremely immature, showed off constantly, wanted to be different and get attention, pushed other children, and was frequently inattentive. At the time of first testing, his Stanford-Binet I.Q. was 124. The reason for the second test was that he created classroom disturbance; he didn't conform, hit other children, and looked unhappy. The teacher thought he probably had an I.Q. of about 140.

Stories

Age 6 years, 10 months

1. What are these, chickens? This chicken was eating badly and spilling and making work for the big chicken, and the big chicken has to spank them and send them back to their grandfather.

Age 8 years, 5 months

1. I wonder what it is. I know! The hen and the naughty little people, when the fox fell in the river! There were three and they were bad and they didn't want to help and they spilled crumbs. And one day the fox came and ate the mother hen up, and then he fell asleep and they put rocks in him and he drowned. (*Mother hen was out when they put rocks in?*) Which would you

---

* From L. Bellak and C. Adelman, the Children's Apperception Test (CAT). In A. I. Rabin and M. R. Haworth (Eds.): *Projective Techniques with Children*. New York, Grune & Stratton, 1960.

Age 6 years, 10 months

Age 8 years, 5 months

rather have, four days of rain, fog, or snow? (*Which would you?*) Snow, then we could have snowball fights. Which would you rather have, three days hot or three days of cold? (*You*) Cold because I don't like short-sleeved shirts (*Want to look at the next one?*) O.K.

3. You wouldn't be able to get near that, would you? Would he eat a mouse? (*Do you think so?*) Yes, I think so, but I don't know if the lion will find him or not. He's waiting for someone to come along that isn't looking what he's doing and he'll eat him.

3. (Timothy voluntarily picked up card 3, looked at it and said:) No, I don't want that; I feel like scaling it out of the window. A lion pooing on his chair. Somebody stole something of his and he was thinking what to do, and there was a little mouse there and he bit his tail and the lion put dynamite in the hole and blew him up. Which would you rather have, calm or a hurricane? (*Calm, and you?*) I don't know, hurricane, maybe.

5. I guess it's the nighttime and someone must be away and it's just getting black and I don't know what this is, I'll call this smoke, and there is a fire outside and when they come back they find their house is all burned down. That would make you cry, wouldn't it?

5. The mother bear and the daddy bear were out and two little bears came in and slept in this crib. And it was dark and father came home it was dark and ran out the back door and when mother and father, came home it was dark and they didn't know what was wrong and they never found 'em. Now, I have 32–38, here comes the kind of flag you have for 39–46. I like a fast wind that blows trees down, do you? (*Not very much.*) (Timothy picked up the next card.)

6. What is those, those swimming? Oh, a bear in his cave and the baby bear is with him. What eats bears, can you think of anything? (*Can you?*) No.

6. What's this! There's three bears and they have no house and they slept in a cave, and one night someone put some mud over it and when they woke up they had to claw their way out. And the next night the same thing happened, and the next night the little bear didn't go to sleep he saw a man there. And the next day he told his mother and daddy and that night they ate the man up. 65, next is, no, 55–65, no, that isn't right. I'm the best in

Age 6 years, 10 months   *Age 8 years, 5 months*

numbers in my class. (Timothy continued to write and say aloud, wind speeds to above 75.) Which would you rather have, above 75 with 10 below zero and cloud, or 8 to 12 with 70 and clear? (*I'll take 10 below.*) Once it was zero and I ran all around, I am just about done, now I want to play a game with you.

Brief Analysis

In both card 1 stories, the children eat badly, are naughty, and antagonize the big chicken, who punishes them and sends them away. In the second testing, an aggressive animal is introduced, a fox, who eats up the mother and is, in turn, drowned for his misdeeds, whereupon the child reverts to an obsessive preoccupation with the weather which went on all through the testing. In the story to card 3, in the first session, he is anxiously concerned with the idea that one has to be careful or else one is devoured. In the second session, he wants to do away with the card altogether by scaling it out the window. There is much more evidence of violence and anal regression here with the lion "pooing" on his chair. The aggressive orality now relates specifically to the castrating notion of biting off the tail. There is also the suggestive evidence of explosive emotional tension in connection with the dynamite and the wish for a hurricane. In story 5, in the first testing, the reference to smoke and fire suggest a great deal of aggressive urethral sexual preoccupation, as does the reference to crying. This would be most suggestive of a history of enuresis (which we were unable to check on) but is certainly consistent with his aggressive behavior, including the aggressive need to show off. The second testing gives a much less clear-cut story, except that the little bears run out when the parents come home and are never discovered. This is followed by some reference to figures and the discussion again of violent weather, in this case a fast wind. Story 6 in the first session introduces water, supporting the notion expressed in story 5, and again a preoccupation with oral incorporation. Story 6 in the second session has to do with being walled up with mud and watchful nighttime observations. This is suggestive of insomnia, perhaps associated with oral incorporation fantasies, and then again comes the preoccupation with numbers, windspeeds, and the weather—his restlessness is also indicated by the reference to running.

An examination of test material suggests not only the marked pathology consistent with the clinical report of aggression and showing off but also that the process is worsening. Judging by the leaving of the stimulus, the inappropriate material, and very poor drive control, this boy is probably on the way towards a psychotic condition. Obsessive preoccupation and acting out have so far served as brakes on the ego disintegration. A school psychiatrist who saw the child suspected that he might be schizophrenic.

CHAPTER XVI

A SUPPLEMENT TO
THE C.A.T.*

A. Purpose of C.A.T.-S.

THE C.A.T. SUPPLEMENT (C.A.T.-S.) WAS DESIGNED TO SUPPLY pictures which might illuminate situations not *necessarily pertaining to universal problems,* but which occur often enough to make it desirable to learn more about them as they exist in a good many children.

Ten pictures have been designed (Fig 9), any single one of which may be presented to children *in addition* to the regular C.A.T. For instance, C.A.T.-S. picture 5 may be given to children with a temporary or permanent physical disability or with a history of disability. It might permit one to learn about the psychological effects of this somatic problem upon the specific child. Or children with any kind of psychosomatic disorder or hypochondriasis might project these onto the stimulus. Picture 10 may permit us to learn what fantasies a boy or girl may have about the mother's pregnancy. If, e.g., a child is brought to a clinic with a number of behavioral problems, and the history shows that the mother is currently pregnant or has delivered relatively recently, then this picture may permit one to learn about the possible relationship between the behavior problems and the fantasies concerning the family event.

In short, the C.A.T.-S. may be used in specific situations for the purpose of eliciting specific themes—as seem indicated (and as discussed below).

A further use of the C.A.T.-S. may lie in its usefulness as material for play techniques. Even though establishing proper rapport will obtain longer and better stories from children than the beginner is likely to think, there remain children severely enough disturbed to be unable to relate stories. For such subjects it may be expedient to make all the pictures of the C.A.T.-S. available at once, upon a table (arranged from 1 to 10, in three rows, the last row having four pictures),

---

* This material was presented as a paper at the 1952 Annual Meeting of the American Orthopsychiatric Association, in Atlantic City, N. J., and is published here independently with the permission of the Editors of the *American Journal of Orthopsychiatry*. I am indebted to L. J. Stone, Professor of Child Study at Vassar College, and C. Fear for supplying data for the CAT-S.

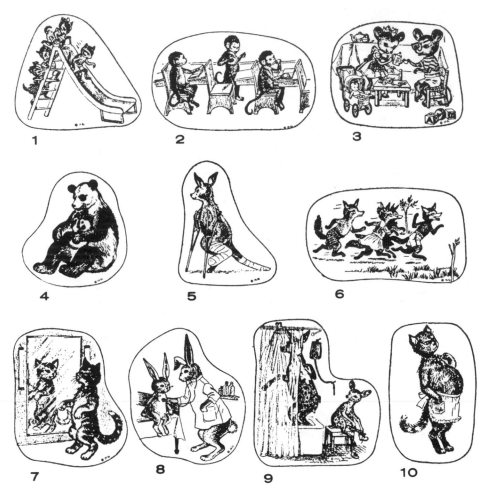

FIG. 9. Pictures for use with the C.A.T.-S.

and to let them see them, handle them, arrange, and talk about them as they will. All of the child's remarks and behavior should be carefully recorded. Also, such use of the pictures may encourage storytelling in children less able to comply immediately with instructions. It should be mentioned, however, that this method is not the most desirable procedure if the stories can be obtained in the regular manner.

By such means one may derive material less reliable for inferences than the regular stories, but more reliable than usual play situations permit; at least we know something empirically about these pictures and will have some norms concerning responses to them. Thus, we may be able to make clinical inferences with some semblance of experimental validity.

For the purpose of adapting it to this kind of play technique, the C.A.T.-S. has been constructed from washable material not too easily marred or destroyed.

B. Administration

The problems of administering the C.A.T.-S. are not different from those of the C.A.T. (and will be only summarized here) except for its special uses, as discussed above.

Proper rapport between child and administrator is most important. It is best to get to know the child before administration, to play games first so as to let him become accustomed to the examiner and to the situation and to reduce anxiety to a minimum.

To younger children particularly, the C.A.T. or the C.A.T.-S. may best be presented as a storytelling game. By far the most successful technique has been to make the test administration *part of a group situation* as often as possible. In a nursery, for example, one may choose the most fear-free and friendly child first, allowing it to appear that this is something of a distinction and something pleasant and interesting. If the first is thus successfully carried off, the rest of the children will compete about who may be next and will be cooperative and interested.

Children usually do not mind at all when recordings are made either by hand or by instrument. It is simple to flatter their narcissism by telling them that one will be able thus to read or play the stories back to them (should they inquire about the recording).

Again, it is important not to permit a child to see more than one picture at a time (unless the play technique is being used) and to conceal (in a desk drawer, for instance) the others lest the child be impatient to cut short the current story in his eagerness to see the next picture.

When the C.A.T.-S. is used as an instrument of play technique, all pictures of the Supplement—and possibly also those of the regular C.A.T.—are exposed simultaneously and, as previously stated, all remarks, manipulations, picture constellations, and combinations are recorded.

C. Inquiry

Special attention needs to be directed to the importance of knowing the behavioral conditions and the real-life situation of the subject. It is entirely true that "blind" interpretations of stories (i.e., interpretations of stories without knowledge of any other data) may lead to impressive and startlingly accurate insights. Nevertheless, *for clinical use it is important that the projective data be seen in conjunction with as much information about the reality situation as possible.*

The inquiry should be directed toward that part of the reality most closely linked with the stories. One should ascertain as often as possible where specific names, places, and other precise references in a story come from. If a plot is taken from TV, radio, films, fairytales, comic strips, or other sources, it is important for the examiner to know it. This does not mean that the story is useless—on the contrary—there will doubtless be individual distortions of the original source which will be particularly illuminating. Even if the story should be a faithful reproduction of the original source (TV, etc.,) it will nevertheless be subjectively indicative that this specific story was elicited by the stimulus card.

Of particular importance for the inquiry is that attempts be made to discover whether a given story or certain details of one reflect a factual or a wishful state of affairs. For instance, if a father figure is seen as especially patient, nurturant, and protective, it should be a simple matter to establish whether this reflects the child's actual conception of the father or whether the father is the opposite in reality and the stories thus primarily reflect a wish.

D. Description of and Typical Responses to Pictures

Picture 1

This picture shows four mice children on a slide. One is just sliding down, one about to start the slide, and two are climbing up the ladder. Numbers one and three suggest males; two and four suggest females (skirts, bows in hair).

A play situation, this picture permits expression of fears of physical activity, of physical harm, and problems in social (play) activities with other children generally, and with the opposite sex specifically. The children may be seen as happy, as fighting, as pushing, frightened, etc.

Picture 2

A classroom situation with three little monkeys, two sitting at typical school desks, one standing with a book in hand, and one of the seated monkeys holding his tail.*

This picture lends itself to a projection of problems with the teacher, schoolmates, and other classroom situations (learning, reciting, etc.). It leaves ample play for ascription of various characteristics to the unseen teacher, and a number of predicaments of the pupil reciting as well as possibilities of wanting to show off knowledge, of relating fears of inadequacy, stagefright, etc. The monkey holding his tail in his hand may give rise to stories concerning masturbation.

Picture 3

This picture shows children "playing house." Father mouse, with eyeglasses much too big for him and obviously belonging to an adult, is receiving a beverage from "Mother mouse" while toys and a baby doll in a carriage are dispersed about them.

Here, children may have a chance to relate their wishful fantasies about being grown up and doing what seems to them desirable and possibly forbidden. The apperceived, imagined relationships in the family will be clearly depicted. Because this picture encourages particular identification with adults, it is more likely to prompt wishful fantasy rather than biographical data. Thus, it is especially necessary to conduct an inquiry at the end of the test to determine—as much as possible—the level from which this story comes.

---

* The situation is frequently not recognized as pertaining to a classroom by preschool children.

Picture 4

A big bear sits crouched forward, holding a baby bear on its lap and in its arms.

This picture may elicit themes of wishes of oral nature, sentiments against infant siblings, regressive tendencies, etc. Light will also be shed upon the conflict between remaining (and wanting) to be dependent and independent, as well as the general relationship to parents.

Picture 5

This picture depicts a kangaroo on crutches and with a bandaged tail and foot.

It prompts stories of fear of injury and castration. It may elicit feelings about a physical handicap or a feeling of general inadequacy, as well as illuminating for us something about the subject's body image (see picture 7). Social rejection related to physical handicap may also be touched upon.

Picture 6

A group of four foxes—two male and two female—are in a race with the goal in sight and one male closest to it.

Competition between siblings and playmates and the accompanying feelings may be dealt with here, as well as themes of success or failure.

Picture 7

A cat stands before a mirror looking at its image.

This should elicit ideas of body image—as Schilder described it: "The image of the human body means the picture of our own body which we form in our mind . . . the way in which the body appears to ourselves." Picture 7 may tell us the ideas the growing child has about himself and his body, the shortcomings, pride. The tail may have phallic significance in the card particularly, and children may express their notions about some people being "so plain" and some "so fancy," as well as their ideas concerning sexual differences, exhibitionism, etc.

Picture 8

A rabbit doctor is examining a rabbit child with a stethoscope; some bottles of medicine are visible in the background.

Here we may be told stories of fears and traumata connected with physical illness, operations, doctors, and hospitals. An impending or past tonsillectomy or some such illness may be clearly revealed in its more or less traumatic and more or less specific meaning for the individual child. We may also obtain biographical or fantasy detail concerning illness of a family member.

Picture 9

A grown deer is taking a shower and is half hidden by a shower curtain. A small deer is looking towards the larger figure. An enema bag hangs against the wall.

Here we hope to learn more about the subject's ideas of sexual differences, nudity, voyeurism, the family bathroom habits; whether or not a child is being overstimulated, what disturbances there may be in this area; the child's handling of the situation, if any. The enema bag may give us biographical data concerning his feelings about enemas. Stories illuminating masturbation practices may appear.

Picture 10

An obviously pregnant cat, standing upright, with large belly, and apron askew.

This is designed to bring out ideas about where a baby comes from and fantasies and/or fear about this. It should be particularly useful with children who are expecting a sibling or who have recently had one and seem to have special problems with the situation.*

E. Interpretation

The basic principles of interpretation need not be discussed here again.

The recording and analysis booklet for the C.A.T. is applicable to the pictures of the C.A.T.-S. without any changes.

The interpretation of the C.A.T.-S. as an instrument of play technique must be predicated upon general clinical experience and theoretical knowledge of psychodynamics. Extreme caution must be preserved lest one read into random behavior or remarks significance which exists only in the examiner's mind and which cannot be clinically and/or historically substantiated.

It has been pointed out [53] that projective techniques make use of several dimensions: content analysis, formal analysis, Gestalt functioning, body image or self-image, and the analysis of choices. Among the techniques using inferences on the basis of choices and preferences are, notably, the Szondi as well as finger painting (choice of colors); in the Rorschach, judgments are made on the basis of rejection of cards and that portion of the inquiry concerning the choices of the best and the least liked pictures. The C.A.T.-S. as a play technique may employ this dimension. For example, if a child has refused to tell stories to any of the 10 C.A.T. cards, and when the C.A.T.-S. is placed before him reaches for the mother bear with the cub; and if—when the C.A.T. pictures are also made available for manipulation—he chooses the first picture and the 4 card and will evince interest in the baby kangaroo in the pouch as well, a tentative inference that this child has oral problems and wants to be cuddled and taken care of is probably safe.

---

* Ideas about the necklace, e.g., its being torn, may well refer to notions about the body.

F. Norms

It has been said that the validity of inferences from projective techniques is based upon three factors:

1. A study of the individual differences and forms of apperceptive distortion by finding repetitive patterns throughout the record: *intratest data;* if there is a theme of lack of support and love and food in nearly every story, we may make the inference that the subject has a strong oral need apparently related to a feeling of deprivation. Similarly, if most stories end upon a hapless note implying that the odds are against one and are just too much, we may again make the inference that this subject feels hopeless and overwhelmed.

2. One may compare the fantasy behavior, as revealed in the test, with manifest behavior and make inferences on this basis: on *intraindividual data.* For instance, if most stories drip with gore as the result of the hero's aggression, and the subject is referred for timidity and shyness, we may make the inference that this child is so full of aggression that he projects it onto other people, and also that he dare not associate socially lest it break through (that is, if other data support this connotation—namely, indication of lack of control, fear of losing control, etc.).

On the basis of these two levels of interpretation we have remarked that norms and normative studies—as is customary with intelligence tests and other quantitative samples of performance—are not a necessity with projective tests despite much academic complaint. Actually, each person and each record constitutes a sample population of needs and behavioral variables which may be studied as mentioned above.

Nevertheless, it is useful—and, in the long run, desirable—to establish norms of apperception concerning our standard stimuli and to be able to make certain quantitative inferences from comparisons of each individual record with a large sample. We speak then, of:

3. A *normative-statistical* approach to the validity of inference on the basis of *interindividual* differences in apperception.

For example, if we should find that 80 per cent of all children tested express fear of falling off the slide, we would consider such a reference in a newly tested child as not of pathological significance. If, on the other hand, a little boy says that the girl on top of the slide has just kicked the little boy below her in the head, and only five out of a sample of 100 children has ever seen some aggression between the two, we may be inclined to infer that this child has a particular fear of aggression from girls.

In a pilot study, Fear and Stone [115] presented the supplement pictures to 40 children of Poughkeepsie schools: 10 girls of 6 years of age; 10 boys of 6 years of age, and 10 boys and girls each aged 7. The stories were told consecutively to each picture.* They tabulated the frequency of themes for each picture, the description of attitudes expressed, and outcome of the stories. Their structural

---

* A tenth picture—the pregnant cat—was added later to the set and three of the pictures had some features added: an enema bag was added to picture 9; the last monkey in 2 was made to play with his tail; the kangaroo in picture 5 had its tail bandaged.

analysis was concerned with the settings for the scene, children departing from the scene, figures used and figures imported, and total story time and wordage per picture (Table 3).

In their study of the 40 children, only a few variables of the many included yielded suggestive differences between boys and girls, and between the ages of 6 and 7. This is not surprising in view of the relative similarity of age and background. Even from the small sample of 40, we can arrive at some notion of what may constitute popular responses, etc. But because of the small numbers involved, it is safe to say only that trends are in the direction expected rather than to consider the data as statistically soundly significant. It is for this reason, too, that we mention only a very few of the more important variables.

TABLE 3. Tabulation of Responses of 40 School Children to the C.A.T.S.*

	Total	Boys	Girls
Frequency of Themes for Picture 1:			
Expected themes			
Peers sliding	29	15	14
Siblings sliding	6	1	5
Having fun	15	7	8
Playing other things, too	9	5	4
Concern with fair play	7	1	6
Other "problems"	20	8	12
Imported themes			
Sibling rivalry	2	1	1
Concern with injury, death	5	3	2
Dangers encountered but children succeed	2	2	—
Interventions but children not successful	2	2	—
Sliding when should be doing something else; being bad	4	1	3
Real parental involvement	4	—	4
Concern for acceptance vs. rejection by peers	1	—	1
Concern for selfish vs. kind children	1	—	1
Birth	1	1	—
Running away	1	1	—
Imported themes only (from responses that did not relate to the stimulus of sliding or playing)			
Concern with danger, death	4	2	2
Self-assertion	2	1	1
Concern with failure, inferiority	1	—	1
Total Wordage for Each Picture:			
1, ranged from 13–528 words, average 98			
2, ranged from 21–388 words, average 80			
3, ranged from 9–476 words, average 83			
4, ranged from 9–234 words, average 68			
5, ranged from 10–306 words, average 68			
6, ranged from 12–227 words, average 81			
7, ranged from 12–348 words, average 76			
8, ranged from 9–288 words, average 74			
9, ranged from 6–346 words, average 88			
Average 79 words			

* Fear, C., and Stone, L. J.: Table from C. Fear's B.A. Thesis, Vassar, 1951, reproduced by permission of the authors.

To picture 1, 31 of the 40 children responded with stories directly concerning the stimulus situation (of a playground with slide). Eleven of this total sample spoke of gaiety, while 10 mentioned apprehensiveness.

To picture 2, 38 responded with stories of a schoolroom. We shall return to speak of the two who did not in greater detail. Twenty-five children introduced a teacher into the story (none being present in the picture).

To picture 3, only 23 children plainly referred to playing house, while 17 introduced themes of their own (27 and 28 respectively identified the male and female figures in the picture correctly); recognition of the stimulus increased with age.

To picture 4, 27 responded strictly to the presented stimulus, while 27 introduced or added stimuli of their own.

To picture 5, 30 children responded with characterization of the kangaroo as hurt, while 10 spoke of it as sick.

To 6, 21 children spoke of the race as dangerous, 12 felt happy, and 13 were apprehensive.

In 7, 23 children referred to the mirror manifestly; the 7 year olds of both sexes did so about twice as much as the 6 year olds.

To 8, 21 spoke of the child as sick, and 22 children introduced the mother as a figure.

To 9 more girls spoke of washing and dressing than did boys, and more so at age 7 than at age 6. Thirty-three children, in all, speak of it manifestly as a bathroom scene.

Thus, such data, when based upon large enough numbers, may permit us to deal with a record in terms of how it meets certain norms and will help us identify a deviation (also such a normative scheme may be useful to demonstrate developmental trends).

For instance, if more than half of our sample introduce the mother in picture 8, it would not be reasonable to infer from such an introduction in any individual record that there is a clinically significantly greater dependence upon the mother than in most children of this age. On the other hand, if 38 out of 40 children speak of picture 2 as a schoolroom situation, any child who does not do so merits special attention. Sure enough, the records of our two deviants are very informative. One of them says this:

Three little monkeys were reading very good. Suddenly a fourth one came in. It said, "Oh, they are reading. What dopes they are. They never knew how to fight teachers." The teacher said, "You must not disturb them." They fought and fought with the teacher and she said, "You must go to the cellar and be drowned." They cried and cried. The three little monkeys had finished their books. She said, "You bad, bad children. You must come to be drowned." So she drowned them (the bad ones). The good monkeys finished another book in a minute. Another and another, seconds and minutes, halves of seconds, fourths of seconds. Finally they read all the books in the world and she said, "What wonderful children you are."

Although implicitly this story refers to a school situation, it does not do so explicitly. At any rate, even without norms, a clinician would have considered this story as indicative of special problems of aggression and fear and compliance.

G. Case Illustrations

The following C.A.T.-S. stories were obtained in a normal sampling of school children.*

Case 1: Jim, 6 Years

Story 1: They went up the slide, and the last one doesn't think the one on top is going fast enough so when they get down the next time she is the first one up the slide. Then she goes down the slide and she can't get off, so the others start to come down and they try to push her off. And then they finally get her off and they get up again and go down, and the first gets stuck again. And they try to push and when the last one comes down the first one goes off. And then the first one goes up again and they go down and they go back up. They can't go down the slide because one gets stuck in the middle and one goes at the bottom and tries to push him up and then goes in the back and tries to push him down. And then they finally get him off and then they go around and play a little and then they try to go up the slide and then go down the stairs. (*Why did they get stuck?*) Because there probably was a little paste on the slide.

Story 2: Here looks like one can't figure out what the word is (points to one on right) and the other one is standing up reading and then the one behind him is looking out the window with his pencil in his hands. And then the teacher tells him something else to do. And then it is time to go out for recess, and then they have about a half an hour out in the morning and then they come in and take a little rest and then they do some more work in their workbooks and then they read in their reading books and then they go down for lunch. They have 15 minutes for lunch, I think, and then they have 10 more minutes until it is time to go home. Then it is time to go home and then they get in the buses. The bus skids. (*Then what happens?*) It gets going.

Story 5: (Laughs) Mother kangaroo when she was hopping hurt her foot. And then they had to take her to the hospital and then they give her some crutches and then they (mother and father) get home and then they eat their supper and then they go to bed and then that night they had a baby—the baby was born. Then the next morning they get up and eat. Then the mother goes shopping and then the bear asks her what happened to her foot. And she said when she was hopping she broke her leg. And then the bear goes on and then she meets the wolf, and the wolf buys some more food at the grocery store and then she goes home. When she gets home she feeds the baby. Then she goes over to see her neighbor. And then the doctor calls her on the phone and then tells her she has to go to the hospital again to have an operation. Then she sleeps there overnight. (*Then what happens?*) Then she goes home and goes to bed.

Story 8: Well, the mother rabbit has a little baby rabbit that goes to school in first grade and the baby has to have an operation at the doctor's. Then that day they go to the doctor's and then it is time for them to go back to their home. Then when they get home they eat their lunch and then the doctor gave them some medicine that the baby should take. Then they take the medicine. Then it's time for the baby to go to bed. And she calls the mother because she feels a little sick to her stomach. (*Then what happens?*) Then she throws up and then the doctor thinks that it is okay for the baby to go to school today. And then when the baby gets to school she feels okay and then she does some work. (*Operation?*) On her stomach—that's why she threw up.

In both stories 1 and 2 there is some disturbance of control; in story 1 the child gets stuck on the slide, and in story 2 the bus skids, suggesting considerable anxiety. This is borne out by the peculiarly hurried tempo of all the stories. Stories 5 and 8 suggest concern with pregnancy.

---

* I am indebted to Miss Clara Fear and Dr. L. J. Stone for permission to reproduce the following CAT-S stories.

Case 2: Burton, 6 Years

Story 1: The little foxes are sliding down the sliding board and they're having fun (pause). (*What happens then?*) They went down and up. The mother snugged them nice and warm when they was in the house. (*Anything else?*) They played. (*What?*) Games.

Story 2: They are in school reading and writing and the teacher is teaching the other kids to learn. The kids are good. They are monkeys. They have a blackboard. They are thinking. They are sitting down. They have lots of kids.

Story 3: The mouses are playing doctor and house. They are having fun. They have a doll carriage. They're playing lady and man. They have a pretty home. They are eating. They are playing. They are pretty. They have coffeepots and spoons and plates. They have clothes. They have two blocks and one ball. They have big ears and pretty chairs. They are nice mouses.

Story 9: The father is getting washed to go out for a big hunt with his little boy. They will have fun. The father is scrubbing and scrubbing and scrubbing. He will get nice and clean. And they are going to stay out nice and late and he doesn't want to get too dirty. The little boy is getting his shoes on. He will tighten them very very tight. They are getting their clothes on and then they will go out and hunt and when they get done they will eat. Now the father is getting out of the bathtub to get on his nice shiny clothes. They are going to have a party out there for every kangaroo. They will have their food—their deer and their wolf food and their tiger food. They will have an awful lot of food. The little boy is not afraid because his father is going to be with him. They have an awful long, long trip for they have good feet and do not get tired for a long while. His father likes his little boy and the little boy likes his father because the father helps the little boy. They are healthy. They eat an awful lot of carrots, cabbage, and lettuce and lots of food. He was a very good little boy and his father is a very good little father. The father is cleaning out the bathtub and then they are going for their trip. The little boy sees a little wolf. The father is shooting the wolf. Then they go on hunting. They see a big moose. The father says, "Here, little boy, you can shoot him." The little boy shot and he missed him. The moose started running. The father took the bow away from the little boy and shot the moose, and the father was very proud. And they went on hunting and got all they could. They got a deer, a rat, a mouse, a tiger, and an elephant, and black bear. They had a very good feast. Everyone caught 20 things. The little boy only caught five. It was a little mouse, a little rat, and a little bear, and a little elephant, and a rabbit. And then they had a very good time and then they lived happily ever after.

These stories are typical of the purely descriptive responses of an apparently rather frightened child. The examiner reports that he seemed very timid in the testing situation and was being cooperative because it was the thing to do. Toward the middle of the administration, Burton became interested in the length of his stories in relation to the rest of the group and in relation to his first few stories. After each story he counted the lines, and seemed proud of his achievement.

Case 3: Clark, 7 Years

Story 4: Once upon a time there was a mother and father and little bear—Jim, Fuzzy, and Andrea (mother's name). They lived happily but one day a mean hunter came along. Fortunately there was a big wise elephant. They all liked him and he liked them. He snatched the gun out of the hunter's hand. "You aren't going to be any more trouble to animals so I'm going to put you in a real strong jail with big double bars." The animals learned how to make guns. After they made guns they caught all hunters that came in the jungle. After that people made pets of elephants and were nice to them and fed them in winter, and didn't hurt them. They lived happily ever after. A mean man came in and tried to kill nice people but all the elephants came up and grabbed the guns and hid them four miles down into the ground. They dug for one year. They hid everything they had in tunnels in the rock.

Story 5: Once upon a time a sad kangaroo had a broken leg. He broke it by having a fight with an ostrich. The ostrich was mean and started the fight. Ostrich didn't like anyone on his land and nobody liked him. He was mean to every animal that passed his home. Kangaroo had a hard time walking 'cause he wasn't a human being. One day his leg healed and he decided to get all the animals and have them break the ostrich's leg so he wouldn't break their legs any more. "Ha, ha, shows what happens to you when you cross my house." Ostrich cried when his leg was broken by the others. He saw how mean he'd been. He was a nice ostrich ever after. He knew he should never fight or same thing would happen to him.

The outstanding feature of these stories is this child's concern with aggression and his use of reaction formation against the aggression. In essence, these stories reflect socialization and internalization of the superego.

Case 4: Myra, 10 Years

The following two stories were told by a 10 year old girl who was in psychotherapy for nausea and vomiting apparently related to unconscious pregnancy fantasies. She was also suffering from a great many fears.

Story 5: I can't think of what kind of an animal this is supposed to be. I know the name of it but I can't remember it. Anyway, the animal broke its leg and it was very hard for it to get about. It can't go any place because of the broken leg and it's always left behind. He doesn't mind; he feels that when his leg is better he'll get along just as well as anyone else.

Story 8: The little rabbit is sick. The doctor is examining it. He tells the rabbit he's got the grippe and he has to stay in bed. The rabbit doesn't want to stay in bed; he wants to go out and play and as a result of that he gets very sick and has to stay in bed for a month. As a result of that, he gets a heart condition and has to be very careful and can't run around like all the other rabbits.

In story 5 she tells in essence her own feelings of bodily inadequacy. She responds with a typical defense of denial, minimizing the emotional implications. Her associations, however, showed her real concern when she told of a man she knew who had had his leg cut off (apparently because of gangrene) and of another man who had both legs cut off in an accident.

Story 8 also shows her fear of illness and the phobic limitations she imposes on herself (having to be very careful).

CHAPTER XVII

REVIEW OF LITERATURE RELEVANT TO THE INTERPRETATION OF THE C.A.T.

A. Use of the C.A.T. in Developmental Assessments of Normal Children

NORMATIVE DATA ARE CRUCIAL FOR THE UNDERSTANDING AND interpretation of thematic protocols of children, since the C.A.T. may be administered to children who have obtained any of several developmental levels. Responses can only be judged "normal" or "disturbed" in terms of the outstanding needs, drives, and abilities that are typical of the child's age level. Many of the recent normative studies using the C.A.T. in the personality evaluation of normal children have been concerned with the assessment of ego functions, their development, and their strength as seen in the C.A.T.

Byrd and Witherspoon [86] conducted a 10 year longitudinal study with preschool children aged from 2 years, 8 months, to 6 years, 5 months, at the first testing. The conclusions were that:

1. Responses to the C.A.T. are largely apperceptive in nature. The frequency of nonapperceptive responses decreases with age and is minimal by age 8.

2. Sex differences in the nature of responses, with the possible exception of those at 3 and 4 years, are very small.

3. Judged by frequency and intensity, the dynamics of parental identification, aggression, and orality are best elicited by the C.A.T., whereas responses concerned with fears, sibling rivalry, the oedipal situation, toileting, cleanliness, and sexuality are infrequent.

Moriarty [241] studied normal preschoolers' reactions to the C.A.T.; prominent perceptual responses suggested the following hypotheses. Misperception is related to sex role confusion and/or feelings of maternal deprivation. Habitual omissions reflect distorted mother-child relationships and/or denial and inhibition of aggressive impulses. Staying concrete in the C.A.T. may be an effective avoidance device, or it may represent a generally passive orientation. Finally, adding ideas beyond those typically given to the objective perceptual stimulus is characteristic of children with high potential for imagination and creativity. Moriarty noted that all the children used maneuvers such as denial, repression, avoidance, and projection of hostility in order to cope with the potentially stressful content. The defenses varied in intensity and effectiveness among the children who employed them.

Rosenblatt [281] examined C.A.T. responses of children in the phallic phase (aged 3–6) and in the latency period (aged 6–10) in an effort to test the effectiveness of the C.A.T. in revealing personality dynamics from the psychoanalytic viewpoint. The younger age group indicated less interaction with threatening figures; children in the latency period indicated more cooperative activities between family members and more independence functions.

It has been demonstrated by Nolan [255] that the motives of achievement, affiliation, and power are expressed in young children's responses. There was a statistically significant increase by age 8–10 for achievement and affiliation, and by age 6–10 for the power motive. Sex differences were not found. Interestingly, the stimulus value of certain cards was much greater than that of others. Sixty-five per cent of the achievement responses were to card 2; cards 3, 5, 8, and 9 elicited 72.5 per cent of the affiliation responses.

Finally, Witherspoon [353] has classified C.A.T. protocols into categories on the basis of content. The nine scoring categories then being studied were: schizothymia, emotionality, character-integrity, basic needs, sex role, activity, description, self-reference, and evasion. The protocols studied were of children aged 3–11 years. Responses scored as schizothymia, emotionality, character-integrity, and basic needs were infrequent at all ages. A continuous increasing trend with increasing age was noted in sex role and activity responses, while with greater age there was also less description, self-reference, and evasion.

B. Sample Variables and Sociocultural Studies

Intelligence level and socioeconomic level are two important variables which must be considered in evaluation of thematic protocols. Kaake [184] studied the relationship between intellectual level and maturity of responses among children 6 years, 3 months, and 7 years of age with slow, average, and superior I.Q.'s. The proportions of interpretive and identification responses increased as intelligence increased, while proportions of enumeration and description decreased. Ginsparg [143] also has concluded that children of lower intelligence have limited ability to express their ideas dynamically.

C.A.T. responses of four socioeconomic groups of Canadian kindergarten children were studied by Lehmann [209]; the groups were low intact, low broken home, average, and high. Differences were obtained on five dynamic themes:

1. *Aggression.* No significant differences, but low-broken groups used the fewest aggressive themes.

2. *Fear.* High group had significantly more fear responses than the low-broken group, but total frequency was low for all groups.

3. *Toileting and cleanliness.* High group mentioned toileting the least and cleanliness the most frequently.

4. *Punishment.* Such themes were most frequently given by high and average groups.

5. *Orality.* Oral themes constituted over half the responses. No significant differences were obtained, although the average group showed the most orality.

A number of sociocultural studies include both normative comparisons of responses of children from two different cultures and comparisons of the responses of children from one culture. Rabin [270] tested 5 and 6 year old *Kibbutz* and non-*Kibbutz* children with the C.A.T. Differences in concern with parental figures, as noted in the responses of these children reared in different family settings, were of interest. *Kibbutz* boys and girls both produced more evaluative responses of parents and higher proportions of positive evaluative responses, compared to non-*Kibbutz* children. This finding was related to the relatively lower oedipal intensity and lower ambivalence in the attitude of *Kibbutz* children to parental figures. Booth [74] compared the C.A.T. responses of 9 year old Latin-American (L.A.) and Anglo-American (A.A.) boys. Differences between the groups, as noted from their responses, were as follows: L.A. boys are more dependent and less in conflict with parental authority; they have clearer male identification, which may be related to their view of the father as the more frequent punisher. A.A. boys have less respect for adults, they regard the mother as the more frequent punisher, and they are more goal-directed and striving.

Chowdhury [90] administered the C.A.T. to children in India and found that some city children could handle the environmental details in the pictures, but that other city children could not, as demonstrated by the fact that their responses did not reflect the problem situations indicated in the cards and did not point to identification with the characters. In her revision for the Indian culture, Chowdbury adapted the original C.A.T. by creating new cards that were more appropriate to the social and environmental situations of the Indian culture specific to it, keeping the additions as close as possible to the original. It is suggested that this technique be followed whenever the pictures must be adapted to another culture. (See Chapter XIII.)

Six to thirteen year old children of Rakau, a Maori community in New Zealand, were studied by Earle [104].. She found that they responded to the C.A.T. quite differently, judging by the reported typical responses of Americans, and interpreted the results in terms of aspects of the Maori culture. When results of the C.A.T. studies of the middle years were compared with doll play responses of 5 year olds and with T.A.T. and Rorschach responses of adolescents, high agreement was noted with respect to modal personality patterns in the culture.

C. Diagnostic Studies

Many diagnostic groups have been studied with the C.A.T. with the purpose of determining any differences in thematic responses obtained from such groups, compared with those found with a normal sample. Bennett and Johannsen [65] have studied the effects of diabetes on the child's personality with the C.A.T., and have found that children who had diabetes the longest had more active and more withdrawing fantasy heroes and fewer heroes who were punished. Katzenstein [191] used the C.A.T. in evaluating children with polio and other physical disabilities, and found that the child's reaction to his disability was reflected in his test responses.

The possible relationships between functional speech disorders and emotional problems were studied by Kagan and Kaufman [188]. First-grade children were given the C.A.T., and children with articulation problems were compared with children with normal speech. The articulation group gave a much lower overall mean number of words per story, significantly more oral aggressive responses, and significantly more themes indicating perception of parental hostility directed toward the child. Fitz-Simons [123] also studied children with functional articulation disturbances and obtained similar results with the C.A.T.

C.A.T. studies with mentally retarded and brain-damaged children have led to essentially similar conclusions in regard to the usefulness of the test with samples such as these. Butler [85] gave the C.A.T. to institutionalized mental retardates whose I.Q.'s ranged from 30–77. Butler stated that, compared to normal children, the retardates' responses were most often just descriptive of the card stimuli, contained fewer words per story, and included little expression of feelings or conflicts. The usefulness of thematic techniques with children of such low intelligence is questioned. Boulanger-Balleyguier [76] administered the C.A.T. to retarded children and obtained these results: a large number of omissions, strong perseverative trends for all picture stimuli, characters were neither named nor described when indicated, and few typical responses expected for the child's chronological age were found. Cerebral palsied children have also been studied with the C.A.T. Holden [167] observed that they tended to get overly involved in the enumeration of small details and that their responses were typically closely bound to the stimuli presented. It was concluded that the brain-injured are unable to assume the abstract attitude necessary to tell a story.

DeSousa [103] administered the C.A.T. to a group of emotionally disturbed children characterized as having behavior problems, and found several differences between their responses and those of a well-adjusted group. Maladjusted children more frequently viewed the identification figure as inferior and rejected, more often identified with the character seen as aggressive, viewed the environment as more threatening, and more frequently expressed antagonism to the mother figure. There was also greater occurrence of the following concepts in the stories of maladjusted children: punishment, violence, accidents, aggression, friends, enemies, injustice, deception, stealing, and weapons. Boulanger-Balleyguier [76] compared 6 and 7 year old normal and disturbed children using the C.A.T. The disturbed were subdivided into two groups of children whose most characteristic behavioral reactions were, respectively, aggression and anxiety. Normal children showed better perception of the stimulus in their stories, and had fewer depressing themes. Aggressives gave stories with little imagination, and indicated emotional immaturity, egocentrism, and retarded conscience development. Anxious children used their imagination freely, reflected high anxiety concerning their own identification, and depicted the hero egocentrically as participating in much aggressive activity. Beller and Haeberle [64] studied the C.A.T. responses of emotionally disturbed preschool children. Children high in dependency motivation responded with more dependent fantasies, more themes of direct need gratification, and tended to deny any threatening characteristics of parental figures. Children with high dependency conflict reacted more frequently with fantasies of threat, pain, and punishment to situations that implied dependency, stressed aggressive features of the parents, and did not adequately differentiate between aggressive and dependent stimuli.

Gurevitz and Kapper [148] administered the C.A.T. to schizophrenic children aged 5 to 12 years. The following was the description of the responses obtained: "Hostility and anxiety were predominant in the responses of this group of children; this could be observed in the content of their stories, the nature of their outcomes, the qualities attributed to the characters, and in the interpersonal relationships, particularly those involving child and adult." The stories were frequently bizarre and the responses dramatized.

Children who have experienced parental loss have also been studied with the C.A.T., with the aim of further clarifying the personality dynamics involved. Stevenson [313] compared the responses of 8 and 9 year old orphanage children to those of control subjects. Twice as many orphanage children felt inadequate; they manifested less aggression, due to repression rather than to lack of hostile feelings. Guilt, especially for aggression, was highest for orphanage children; sex typing was not as clearly defined for orphanage children; and orphanage children showed more intense fears. Haworth [157] tested children between the ages of 6–14, who had lost one or both parents before age 6, with the Rorschach, the T.A.T., and the C.A.T. These children responded much more frequently than a group of control children with themes of damage, contrasts, separations, successive attacks, and death. The themes used most often by the loss group indicated the depressive aspects of the fantasies of these children, and suggested an unusual amount of concern with matters of hostility, ambivalence, sexuality, origins, and death. The degree of deviation from typical responses for children in the loss group varied, depending on factors such as whether one or both parents had been lost, sex of the child, and sex of the parent lost.

Zimmerman, et al., in the study of sex differences in childrens' perceptions of their parents as inferred from the C.A.T. and Rorschach, present responses of two hundred "normal" six year old caucasian boys and girls to the Rorschach cards frequently considered to evoke parental images (cards 3 and 4) and compared these with responses to C.A.T. cards (1, 2, 5, 6 and 9) which clinical judgement suggests are likely to elicit specific themes or support or nurturance from parental figures. Responses were scored for parent mentioned as negative, positive, or not identified, and scores on the C.A.T. and Rorschach were combined for each parent to produce an overall score for each, designated as negative (nonsupportive), positive (supportive), or both (ambivalent).

When responses given to the C.A.T. and Rorschach were summed, to check on the consistency of perception from one measure to another, both parents were seen positively or negatively to a similar extent: fathers 27% positive, 22% negative, mothers 31% positive, 24% negative. Examined for differences attributable to sex, both boys and girls perceived the father similarly. However, the perception of the mother figure differed between boys and girls, with 43% of the girls reporting a positive figure, vs. only 20% of the boys.

From a psychoanalytic viewpoint, at this age level, boys could be seen as rejecting the mother, as a resolution of the Oedipal strivings, while girls turn back to the mother as an identification figure. "More pragmatically, Maccoby and Jaclin (1974) in their review of sex differences note that boys are punished more frequently and harshly than girls, while girls are given more maternal affection. Perhaps this helps explain why girls respond more favorably to the maternal figure."

D. Bases for Interpretations

Haworth [160] has noted three major bases for interpretations made from C.A.T. data:

1. *Recurrent themes.*

2. *Sequence analysis.* Haworth [155], for example, has found a sequential pattern from card 6 to card 9. Neither card portrays aggression (both suggest sleep), but she obtained the following results in studying a group of neurotic and control children. Neurotics all told attack stories to both cards, with stories to card 6 generally indicating fears that an attack was imminent, while all stories to card 9 described an actual attack occurring. For control children, an attack theme was rarely given to card 6, and any fantasy attacks given for Card 9 did not actually take place. Examination of stories to these two cards is suggested as a possible indicator of phobic or panic reactions.

3. *Use of case history information.* It is advisable to be aware of the child's home situation and any recent or impending crisis events before one undertakes interpretation of the C.A.T., since such information can frequently alter the meanings attributed to test responses.

Assessment of Identification Patterns

The assessment of identification from child-parent situations depicted in C.A.T. themes requires more than naming of the parent figure. Haworth [160] has stated that other factors to be considered are: sex of the child in relation to sex of the parent, the role function portrayed in the specific situation, the affects by which each figure in the card is characterized, and the sex ascribed by the child to child characters in the stories. This last method is probably better for assessing identification patterns of boys as compared to girls, due to the cultural stereotype of characterizing figures whose sex is ambiguous as masculine. King and King [196] also question the validity of feminine identification on verbal tests such as the C.A.T. since girls' responses would be more likely to contain more cross-sex identifications than boys' stories on the basis of cultural and linguistic factors. Haworth [160] states that, in regard to child characters, the main significance is in the attribution of feminine characteristics, with opposite-sex identification indicated when given by a boy and same-sex identification when supplied by a girl.

Because of the tendency to see child figures as males, and because of the child's limited abstracting abilities, it is suggested that expressed attitudes and activities of parent figures be interpreted in relation to the actual sex of the child instead of in relation to the sex attributed to the child figure.

Overt versus Fantasy Behavior

Lindzey [218] proposed that thematic content which can be directly connected to elements in the presented stimulus is less likely to be significant in interpretation than that which has been added or is only indirectly related to the stimulus. This statement implies that thematic material not closely tied to the stimulus is more likely to be relevant to overt behavior.

Kagan [185] investigated the problem of manifest versus latent levels of fantasy, and presented groups of aggressive and nonaggressive boys with pictures ambiguous for aggression and pictures which implied aggressive actions. Ambiguous pictures did not differentiate between groups, whereas aggressive children responded to aggressive stimuli with significantly more aggressive stories. It would seem that aggressive boys had less anxiety about telling aggressive stories to aggressive stimuli.

Lesser [210] presented children with aggressive and nonaggressive pictures. It was found that, for boys whose mothers encouraged aggression, there was a positive correlation between overt and fantasy aggression; for those whose mothers discouraged aggression the correlation was negative.

It has been concluded (Kagan, [187]) from these findings and others that, in predicting overt aggression in children, the following should be attended to: fantasy content that indicates anxiety over aggression, and distortions and sudden changes in fantasy responses to stimuli that suggest aggressive behavior. Kagan [187] believes that these statements about aggression are relevant to other areas of conflict.

Kenny [192] has suggested that the C.A.T. is best used now as a source of hypotheses to be checked against other clinical procedures. More information is needed about how much the thematic content reflects the conditions immediately preceding the testing, the atmosphere of the test administration itself, and the thematic stimuli. Once this has been obtained, those aspects of the story content which actually reflect the underlying structure of the child will be susceptible to clearer delineation.

E. Interpretive Outlines

There are two interpretive outlines that are relevant to the C.A.T. They are Bellak's T.A.T. and C.A.T. Blank (Short Form), which was outlined in Chapter XII, and Haworth's "A Schedule of Adaptive Mechanisms in C.A.T. Responses" (Fig. 8, Chapter XIV).

The Schedule of Adaptive Mechanisms was developed by Haworth [156, 159] mainly for the purpose of delineating defense mechanisms and assessing identification patterns, as manifested in C.A.T. themes. The schedule basically provides a foundation for qualitative evaluation of the stories, and secondarily affords a way of obtaining rough quantitative scores which can be used for comparisons between children and groups.

Haworth [160] describes the schedule in this way:

> The schedule provides a quick summary of the number and kinds of defenses employed as well as the content of items frequently used. The categories are arranged as nearly as possible on a continuum from measures indicating a high degree of control and constriction to indicators of disorganization and loosening of reality ties. In individual qualitative assessment, the total number of responses within a category and their distribution among the various subitems provide a meaningful summary picture when making personality evaluations. However, for research purposes, the quantitative measure used consists of the number of categories "receiving critical scores.' The latter are determined by comparing the number of responses checked under each category with a pre-established cut-off point for that category. If the number of responses exceeds the cut-off point, a "critical score' is assigned to that category.

It is suggested that five or more critical scores indicate some degree of emotional disturbance; 8–10 such scores imply that the child uses various defenses in attempts to control his anxiety, but that these defenses are not working successfully.

CHAPTER XVIII

THE S.A.T.*

THE SENIOR APPERCEPTION TECHNIQUE (S.A.T.) IS AN EXTENsion of the T.A.T. designed to elucidate the problems of elderly individuals. At present, 10 per cent of the population, 20 million Americans, are over 65 years old, and their number will grow steadily. Our society has been no better prepared for the population explosion of the aged than it has been for the ecological effects of population growth, the development of atomic power, or for any of the other changes in geometric proportions so typical of our era.

The problems of the aged are therefore plentiful, as described, for instance, by Sloate [308], in comprehensive reviews published by the American Psychiatric Association [84], in a volume with sociological as well as psychological implications by Geist [139], and in a practical handbook about aging by Bellak [42a].

A. Nature and Purpose of the Technique

The concerns of the aged frequently are thought to be centered around loneliness, uselessness, illness, helplessness, and lowered self-esteem. Many of the infirmities associated with old age may be alleviated or eliminated by advances in medicine, and many of the social, economic, and psychological problems of the aged are consequences of social policies that could be altered. Aging is treated differently in other cultures.

In providing apperceptive stimuli to reflect the problems of old age, we could not be utopian. We had to design pictures which, though ambiguous enough to give individual leeway, were likely to reflect such situations and problems as exist for the aged to be useful now.

While this means that we provide stimuli which permit ascription of themes of loneliness, illness, and other vicissitudes, we also provide pictures which lend themselves to the reflection of happy sentiments such as joy in grandchildren, pleasures of a social dance, and social interaction game playing [10, 42a], and five pictures which are ambiguous enough to lend themselves either to happy themes or some reflection of difficulties [5, 16, 32, 40, 63]. A family setting, a scene in a center for the aged, fall into this group.

---

* L. Bellak, M.D. and S. S. Bellak, C.P.S., Inc., P.O. Box 83, Larchmont, New York 10538, 1973.

Compared with the T.A.T. and the C.A.T., we see the use of the S.A.T. as both broader and narrower. We see its applicability *broader* than the other two as we believe that certain relatively superficial problems revealed through the S.A.T. may be useful to professionals such as physicians, social workers, and nurses, not specifically trained in clinical psychology.

The stories told in response to the S.A.T. are often a good concrete guide to manifest concerns about getting along with peers and juniors, about health, or entering a home for the aged. More often than young adults, and more than some young children, the aged give relatively concrete stories with a great deal of self-reference, thus lending themselves to that level of inference. In *that* sense, utilization of the S.A.T. is narrower than the use of the T.A.T. and C.A.T. for insight into general personality dynamics.

This view is, for instance, in accordance with that of Pfeiffer and Busse (p. 124); "The psychological disturbances which occur commonly in old age tend to be rather simple direct reactions to stressful circumstances, making use of relatively simple, even primitive psychological defense mechanisms. Thus, the defenses seen most prominently in this age group are withdrawal, denial, projection, and somatization; all of them mechanisms for dealing with anxiety that become available early in life. Sometimes not even these simple mechanisms are used by older persons, and the anxiety evoked by adverse circumstances is experienced in totally unmodified form. It is the use of these relatively simple defenses, or no defenses, which shapes the clinical manifestations of psychiatric disorders in old age, and which dictates modifications in diagnostic and therapeutic technique. These modifications . . . seek to take into account the special needs, limitations, and circumstances of older persons" [84].

At the same time, of course, many stories are amenable to the type of sophisticated interpretation of unconscious drive representation, conflicts, anxieties and ego functioning for which the T.A.T. and C.A.T. are useful.

The aims of the S.A.T. are modest to the same extent that they are also specific. In most instances, it does not need a great deal of clinical acumen, and surely no test, to discover that an aged person suffers from depression, from loneliness or rage. What the S.A.T. may be able to add in information are the specific forms which these general states may take or be caused by in a given individual. Is the aged woman depressed because she specifically feels deserted by her oldest daughter, rather than because she feels let down by the other daughter, or the son? Or is she depressed because she is acutely aware of some loss of her faculties, or because of injury to her pride over the loss of her desirability as a sexual object? And what defenses and other drives does her story suggest? Often the stories reflect problems the patient cannot verbalize directly.

One may not be able to do anything about the chronological facts of age or the disease processes responsible for what is often wrongly considered aging, or about some of the current social burdens imposed on the elderly. There is something that can be done about the specific meaning of various emotional states if one understands the specific set of circumstances which precedes or precipitates them.

In this respect, the afflictions of old age do not represent different therapeutic problems from those conditions at any other age which have a more or less precipitating factor. Long ago, it was noted that heart disease [34] or tuberculosis [24] had specific meanings for those afflicted, as did other illnesses [24]. As suggested particularly in the volume on emergency and brief psychotherapy [63], it is essential that the unique and specific causes and precipitating factors of panic, depression, and others to be understood and dynamically formulated before intervention takes place. *Brief, limited intervention is often all that is needed, as* Berezin [66] and Goldfarb [16] also point out.

Again, following the general principles of psychotherapy, it is important to understand and place in sequence a current chief complaint in terms of the preexisting personality. People react differently to fire, rape, the loss of a person dear to one, retirement, removal—and so they do to aging. Very often a person who had a great deal of body narcissism and vanity in earlier life will react with excessive narcissistic injury to aging. A man whose main defense against anxiety and depression lay in his pride of masculine prowess will suffer more from infirmity than another man.

To the extent, then, to which life history and S.A.T. data give a general picture of personality structure and dynamics, they furnish the specific data concerning the acute upset; it can be seen in perspective of the larger picture. In this way also the S.A.T. can be used for effective therapeutic intervention and/or restructuring of the situation.

The history of dynamic psychotherapy, even for the dying, is fairly old. Sigmund Freud treated a Hungarian baron during his terminal illness so successfully that the grateful patient, Anton von Freund, endowed what was to become the International Psychoanalytic Publishing Company.

One can only hope that the S.A.T. will be used by psychologists, physicians, psychiatrists, rehabilitation workers, nurses, therapists, and other professionals concerned with the care of the aged. It is designed to help them reduce for the aged the irrational overlay of unrelenting facts of their existence in order to make their lives, as well as the lives of those concerned with them, more comfortable and bearable.

Construction of the Senior Apperception Technique

We had to start with some working notions concerning those themes we wanted to highlight. Aside from personal clinical experience, themes discussed in the gerontological literature appeared to be relevant [96, 105, 140, 141, 174].

We set out to design pictures which were likely to pull themes we had learned are of significance for the aged as seen in private practice, clinics, and other settings. Sonya Sorel Bellak drew a successive series of 44 pictures which were photocopied and administered to a stratified sampling of the aged—some working, some retired, some institutionalized, some living at home, etc.

In the course of story collecting (almost all were taped), it became obvious that some of the pictures rarely elicited good stories while others stimulated stories very limited in variety. Out of 44 pictures, we rejected or modified 30 to arrive at the current set of 16.

By clinical inspection, some pictures failed to have a pull due to insufficient ambiguity as well as lack of interest in the particular theme. To the latter belonged, surprisingly, the picture of a mourning family behind a casket in a funeral home. The lack of rich stories in response to this picture may be consistent with the widespread clinical impression that the elderly tend to feel very matter-of-fact about death, or simply avoid concern with it.

In other instances, pictures were redrawn or dropped because they failed to produce expected results. We thought that the problem of motor control and its loss would be an outstanding concern of the aged. We presented the picture of an elderly person dropping one of two crutches, expecting to elicit such themes, but found little response; the stories showed no specific attempt to deal with loss, or fear of loss of control and generally did not rouse much interest in terms of length of stories or liveliness of themes.

We attempted to approach this problem with a different picture—an elderly person stands at the curb while a young boy runs across a street filled with trucks and cars. A situation frequent in urban settings, we thought, would lead to generalized reflections on loss of speed and agility and the resulting dangers for the elderly. It also seemed likely that stories noting the ease with which the youth could cross the street, in contrast to the difficulties facing the old person, would result in various individual features: anger, self-pity, adaptation, fear of injury, withdrawal, and envy of the young. However, even when the picture was twice re-drawn to emphasize the problem, most responses simply dealt with the boy and did not mention the street-crossing problem at all. Even after removing the boy, no stories concerned with the traffic problem materialized, so we dropped the picture from the series.

Another picture showing the check-out counter of a supermarket was meant to produce responses about economic concerns (thought to be such a common problem of the aged), and possibly to reflect individual and even irrational anxieties above and beyond the ordinary concerns. It, too, was not productive and was dropped.

We decided to have most figures ambiguous for sex. We designed the cards in a slightly larger format than the C.A.T. or T.A.T. pictures, as poor eyesight is a frequent problem of the aged.

The mood of the pictures was a special problem. These stimuli are designed to elicit possible psychological problems. By that definition, they cannot be expected to be pictures of gaiety, just as the T.A.T., and to a certain extent the C.A.T., are not cheerful. Some attempt was made to keep them from being too depressing or wholly gloomy in order not to discourage the subjects more than may be unavoidable for this sort of task.

A good deal of thought was given to attempts to make the settings suitable for various socio-economic, ethnic, and personal life situations.

Anyone who has had dealings with the elderly at all will have experienced the fact that an eighty-year-old is likely to speak of another eighty-year-old as "that old man" or "that old woman"; a certain degree of denial of one's own age seems very common. From that standpoint, some resistance to relating to clearly aged figures in the pictures seemed almost unavoidable. (One is reminded of the Thompson modification of the T.A.T. for Blacks which, at the time it was published, was found less acceptable to blacks than the regular T.A.T.)

B. Administration

The S.A.T. is a technique that lends itself to many different uses. Therefore the qualifications of people administering this technique (as well as interpreting it) depends on the use to which it is put. If a general practitioner of medicine or a social worker without specific psychiatric or psychological training merely wishes to enlarge his ordinary questioning by getting some responses to these pictures as additional information virtually on the conscious level, no further qualifications for administration or interpretation are indicated; that is, none with regard to administration beyond ordinary clinical prudence in showing the pictures with tact and with the words recommended here.

In administering the S.A.T., the general principles of establishing psychological rapport and a general working alliance must be kept in mind. In addition, some factors which might be specific for the age group over 65 also have to be remembered.

Among the general factors are that the patient be comfortably seated, that a friendly atmosphere be established, and that some ordinary human interest be exhibited. This should under no circumstances involve a condescending attitude, such as referring to them as "Pop" or "Grandma". Elderly patients may claim to be too tired, not to be alert enough, or not able to see well (which may be true; on the other hand this may often turn out to be wrong; occasionally it may be found that small objects were seen quite well while large objects were not seen at all).

Elderly people, indeed often have a limited attention span or tend to be concrete more readily than younger adults. They lack distance to the picture. They are likely to refer the content to themselves. "Leaving stimulus" is also more frequent in this age group and attempts to lead them back to the stimulus picture may have to be made gently while keeping a record of their spontaneous productions. An interruption of the story-telling with a drink of water for the subject may be necessary or appropriate.

As with the C.A.T. and the T.A.T., after presentation of the pictures has been completed, one may go back and ask specific questions on some aspects of the responses.

Instructions

A. Each interview should last at most half an hour, depending upon the responsiveness of the subject and how easily he or she tires. Allow no more than five minutes per picture unless you are getting a lot of rejections; in that case, allow more time to pictures with which the subject is willing to deal. If there is no response to a given picture, say "Maybe we will come back to this one."

B. Keep the microphone out of reach of the subject, using the mike stand. (If you tape the stories, it must be with the patient's permission.)

C. While the S.A.T. consists of 16 pictures, there is no need to administer all of them, especially if the subject is likely to be easily fatigued or to have a brief attention span. One may choose those pictures which, judging from the clinical data, are most likely to illuminate the problems at hand.

If this is done, it is still useful to select the pictures in such a way as to administer them within the order in which they are arranged (e.g. #5, 7, 8, 9), and clearly record which pictures were used. If the subject is not fatigued at the end of this series and there is some use for further information, then more pictures can be shown.

Most of the pictures of the S.A.T. are left ambiguous with regard to sex. However, even the two clearly identified as females and the one as a male could be given to the opposite sex. While the obvious identification may not be as clear for the like-sexed figures as for the ambiguous figures, the subject may be all the readier to reflect on some deeper lying problem. This tendency to ascribe problems to other than immediate identification figures has been spoken of by Murray as object needs, i.e. needs (of the subject) ascribed to other objects. It has been suggested that such needs or problems are often of the kind especially unacceptable to the subject and therefore rather removed one step; that is, permitted to be expressed because they seem removed from him or her by obvious identification.

This point is relevant for *Picture 16,* for which there are *special instructions.* When this last picture is presented, the test administrator should say: *"Here is the picture of a sleeping person having a dream.* Tell me in some detail what the dream might be about—make it a lively dream." This picture, though of a woman, should also elicit very useful information from men, possibly even somewhat less guarded material.

D. Keep all pictures face down both before and after showing. Keep the pictures out of reach of the subject until ready to show the next one. Hand each picture to the subject for viewing. If necessary, place the next picture over the one being viewed, gently remove the previous picture and place it down on the side.

C. Description of, and Typical Responses to Pictures

As noted earlier, the pictures were designed to reflect thoughts and feelings of the elderly. We start with a rather bland picture, follow with one relating to a concrete problem of economic nature because its very concreteness, like the blandness of the first one, should ease the subject into the task. Number three is one of the pictures often seen as an outright pleasant one; while there is obviously reason why we arranged the pictures in the way that we did, each administrator will have to use his own judgment, in varying administrations, by starting, for instance, with the happy number three and possibly following with the happy scene in number 15 to encourage an unhappy person.

Below we present typical themes seen as responses to the various pictures (Fig. 1).

Picture 1

Three elderly figures in discussion. The middle one is frequently seen as a male. This picture was chosen as the first shown because it is innocuous and some kind of social relations can be easily related to it.

FIG. 10. Pictures for use with the S.A.T.

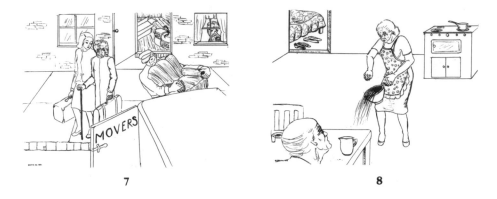

7   8

9

10   11

FIG. 10. (cont.)

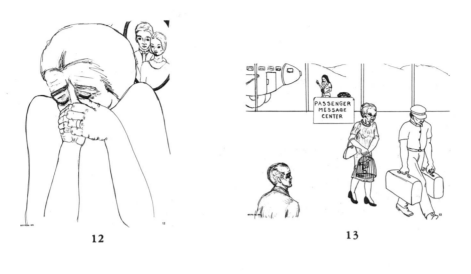

12   13

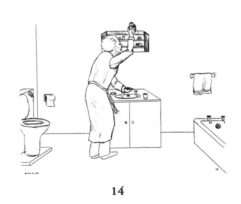

14

15   16

FIG. 10. (cont.)

Themes elicited often revolve around social interaction—two women competing for the man's attention, arguments, or references to social arrangements. They often show clearly how the subject relates to her peers, whether she is actively involved, somewhat withdrawn, critical, bides her time, whatever. There have also been introduced themes of sex, adultery, and rivalry—rivalry between older people for son or daughter, or of a mother in relation to the daughter where men were concerned.

Doctors are introduced. There are also themes of two of the figures giving advice to the third who may be in trouble or ill.

Picture 2

An elderly couple looking through a store window containing a display of food, with the prices conspicuously marked.

This picture especially elicits concerns of a financial nature and oral themes, as well as reflections on the relationship between the two figures.

Picture 3

An elderly woman on the right and an elderly man on the left, both with their hands stretched out towards the figure, presumably of a child, in the middle.

Aside from the expected pleasure of the grandparents, this scene elicits competitiveness for the attentions of the child. We get hostility between the elderly people, and veiled hostility toward the grandchild and the parents of the child. Stories of being visited or of visiting, and their attendant themes also emerge.

Picture 4

At the right foreground, an elderly woman; on the left a somewhat nondescript figure holding a small child; a teenager sprawled on the floor using the telephone with a display of miniskirt and thighs, and the partially visible figure of a presumably middle-aged woman at the kitchen range; in the background, a table with chairs.

Themes elicited are those of family relations, possibly competitive ones toward grandchildren, attitudes toward adolescents and sex, living and/or visiting in the home of the family presumably.

The elderly woman at the right is identified with the male on the left (the young male) as her spouse; occasionally he is seen as the son, and the baby thus becomes the grandchild. There is a confusion of identity, the male seen as grandfather as well as father.

The figure in the background has been made into a servant by some. By others she is seen as the mother of the teenager and the baby, and thus the young man's wife, too busy to participate in the family activities because she is providing the evening meal. There has been evidence of rivalry between the elderly female and this younger women in disguised form, mainly when the young man is seen as the spouse of the older female rather than as her son. The wish to take the younger woman's place becomes very clear again and again in the misinterpretation of the male figure who is obviously young compared with the woman in the foreground. It is the only consistent way in which rivalry for a son's favors emerges.

The teenager is often patronizingly referred to as "a teenager on the phone— of course, aren't they all?" She is occasionally referred to as being "spread out". Indirect allusion to the sexuality implied in the drawing emerges.

Picture 5

Eight figures, grouped and individual, in a setting that could be a comfortable home for the aged or a private home. A large picture window; a small old lady looking out of it with her back to the room; four card players in the foreground; two ladies on the right gossiping; a man on the left reading a newspaper.

This picture lends itself to elucidation of social feelings and needs, in an institutional setting especially. The old lady in the background is pictured as a great-grandmother, and the bridge foursome as perhaps cronies either enjoying their game or in keen competition. Grandfather, the figure on the left, is often spoken of either as relaxed or disengaged, and the "two gossips on the right" are talking about members of their family or what they disapprove of in their neighbors' lives. It is described as a big party or a gathering in an institutional social room.

The two ladies on the right are seen as envious of the females in the foreground because they have a man with them. The woman looking out of the window has been seen as not caring about cards or gossip; she is watching the road, perhaps waiting for someone to visit her.

Picture 6

An elderly woman staring at the telephone.

Reactions to this picture deal mainly with loneliness, neglect, distress. It also brings out themes of anxiety—waiting for a phone call that may or may not come, or that will bring bad news. Feelings of neglect, feelings of anger at family mistreatment of the subject, and contemplation by the subject of making a phone call to air her complaint.

Another theme is that of a woman waiting for her husband to come home, an overdue husband. There are stories in which the subject wonders why she is neglected; she has done her best and will do her best to try not to make demands.

Picture 7

A moving van. A mover carries an armchair while an elderly woman and a younger woman carry hand luggage.

This scene is likely to bring out themes rather typical for aged people, either leaving a home of their own to join someone else's, or going to an institution. Though the two female figures are facing away from the house, there are occasional stories of moving in rather than out, frequently defensive in nature.

The old figure is ambiguous and is seen just as often as an old man as an old woman. We have a daughter taking the parent to live with her, or to an institution or other living situation, or to a hospital. The young woman is seen as benign more often than not.

The figure in the window is often described as a nosy neighbor, sometimes as the spouse of the elderly figure in the street. When seen as a spouse, he or she is left behind and does not know, the stories go, whether she will remain there, join her husband, or go elsewhere, to live in a home or with another child. Almost invariably there is grief about breaking up the home; the armchair is sometimes seen as a prized possession, going with them or, less happily, being given away. All regret leaving the home, or wish they did not have to go.

Some subjects actually make the pair on the sidewalk a contemporary couple. Even in otherwise intact protocols, they are sometimes perceived as a young married couple.

Sometimes it is the figure in the window who is moving and is watching her belongings being removed. The elderly person on the sidewalk has been seen as helping with the young woman's moving. Some subjects turn the picture into something relatively innocuous such as the elderly person going on a trip with the daughter. Peeping Tommery was introduced.

There is fear of the furniture being mishandled or stolen. Attitudes by women in relation to men's ineptitude appear in this context.

Varying degrees in attitudes emerge about being moved into an old age home—from attempts to be understanding and to take it gracefully, to rage at being "shoved off" because children do not want parents to be a burden. Younger people are seen as not really interested in the elderly while the older people are interested only in them. Old age is seen as not being needed any more and being disposed of, however kindly.

This picture elicits or engenders more confusion in otherwise fairly intact protocols than do any of the others.

Picture 8

A woman carrying a deep bowl and dropping it on her way to the table at which an elderly man is seated. Through a doorway, two pairs of slippers are seen next to a bed.

This picture lends itself to surfacing of feelings about loss of bodily control and attitudes toward that phenomenon, towards one's own body, and to aging in that context.

In some people it brings out aggression, remarks that the spilled matter is scalding hot and spills all over, or that the person at the table will not (or refuses to) help.

Picture 9

An elderly couple seated at opposite corners of a bench, facing a young couple in embrace.

This picture is likely to lend itself to feelings of companionship and sex among the aged, as well as to sentiments about the younger generation.

Among the most common responses are: nostalgia, estrangement, wish for companionship, envy, disapproval. There emerge clear indications of coping mechanisms and reality testing.

Picture 10

A lone figure is in bed in a sparsely furnished room with a spoon, glass, a clock and bottle on the night chest beside him.

This picture suggests stories of loneliness, illness, feelings of isolation and poverty. Suicidal thoughts might be elicited by the medicine.

We heard occasional stories in which merely the facts were related: someone who is ill will take his medicine, get a good night's rest, and recover; a woman is crying or merely being awakened too early by the staff and would like to sleep longer; a poor old man is waiting for the time when he can take his medicine; he is trying to stay awake, he looks pretty sick, even the doctor cannot tell if he will die.

Hangover is another suggested theme.

Picture 11

A man with the "Help Wanted" section of the newspaper in his hands. From his window a man getting into a car and a young couple carrying ice skates can be seen.

This picture is likely to elicit themes concerned with envy of those better off, and themes about the young. We have mainly stories indicating envy both of the youths and of the man getting into his own auto while he himself has to look for a job and cannot enjoy himself. Feelings of depression emerge and hopelessness is mentioned in connection with the job-hunting. The cozy cat is noticed, as well as the other objects.

Picture 12

A grieving woman, head held in her hands, a wedding band visible on her finger. The picture over her left shoulder shows a younger couple, which may lead to reverie about her own life in younger days with husband and mate, or bring out stories relating to children.

Themes revolve around grief over death, illness, bad news, a runaway or philandering husband, problems with children. Grief is attributed to an overwhelming feeling of helplessness; to loss of a pocketbook with all her money; bereavement; fear of the future. A mother's grief for her children emerges stronger than that for her husband.

Picture 13

An airport scene showing an elderly woman carrying a bird in a cage and a porter carrying hand luggage. A man is off to the left.

This picture lends itself to many interpretations: themes of leaving someplace or joining someone, or going on a trip (less likely because of the bird). Display of the passenger message center lends itself to feelings of disappointment at not being met and to feelings of being lost.

Stories range from an innocuous lady who has been away and returning home; an old man who is also coming home; to taking a trip to visit a child; carrying candy for someone; going to visit some member of the family because of being unhappy alone; leaving home possibly after a fight with her husband. There are stories of jealousy and separation, and remarks about a busy, busy world in which no one is concerned with anyone but themselves. Feelings of anxiety over reception at destination were expressed.

Picture 14

A bathroom scene showing a person getting a medicine bottle from the top of the chest.

This frequently produces a measure of shock, and then elicits stories mainly concerned with physical ailments, medicine, hypochondriacal thoughts, or suicidal thoughts. Most references are fairly innocuous: mention of indigestion, sleeping tablets to help through the night, constipation, cleaning the bathroom. A number of protocols produced references, both overt and covert, to suicide and to alcoholism or secret tippling. There are also frequent references to being old and of trying to manage as best one can.

Picture 15

A relief from the previous pictures. An older man dancing with a younger woman and an older woman with a younger man; two older figures are off in the corners.

This lends itself to a variety of themes—the relations between the generations on a social and sexual level; sexual feelings of elderly people toward much younger men and women; competitiveness, impotence, jealousy, resentment, anger and disapproval. We had also benign stories of young people dancing with older ones, pleased to be making the old people happy, as perhaps at a family function. It frequently illuminates the intactness or failure of reality testing.

Picture 16

The figure of a woman reclining and sleeping.

For this picture we have specific instructions: "This is a person having a dream. I would like you to tell me what the dream is about in as much detail as possible and as lively as possible."

People who have had difficulty in relating specific content before may be able to do it with these specific instructions and be somewhat less guarded in reporting a dream.

No examples are given here because of the broad range of material that is elicited.

D. Interpretation

As mentioned earlier, we prefer to think of the S.A.T. as a technique rather than as a "test". It is only a slight variation on the clinical technique of asking people to tell us what ails them. It does not make more claims than to facilitate the process of communicating one's feelings and thoughts by responding to standard stimuli rather than to standard clinical questions.

If inferences are to be made about the preconscious and unconscious implications of the test responses, this should be done only by fully qualified clinical psychologists and psychiatrists trained in and acquainted with the uses of projective techniques.

Interpretation of the S.A.T. can be done by the identical technique which Bellak described for the C.A.T. and the T.A.T. [41].

E. Data Concerning the Senior Apperception Technique

By tradition, the S.A.T. falls into the class of projective techniques: a stimulus is presented to a subject whose responses in the form of stories, words and behavior are scrutinized for whatever they may reveal about that subject.

In 1950 Bellak introduced the study of the defenses in projective techniques [25] and enlarged on the application of ego psychology to them in a paper in 1954 [32] and further extended the concept in his volume on the T.A.T. and C.A.T. [41].

"Cognitive style" is the term now generally used to comprise the totality of responses, somewhat anticipated in the above references. To the extent that we study each person as an individual, idiosyncratic ideographic ways of dealing with a particular stimulus situation affect the process we are studying. For this reason, Herman Rorschach's term for his ink blot inquiry was a "Versuch", an experiment, and it is still by far the best term and much to be preferred to "test", with its normative connotations in American psychology. For this reason, the title Senior Apperception *Technique* is preferable to Senior Apperception Test.

This is true for the T.A.T. and C.A.T. also. In responses to these picture stimuli, we are dealing with the unique Gestalt of thought processes, of structure as well as content.

To the extent to which inferences about a person are made from comparisons of one person's responses to a group of other people's responses, certain norms are indicated and useful. The American Psychological Association publication on test standards goes into a great deal of detail on these points [10].

What are the basic data that should be available for a technique such as the S.A.T.?

1. Some assurances that people will indeed tell stories of some length and meaningful content. In the present cases, it means that the pictures should elicit stories that reveal something about the personalities and problems of people in the target population of above 65 years of age.

By our procedure, starting experimentally with a large number of pictures and finding some of them useless, we did something akin to proving the null hypothesis: some pictures (28 out of 44) had to be dropped because the stories were short, banal, or not reflective of the problem we wanted illuminated.

2. The length of stories related to the picture themselves seems highly correlated to the Ambiguity Index, according to Prola [268] and therefore it is a measure of the usefulness of a picture by this generally accepted criterion.

3. An account of themes and a study of the frequency of themes is a further way of meeting this need; another is face validity by consistency with—and by internally consistent amplification of clinical information; even though face validity is not highly thought of in tests of skill and intelligence, the internal consistency with sets of dynamic data and reality obtained from interview and history give it greater value here.

4. There should be enough of a general idea about "popular" themes, that is, themes frequently elicited by the stimuli. On the one hand this justifies and provides the basis for selection of certain pictures generally, and selection of some of them for some people specifically. Also, the establishment of some popular themes should make it possible to make some tentative inferences when individual responses deviate significantly from the expected norm.

No statistically sophisticated claims for validity and reliability are being made for this Technique except for the fact that the pictures represent situations frequently met in everyday life and are therefore likely to elicit typical responses, feelings, and thoughts about such situations.

The present information on the S.A.T. is predicated on responses from a hundred people (not counting previously discarded ones), the four pilot studies discussed below, and clinical data since obtained. There were 46 males and 54 females between the ages of 65 and 84 years of age. We tried to have some socio-economic cross-section. It is doubtful that we succeeded in drawing equally from all of the classes, for instance, of the Hollingshead Index. We did administer the S.A.T. in a variety of settings (see Acknowledgments).

Among the stories from these hundred people, the average length in terms of word count was 112, with the mean 138 and the mode of 280. The average length of time for administration of ten pictures ranged from 20 to 30 minutes.

As a further generalization, it can be said that the aged seem to tell more concrete stories than either children in response to the C.A.T. or adults of 18 to 65 years to the T.A.T. This observation is by no means established beyond mere clinical impressions, but is consistent with a widely held assumption that there is a tendency toward constriction of the field of interest among many aged people.

F. Four Pilot Studies Based on the S.A.T.*

The thesis by Nancy Altobello [9] studies hope and despair by utilizing the S.A.T. It produced interesting results contradicting Neugarten's (1968) hypothe-

* We would like to express our appreciation to Dr. Bernard Landis, Associate Professor at the State University of New York College at Purchase for his counsel and for supervision of these studies which are on file at the library, S.U.N.Y. College at Purchase.

ses of disengagement and supporting her later study (1972) that elderly persons, if given a relatively supporting social environment, will choose personal involvement.

The "disengagement theory", originally stated by Cummings and Henry [96], was investigated and later propounded by Neugarten. She originally proposed that elderly persons experience a decrease in emotional involvement during the aging process and therefore withdraw from those activities which once characterized their lives; these disengaged persons, she hypothesized, maintained a sense of psychological well-being and of life satisfaction. In a later study, however, Neugarten found that those aged persons who were socially active and involved, rather than the uninvolved, retained a high degree of life satisfaction [254].

Altobello set out not only to test hypotheses that elderly people convey more experience of despair, death, and a feeling of struggling than a control group of students, but also to explore whether the disengagement theory held. She attempted to estimate involvement by word count, made estimates of degree of involvement, and compared the kinds of hope and despair experienced by the elderly as compared with young people. In the process, she also compared the S.A.T. with the T.A.T. For the elderly subjects she used three of the T.A.T. cards and twenty S.A.T. cards, some of which have been modified or dropped from the present series. The younger subjects were given the same set of S.A.T. cards in the same way, but because of time limitations they were not given the T.A.T. cards. Each story was evaluated with regard to kinds of activity, degree of interpersonal involvement, themes of despair, outcome, and word count. Each scoring category was examined with regard to age and sex differences between the S.A.T. and the T.A.T.

In terms of the five sub-categories of Activities (day-dreaming, daily routine, passivity, conflict and affiliation) there were no sex differences for the elderly subjects nor for the students. It also is striking that the main Activities for the students were the same as those for the elderly, with the exception of daily routine which was slightly higher for the students.

In terms of the five sub-categories of Hope for the S.A.T. (happiness, optimism, effort to maintain self, meaning kinship and interest in people), there was no difference between the age groups.

The degrees of Social Involvement also showed no differences between the students and elderly. The men in both groups seem to have more scores of moderate involvement while the women in both groups had more scores of low involvement. In accordance with Prola's findings [144], the categories of Word Count and Involvement seem to be related. Subjects with higher word counts tend to have more scores for high degree of Involvement.

With regard to the three T.A.T. cards, administered to see what might be elicited from pictures of younger people, the Activities scored were consistent with the S.A.T. results, showing similar rankings for affiliation, daily routine and passivity. Although too small a number of T.A.T. cards was used to draw conclusions, it is significant that quite different stimuli resulted in similar thematic contents. The hypothesis that the T.A.T. cards would elicit more responses of hope and fewer of despair in comparison with the S.A.T. cards was not supported in this study. The T.A.T. outcomes were actually more despairing than the S.A.T. outcomes, and the S.A.T. cards did not produce the grimness that might have been expected.

The prediction that elderly people would overwhelmingly respond with images of despair and death was not supported by this study. The stories elicited by the S.A.T. showed a yearning for connectedness and activity in the elderly. Despite the fear of infirmity and death, these stimuli elicited aspects of hope, indicating that aging need not be viewed as depressing, unhopeful, and isolating.

Overall the control group of students did not differ substantially from the elderly. The only notable differences were between the two sexes.

In an investigation of the elderly person's psychosexual concerns and the effects that aging may have upon their sexual ideation, Lynette Ackerly used the S.A.T., as well as the T.A.T. and Rorschach [5].

Ackerly's hypotheses were that older people will reveal their interest in sex through stories they will tell to various picture stimuli; that the T.A.T. would elicit a higher rate of sexual imagery than the S.A.T. because of stereotyped attitudes about sexual feelings in older people; that there would be a higher percentage of sexual images in the elderly as compensation for unfulfilled sexual longings; and that individual differences, more than age differences, should be reflected in the degrees of sexual responsiveness to the projective materials.

Her fifteen subjects ranged from 65 to 86 years, with an average of 75.6 years. Of the seven men, two were single, three widowed, and two presently married. Among the eight women, one was single, four widowed, and three presently married She studied the frequency of seven themes: depression and loneliness; competition, antagonism and aggression; discouragement and disappointment; security and health concerns; needs for nurturance; affiliation and compassion; and sexuality.

Subjects were given 21 S.A.T. cards, 4 T.A.T. cards, and the 10 Rorschach cards. Seven of the subjects were given the S.A.T. first while eight were given the T.A.T. and Rorschach first.

The most striking finding was that sexuality did not drop out as people age; among the seven themes, it was fifth in prevalence on the S.A.T., but second highest on the T.A.T. Generally, the older half of the subjects showed as much interest in sexual subjects as the younger half. No significant difference was found between the level of sexual interest in men and women. There were marked individual differences.

Deanna Toone investigated whether old age is accompanied by a constricted world view. She considered the degree and breadth of responses to S.A.T. pictures as an indication of respondents' engagement in the external world and hypothesized that older subjects would score lower on all measures than the younger group.

In her review of the literature, she calls attention to the importance of individual personality characteristics and to the concept of stages of development during adulthood as factors affecting engagement as noted in studies that tend to support the theory of disengagement during old age (Cummings and Henry 1967; Parla-greco et al., 1960; Cumming et al., 1972), in studies of persistence of life style (Maddox, 1968) and of isolation (Lowenthal, 1965) [9].

Toone administered a questionnaire and ten S.A.T. pictures to a group of 15 healthy black women aged 60 to 81 years. Responses were scored for mentioning the physical setting, describing a person, describing interaction between charac-ters, and introducing content not specifically present in the picture. Word count was employed as an additional measure of involvement and stories were also scored for positive, negative, or neutral outcome.

The disengagement theory did not hold for Toone's sample. In fact, the older subjects scored higher on measures of involvement and introduction of new ideas, although none of the scores was significant. The mean number of words was very close between the two groups, the measure for the younger women being slightly higher. Finally, the older respondents told more stories with posi-tive or neutral outcomes, while the outcomes of the younger groups' stories were more often neutral and negative than positive. Toone suggests the possibility that the high involvement of the older subjects was due in part to the particular relevance of the stimuli to them, and also that her sample, as members of a senior citizens club, was predisposed to social interaction.

Finally, Toone points to the limited attention to women in the literature on aging, and especially, to the virtual absence of studies of black women. She sees a need for studies comparing the adjustment of women who have been employed with those who have been "housewives".

Clio Garland used the S.A.T. to study the degree and kinds of dependency that may accompany old age. She hypothesized that there will be a significant increase in over-all dependency among the aged, but "it remains an open question as to whether there will be different kinds of dependency manifested by elderly and young people." She believes that the impairments that accompany old age and individual personality characteristics, rather than age itself, are important factors affecting dependency.

Garland administered a questionnaire and ten S.A.T. plates to two groups of 15 white women: the older group ranged in age from 65 to 81 with various marital histories; the younger, mostly unmarried college students, were aged 20 to 25 years. Each subject was scored for the number and categories of themes of dependency they mentioned as follows: passive orientation; need for proximity; inability to make decisions; reliance on others or on institutions; feelings of rejection; exaggerated need for attachment; regressive imagery; inability to func-tion alone.

There were no significant differences between the two age groups as far as the kinds of dependency themes mentioned. In keeping with a view that regression is typical of old age, older respondents had three regressive responses and the younger women, none. Surprisingly, younger subjects more frequently men-tioned themes of rejection and the kind of rejection they conveyed was more general than was the case for the older women. Educational level and health were not related to dependency; it was unclear from this sample whether or not marital status might be related to dependency. Garland also divided her older subjects into two age groups: those over 70 and those younger. The older women averaged less themes of dependency than the younger ones.

G. Suggestions for Future Research

Researchers in the future may be interested in a comparative analysis by "idea count" between younger and older age groups. It seems of interest, for example, to count the number of words relating to hope, despair, affiliative tendencies, and sex, as was done in the modest pilot studies reported above. One might also count words relating to death and aggression, and the number of affective adjectives and adverbs.

Future research might include a variety of content analytic studies by word count. A content analytic study (by word count) of love and death in the short stories of Somerset Maugham by Judson [183] led to results remarkably similar to those obtained by Bellak [5]. It may be of interest to see if such divergent approaches to S.A.T. stories in the future will bring a similar convergence of data. A comparison of this kind between the group over 65 and those of younger adults should be of additional interest.

It should be possible to define other criterion words or criteria of depression, disorientation, deterioration (in terms of the organic brain syndrome), or evidence of a thought disorder. It should be entirely possible to define criteria in responses to the S.A.T. and correlate them with criteria of established tests on thought disorder, deterioration, or depression scales and get measures of validity.

Other studies might rate patients for their social relations in an old age home on behavioral rating scales and get correlation coefficients on measures of sociability derived from the S.A.T. It should also be possible to compare performance on the S.A.T. to performance on the T.A.T. and on the Rorschach or other personality tests. This, however, is likely to be an exercise of limited value since even these old and well-established techniques in turn have never fulfilled criteria of validity such as are required by their very nature for intelligence tests or ability tests. Neugarten's disengagement construct could be investigated by defining it carefully for a sample population, establishing content variables of social relations or disengagement on the S.A.T., and computing correlations between the observed behavior and the one reflected in the S.A.T.

CHAPTER XIX

THE PSYCHODIAGNOSTIC TEST REPORT BLANK

Figure 10 shows this Report Blank, which is a logical extension of the forms developed for the T.A.T. and the C.A.T. It permits recording not only of these tests but also of the basic data of an entire test battery. The emphasis is again on the practicality of an overview and the provision of a systematic framework for the formulation of diagnostic inferences.

The Report Blank is meant primarily to be used by the psychologist for imparting information he has derived from a detailed study of the tests to the referring psychiatrist, psychologist, social worker, etc.; some psychologists might also want to use it as their worksheet, supplemented by scratch paper and necessary modifications, though it is not specifically designed for this purpose. However, the Report Blank should lend itself especially well to teaching and training purposes.

It was designed in the hope that it will:

1. Make test reporting intellectually less of a chore by providing a frame of reference and a set of variables which in part need only be check rated—rather than having to write a lengthy essay.

2. Provide a somewhat standardized basis for test reporting. The problems of test reporting are numerous [49]. One of the most frequent problems is doubtless that the peruser of the report does not get enough of an idea of the test reporter's progression from raw data to inference.

3. Provide a more orderly form in which to submit the report than the frequently used personal stationery or blank pieces of paper. It will make individual test reports comparable to others.

For the purpose of providing an overall view of the data, the fold-out style, which has been found helpful in the Bellak Short Form T.A.T. and C.A.T. Blank, of the actual form is arranged so that the summary and the final report can be in simultaneous view, both for test reporter and test user.

Designed by
Leopold Bellak, M.D.

© C. P. S. Inc. 1965
Box 83, Larchmont, N.Y.
Revised 1974

PSYCHODIAGNOSTIC TEST REPORT BLANK

Grade_____

Name_____Age_____Birthdate_____Sex_____Education_____Occupation_____

Married_____Single_____Divorced_____Widowed_____

Tests administered:

WISC	☐	Rorschach	☐	Figure Drawing	☐
WAIS	☐	TAT	☐	Bender Gestalt	☐
Stanford Binet	☐	CAT-A-H-S	☐	Other	☐
School Achievement	☐	SAT	☐	Other	☐

FINAL REPORT:

(See Summary page for details)

Test Behavior:

Diagnostically, the findings are consistent with:

    Dynamically:

    Therapeutically:

Recommendations:

Tested by: _____
                                         Signature

FIG. 11. The Psychodiagnostic Test Report Blank.

WECHSLER INTELLIGENCE SCALE

	Weighted Score	Selected Illustrative Responses	Inference or Conclusion
1. Information			
2. Comprehension			
3. Digit Span			
4. Arithmetic			
5. Similarities			
6. (Vocabulary)			
Verbal Score			
7. P. Arrangement			
8. P. Completion			
9. Block Design			
10. Object Assembly			
11. Digit Symbol			
Performance Score			
Total Score			
I.Q. Verbal Scale			
I.Q. Perform. Scale			
I.Q. Full Scale			

Functioning Intellectually:

    At optimum: ☐

☐ Below optimum because of:

    Anxieties ☐

    Constriction ☐

    Deterioration ☐

    Organic factors ☐

    Other ☐

Functioning Psychodynamically:

Test Behavior and
Other:

FIG. 11. (cont.)

RORSCHACH

Card	Selected Illustrative Responses	Inference or Conclusion
1.		
2.		
3.		
4.		
5.		
6.		
7.		
8.		
9.		
10.		

Test Behavior:

FIG. 11. (cont.)

T.A.T. or C.A.T. or S.A.T.

Card TAT ☐ SAT ☐	CAT-A ☐ CAT-H ☐ CAT-S ☐	Selected Illustrative Responses	Inference or Conclusion

1.

2.

3.

4.

5.

6.

7.

8.

9.

10.

Other:

FIG. 11. (cont.)

Illustrative Data	Inference or Conclusion

Bender Gestalt:

Figure Drawing:

Other:

FIG. 11. (cont.)

SUMMARY:

1. Intellectual functioning

2. Significant drives and conflicts

3. Nature of anxieties

4. Ego functions

    a) reality testing

    b) judgment

    c) sense of reality and of self

    d) regulation and control of drives

    e) object relations

    f) thought processes

    g) ARISE (adaptive regression in the service of the ego)

    h) defensive functioning

    i) stimulus barrier

    j) autonomous functioning

    k) synthetic—integrating functioning

    l) mastery—competence

5. Superego function

6. Organic disturbances

Other:

FIG. 11. (cont.)

EGO FUNCTION ASSESSMENT FROM TEST DATA

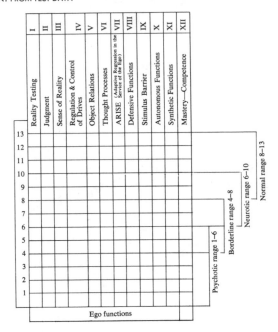

(From Bellak, Hurvich & Gediman, *Ego Functions in Schizophrenics, Neurotics, and Normals.* Copyright © 1973, by C.P.S., Inc. Reprinted by permission of John Wiley & Sons, Inc.)

You may decide to record only current overall ego functions or may draw in graphs indicating what you consider optimal, minimal or characteristic levels for any or all ego functions.

EGO FUNCTIONS OBSERVED IN TEST BEHAVIOR

FIG. 11. (cont.)

BIBLIOGRAPHY

1. AARON, N.: Some personality differences between asthmatic, allergic, and normal children. J. Clin. Psychol., no. 3, 336–340, 1967.

2. ABEND, S. M., PORTER, M. S., AND WILLICK, M. S.: (Kris Study Group) Borderline Patients: Psychoanalytic Perspectives. International Universities Press, 1983.

3. ABRAMS, D. M.: Conflict resolution in children's storytelling: An application of Erikson's theory and the conflict-enculturation model. Unpublished doctoral dissertation, Columbia University, 1977.

4. ABT, L., AND BELLAK, L.: Projective Psychology. New York, Knopf, 1950.

5. ACKERLY, L.: Sexual Fantasies of Elderly People. Thesis for the B.S. degree, State University of New York College at Purchase, 1973.

6. ALLPORT, G., AND VERNON, F.: Studies in Expressive Movement. New York, Macmillan, 1933, pp. 131–134, 230, 231.

7. ——: Personality: A Psychological Interpretation. New York, Holt, 1937.

8. ——: The Use of Personal Documents in Psychological Science. Social Science Research Council Bulletin, No. 49, 1942.

9. ALTOBELLO, N.: Hope and Despair in Old Age. Thesis for the B.A. degree, State University of New York College at Purchase, 1973.

10. American Psychological Association: Standards for development and use of educational and psychological tests. 3rd draft, Washington, D.C., 1973. 15 pp.

11. American Psychological Association DSM-III. Washington, D.C., 1980.

12. ARMSTRONG, M.: Children's responses to animal and human figures in thematic pictures. J. Consult. Psychol. 18:67–70, 1954.

13. ARNOLD, M.: In Shneidman, E. S. (ed.): Thematic Test Analysis. New York, Grune & Stratton, 1951.

14. ARON, B.: In Shneidman, E. S. (ed.): Thematic Test Analysis. New York, Grune & Stratton, 1951.

15. ATKINSON, J., HEYNS, R., AND VEROFF, J.: The effect of experimental arousal of the affiliation motive on thematic apperception. J. Abnorm. Soc. Psychol. 49:405–417, 1954.

16. BALIER, C.: Les comportements psychiques des personnes agees. Reprint from Evolutions Medicales, No. 5, Tome 13:417–21. Paris, Les imprimeries reunies moulins, n.d.

17. BALKEN, E. R., AND MASSERMAN, J. H.: The language of phantasy. III. The language of the phantasies of patients with conversion hysteria, anxiety state, and obsessive compulsive neurosis. J. Psychol. 10:75–86, 1940.

18. BELL, J. E.: Projective Techniques: A Dynamic Approach to the Study of Personality. New York, Longmans, Green, 1948.

19. BELLAK, L.: A note about the Adam's apple. Psychoanal. Rev. vol. 29, no. 3, 1942.

20. ——: The concept of projection: an experimental investigation and study of the concept. Psychiatry 4:353–370, 1944.

21. ——: A note of some basic concepts of psychotherapy. J. Nerv. Ment. Dis. 108:137–141, 1948.

22. ——: On the problems of the concept of projection. In Abt, L., and Bellak, L. (eds.): Projective Psychology. New York, Knopf, 1950.

23. ——: Projection and the Thematic Apperception Test. In Crafts, L. W., Schneirla, T. C., Robinson, E. E., and Gilbert, R. W. (eds.): Recent Experiments in Psychology. New York, McGraw-Hill, 1950.

24. ——: Psychiatric aspects of tuberculosis. Soc. Casework, May, 1950.

25. ——: Thematic apperception: failures and the defenses. Trans. N.Y. Acad. Sci. 12:4, 1950.

26. ——: The emergency psychotherapy of depression. In: Specialized Techniques in Psychotherapy, New York, Basic Books, 1952.

27. ——: Manic-Depressive Psychosis and Allied Disorders. New York, Grune & Stratton, 1952.

28. ——: Psychology of Physical Illness: Psychiatry Applied to Medicine, Surgery, and the Specialities. New York, Grune & Stratton, 1952.

29. ——: The Psychology of Physical Illness. New York, Grune & Stratton, 1952, 243 pp.

30. ——: Revised Manual for the TAT. New York, Psychological Corp., 1952.

31. ——: A further experimental investigation of projection by means of hypnosis. (Unpublished, summarized in reference 20).

32. ——: A study of limitations and "failures":

toward an ego psychology of projective techniques. J. Project. Techn. 18:279–293, 1954.

33. ——: An ego-psychological theory of hypnosis. Int. J. Psychoanal. 36:375–378, 1955.

34. ——: Psychiatric aspects of cardiac illness and rehabilitation. Soc. Casework 37:482–9, 1956.

35. ——: Creativity: some random notes to a systematic consideration. J. Project. Techn. vol. 22, no. 4, 1958.

36. ——: The unconscious. Ann. N.Y. Acad. Sci. 76:1066–1081, 1959.

37. ——: Free association. Int. J. Psychoanal. 42:9–20, 1961.

38. ——: Somerset Maugham: A study of some of his stories. In R. White (ed.): The Study of Lives. New York, Atherton Press, 1963.

39. ——: Depersonalization as a variant of self-awareness. In Abrams, A. (ed.): Unfinished Tasks in the Behavioral Sciences. Baltimore, Williams & Wilkins, 1964.

40. ——: A psychological study of the stories of Somerset Maugham: a profile of a creative personality. In White, R. (ed.): The Study of Lives. New York, Atherton Press, 1963; and In Spence, D. P. (ed): The Broad Scope of Psychoanalysis: Selected Papers of Leopold Bellak. New York, Grune & Stratton, 1967.

41. ——: The T.A.T. and C.A.T. in Clinical Use. 2nd ed. New York, Grune & Stratton, 1971.

42. ——: Ego Functions in Schizophrenia, Neurotics, and Normals (with Marvin Hurvitch and Helen Gediman,) New York: John Wiley & Sons, 1973.

42a. ——: The Best Years of your Life. A Guide to the Art and Science of Aging. New York, Atheneum, 1975.

43. ——: Psychiatric Aspects of Minimal Brain Dysfunction in Adults. New York: Grune & Stratton, 1979.

44. ——: Current Status of Classical Freudian Psychoanalysis. Chapters 9, 10, 11, Directions in Psychiatry, June, 1982.

45. ——: Psychoanalysis in the 1980's. Am. J. Psychotherapy, Vol. XXXVII, No. 4, October 1983.

46. ——: The Broad Scope of Ego Function Assessment (ed. and contributor, Lisa Goldsmith, Ph.D.). New York: John Wiley & Sons, 1984.

47. ——: A.D.D. Psychosis: A Separate Entity. Schizophrenia Bulletin, Vol. II, #4, 1985.

48. —— ET AL.: The use of the TAT in psychotherapy. J. Nerv. Ment. Dis. 110:51–65, 1949.

49. —— ET AL.: Psychological test reporting: a problem in communication between psychologists and psychiatrists. J. Nerv. Ment. Dis. 129:76–91, 1959.

50. —— AND BARTEN, H.: Progress in Community Mental Health, vol. 1. New York, Grune & Stratton, 1969.

51. —— AND BARTEN, H.: The validity and usefulness of the concept of the schizophrenic syndrome. In Cancro, R. (ed.): The Schizophrenic Reactions. New York, Brunner/Mazel, 1970.

52. —— AND BELLAK, S.: The C.A.T.-H.—A Human Modification. Larchmont, N.Y., C.P.S. Inc., 1965.

53. —— AND BROWER, D.: Projective methods. In: Progress in Neurology and Psychiatry, New York, Grune & Stratton, 1951, vol. 6.

54. —— AND CHASSAN, J.: An approach to the evaluation of drug effect during psychotherapy: a double bind study of a single case. J. Nerv. Dis. 139:20–30, 1964.

55. —— AND HURVICH, M.: A human modification of the Children's Apperception Test. J. Project Techn. 30:228–242, 1966.

56. ——, HURVICH, M., AND CRAWFORD, P.: Psychotic egos. Psychoanal. Review, vol. 56, no. 4, 1970.

57. ——: A study of ego functions in the schizophrenic syndrome. Arch. Gen. Psychiat., vol. 23, October, 1970.

58. ——, HURVICH, M., GEDIMAN, H.: Ego Functions in Schizophrenics, Neurotics, and Normals. New York, John Wiley & Sons, 1973.

59. ——, HURVICH, M., GEDIMAN, H. AND CRAWFORD, P.: The systematic diagnosis of the schizophrenic syndrome. Dynamic Psychiat., October, 1969.

60. ——, LEVINGER, L., AND LIPSKY, E.: An adolescent problem reflected in the TAT. J. Clin. Pschol. 6:295–297, 1950.

61. —— AND LOEB, L.: The Schizophrenic Syndrome. New York, Grune & Stratton, 1969.

62. —— AND MURRAY, H. A.: Thematic Apperception Test Blank. Cambridge, Harvard Psychological Clinic, 1941. (Mimeographed and privately distributed.)

63. —— AND SMALL, L.: Emergency Psychotherapy and Brief Psychotherapy. Grune & Stratton, 1965, 253 pp.

64. BELLER, E., AND HAEBERLE, A.: Motivation and conflict in relation to phantasy responses of young children. Paper read at meeting of the Society for Research in Child Development, Bethesda, Md., March, 1959.

64a. BENDER, L., AND RAPAPORT, J.: Animal drawings of children. Am. J. Orthopsychiat. 14:521–527, 1944.

65. BENNETT, E., AND JOHANNSEN, D.: Psychodynamics in the diabetic child. Psychol. Monogr., vol. 68, no. 11, 1954.

66. BEREZIN, M. A.: Some Intrapsychic Aspects of Aging. In Zinberg, N. E. and Kaufman, I. (eds.): Normal Psychology of the Aging Process. New York, International Universities Press, 1963.

67. BERNSTEIN, L.: The examiner as an inhibiting factor in clinical testing. J. Consult. Psychol. 20:287–290, 1956.

68. BEXTON, W., HERON, W., AND SCOTT, T.: Effects of decreased variation in the sensory environment. Canad. J. Psychol. 8:70–76, 1954.

69. BIERSDORF, K. R., AND MARCUSE, F. L.: Responses of children to human and animal pictures. J. Proj. Tech. 17:455–459, 1953.

70. BILLS, R. E.: Animal pictures for obtaining children's projections. J. Clin. Psychol. 6:291–293, 1950.

71. BILLS, R., LEIMAN, C., AND THOMAS, R.: A study of the validity of the T.A.T. and a set of animal pictures. J. Clin. Psychol. 6:293–295, 1950.

72. BLATT, S., ENGEL, M., AND MIRMOW, E.: When inquiry fails. J. Project. Techn. 25:32–37, 1961.

73. BLUM, G., AND HUNT, H. F.: The validity of the Blacky pictures. Psychol. Bull. 49:238–250, 1952.

74. BOOTH, L.: A Normative Comparison of the Responses of Latin-American and Anglo-American Children to the Children's Apperception Test. Unpublished doctoral dissertation, Texas Technological College, Lubbock, Texas, 1953.

75. BOULANGER-BALLEYGUIER, G.: Études sur le C.A.T.: influence du stimulus sur les récits d'enfants de 3 à 8 ans. Rev. Psychol. Appl. 7:1–28, 1957.

76. ——: La personalité des enfants normaux et caractériels à travers le test d'apperception C.A.T. Monogr. Franc. Psychol., no. 4, 1960.

77. BOYD, N., AND MANDLER, G.: Children's responses to human and animal stories and pictures. J. Consult. Psychol. 19:367–371, 1955.

78. BROVERMAN, D., JORDAN, E., AND PHILLIPS, L.: Achievement motivation in fantasy and behavior. J. Abnorm. Soc. Psychol. 60:374–378, 1960.

79. BRITTAIN, H. L.: A study in imagination. Ped. Seminars 14:137–207, 1907.

80. BRUNER, J. S., AND POSTMAN, L.: Tension and tension-release as organizing factors in perception. J. Personality 15:300–308.

81. —— AND GOODMAN, C.: Value and need as organizing factors in perception. J. Abnorm. Soc. Psychol. 42:33–44, 1947.

82. BUDOFF, M.: The relative utility of animal and human figures in a picture story test for young children. J. Project. Techn. 42:347–352, 1960.

83. BUEHLER, C., ET AL.: Development of Basic Rorschach Score with Manual for Directions, No. 1 of Rorschach Standardization Studies. Los Angeles, 1949.

84. BUSSE, E. AND PFEIFFER, E.: Mental Illness in Later Life. Washington, D.C. American Psychiatric Association, 1973.

85. BUTLER, R.: Responses of institutionalized mentally retarded children to human and to animal pictures. Amer. J. Ment. Defic. 65:620–622, 1961.

86. BYRD, E., AND WITHERSPOON, R.: Responses of preschool children to the Children's Apperception Test. Child Develop. 25:35–44, 1954.

87. CAIN, A.: A supplementary dream technique with the Children's Apperception Test. J. Clin. Psychol. 17:181–184, 1961.

88. CATTELL, R. B.: Principles of designs in "projective" or misperception tests of personality. In Anderson, H. H., and Anderson, G. L. (eds.): An Introduction to Projective Psychology. New York, Prentice-Hall, 1951.

89. CHAMSON, S. F.: An Investigation of T.A.T. Responses as a Function of Figure-Ground Deficits. Unpublished Ph.D. thesis, School of Professional Psychology, Florida Institute of Technology, 1983.

90. CHOWDHURY, U.: An Indian Adaptation of the Children's Apperception Test. Delhi, India, Manasayan, 1960.

91. CLARK, A.: A method of administering and evaluating the Thematic Apperception Test in group situations. Genet. Psychol. Monogr. 30:3–55, 1944.

92. CLARK, R.: The projective measurement of experimentally induced levels of sexual motivation. J. Exp. Psychol. 44:391–399, 1952.

93. COLEMAN, W.: The Thematic Apperception Test. I. Effect of recent experience. II. Some quantitative observations. J. Clin. Psychol. 3:257–264, 1947.

94. COMBS, A.: The use of personal experience in Thematic Apperception Test story plots. J. Clin. Psychol. 2:357–363, 1946.

95. COWEN, G., AND GOLDBERG, F.: Need achievement as a function of the race and sex of

figures in selected T.A.T. cards. J. Personality Soc. Psychol. 5:245–249, 1967.

96. CUMMINGS, E. AND HENRY, W. E.: Growing Old. New York, Basic Books, 1961.

97. DANA, R.: Thematic techniques and clinical practice. J. Project Techn. 32:204–214, 1968.

98. DANA, R. G.: Cross validation of objective T.A.T. scoring. J. Consult. Psychol. 20:33–36, 1956.

99. DANA, R. H.: Clinical diagnosis and objective T.A.T. scoring. J. Abnormal and Soc. Psychol. 50:19–25, 1955.

100. DANA, R. H.: A proposal for the objective scoring of the T.A.T. Perceptual Motor Skills 9:27–43, 1959.

101. DAVIDS, A., AND DEVAULT, S.: Use of the T.A.T. and Human Figure Drawings in research on personality, pregnancy, and perception. J. Project. Techn. 24(4):362–365, 1960.

102. DAVISON, A.: A comparison of fantasy productions on the T.A.T. of 60 hospitalized psychoneurotic and psychotic patients. J. Project Techn. 17:20–33, 1953.

103. DESOUSA, T.: A Comparison of the Responses of Adjusted and Maladjusted Children on a Thematic Apperception Test. Unpublished master's thesis, Loyola University, Chicago, 1952.

104. EARLE, M.: Rakau children: from six to thirteen years, Wellington, New Zealand. Victoria University Publications in Psychology, no. 11, 1958. (Monographs on Maori Social Life and Personality, no. 4.)

105. EISDORFER, C. AND LAWTON, M. P.: The Psychology of Adult Development and Aging. Washington, D. C., American Psychological Association, 1973.

106. EISSLER, K.: Notes upon defects of ego structure in schizophrenia. Int. J. Psychoanal. 35:141, 1954.

107. EPSTEIN, S.: The measurement of drive and conflict in humans: theory and experiment. In Jones, M. (ed.): Nebraska Symposium on Motivation. Lincoln, Nebr., University of Nebraska Press, 1962.

108. ERIKSEN, C. W.: Some implications for T.A.T. interpretations arising from need and perception experiments. J. Personality 19:282–288, 1951.

109. ERON, L. D.: Frequencies of themes and identifications in the stories of schizophrenics and nonhospitalized college students. J. Consult. Psychol. 12:387–395, 1948.

110. ———: A normative study of the Thematic Apperception Test. Psychol. Monographs 64 (Whole No. 315), 1950.

111. ——— AND RITTER, A. M.: A comparison of two methods of administration of the Thematic Apperception Test. J. Consult. Psychol. 15:55–61, 1951.

112. ——— In Shneidman, E. S. (ed.): Thematic Test Analysis. New York, Grune & Stratton, 1951, p. 55.

113. FAIRBAIRN, W. R. D.: An Object-Relations Theory of the Personality. New York, Basic Books, 1954.

114. FAIRWEATHER, G., SIMON, R., GEBHARD, M., WEINGARTEN, E., HOLLAND, J., SANDERS, R., STONE, G., AND REAHL, J.: Relative Effectiveness of Psychotherapeutic Programs: A Multicriteria Comparison of Four Programs for Three Different Patient Groups. Psychol. Monogr., no. 5, vol. 74, 1960.

115. FEAR, C., AND STONE, L. J.: A Study of 40 School Children with the C.A.T.-S. Thesis filed at Vassar College Library, Poughkeepsie, N.Y., 1951.

116. FEIFEL, H.: Psychological test report: a communication between psychologist and psychiatrist (L. Bellak, Chairman). J. Nerv. Ment. Dis. 129(1):76–91, July, 1959.

117. FENICHEL, O.: The Psychoanalytic Theory of Neurosis. New York, Norton, 1945.

118. FESTINGER, L.: The Theory of Cognitive Dissonance. New York, Harper, 1957.

119. FINE, R.: In Shneidman, E. S. (ed.): Thematic Test Analysis. New York, Grune & Stratton, 1951, p. 64.

120. FINN, M.: An Investigation of Apperceptive Distortion in the Obsessive-Compulsive Character Structure by Three Methods, Verbal, Graphic-Emotional, and Graphic-Geometric. Ph.D. Thesis, New York University, New York, N.Y., 1951.

121. FISHER, C.: Dreams and perception: the role of preconscious and primary modes of perception in dream formation. J. Amer. Psychoanal. Ass. 11:389–445, 1954.

122. FITZGERALD, B.: Some relationships among projective test, interview, and sociometric measures of dependent behavior. J. Abnorm. Soc. Psychol. 56:199–203, 1958.

123. FITZSIMONS, R.: Developmental, psychosocial, and educational factors in children with non-organic articulation problems. Child Develop. 29:481–489, 1958.

124. FOGEL, M. L.: Picture description and interpretation in brain-damaged patients. Cortex, 1967, pp. 3, 443, 448.

125. FOULDS, G.: A method of scoring the

T.A.T. applied to psychoneurotics. J. Ment. Sci. 99:235–246, 1953.

126. FRANK, L. K.: Projective methods for the study of personality. J. Psychol. 8:389–413, 1939.

127. FREUD, A.: The Ego and the Mechanisms of Defense. London, Hogarth Press, 1937.

128. ——: Normality and Pathology of Childhood. New York, International Universities Press, 1965.

129. FREUD, S.: The anxiety neurosis. In: Collected Papers, International Psychoanalytic Library. London, Hogarth Press, 1940, vol. 1.

130. ——: The Future of an Illusion, International Psychoanalytic Library, No. 15. Hogarth Press, 1940.

131. ——: Group Psychology and the Analysis of the Ego, International Psychoanalytic Library, No. 6. London, Hogarth Press, 1940.

132. ——: Neuropsychoses, International Psychoanalytic Library. London, Hogarth Press, 1940, vol. 1.

133. ——: Psychoanalytic notes on an autobiographical account of a case of paranoia (dementia paranoides). In: Collected Papers, International Psychoanalytic Library. London, Hogarth Press, 1943, vol. 3.

134. ——: Totem and taboo. In Brill, A. A. (ed.): Basic Writings of Sigmund Freud. New York, Modern Library, 1938.

135. FURUYA, K.: Responses of school children to human and animal pictures. J. Project. Techn. 21:248–252, 1957.

136. GARDNER, R., AND LOHRENZ, L.: Leveling-sharpening and serial reproduction of a story. Bull. Menninger Clin. 24:295–304, 1960.

137. GARFIELD, S. L. AND EFRON, L. D.: Interpreting mood and activity in T.A.T. stories. J. Abnormal Social Psychol. 43:338–345, 1948.

138. GARLAND, C.: The Experience of Dependency in the Elderly. Thesis for the B.A. degree, State University of New York College at Purchase, 1974.

139. GEIST, H.: The Psychological Aspects of the Aging Process. St. Louis, Warren H. Green, Inc., 1968.

140. Geriatrics. In Medical World News, New York, McGraw Hill, Inc., 1972.

141. Gerontologie Mars, 1973. No. 10. 75011 France.

142. GILBERT, G. M.: The Nüremberg Diary. New York, Prentice-Hall, 1947.

143. GINSPARG, H.: A Study of the Children's Apperception Test. Unpublished doctoral dissertation, Washington University, Seattle, Wash., 1957.

144. GOLDFARB, A.: How to stay young: probing the mysteries of aging. Newsweek, April 16, 1973.

145. GOLDFARB, W.: The animal symbol in the Rorschach test and in animal association test. Rorschach Res. Exch. J. Project. Techn. 9:8–22, 1945.

146. GOLDFRIED, M., AND ZAX, M.: The stimulus value of the T.A.T. J. Project. Techn. 29(1):46–57, 1965.

147. GREENACRE, P.: Trauma, Growth, and Personality. New York, International Universities, 1952.

148. GUREVITZ, S., AND KAPPER, Z.: Techniques for and evaluation of the responses of schizophrenic and cerebral palsied children to the Children's Apperception Test (C.A.T.). Quart. J. Child Behav. 3:38–65, 1951.

149. GUTHRIE, E. R. AND HORTON, G. P.: Cats in a Puzzle Box. New York, Rinehart, 1946.

150. HAFNER, J., AND KAPLAN, A.: Hostility content analysis of the Rorschach and T.A.T. J. Project. Techn. 24:137–143, 1960.

151. HARROWER, M.: Group techniques for the Rorschach protocol. In Abt, L. and Bellak, L. (eds.): Projective Psychology. New York, Knopf, 1950.

152. HARTMAN, A. A.: In Shneidman, E. S. (ed.): Thematic Test Analysis. New York, Grune & Stratton, 1951, p. 83.

153. HARTMANN, H.: Comments on the psychoanalytic theory of the ego. In: The Psychoanalytic Study of the Child, vol. 5, New York, International Universities, 1950, pp. 75–96.

154. ——: Ego psychology and the problems of adaptation. In Rapaport, D. (ed.): Organization and Pathology of Thought. New York, Columbia University Press, 1951.

155. HAWORTH, M.: Responses of children to a group projective film and to the Rorschach, C.A.T., Despert Fables, and D-A-P. J. Project. Techn. 26:47–60, 1962.

156. ——: A schedule for the analysis of C.A.T. responses. J. Project. Techn. 27:181–184, 1963.

157. ——: Parental loss in children as reflected in projected responses. J. Project. Techn. 28(1):31–45, 1964.

158. ——: C.A.T. vs. C.A.T.-H. with a clinic sample. Unpublished manuscript, 1964.

159. ——: A Schedule of Adaptive Mechanisms in C.A.T. Responses. Larchmont, N.Y., C.P.S. Inc., 1965.

160. ——: The C.A.T.: Facts about Fantasy. New York, Grune & Stratton, 1966.

161. HEALY, W. A., BRONNER, A. F. AND BOWERS, A. M.: The Structure and Meaning of Psychoanalysis. New York, Knopf, 1930.

162. HENRY, W.: The Analysis of Fantasy. New York, Wiley, 1956.

163. HENRY, W. E., AND GUETZKOW, H.: Group projection sketches for the study of small groups, Publication 4 of the Conference Research Project at the University of Michigan. J. Soc. Psychol. 33:77–102, 1951.

164. ——: In Wyatt, F.: The scoring and analysis of the Thematic Apperception Test. J. Psychol. 24:319–330, 1947.

165. HERTZ, M.: A further study of suicidal configurations in Rorschach records. Rorschach Res. Exch. J. Project. Techn. 13:1, 1939.

166. HILGARD, E. R.: Theories of Learning. New York, Appleton-Century-Crofts, 1948.

167. HOLDEN, R.: The Children's Apperception Test with cerebral palsied and normal children. Child Develop. 27:3–8, 1956.

168. HOLT, R.: In Shneidman, E. S. (ed.): Thematic Test Analysis. New York, Grune & Stratton, 1951, p. 101.

169. HOLT, R.: Gauging primary and secondary processes in Rorschach responses. J. Project. Techn. 20:14–25, 1956.

170. HOLZBERG, J.: Projective techniques and resistance to change in psychotherapy as viewed through a communications model. J. Project. Techn. 27:430–435, 1963.

171. HOLZMAN, P., AND KLEIN, G.: Cognitive system-principles of leveling and sharpening: individual differences in assimilation effects in visual time-error. J. Psychol. 37:105–122, 1954.

172. ——: Highlights: The Menninger Foundation Conference on the Schizophrenic Syndrome. Psychiat. Spectator, Topeka, Kansas, April 3–5, 1969.

173. HORWITZ, M., AND CARTWRIGHT, D.: A projective method for the diagnosis of groups. Human Relations, 1951.

174. How to stay young: probing the mysteries of aging. Newsweek, April 16, 1973.

175. HUNT, R., AND SMITH, M.: Cultural symbols and response to thematic test materials. J. Project. Techn. 30(6):587–590, 1966.

176. ICHHEISER, G.: Projection and the mote-beam mechanism. J. Abnorm. Soc. Psychol. 42:131–133, 1947.

177. ISAACS, S.: Social Development in Young Children. London, Routledge & Kegan Paul, 1933.

178. ISAKOWER, O.: A contribution to the pathopsychology of phenomena associated with falling asleep. Internat. J. Psychoana. 19:331–345, 1938.

179. JACOBSON, E.: The Self and the Object World. International Universities Press, Inc., 1964.

180. JAMES, P., AND MOSHER, D.: Thematic aggression, hostility-guilt and aggressive behavior. J. Project. Techn. 31(1):61–68, 1967.

181. JOEL, W., AND SHAPIRO, D.: In Shneidman, E. S. (ed.): Thematic Test Analysis. New York, Grune & Stratton, 1951, p. 119.

182. JOHNSON, D., AND SIKES, M.: Rorschach and T.A.T. responses of Negro, Mexican-American, and Anglo psychiatric patients. J. Project. Techn. 29(2):183–188, 1965.

183. JUDSON, A.: Love and death in the short stories of W. Somerset Maugham: a psychological analysis. Psychiat. Quart. Suppl., 37:250–262, Pt. 2, 1963.

184. KAAKE, N.: The Relationship between Intelligence Level and Responses to the Children's Apperception Test. Unpublished master's thesis, Cornell University, Ithaca, N.Y., 1951.

185. KAGAN, J.: The measurement of overt aggression from fantasy. J. Abnorm. Soc. Psychol. 52:390–393, 1956.

186. ——: The stability of T.A.T. fantasy and stimulus ambiguity. J. Consult. Psychol. 23:266–271, 1959.

187. ——: Thematic apperceptive techniques with children. In Rabin, A. I., Haworth, M. R. (eds.): Projective Techniques with Children. New York, Grune & Stratton, 1960.

188. KAGAN, M., AND KAUFMAN, M.: A Preliminary Investigation of Some Relationships between Functional Articulation Disorders and Responses to the Children's Apperception Test. Unpublished master's thesis, Boston University, Boston, Mass., 1954.

189. KARDINER, E. T.: A Comparison of T.A.T. Readings with Psychoanalytic Findings. M.A. Thesis, The City College, New York, N.Y. 1951 (unpublished).

190. KARON, B.: The resolution of acute schizophrenic reactions: a contribution to the development of non-classical psychotherapeutic techniques. Psychotherapy, no. 1, pp. 27–43, 1963.

191. KATZENSTEIN, B.: Estudos individuais e orientação psico-pedagógica de criancas acornetidas de poliomielite (Case studies and psycho-pedagogical guidance of children attacked by poliomyelitis.) Rev. Psicol. Norm. Patol. 3:77–85, 1957.

192. KENNY, D.: The Children's Apperception Test. In Buros (ed.): The Fifth Mental Measurements Yearbook. Highland Park, N.J., Gryphon, 1959.

193. KERNBERG, O.: Borderline Conditions and Pathological Narcissism. New York: Aronson, 1975.

194. ——: Object Relations Theory and Clinical Psychoanalysis (New York: Jason-Aronson, 1976).

195. ——: Internal World and External Reality. New York: Aronson, 1980.

196. KING, F., AND KING, D.: The projective assessment of the female's sexual identification, with special reference to the Blacky pictures. J. Project. Techn. 28:293–299, 1964.

197. KLEBANOFF, S.: Shneidman, E. S. (ed.): Thematic Test Analysis. New York, Grune & Stratton 1951, p. 126.

198. KLEIN, M.: Contribution to Psycho-Analysis, 1921–1945 (London: Hogarth Press, 1948).

199. KLEIN, G.: Need and regulation. In Jones, M. (ed.): Current Theory and Research in Motivation: A Symposium. Lincoln, Nebr., University of Nebraska Press, 1954.

200. KOHUT, H.: The Analysis of the Self International Universities Press, 1971.

201. ——. The Restoration of the Self. New York: International Universities Press, 1977.

202. KORCHIN, S.: Shneidman, E. S. (ed.): Thematic Test Analysis. New York, Grune & Stratton, 1951, p. 132.

203. KORCHIN, S., MITCHELL, H., AND MELTZOFF, J.: A critical evaluation of the Thompson Thematic Apperception Test. J. Project. Techn. 14:445–452, 1950.

204. KRIS, E.: On preconscious mental processes. Psychoanal. Quart. 19:540–560, 1950.

205. LASAGA, J. I.: In Shneidman, E. S. (ed.): Thematic Test Analysis. New York, Grune & Stratton, 1951, p. 144.

206. LAWTON, M.: Animal and human C.A.T.'s with a school sample. J. Project. Techn. 30(3):243–246, 1966.

207. LAZARUS, R.: Ambiguity and nonambiguity in projective testing. J. Abnorm. Soc. Psychol. vol. 17, 1953.

208. LAZARUS, R. S.: The influence of color on the protocol of the Rorschach Test. J. Abnorm. Soc. Psychol. 4:506, 1949.

209. LEHMANN, I.: Responses of kindergarten children to the Children's Apperception Test. J. Clin. Psychol. 15:60–63, 1959.

210. LESSER, G.: The relationship between overt and fantasy aggression as a function of maternal response to aggression. J. Abnorm. Soc. Psychol. 55:218–221, 1957.

211. LEVINE, F.: Thematic drive expression in three occupational groups. J. Project. Techn. 33(4):357–364, 1969.

212. LEVINE, R., CHEIN, I., AND MURPHY, G.: The relationship of the intensity of a need to the amount of perceptual distortion: a preliminary report. J. Psychol. 13:283–293, 1943.

213. LEWIN, B.: Sleep, the mouth and the dream screen. Psychiat. Quart., vol. 15, 1946.

214. ——: Psychoanalysis of Elation. New York, Norton, 1950.

215. LEZAK, M. D.: Neuropsychological Assessment. New York: Oxford University Press, 1976.

216. LIBBY, W.: The imagination of adolescents. Amer. J. Psychol. 19:249–252, 1908.

217. LIGHT, B.: Comparative study of a series of C.A.T. and T.A.T. cards. J. Clin. Psychol. 10:179–181, 1954.

218. LINDZEY, G.: TAT: Assumptions and related empirical evidence. Psychol. Bull. 49:1–25, 1952.

219. ——, AND SILVERMAN, M.: Thematic Apperception Test: techniques of group administration, sex differences, and the role of verbal productivity. J. Personality 27:311–323, 1959.

220. LUBIN, B.: Some effects of set and stimulus properties on T.A.T. stories. J. Project. Techn. 24:11–16, 1960.

221. LUNDY, A.: The Reliability of the Thematic Apperception Test. J. Person. Assess. Vol. 49, No. 2, 1985.

222. LYLES, W.: The Effects of Examiner Attitudes on the Projective Test Responses of Children. Unpublished doctoral dissertation, New York University (School of Education), New York, N.Y., 1958.

223. MAHLER, M. S.: On Human Symbiosis and the Vicissitudes of Individuation. New York: International Universities Press, 1968.

224. MAINFORD, F., AND MARCUSE, F.: Responses of disturbed children to human and animal pictures. J. Project. Techn. 18:475–477, 1954.

225. MARTIN, B.: Expression and inhibition of sex motive arousal in college males. J. Abnorm. Soc. Psychol. 68:307–312, 1964.

226. MAUGHAM, M. S.: Complete Short Stories, vol. I and II. New York, Doubleday, 1953.

227. MAY, R.: Sex differences in fantasy patterns. J. Project. Techn. 30(6):576–586, 1966.

228. MCARTHUR, C.: The effects of need achievement on the content of T.A.T. stories: a

reexamination. J. Abnorm. Soc. Psychol., vol. 45, 1953.

229. McCLELLAND, D., ATKINSON, J., CLARK, R., AND LOWELL, E.: The Achievement Motive. New York, Appleton-Century-Crofts, 1953.

230. MEGAREE, E.: A comparison of the scores of white and Negro male juvenile delinquents on three projective tests. J. Project. Techn. 30(6):530–535, 1966.

231. ———: Hostility on the T.A.T. as a function of defensive inhibition and stimulus situation. J. Proj. Techn. 31(4):73–79, 1967.

232. MELTZOFF, J.: The effect of mental set and item structure upon response to a projective test. J. Abnorm. Soc. Psychol. 46:177, 1951.

233. MENNINGER, K.: Psychological aspects of the organism under stress, Parts I and II. J. Amer. Psychoanal. Ass., vol. 2, 1954.

234. MEYER, B. T.: An investigation of color shock in the Rorschach Test. J. Clin. Psychol. 7:367, 1951.

235. MEYER, M. M.: The direct use of projective techniques in psychotherapy. J. Project. Techn. 15:263, 1951.

236. MIRA, E.: Myokinetic psychodiagnosis. Proc. Roy. Soc. Med., 1940.

237. MITCHELL, K.: An analysis of the schizophrenic mother concept by means of the Thematic Apperception Test. J. Abnorm. Soc. Psychol. 6:571–574, 1968.

238. MOLISH, H. B.: The quest for charisma. J. Project. Techn. vol. 33, no. 2, 1969.

239. MORGAN, C. D., AND MURRAY, H. A.: A method for investigating phantasies: the Thematic Apperception Test, Arch. Neurol. Psychiat. 34:289–306, 1935.

240. MORIARTY, A., AND MURPHY, L.: Observations of Patterns in Perception Related to Basic Motivations of Children. Unpublished, Menninger Foundation, Topeka, Kans., 1960.

241. ———: Normal preschoolers' reactions to the C.A.T.: some implications for later development. J. Project. Techn. 32(5):413–419, 1968.

242. MOWRER, O. J.: An experimental analogue of "regression" with incidental observations on "reaction-formation." J. Abnorm. Soc. Psychol. 135:56–87, 1940.

243. MUNROE, R.: Film: The Administration of Projective Tests. Pennsylvania State College, Psychological Cinema Register, 1951.

244. MURRAY, H. A.: Explorations in Personality. New York, Oxford University Press, 1938.

245. ———: Thematic Apperception Test Manual. Cambridge, Mass., Harvard University Press, 1943.

246. ———: Uses of the T.A.T. Amer. J. Psychiat. 107:577–581, 1951.

247. ———: Foreword. In Anderson, H. H., and Anderson, G. L. (eds.): An Introduction to Projective Techniques. New York, Prentice-Hall, 1951.

248. MURSTEIN, B.: The Projection of Hostility on the T.A.T. as a Function of Stimulus, Background, and Personality Variables. Unpublished manuscript, Interfaith Counseling Center, Portland, Ore., 1962.

249. ———: The relationship of expectancy of reward to achievement performance on an arithmetic and thematic test. J. Consult. Psychol. 27:394–399, 1963.

250. ———: Theory and Research in Projective Techniques. New York, Wiley, 1963.

251. ———: New thoughts about ambiguity and the T.A.T. J. Project. Techn. 29(2):219–226, 1965.

252. MUSSEN, P.: Differences between the T.A.T. responses of Negro and white boys. J. Consult. Psychol. 17:373–376, 1953.

253. ——— AND NAYLOR, H.: The relationships between overt and fantasy aggression. J. Abnorm. Soc. Psychol. 49:235–240, 1954.

254. NEUGARTEN, B.: Personality and the aging process. Gerontologist. Vol. 12 (1):9–15, Spring, 1972.

255. NOLAN, R.: A Longitudinal Comparison of Motives in Children's Fantasy Stories as Revealed by the Children's Apperception Test. Unpublished doctoral dissertation, The Florida State University, Tallahassee, Fla., 1959.

256. NUTTALL, R.: Some correlates of high need for achievement among urban northern Negroes. J. Abnorm. Soc. Psychol. 68:593–600, 1964.

257. OBER, W.: A few kind words about W. Somerset Maugham (1874–1965). New York J. Med., October, 1969.

258. OLNEY, E. E., AND CUSING, H. M.: A brief report of the responses of preschool children to commercially available pictorial material. Child Develop. 6:52–55, 1935.

259. ORSO, D.: Comparison of achievement and affiliation arousal of n Arch. J. Project. Techn. 33(3):230–233, 1969.

260. PIAGET, J.: The Language and Thought of the Child. London, Routledge & Kegan Paul, 1932.

261. PINE, F.: A manual for rating drive content in the Thematic Apperception Test. J. Project. Techn. 24, No. 1, 32–45, 1960.

262. PIOTROWSKI, Z.: The Rorschach inkblot method in organic disturbances of the central

nervous system. J. Nervous Mental Dis. 86:525–537, 1937.

263. PIOTROWSKI, Z.: A new evaluation of the Thematic Apperception Test. Psychoanal. Rev. April, 1950, pp. 101–127.

264. ——: A TAT of a schizophrenic interpreted according to new rules. Psychoanal. Rev. 39:230–249, 1952.

265. POE, W.: The Old Person in Your Home. New York, Chas. Scribners' Sons, 1969.

266. PORTERFIELD, C.: Adaptive mechanisms of young disadvantaged stutterers and non-stutterers. J. Project. Techn. 33(4):371–376, 1969.

267. POSTMAN, L., BRUNER, J. S., AND McGINNIES, E.: Personal values as selective factors in perception. J. Abnorm. Soc. Psychol. 43:142–154, 1948.

268. PROLA, M.: Verbal Productivity and Transcendence. J. of Personality Assessment, Vol. 36, No. 5, p. 445–46, Oct. 1972.

269. PURCELL, K.: The T.A.T. and antisocial behavior. J. Consult. Psychol. 20:449–456, 1956.

270. RABIN, A.: Children's Apperception Test Findings with Kibbutz and non-Kibbutz preschoolers. J. Project. Techn. 32(5):420–424, 1968.

271. RAPAPORT, D.: Diagnostic Psychological Testing. Chicago, Yearbook, 1946.

272. —— (ed.): Organization and Pathology of Thought. New York, Columbia University Press, 1951.

273. ——: Projective techniques and the theory of thinking. J. Project. Techn. 16:3, 269–275, 1952.

274. RAPAPORT, D.: In Wyatt, F.: The scoring and analysis of the Thematic Apperception Test. J. Psychol. 24:319–330, 1947.

275. REZNIKOFF, M., AND DOLLIN, A.: Social desirability and the type of hostility expressed on the T.A.T. J. Clin. Psychol. 17:315–317, 1961.

276. RIESS, B., SCHWARTZ, E., AND COTTINGHAM, A.: An experimental critique of assumptions underlying the Negro version of the T.A.T. J. Abnorm. Soc. Psychol. 45:700–709, 1950.

277. RITTER, A., AND EFFRON, L. D.: The use of the Thematic Apperception Test to differentiate normal from abnormal groups. J. Abnorm. Soc. Psychol. 47:147–158, 1952.

278. ROCKWELL, F. V., ET AL.: Changes in palmar skin resistance during the Rorschach Test. II. The effect of repetition with color removed. Mschr. Psychiat. Neurol. 116:321, 1948.

279. ROSEN, B.: The achievement syndrome: a psychocultural dimension of social stratification. In Atkinson, J. (ed.): Motives in Fantasy Action and Society. Princeton, N.J., Van Nostrand, 1958.

280. ——: Family structure and achievement motivations. Amer. Sociol. Rev. 26:574–585, 1961.

281. ROSENBLATT, M.: The Development of Norms for the Children's Apperception Test. Unpublished doctoral dissertation, Florida State University, Tallahassee, Fla., 1958.

282. ROSENZWEIG, S., Apperception norms for the Thematic Apperception Test: the problem of norms in projective methods. J. Personality vol. 17, no. 4, 1949.

283. —— AND FLEMING, E. S.: II. An empirical investigation. J. Personality vol. 17, No. 4, June, 1949.

284. Rossman, I. (ed): Clinical Geriatrics. Philadelphia, J. B. Lippincott Co., 1971.

285. ROTTER, J.: Some implications of a social learning theory for the prediction of goal-directed behavior from testing procedures. Psychol. Rev. 67:301–316, 1960.

286. ROTTER, J. B.: In Wyatt, F.: The scoring and analysis of the Thematic Apperception Test. J. Psychol. 24:319–330, 1947.

287. ROTTER, J. B., AND JESSOR, S.: in Shneidman, E. S. (ed.): Thematic Test Analysis. New York, Grune & Stratton, 1951, p. 163.

288. RUBIN, S.: A comparison of the Thematic Apperception Test stories of two IQ groups. J. Project. Techn. 28:81–85, 1964.

289. Runes, D. (ed.): Dictionary of Philosophy, Patterson, N.J., Littlefield, 1955.

290. SAMPSON, E.: Achievement in conflict. J. Personality 31:510–516, 1963.

291. SANDLER, J., AND ROSENBLATT, B.: The Concept of the Representational World. Psychoanalytic Study of the Child, Vol. 17, 1962.

292. SANFORD, R. N.: The effects of abstinence from food upon imaginal processes: a further experiment. J. Psychol. 3:145–159, 1936.

293. —— ET AL.: Physique, Personality and Scholarship. Washington, D. C., Society for Research in Child Development, 1943.

294. SARGENT, H.: The Insight Test. New York, Grune & Stratton, 1953.

295. ——: In Shneidman, E. S. (ed.): Thematic Test Analysis. New York, Grune & Stratton, 1951, p. 180.

296. SCHAFER, R.: The Clinical Application of Psychological Tests. New York, International Universities, 1948.

297. SCHILDER, P.: Entwurf zu einer Psychiatrie auf Psychoanalytischer Grundlage. Leipzig,

Wien, Zürich, Internationale Psychoanalytische Bibliothek, 1925, no. 17.

298. ——: Image and Appearance of the Human Body. London, Routledge, 1935.

299. SCHWARTZ, L. A.: Social-situation pictures in the psychiatric interview. Amer. J. Orthopsychiat. 2:124–132, 1932.

300. SEARS, R. R.: Survey of objective studies of psychoanalytic concepts, Social Science Research Council Bulletin, no. 51, 1943.

301. SHARKEY, K. J. AND RITZLER, B. A.: Comparing Diagnostic Validity of the T.A.T. and a New Picture Projective Test, J. Person. Assess, vol. 49, No. 4, August 1985.

302. SHIPLEY, T., AND VEROFF, J.: A projective measure of need for affiliation. J. Exp. Psychol. 43:349–356, 1952.

303. Shneidman, E. S. (ed.): Thematic Test Analysis. New York, Grune & Stratton, 1951.

304. SHPOLA, E. M.: Influence of color on reactions to ink-blots. J. Personality 18:358, 1950.

305. SILBERER, H.: Report on a method of eliciting and observing certain symbolic hallucination phenomena. In Rapaport, D. (ed.): Organization and Pathology of Thought. New York, Columbia University Press, 1951.

306. SIMSON, E.: Vergleich von C.A.T. und einer inhaltsanalogen Mensch-Bilderserie. Sonderdr. Diagnost. 5:54–62, 1959.

307. SINGER, R.: A cognitive view of rationalized projection. J. Project. Techn. 27:235–243, 1963.

308. SLOATE, N.: Aging and community health problems. In Bellak, L. (ed.): A concise handbook of community psychiatry and community mental health. New York, Grune & Stratton, 1974.

309. SPIEGELMAN, M., TERWILLIGER, C., AND FEARING, F.: The content of comic strips: a study of a mass medium of communication. J. Soc. Psychol. 35:37–57, 1952.

310. SPITZ, R.: The primal cavity: a contribution to the genesis of perception and its role for psychoanalytic theory. In: The Psychoanalytic Study of the Child, vol. 10. New York. International Universities, 1955.

311. STABENAU, J., TURPIN, J., WERNER, M., AND POLLIN, W.: A comparative study of families of schizophrenics, delinquents, and normals. Psychiatry, vol. 28, no. 1, February, 1965.

312. STEIN, M. I.: Personality factors involved in the temporal development of Rorschach responses. Rorschach Res. Exch. J. Project. Techn. 13:355–414, 1949.

313. STEVENSON, M.: Some emotional problems of orphanage children. Canad. J. Psychol. 6:179–182, 1952.

314. STONE, H.: The T.A.T. aggressive content scale. J. Project. Techn. 20:445–452, 1956.

315. —— AND DELLIS, N.: An exploratory investigation into the levels hypothesis. J. Project. Techn. 24:333–340, 1960.

316. Strachey, J. (ed.): The Standard Edition of the Complete Psychological Works of Sigmund Freud, London: Hogarth Press (containing "mourning and Melancholia," 1917).

317. —— (ed.): The Standard Edition of the Complete Psychological Works of Sigmund Freud. London: Hogarth Press (containing the "Ego and the Id," 1923).

318. STRIZVER, G.: Thematic, sexual, and guilt responses as related to stimulus-relevance and experimentally induced drive and inhibition. In Epstein, S. (principal investigator): The Influence of Drive and Conflict upon Apperception. Progress report of NIMH Grant M-1293, 1961, pp. 10–11.

319. SULLIVAN, H. S.: Conceptions of modern psychiatry. Psychiatry 3:147, 1940.

320. SUTTON-SMITH, B., ABRAMS, D. M., BOTVIN, G. J., CARING, M., GILDESGAME, D. P., MAHONY, D. H., AND STEVENS, T. R.: *The Folkstories of Children.* Philadelphia, PA: University of Pennsylvania Press, 1981.

321. SYMONDS, P. M.: In Shneidman, E. S. (ed.): Thematic Test Analysis. New York, Grune & Stratton, 1951, p. 185.

322. T.A.T. Newsletter. J. Project. Techn. vol. 17, no. 1, 1953.

323. THEINER, E.: Experimental needs are expressed by projective techniques. J. Project. Techn. 26:354–363, 1962.

324. THOMPSON, C., The Thompson modification of the Thematic Apperception Test. J. Project. Techn. 13:469–478, 1949.

325. TOMKINS, S.: The Thematic Apperception Test: The Theory and Technique of Interpretation. New York, Grune & Stratton, 1947.

326. TOOLEY, K.: Expressive style as a development index in late adolescence. J. Project. Techn. 31(6):51–60, 1967.

327. TOONE, D.: Is Old Age Accompanied by a Constricted View of the World? Thesis for the B.A. degree, State University of New York College at Purchase, 1974.

328. ULLMANN, L.: Selection of neuropsychiatric patients for group psychotherapy. J. Consult. Psychol., no. 21, pp. 277–280, 1957.

329. VARENDONCK, J.: The Psychology of Daydreams. New York, Macmillan, 1931.

330. ——, ATKINSON, J., FELD, S., AND

GURIN, S.: The use of thematic apperception to assess motivation in a nationwide interview study. Psychol. Monogr. 12:74, 1960.

331. ——, FELD, S., AND CROCKETT, H.: Explorations into the effects of picture cues on thematic apperceptive expression of achievement motivation. J. Personality 3:171–181, 1966.

332. ——, FELD, S., AND GURIN, G.: Achievement motivation and religious background. Amer. Sociol. Rev. 27:205–217, 1962.

333. VEROFF, J., WILCOX, S., AND ATKINSON, J.: The achievement motive in high school and college-age women. J. Abnorm. Soc. Psychol. 48:108–119, 1953.

334. VOLKAN, V. D.: *Primitive Internalized Object Relations*. New York: International Universities Press, 1976.

335. VUYK, R.: Plaatjes als Hulpmiddel bij het Kinderpsychologisch Onderzoek. Leiden, H. E. Stenfert Kroese N.V., 1954.

336. WEINER, I. B.: Psychodiagnosis of Schizophrenia. New York, Wiley & Sons, 1966.

337. WEISSKOPF, E. A.: An experimental study of the effect of brightness and ambiguity on projection in the Thematic Apperception Test. J. Psychol. 29:107–116, 1950.

338. ——: A transcendence index as a proposed measure in the T.A.T. J. Psychol. 29:379–390, 1950.

339. —— AND DIEPPA, J. J.: Experimentally induced faking of TAT responses. J. Consult. Psychol. 15:469–474, 1951.

340. —— AND DUNDLEVY, G.: Bodily similarity between subject and central figure in the T.A.T. as an influence on projection. J. Abnorm. Soc. Psychol. 47:441–445, 1952.

341. —— AND LYNN, D. B.: The effect of variations in ambiguity on projection in the Children's Apperception Test. J. Consult. Psychol. 17:67–70, 1953.

342. WEISSKOPF-JOELSON AND MONEY, L.: Facial similarity between subject and central figure in the T.A.T. as an influence on projection. J. Abnorm. Soc. Psychol., vol. 48, 1953.

343. —— AND FOSTER, H.: An experimental study of the effect of stimulus variation upon projection. J. Project. Techn. 26:366–370, 1962.

344. WEISSMAN, S.: Some indicators of acting out behavior from the Thematic Apperception Test. J. Project. Techn. 28:366–375, 1964.

345. WERNER, H.: The Acquisition of Word Meanings: A Developmental Study. Society for Research in Child Development, vol. XV, no. 1, 1950.

346. WERNER, M., STABENAU, J., AND POLLIN, W.: A T.A.T. method for the differentiation of families of schizophrenics, delinquents, and normals, NIMH. To be published.

347. WHITE, R. K.: In Shneidman, E. S. (ed.): Thematic Test Analysis. New York, Grune & Stratton, 1951, p. 188.

348. WHITE, R. W., AND SANFORD, R. N.: Thematic Apperception Test Manual (mimeographed). Cambridge, Mass., Harvard Psychological Clinic, 1941.

349. WEINER, N.: Cybernetics. New York, Wiley, 1948.

350. WINDLEBAND, W.: Geschichte und Naturwissenschaft, Ed. 3, 1904.

351. WINNICOTT, D. W. *The Maturational Process and the Facilitating Environment*. International Universities Press, 1965.

352. WINTER, W., FERREIRA, A., AND OLSON, J.: Hostility themes in the family T.A.T. J. Project. Techn. 3:270–274, 1966.

353. WITHERSPOON, R.: Development of objective scoring methods for longitudinal C.A.T. data. J. Project. Techn. 32(5):407, 1968.

354. WOLOWITZ, H., AND SHORKEY, C.: Power themes in the T.A.T. stories of paranoid and schizophrenic males. J. Project. Techn. 30(6):591–596, 1966.

355. WYATT, F.: The scoring and analysis of the Thematic Apperception Test. J. Psychol. 24:319–330, 1947.

ADDITIONAL BIBLIOGRAPHY

Bellak, L.: The Best Years of Your Life: A Guide to the Art and Science of Aging. New York, Atheneum, 1975.

Bellak, L.: Contemporary character as crisis adaptation. Am. J. Psychotherapy, Vol. 28 (1), 1974, pp. 46–58.

Bellak, L.: Overload: The New Human Condition. New York, Human Sciences Press, 1975.

Bellak, L., Small, L. *Emergency Psychotherapy and Brief Psychotherapy.* Grune & Stratton, New York, and C.P.S., Inc., Larchmont, New York, 1978.

Bellak, L., Siegel, H. *Handbook of Intensive Brief and Emergency Psychotherapy.* C.P.S., Inc., Larchmont, New York, 1984.

Bellak, L. and Antell, M.: An intercultural study of aggressive behavior on children's playgrounds. Am. J. Orthopsychiat, Vol. 44 (4), July, 1974, pp. 503–511.

Bellak, L., Chassan, J. B., Gediman, H. K., and Hurvich, M.: Ego function assessment of analytic psychotherapy combined with drug therapy. J. Nervous and Mental Disease, Vol. 157 (6), 1973, pp. 465–469.

Bellak, L., Hurvich, M., and Gediman, H.: Ego Functions In Schizophrenics, Neurotics, and Normals. New York, John Wiley and Sons, 1973.

Bellak, L., and Karasu, T.: Geriatric Psychiatry: A Handbook for Psychiatrists and Primary Care Physicians. New York, Grune & Stratton, in press.

de la Cruz, F., Fox, B. H., and Roberts, R., eds.: Minimal brain dysfunction. Annals of the N.Y. Academy of Sciences, Vol. 205, Feb. 1973.

Gottschalk, L. A. (ed.): The Content Analysis of Verbal Behavior: Further Studies. Jamaica, New York: Spectrum Publications, 1978.

Myler, B., Rosenkrantz, A., and Holmes, G. A.: Comparison of the T.A.T., C.A.T., and C.A.T.-H. among second grade girls. Journal of Personality Assessment, Vol. 36 (5), 1972, pp. 440–444.

Neuringer, C. and Livesay, R. C.: projective fantasy on the C.A.T. and C.A.T.-H. Journal of Projective Techniques and Personality Assessment, Vol. 34 (6), 1970, 487–491.

Phillipson, H.: The Object Relations Technique. The Free Press, 1955.

"Sex Differences in Childrens' Perceptions of their Parents as Inferred from the Children's Apperception Test and the Rorschach." Irla Lee Zimmerman, Maurine Bernstein, Bernie T. Eideson. VCLA-NPI.

INDEX